British Main Line Services

IN THE AGE OF STEAM 1900-1968

MICHAEL HARRIS

Dedication

To my dearest daughter, Georgia, with all my love.
She has seen a little of the magic of the steam age.

Title page: In the early days of the 'Britannias' on the Great Eastern lines, No. 70013 *Oliver Cromwell* passes Trowse Upper Junction on the exit from Norwich with the up 'East Anglian' of 31 August 1951. Some of the prewar stock built for this service remains in the formation.

A catalogue record for this book is available from the British Library.

ISBN 0-86093-536-1

Oxford Publishing Co. is an imprint of Haynes Publishing, Sparkford, Nr Yeovil, Somerset BA22 7JJ

Printed in Hong Kong

Typset in Times Roman Medium

As part of our ongoing market research, we are always pleased to receive comments about our books, suggestions for new titles, or requests for catalogues. Please write to: The Editorial Director, Oxford Publishing Co., Sparkford, Near Yeovil, Somerset, BA22 7JJ

CONTENTS

INTRODUCTION   5

The pre-Grouping railways 1900 - 1922
CHAPTER 1 Great Western Railway and South Wales railways to 1922   7
CHAPTER 2 The Southern group of companies to 1922   14
CHAPTER 3 The East Coast, Great Northern, and North Eastern to 1922   31
CHAPTER 4 The Great Eastern and Great Central to 1922   42
CHAPTER 5 The West Coast services and London & North Western to 1922   59
CHAPTER 6 The Midland, and Lancashire & Yorkshire to 1922   76
CHAPTER 7 The Scottish companies to 1922   89
CHAPTER 8 Cross-country inter-railway services to 1922   105

The Big Four - January 1923 - December 1947
CHAPTER 9 The Great Western Railway from 1923   119
CHAPTER 10 The Southern Railway   126
CHAPTER 11 The London Midland & Scottish Railway   136
CHAPTER 12 The London & North Eastern Railway   148
CHAPTER 13 Scottish railways from Grouping   163
CHAPTER 14 Cross-country inter-railway services 1923-1947   171

The Nationalised railway to the end of Steam
CHAPTER 15 The Western Region   180
CHAPTER 16 The Southern Region   186
CHAPTER 17 The London Midland Region   192
CHAPTER 18 The Eastern and North Eastern Regions   201
CHAPTER 19 The Scottish Region and cross-country expresses   210

ACKNOWLEDGEMENTS   220
INDEX   221

The first part of the 2pm Victoria–Dover Marine boat train passes Orpington during the winter of 1928/9 behind 'Lord Nelson' 4-6-0 No. E853 *Sir Richard Grenville*, one of the class with a six-wheeled tender. Most of the train is made up of recently built SR gangwayed stock, and there are two Pullman cars, too.

Photographic credits
The following photographs are reproduced by courtesy of the respective photographers or owners of collections:
the late W. J. V. Anderson/Rail Archive Stephenson photographs pages 196; 197 (upper); 211.
D. H. Ballantyne photograph page 184 (upper).
C. R. L. Coles photographs pages 124; 135.
K. L. Cook/Rail Archive Stephenson photograph page 190.
Derek Cross photograph page 184 (lower).
J. F. Davies/Photomatic Rail Archive Stephenson photograph page 183.
Fastline Group Ltd photograph page 162.
Kenneth Field photograph page 209.
W. S. Garth/Rail Archive Stephenson photograph page 1.
D. T. Greenwood/Rail Archive Stephenson photographs pages 195; 200; 202 (lower).
F. R. Hebron/Rail Archive Stephenson photographs pages 4; 121; 127; 128 (upper); 137 (upper); 149; 160; 164; 166; 168 (lower); 174 (upper); 179; 182.
T. G. Hepburn/Rail Archive Stephenson photographs pages 50; 154; 155; 158; 198; 199; 202 (upper); 206; 207; 216.
D. M. C. Hepburne-Scott/Rail Archive Stephenson photographs pages 6; 189; 197 (lower); 205; 21 (both); 218; 219 (upper).
H. L. Hopwood Collection/Ken Nunn Collection photographs pages 8; 13; 16; 19; 21; 24; 26; 36; 39; 40; 47; 57; 68; 74; 78; 94; 99; 128 (lower); 148; 152.

Lens of Sutton photographs pages 12; 30; 53; 122; 134; 147; 173; 177; 188.
L. W. H. Lowther Collection photograph pages 102/103.
K. A. C. R. Nunn/Ken Nunn Collection photographs pages 9; 14; 32; 38; 45; 54; 62; 65; 70; 73; 85; 87; 91; 92; 96; 104; 111; 113; 117; 131; 132; 137 (lower); 139; 161 (upper); 168 (upper); 187 (both photographs); 193; 203; 215.
Photomatic/Rail Archive Stephenson photograph page 97.
Rail Archive Stephenson photographs pages 140; 142; 144.
C. J. L. Romanes/Locomotive & General Photographs photograph page 165.
H. L. Salmon/Locomotive & General Photographs photographs pages 79; 81.
E. E. Smith photographs pages 120; 161 (lower).
H. Gordon Tidey photographs pages 11; 172; 175.
Colling Turner/Photomatic Rail Archive Stephenson photograph page 145.
W. Vaughan Jenkins/Locomotive & General Photographs photographs pages 125; 178.
E. R. Wethersett photograph page 170.
J. P. Wilson/Rail Archive Stephenson photographs pages 129; 159; 169; 174; 194.

Photographs from the Ken Nunn Collection are reproduced by courtesy of the Locomotive Club of Great Britain.

INTRODUCTION

When musing over sources of information, it is always reckless to think that there should be a book on the subject. So it was with *British Main Line Services in the Age of Steam*.

Did the Glasgow–Plymouth run as complete train all the way or not? When did the Colchester–York start running? Why not find out . . . and so the idea of the book was born.

Does it matter, or is it just another contribution to trivia? I think it does, because the railway has shaped the lives of British people in the last 170 years, and there is something of the fabric of our society in the bygone services of our railways. Why was there a through coach from Whitehaven to Southampton before World War 1? – because with the collapse of the iron ore industry in West Cumberland, people wanted to seek their fortune elsewhere. This book has had to be selective, otherwise it would have something to say in its chapters of the thousands who escaped from Central and Eastern Europe before 1914 by boat to Hull, to join trains there for Liverpool, where they embarked on ships for the New World to try to make a new start. They constituted a major and regular flow of passengers.

But perhaps, as elsewhere, history books tend to honour the successful so that we risk being more intrigued to hear of the Club saloons patronised by wealthy Lancastrians travelling from their villas in the Fylde to work in Salford or Manchester, or of city slickers ensconced in the 'City Limited' between Brighton and London Bridge.

Main line services have been interpreted a little literally. Not all the trains in this book necessarily were belled forward by signalmen as express passenger workings but most of them were. An attempt has been made to cover as many as possible of the scheduled services, and to sketch in some of the prominent specials such as the annual Pullman train from King's Cross to Aintree for the Grand National, or the Plymouth–Paddington Ocean Liner expresses.

The period featured is from 1900 until 3 August 1968, the day that the last Class '1' steam-worked service puffed itself to a standstill on British Rail. In those 68 years the railways were transformed, largely because of the new construction of railways before World War I.

There was never a Golden Age of railways. The years 1910-14 were seldom free of industrial disputes, then there was the war and government control, followed by the debate over whether the system should have been nationalised. It wasn't and, in the wasted years of 1918-22, the railways failed to respond to the beginnings of the motor age. Then came the General Strike, the Depression, and afterwards a clear period – until 1939. From 1945, the railways were seldom out of the firing line. So, no, there wasn't much of a Golden Age but there were some better years than others – 1900-9 and 1934-39, perhaps.

Any mistakes are the author's alone. A proportion of the information on train services already in print must be taken with a pinch of salt. Much was based on the summer services of the past, particularly when drawing comparisons with the present. Summer services were – and are – always better: more trains, faster trains and more revenue – in the past, typically 40% more than in winter. Most of what appeared in print under the by-line of the railway writers and editorial staff of the past was derived from publicity hand-outs provided by the railway companies. These mentioned what the railways wanted to, and omitted what was embarrassing. Sometimes the commentators perpetuated mistakes, sometimes their transcriptions were incorrect, sometimes they relied on memory, and got it wrong. Some of the writers had hobbyhorses which were ridden to death in their regular columns. It tends to be a minefield.

Source material is invaluable, often sets the record straight and, where possible, it has been used. The timetables themselves are often confusing. *Bradshaw* and the others frequently did not make clear whether there were through *coaches* or a through *train*.

Within the book the pre-1964 railway convention of am or pm has been used, rather than the 24hr clock. Time has been generally shown in minutes, abbreviated to min, rather than parts of hours which are less precise though reference to a Birmingham '2hr train' describes a service rather than the time taken. Miles are shown in fractions, not decimal points. Abbreviations are often irritating and an attempt has been made to keep them to a minimum. But those employed include: 'From' and 'to' abbreviated to 'London–Manchester'; days of the week follow the railway convention, ie, M, T, W, Th, F, S, Su for Monday to Sunday inclusive, with X to indicate that the train did not run on that/those days, and O to denote that the train ran on that/those days only; Used sparingly TC indicates 'Through coaches' and EWD is 'each working day'.

The Grouping of 1923 might well have produced a separate Scottish group of railways. In this book it seemed sensible to cover the LNER and LMS internal services within Scotland in one chapter, entitled the 'Scottish railways from Grouping' – Chapter 13.

The years from 1900 to 1968 may have been part of the steam age, but 1968 was not the end of our railways which are still very much alive and developing when they are allowed to do so. Some passenger services are immeasurably better than before. There was and – is – no Golden Age...

Michael Harris
Ottershaw, Surrey
August 1995

The accelerated timings of the 'Pembroke Coast Express' brought some sparkle to the Western Region's Paddington–South Wales service. This view, dated 10 December 1955, shows 'Castle' No. 7028 *Cadbury Castle* at speed near Wantage Road with the down express.

CHAPTER ONE

GREAT WESTERN RAILWAY AND SOUTH WALES RAILWAYS TO 1922

The Great Western Railway

The major transformation of the GWR's main line passenger service between 1900 and 1914 is one of the most striking developments of any of the pre-Grouping British railways. It entailed the extensive construction of new lines, totalling 150 miles, and for the most part more easily graded and aligned than the old routes. No longer was it a matter of the Great Way Round for the shortened or new routes available by 1914 reduced mileages appreciably, notably 20 from Reading to Taunton, 19 from Paddington to Banbury and ten miles (and many more minutes) saved by the construction of the Badminton line. New routes were created too, such as from Birmingham to Bristol via Honeybourne. In association with the Great Central Railway's London Extension, the GWR also had an opportunity to offer new cross-country services.

The programme associated with the Great Awakening of the GWR involved the construction of no fewer than seven stretches of main line: Stert, near Patney & Chirton, to Westbury, opened 1900; Wootton Bassett to Patchway, opened 1903; Castle Cary to Curry Rivel, and improvements to the existing line on to Cogload Junction, the new through route opening in 1906; Old Oak Common to High Wycombe and Princes Risborough to Aynho Junction, through route completed 1910, in association with the GCR; Tyseley to Bearley West Junction, and Honeybourne East Junction to Cheltenham Malvern Road and associated lines, new through route available, 1908. Loop lines installed in 1906 on the Banbury and Cheltenham line permitted through

running from the east to Gloucester, of main advantage to cross-country services. Often overlooked is the cumulative effect of the series of improvements west of Exeter, notably doubling of the Cornish main line in association with viaduct rebuilding and track relaying, the doubling of the approach to Penzance in 1893, and the provision of double track throughout from Exeter to Plymouth which took until 1905 to effect.

By 1910, the GWR's express passenger service had greatly changed from that of 1900. Then, expresses had run from Paddington to Weymouth via Chippenham; to Devon and Cornwall via Bristol; to South Wales via Bath and Stapleton Road, or via Swindon–Gloucester, and to Birmingham via Oxford.

In 1900, the best times were made by Paddington–Bristol expresses, the 10.35am down and 4.45pm being booked in 135 min for 118½ miles. There was also a service via Devizes, introduced in 1895, at 11.36am from Bristol, and taking 3hr over its journey to Paddington. This train survived the altered West of England services of 1906 when it was joined by a 3pm return from Paddington via Devizes which slipped at Savernake. The line to Newbury also featured a 'Southampton express' in the early years of the century, and a vestige survived in 1910 as through coaches to Southampton Town from Paddington, at 9.35am and 5.25pm return.

Notable was the through express in summer months, to Newquay and Falmouth, at 10.30am from Paddington, and 10.45am return from Falmouth, formed of Dean's corridor stock and offering the longest non-stop runs in Britain. From July 1901, the

An unidentified down express, made up of Dean non-gangwayed clerestory stock, sets out from Paddington in 1908 behind Dean Single No. 3040 *Empress of India*.

'Cornishman' had been accelerated, to run non-stop to Exeter, and to reach Plymouth in 5hr, and Penzance in 7hr 52min. In those days when all West of England trains ran via Bristol, the overall times between that city and Plymouth were not much slower than after 1923. The principal South Wales trains ran via Bath, with the 4.30pm Cork boat train, taking 6½ hours for its 270-mile journey to New Milford. There was also a boat connection to Waterford from New Milford off the 6.10pm from Paddington dining car express which ran via Gloucester. Restaurant cars had been introduced in 1896, and sleeping cars in 1877, these working between Paddington and Plymouth and to South Wales.

The Gloucester line also had its own expresses for Cheltenham. Generally these had connections at Gloucester to Hereford via Ross, whereas before long the emphasis would switch to a service via Worcester which, in 1900, had just one express from and to Paddington. The Honeybourne route would in time see Birmingham–South Wales expresses, but in 1900 these were routed via the Worcester–Hereford line. On the North and West line along the Welsh Border, many of the trains from/to Shrewsbury conveyed through coaches to/from Bristol and Cardiff, and Birmingham and Birkenhead.

The disadvantage of the Great Way Round to

Birmingham was obvious in that the best down northern line express was the 9.30am, making its first stop at Birmingham Snow Hill in 147min (129¼ miles) and, although making intermediate calls through to its Birkenhead destination, avoided Chester by taking the avoiding curve. The 11.47am Birkenhead–Paddington and 4.45pm return were known as the 'Zulu'. By 1902 half of the principal expresses on the route were shown as 'Corridor Trains'. Indeed, the emphasis in the timetables detailing the northern line service was on travel to Liverpool and Manchester, with through coaches to/from the latter and Paddington via Crewe and Wellington. Several of the Birkenhead expresses also conveyed through coaches for or from the West Country, and there was one return working of through coaches between Paddington and Barmouth via Ruabon. Generally, Birmingham involved three hours' travelling from Paddington for passengers who had chosen the GWR, but the company took trouble to cultivate travel to destinations en route by an extraordinary variety of slip coaches, those slipped at Hatton from up trains usually working forward to Stratford-upon-Avon.

The new century saw the introduction of the Oxford–Leicester trains, described in **Cross-Country services** (Chapter 8) then came the introduction, from

July 1901, of Paddington–Weymouth expresses, now routed via Newbury and the short-cut to Westbury, and taking some 25min or so less on their throughout journey than over their old route via Chippenham. T. I. Allen had been appointed in 1894 as Superintendent of the Line, and he was largely responsible for the energy in improving the main line trains, with the result that whereas in 1888 there were just nine trains with runs of 50mph-plus, by 1901 the total was 54. Also significant was the gradual availability of a fleet of modern locomotives, beginning with the Dean Singles and 'Atbara' 4-4-0s, able to make long and relatively fast non-stop runs, helped of course by the provision of water-troughs, such as at Goring, Fox's Wood, near Bristol, Creech, near Taunton (1902) and Exminster.

Consequently, it was possible to operate non-stop runs Paddington–Plymouth, the pioneer being the Royal Train run in March 1902 for King Edward VII. This and another royal special to Plymouth, the latter run in the record time of 233min on 14 July 1903, paved the way from July 1904 for the regular summer Paddington–Plymouth non-stop runs by the 'Cornish Riviera Express', at the time the longest regular non-stop working in the world. The general introduction from the late summer of 1904 of the Churchward 4-6-0s (and Atlantics) allowed the reduced journey times to be maintained with heavier loads. Fast runs were also made from Plymouth Docks to Paddington by specials conveying passengers and mails landed from ocean liners. The most significant of these was the record run of 9 May 1904 which gave rise to *City of Truro's* 100+mph speed down Wellington bank. The frantic competition between the GWR and LSWR for the Plymouth ocean liner traffic ceased in 1910 when the latter withdrew and a peace treaty was signed.

Improvements continued on other GWR routes, from the end of 1903 under the management of a new Superintendent of the Line, Joseph Morris. From July 1902 the Paddington–Birmingham Snow Hill trains had been accelerated, with four trains in all taking 140min (one summer North Wales service took 137min) while from July 1903 four South Wales trains began to use the Badminton route, with times to Swansea, for example, reduced by 30min. In October 1903, the 10.50am was the first Paddington–Bristol two-hour train. The next was the first portion of the 'Dutchman' from Penzance, leaving Bristol at noon and routed over the Badminton line. Both these expresses were worked by the capable 'City' 4-4-0s

The new Great Western – the 4.15pm Paddington–Bristol Temple Meads and Plymouth express passes Iver on 1 July 1911 behind Atlantic No. 190 *Waverley* (rebuilt as a 4-6-0 the next year). The train represents a major advance on the Dean Single and its clerestory stock. Behind the engine is the 'Tea and Dining Car'; like several of the other vehicles in the train it is an example of Churchward's 70ft gangwayed stock.

which, with 150ton loads, had no difficulty in maintaining 70 mph on level track.

Non-stop running between Paddington and Plymouth allowed Penzance to be reached in 7hr from London, and the inaugural 'Cornish Riviera Limited' first ran to this timing on 1 July 1904. At this stage, it ran in summer only. Including a restaurant car and a through portion to Falmouth, the load was limited to seven coaches, hence the use of the term 'Limited' for this Penzance service, for which new 'Dreadnought' elliptical-roofed stock was built in 1905 for that season's operations. Two other innovations to signify the 'new' Great Western were the absence of any second-class accommodation on the 'Limited', and the introduction of seat reservations. The following year, the opening of the Castle Cary–Cogload cut-off reduced the distance to Taunton and beyond by 20 miles, and from July 1906 the 10.30 am Paddington–Penzance 'Limited' and return working became year-round services, the down train now taking 4hr 10min (3min less from 1907), and slipping coaches at Westbury, Taunton and Exeter.

In contrast to 1900, Worcester had a good service in 1905, better indeed than in the 1950s, with non-stop expresses covering the 120 miles in 135 min – the 1.40pm and 4.45pm – and one up express in 135, another in 140min. As late as 1914, Dean Singles continued to appear on the 8.55am Worcester–Paddington and 1.40pm return. By 1905, there were restaurant cars on five expresses each way between Paddington, Bristol and beyond, two each way on the South Wales and Birmingham services, but none, for instance, to/from Worcester. No less than 79 slip coaches were detached at some 25 locations in 1908, not necessarily to serve destinations further afield as there were six slips at Slough (for Windsor or Taplow), and no less than a dozen at Reading.

The next development was the inauguration of steamer services between Fishguard and Rosslare at the end of 1906, with day and night services in each direction, booked in 5½hr for the 261 miles and provided with the latest 'Toplight' corridor stock. Fishguard was also briefly an ocean port, and boat train specials were run from 1909 to 1914 (with running times to/from Paddington of just over 4½hr). Another initiative was the promotion of day excursions from 1907 between Paddington and the lakes of Killarney, the special trains running non-stop to/from Fishguard.

The enormous investment to create Fishguard and its associated new lines was never realised, and the same must be said of the next development, the creation of a new route from Birmingham to Bristol

and South Wales. The first section of this enterprise was some clue to the GWR's motivation. The North Warwickshire line had been promoted by an independent company which looked as though it might fall into the clutches of the Manchester, Sheffield & Lincolnshire Railway or, alternatively, the Midland & South Western Junction Railway. By backstage manoeuvring, the upshot was that the GWR evolved a fresh scheme, by which it created a through route from Tyseley to Cheltenham. Construction started during 1902 south of Cheltenham, and in 1905 north thereof, and a through regular passenger service from Birmingham was on the cards for 1908. This depended on the GWR being able to exercise running powers it already possessed over the Midland Railway between Standish Junction, south of Gloucester, and Yate, just north of Bristol.

That was debatable, said the Midland, when it came to Birmingham–Bristol trains, and the dispute went to the Court of Chancery which found in favour of the Midland. The GWR trains now faced unnecessary mileage over rival metals, and likely delays in running south of Mangotsfield. So the GWR decided to appeal, but in the meantime commenced running a Wolverhampton and Penzance service each way, using the Midland route south of Yate. A costly legal dispute now developed, the result being that the GWR triumphed, and so from 2 November 1908 the pair of expresses were diverted into Bristol over their own line from Yate South Junction. At this stage, their only companions on the Honeybourne route were less expected: a Cardiff–Yarmouth/Lowestoft and return trains that began running from 10 July 1908, but did not reappear after the summer of 1909. By April 1910, there were three expresses each way over the line: Wolverhampton–Penzance and reverse; Wolverhampton–Weston-super-Mare (from Torquay northbound), and the 'Shakespeare Express' from Wolverhampton to Bristol, with through coaches from/to Birkenhead, the latter from Weston-super-Mare northbound. By August 1914, there were no more than four expresses each way and the service was reduced during World War I. Even in their early days, the route's expresses were not particularly fast, taking 135min or so for the 98 miles between Birmingham and Bristol.

One other service on the Honeybourne line was that between Paddington and Stratford-upon-Avon and Cheltenham St James, by virtue of a two-coach portion slipped at Moreton-in-Marsh from the 4.45pm down Worcester express as from July 1907. The coaches were worked to Honeybourne, and each then went on its own way, the time to Cheltenham being 170min.

Typical of the lightweight expresses to be found on the GWR Birmingham–Paddington service. Hauled by a 'Saint', this train on Lapworth troughs comprises just two passenger coaches and two full brakes.

This was 10min faster than the best services via Swindon and Gloucester, but 18 min slower overall than provided from May 1906 by the Cheltenham slip made at Chipping Norton Junction (Kingham after 1909) off the 1.40pm Paddington–Worcester. Such speedy slip-coach journeys had the disadvantage of being unable to be matched in the return direction.

The diversion of most of the northern expresses to the new short-cut via High Wycombe and Bicester in July 1910 brought the Paddington–Birmingham time down to exactly 2hr, to provide effective competition to the existing two-hour LNWR expresses from Euston. At first, there were five down 2hr expresses, with Leamington served by slip (which generally continued to Stratford-upon-Avon) while the principal up workings took 5min more as they stopped at Leamington, and usually made one other stop. Five trains each way daily ran north of Wolverhampton.

Until 1914, most trains loaded lightly, and timekeeping was variable, as speed slacks were imposed over the newly-built embankments, and station times tended to be exceeded. By April 1913, the 4.50pm Birmingham–Paddington ran from the Banbury stop in 67min, the GWR's first mile-a-minute booking. To accommodate these and other new services such as those over the Honeybourne route, the GWR rebuilt Snow Hill station, Birmingham, the work being completed early in 1913. In 1911/12 there were through trains between

Wolverhampton and Victoria via the West London Extension line – see Chapter 8. In 1906/7, there had been a Paddington–Kensington Addison Road–Brighton train – see **London, Brighton & South Coast Railway.**

Signs of changing attitudes came in 1913 with the introduction of third-class only, reserved seat facility, restaurant car holiday expresses: a ThFSO peak train of the latest stock, at 9.30am from Paddington, non-stop to Newton Abbot, and arriving in Falmouth at 6.5pm, and conveying portions for Newquay and Paignton. The GWR reported that the train was an 'unqualified success' and it was repeated in 1914. During the same summer peak, there was a third-class relief to the 'Cornish Riviera'. Torquay was served by an 11.50am (12noon from c1914) from Paddington, booked non-stop to Exeter, and conveying coaches – including uniquely a restaurant car – slipped at Taunton (for Ilfracombe, to arrive at 6.6pm, and with its own restaurant car in summer). There was no up through train, but Torbay portions were attached to Plymouth trains at Newton Abbot.

Splendid though these new services and facilities were, and encouraging though the increase in passenger numbers appeared at first sight, the GWR's investments must overall be regarded as questionable. While from 1890 passenger travel exceeded the increase in train-miles, from 1904 the increase in train-miles outstripped the rate of growth

Into the new age the GWR dispensed with its trademark of chocolate and cream liveried stock in favour of a single colour. The engine is a 'Saint' 4-6-0, and its train includes both 57ft and 70ft Toplight stock.

in passenger numbers although admittedly the average length of journey was longer. In the decade to 1916, the greatly improved main line service had been the motivation for extensive and costly improvements to the approaches to Paddington, and at the terminus itself.

The first major changes to services during World War I came from 1 January 1917 when most of the principal expresses were withdrawn, others became slower and made more stops, and restaurant and sleeping cars and slip coaches were discontinued. Further cut-backs occurred in November 1917, and again in April 1918, by which time the fastest times from Paddington to Bristol were 135min, to Plymouth 5hr and Birmingham 150min, the last-named having just three down and two up expresses from Paddington.

On 5 May 1919, many expresses were reinstated including the 'Cornish Riviera Limited' which, on 7 July 1919, regained its non-stop run to Plymouth, last made in 1916. Restaurant cars and slip coaches reappeared. In the summer 1920 timetable the GWR was seen to have recovered to its 1914 standards more quickly than other railways, and there were new non-stop runs from Paddington to Torquay – the noon express, in 3hr 49min – and to Worcester in 135min by the 1.30pm down, and non-stop running was resumed between Paddington and Bristol, in 135min each way. All told, there were 20 non-stop runs of 100 miles or over, including the down 'Cornish Riviera' booked to Plymouth in 4hr 23min, and no less than 99

runs on the GWR were booked at 50mph or over. But prewar standards of speed were not really achieved until October 1921. The July 1922 timetable featured five expresses over the Stratford–Cheltenham route – the Penzance, one to Plymouth, two to Bristol and a Birmingham–Cardiff and return – increased by one from the 1914 total.

The South Wales railways

By their nature the various independent railways in South Wales were concerned with local services, so main line workings were limited.

The Barry Railway was concerned to project itself as an expanding, integrated operator of rail and dock services. It developed Barry Island as a resort, and encouraged the operation of through excursion trains from the Welsh valleys. To cash in on the demand for leisure travel, the Barry Railway built up a fleet of steamers from 1905 to serve resorts on the south side of the Bristol Channel. In connection with sailings the 'Ilfracombe Boat Express' was run from Clarence Road to Barry Pier, running non-stop from Cardiff Great Western station. The steamship venture was short-lived and the vessels disposed of in 1910. Longer-lasting was the Barry's involvement with the 'Ports-to-Ports Express', see Chapter 8, the Barry Railway persuading the GWR to extend the service to Barry, and one of its engines worked the train to and from Cardiff. Suspended during World War I, the 'Ports-to-Ports' was reintroduced on 12 July 1919, and the following year was extended to/from

Swansea working forward over the Vale of Glamorgan line to Bridgend. The engine used from Cardiff was a GWR 2-6-0 or 4-4-0.

The Brecon & Merthyr Railway's principal service was between Newport and Brecon, and although these were local trains their journey time occupied 135-180min. The only main line service worked by the company was through participation in the Cardiff/Rhondda Valley stations–Aberystwyth summer trains, see below, in which the Rhymney/Taff Vale portions were combined at Pontsticill Junction and worked over the B&M to Brecon by a Cambrian 4-4-0 during the early 1900s, and by a Taff Vale locomotive after 1908. On reintroduction after World War I, the train was worked through to Talyllyn and back by a Taff Vale 0-6-2T. In the 1925 timetable, the train ran MSO and left Treherbert at 9.40am, routed via Merthyr, Builth Road, Rhayader and Moat Lane Junction to arrive in Aberystwyth at 4.40pm, with the return working from there at 2.20pm.

Apart from the summer Aberystwyth service, the Rhymney Railway had a hand in another longer distance service as a consequence of the joint LNWR/Rhymney line between Nantybwch and Rhymney Bridge which had given the larger company access to Cardiff. The facility did not involve regular through passenger trains but LNWR coaches were operated from Cardiff to Crewe, and to Liverpool and Manchester from 1897 and up to 1914. There were also through excursion trains between these places, worked by Rhymney engines between Cardiff and Rhymney Bridge.

As noted, the Taff Vale Railway contributed to the summer Aberystwyth train, its main section starting from Cardiff, combining at Pontypridd with through coaches from the Rhondda. The company extended some of its trains from Cardiff to Treherbert over the Rhondda & Swansea Bay Railway to Swansea, the latter company's trains making reciprocal appearances at Cardiff.

A summer FSO 12.45pm Newport–Aberystwyth and 1.10pm return began running in August 1920, with an alternative routing via Pontypridd, Treherbert, over the Rhondda and Swansea Bay line to Court Sart, then the Swansea District line to Llanelly, to Carmarthen and over the Manchester & Milford line. The overall journey was 5hr 20-50min. In early GWR days the train started from Cardiff Parade at 7.40am and was formed of gangwayed stock and usually headed by an 'Aberdare' 2-6-0. The return working left Aberystwyth at noon and was due in Cardiff at 7.20pm. The 1923-5 summer timetables also featured a summer FSO through train between Barry, Cardiff and Llandrindod Wells via Merthyr, Talybont, Builth Wells and Road.

An example of one of the through summer trains from the Welsh Valleys to Welsh holiday resorts – this is the Barry–Llandrindod Wells train introduced by the GWR and it is seen near Cefn Coed, soon after departure from Merthyr. Quite a smart-looking train, including Dean gangwayed stock and headed by Dean Goods 0-6-0 No. 2381.

CHAPTER TWO

THE SOUTHERN GROUP OF COMPANIES TO 1922

London & South Western Railway

A railway generally thought of nowadays in terms of its holiday and residential traffic to Bournemouth and the West Country. In its heyday however, more emphasis was placed on its importance in serving the military establishments at Portsmouth, Portland and Plymouth, on Salisbury Plain, and the Hampshire garrison towns. In addition, Southampton Docks was effectively the real heart of the LSWR, and again the military traffic passing to the outposts of Empire was a major source of revenue, the company making more out of its docks

The 12.50pm Waterloo–Portsmouth Harbour approaches Vauxhall on 27 March 1909, hauled by T9 class 4-4-0 No. 721.

and shipping than any other pre-Grouping company. Into Exeter, Plymouth, Weymouth and Portsmouth the LSWR was dependent on running powers granted by other railways. Such influences should serve as a perspective to its express services.

Competition with the London, Brighton & South Coast Railway for traffic between London and Portsmouth might have been expected to result in fast journey times, but at the turn of the century the best times made over the 74 miles of the LSWR's routes were 125/126min. Then, as now, the faster trains ran via the Guildford New Line, at 3.40pm down, and at 2.45pm and 5.40pm up. Other semi-fasts – up to eight stops were made – ran via Woking and, to be fair, some of their intermediate bookings were fairly demanding. There were also trains such as the 2.20pm from Waterloo, which comprised sections for Bournemouth and Portsmouth, the train dividing at Eastleigh.

The best times on the Southampton line via Basingstoke were made by the Channel Islands boat trains (up to nine weekly were run in summer) and these averaged 46mph. At this stage there was spirited competition between the LSWR and GWR for this traffic, and in 1899 the former had cut its boat train schedules appreciably. Of the other trains, the 12.30pm from Waterloo reached Southampton West non-stop in 104min for 79 miles, and the 4.55pm down called at Basingstoke and slipped at Winchester, to arrive at Southampton in 109min, but three other trains could do no better than 150min. Coming up, the fastest working was the 2.58pm, non-stop Southampton West–Vauxhall (for ticket collection) in 101min, and other trains took 111-135min. Although a non-stop run was made by the 2.5pm from Bournemouth Central (East, until May 1899) getting to Vauxhall in 132min, and the 2.15pm down called only at Christchurch to reach Bournemouth in 143min, other times tended to be 160min. First introduced in 1890, Pullman parlour cars were worked on the 2pm down, and on other trains.

Waterloo–Weymouth trains had earlier run over 'Castleman's Corkscrew' from Brockenhurst to Hamworthy Junction, as well as via Bournemouth. The decline of the 'Corkscrew' dated from the opening in 1893 of avoiding lines past Branksome and Holes Bay, after which Weymouth trains increasingly ran via Bournemouth. In 1898, Weymouth was usually 180-240min travelling from Waterloo, but during the following year two fast trains were introduced each way, with a best time of just over 3hr to/from Weymouth. The new T9 class 4-4-0s were loaded to no more than six coaches on

these workings but such enterprise was short-lived: two trains were soon withdrawn, and the others decelerated. Before that happened there had been a working timetable booking of 15min from Dorchester to Wareham for the up morning train which the enginemen delighted in trying to keep!

A feature of later LSWR services was the regular interval timetable. At the turn of the century, the West of England service had trains 'on the hour', at 11am, 1pm and 3pm, and these were to become time-honoured departures, supplemented by others at 9.15am and 5.50pm. Even by 1901, there were summer-only expresses, at 10.50am, for Plymouth, and 11.10am for North Cornwall. These were supplemented by a Friday night excursion train from Waterloo at 11.25pm, arriving at Padstow at 8.31am. As yet, the early morning van train to the West of England was unadvertised for passengers west of Salisbury. The fastest of the West of Englands was the 3pm down, timed in 3hr 46min for the 171¾ miles to Exeter Queen St, and calling at Salisbury (to change engines, as did all West of England trains), and Sherborne. The other expresses took 4hr or so to Exeter, and made more intermediate stops, notably at Templecombe where there were good connections with the Somerset & Dorset line. The five (one additional in summer) principal up departures from Exeter were at irregular intervals. Some timings were fast, given the switchback gradients west of Salisbury, such as 45min for the 36¾ miles from Sidmouth Junction to Yeovil Junction. This energy continued west of Exeter too, on the lines to Plymouth and Barnstaple. Until 1906, the LSWR enjoyed its advantage over the GWR of a shorter route to Exeter (nearly 22 miles) and Plymouth (15 miles).

The LSWR invested heavily in new running lines and flying junctions, such that by 1905 there was quadruple track throughout from Clapham Junction to Basingstoke. The fortunes of the LSWR's express services also changed for the better with the appointment in 1899 of Sam Fay as Superintendent of the Line. The best times on the West of England line had greatly improved by 1905, with the 11am and 3.30pm from Waterloo running, as they had from June 1903, to Exeter in 3¼hr (15min faster than the GWR), then non-stop to Exeter and to Plymouth in just under 5hr. A 4hr 53min time to Waterloo from Plymouth North Road was achieved by the 10.22am up, with 3¼hr spent east of Exeter Queen St., while the 10.20am from that station took 3hr 25min to Waterloo, calling at Templecombe and Salisbury. From the latter city, best up times were 91min, the fastest down trains taking 1min longer, and the times

With clerestoried restaurant car next Drummond Double Single No. 720, the 4.10pm from Waterloo nears journey's end at Bournemouth West on 31 May 1913. This train was non-stop to Bournemouth Central.

of 98/99min for Salisbury–Exeter were creditable. Speeds of to 80mph+ were not unusual with the capable T9 4-4-0s. From 1901, two West of England expresses in each direction had open layout coaches converted from 'Eagle' Plymouth boat stock and featured an at-seat service of meals from a kitchen brake vehicle.

Fast running on the West of England main line was to have tragic consequences, with the derailment at Salisbury on 1 July 1906 of a Devonport–Waterloo boat train which was conveying passengers, some say millionaires, from a transatlantic liner. Concern about speeding with these boat trains had been expressed from their introduction in 1904. Usually they ran once-weekly, at night, and were composed of the 'American Eagle Express' stock built in 1893 for Southampton transatlantic boat trains. In April 1904, a best time of 4hr 13min was set up between Stonehouse Pool Junction and Waterloo – 230 miles – with a 105 ton train. After the 1906 accident, the LSWR curbed any speeding but, with the GWR's shortened route to Plymouth, competition was in terms of creature comforts, and the LSWR introduced some fine new sleeping cars in 1908. It sold them to its rival in 1910 when a working agreement brought the striving between the companies to an end. From March 1908, a stop at Salisbury had become mandatory for all trains, less a

consequence of the accident there than for signalling reasons.

Holiday traffic to the West Country grew markedly during the Edwardian years. A North Cornwall express had begun running from July 1907, at 10.45am, the Plymouth portion of this train being booked to run non-stop from Exeter Queen St. to Devonport; in practice, the GWR observed its right to bring it to a stand at St Davids. By 1911, the 11am down was the main summer North Cornwall train, and complete with restaurant car reached Padstow in 6hr 4min for 259 miles, detaching coaches for Bude at Halwill Junction. Ilfracombe had a 10.28am to Waterloo which in taking 5hr 5min was considerably faster than the GWR service to/from Paddington. A later summer Saturdays train was introduced in July 1913, at 12.50pm to Ilfracombe/Torrington, returning at 9.55am from the latter. A short-lived experiment on the Salisbury line involved the running of the 9.35am Richmond–Salisbury and 4.25pm semi-fasts, a feature in the summer timetables of 1907/8.

By 1905, matters had also greatly improved on the Bournemouth line, with the 4.10pm from Waterloo to Weymouth and Swanage (dividing at Wareham), booked non-stop in 126min to Bournemouth Central, and the best up trains, also non-stop, at 9am and 1.57pm and taking 130/133min respectively. The afternoon train which made its first call at Christchurch now left at 2pm. The principal morning express was the undistinguished 10.15am Waterloo–Weymouth, taking a leisurely 148min to Bournemouth, and 3hr 27min to its destination; like most of the Weymouth expresses of that time it passed Wareham without stopping.

In 1899, Fay ran an experimental Sunday excursion train from Waterloo to Bournemouth in 110min, and intended to introduce a fastest time of 115min for service trains as from July that year. This initiative was vetoed by his chairman, and it took until July 1911 for two-hour timings to Bournemouth to materialise: by the 4.10pm down, and 9.8am and 2pm up. The last-mentioned started from Weymouth at 12.55pm and offered a 3hr 5min journey to Waterloo, not bettered until 1934. The 2pm down continued to make Christchurch its first call, and took 126min to Bournemouth. In charge of these trains were the Drummond 'Paddlebox' 4-6-0s built from 1910, and the designer's larger 4-4-0s. Non-stop running in the absence of water-troughs on the LSWR was made possible by the provision of tenders with a water capacity of 5,800 gallons. With the introduction of corridor stock and restaurant cars on the Bournemouth line, all Pullman cars had been withdrawn by 1911. One innovation in July 1905 was the facility of through coaches between Weymouth (dep 9.55am) and King's Cross (arr 2.5pm), to connect into afternoon GNR expresses. The return working left King's Cross at 2.40pm. The coaches were attached/detached at Clapham Junction and ran via Loughborough Junction and Ludgate Hill; into Clapham Junction from the south the train ran via Wimbledon and East Putney. The workings continued every summer up to and including 1910, but did not run beyond Bournemouth after the 1908 season. The Bournemouth departure was 10.5am, to arrive in King's Cross at 1.34pm. The return working remained at 2.40pm.

The LSWR worked hard to develop its rail/steamer services, particularly to France although the Le Havre service in particular barely paid its way. By 1913, the principal service was by the 9.45pm restaurant car express from Waterloo to Southampton Docks for passengers travelling to Le Havre (offering an arrival in Paris at 11.24am), and to the Channel Islands. The return working arrived at Waterloo at 9am. The departure was delayed to 10.30pm in June 1914. There was also a Southampton–Cherbourg service, with a boat train from Waterloo at 8.15pm, and more limited sailings to St Malo with, at times, a connecting train from Waterloo.

On the lines to the Hampshire coast, the opening in 1903 of the Meon Valley line, from Butts Junction, Alton, to just short of Fareham, was intended to develop a main route to Gosport and to Stokes Bay (to connect with LSWR steamers for Ryde). Through trains were provided from Waterloo but traffic did not develop as hoped. The schedules of the LSWR's service between Waterloo and Portsmouth via Guildford remained disappointing even in June 1914, when the fastest train reached Portsmouth Harbour from Waterloo in no better a time than 116min. This was the 6.40pm down, with restaurant car, and it returned as a semi-fast at 12noon the next day, taking 140min to Waterloo. Only the 12.45pm down – with restaurant car – was timed in less than 2hr. Many of the other Portsmouth trains stopped at most stations south of Guildford, and spent up to 150min on their journeys.

Whatever the merits of the train service, the old Waterloo terminus was inadequate on many scores, and in 1899 the LSWR obtained powers for its total rebuilding which took from 1902 until 1922 to complete. By October 1918, express schedules had deteriorated sadly, with best times of 159min from Waterloo to Bournemouth, and 3hr 57min to Exeter, the latter very much slower than the GWR. The mid-morning Waterloo–West of England express had however retained its restaurant car throughout the war.

In the Summer 1920 timetable there were limited accelerations of the wartime schedules, but more notable was the introduction of systematised departure times 'on the hour' from Waterloo for the West of England trains. There were three non-stop runs in each direction between Salisbury and Exeter, one each way made by a new restaurant car express between Portsmouth, Exeter and Plymouth which quickly became popular with naval officers travelling between the two centres. The disappointing schedules reflected the imposition of a maximum line speed of 60mph rather than available motive power. By 1920, there were ten Urie N15 class 4-6-0s at work on the principal Bournemouth and West of England duties. Even in the depth of winter in February 1921, over 93% of LSWR trains were right time-5min late, with an average lateness of no more than 1.35min.

With the Summer 1921 timetable, the West of England service was improved by a better spacing of expresses, giving hourly departures from Waterloo to Exeter between 8am and 5pm – excepting 2pm and 4pm – and a 6pm to Yeovil; a similar process of tidying-up and accelerations was applied to the up expresses. Two trains in each direction were summer peak workings between Waterloo and Padstow/Bude, and Sidmouth/Exmouth respectively. Similarly revivified was the Bournemouth line, with hourly departures at 30min past from Waterloo between 9.30am and 7.30pm, excepting 11.30am, 1.30 and 5.30pm. The fastest timing to Bournemouth Central was now 135min down, and 137min up. The Portsmouth trains followed a systematic departure pattern too, at 50min past the hour from Waterloo.

Two expresses each way on the Bournemouth and West of England main lines were withdrawn with the winter timetable, but the improvements of 1921 were consolidated the next summer when the West of England expresses lost a number of intermediate calls. By now, the 9.53am Portsmouth–Plymouth Friary and 9.35am return expresses were accompanied by another cross-country service, leaving Brighton at 11.20am with through coaches to Bournemouth, Ilfracombe and Cardiff – see **Cross-Country services** (Chapter 8).

By this time, and resplendent in the LSWR's recently adopted dark-green paintwork, there were four new five-coach sets of so-called 'Ironclad' gangwayed stock at work on the Bournemouth expresses; a pantry compartment was included in one coach for the service of light refreshments. Two trains of similar stock including pantry brake firsts were built the following year for the Southampton boat trains.

The Summer 1921 and 1922 timetables featured a 12.40pm Guildford–Havant–Bournemouth West which included through coaches from Deal via Tonbridge (high summer only) and from Portsmouth, with return from Bournemouth at 11.30am (10.30 in 1922). Another curiosity of these times was a short-lived 3.34pm Waterloo–Guildford–Redhill semi-fast worked throughout by an LSWR engine.

The Somerset & Dorset Joint Railway
Originally conceived of as two local undertakings which came together to form a system linking the Bristol and English Channels, the completion of the line to Bath in 1874 resulted in greatly increased traffic, ironically accompanied by a financial crisis for the company. The Somerset & Dorset Railway Company's management reacted by approaching the GWR with the hope that the company might take over their railway. In turn, the GWR decided to involve the London & South Western as the latter had an obvious interest in the portion of the S&D south of Templecombe. But, instead of concluding a deal with the GWR, the Waterloo management

conferred with the Midland Railway, and these companies made a better offer to the S&D. This involved a joint lease of the company for a term of 999 years from 1 November 1875, and the partners set up a Joint Committee to run the enterprise, with local management based at Bath. The *raison d'être* of the S&D was therefore to serve the interests of its joint masters, by feeding traffic to their main lines.

Although there was sufficient local freight and perishables traffic, by the 1880s the S&D's operations were beginning to be dominated by passenger traffic to and from Bournemouth. Through coaches to/from Birmingham had been operated, if none too successfully, from 1874, and from Bradford from 1880. To improve operations and schedules, the infrastructure was improved at the southern end of the line, and some doubling was carried out up to and including 1904. Even so, the S&D remained a predominantly single-line railway, the resultant speed restrictions combining with the severe gradients to limit service speeds.

The LSWR's involvement meant that adequate connections with its West of England main line were essential. By 1900, there were four principal Bath–Bournemouth trains each way, making connection with Midland Railway services north of Bath Queen Square station. The best time was 130min for the 71½ miles to Bournemouth. With the completion of doubling, and the introduction of tablet-exchanging apparatus and more powerful 4-4-0s by 1904, the winter timetable included a 'Bournemouth Express' booked in 122min for Bath–Bournemouth, despite three stops, while the corresponding 9.45am from the resort took 1min longer with no less than six calls. During the summer timetable, two expresses each way took just 110min while a two days a week relief bettered this by 3min – so achieving an all-time record for the S&D.

In the summer of 1913 the 10.38am from Bournemouth West took no more than 114min to reach Bath, running non-stop from Poole to Bath at an average speed of 38mph despite the fearsome five-mile climb at 1 in 50 from Evercreech Junction up to the Mendips. The return 2.13pm from Bath (originating as a restaurant car express from Nottingham) also achieved the same overall timing and non-stop run to Poole. The S&D was to see a procession of holiday trains over the line in early BR days which might have given the impression that this was the height of operations on the railway.

Actually, the heyday was achieved in 1914 so far as *year-round* volume and frequency of passenger services were concerned. Then there were five

A Somerset & Dorset Joint Railway train from Bath drifts down to Bournemouth West on 31 May 1913 behind 4-4-0 No. 18. All but the first coach is S&D stock, and next the engine is a through Midland gangwayed brake composite, possibly from Bradford Market Street.

through down trains, all but one fast, and five up; there were shorter distance stopping trains in addition. Principal trains were the 8.37am from Bournemouth West to Manchester, with restaurant car to Derby (Nottingham in summer), and the 9.20am Manchester–Bournemouth, with restaurant car from Birmingham New St., and a summer 1.45pm Birmingham New St.–Bournemouth. The all year-round Manchester trains had been introduced on 1 October 1910, the response from the Midland and LNWR no less to a GWR/LSWR express from Birkenhead to Oxford and Bournemouth inaugurated in that year's summer timetable – see **Cross-Country services**. Between June and September there were at least a couple of other seasonal weekday fast through trains each way on the S&D.

Other S&D trains conveyed through coaches between Bristol Temple Meads or St Philip's and Bournemouth. Efforts had been made earlier to develop traffic to/from Bridgwater and LSWR stations, and up until 1914 semi-fast trains continued to run between this Somerset town and Templecombe.

The recovery of services from World War I was quite rapid, and by May 1919 there was a through Derby–Bournemouth express booked for Bournemouth–Bath in 122min. The best down train of 1920 took 125min, with two stops. By now, there

were five rebuilt Johnson 4-4-0s at work – virtually standard Midland Class 2s – and they worked the Manchester–Bournemouth express which even in winter loaded to six coaches. Generally, the S&D Class 2s were worked much harder than on the MR with the route's expresses, and fruitless attempts were made to allocate more powerful engines to the line, such as Compounds and the ex-MR 990 class 4-4-0s.

In the 1923 summer timetable there were expresses south from Bath at 2.30pm (Liverpool, Manchester and Leicester through coaches), 2.40 (coaches from Bradford including restaurant car, and from Newcastle and Hull), 4pm (restaurant car from Nottingham, TC from Lincoln St Marks) and a 6.35pm, all trains booked in 123-133min. There were four departures with long-distance through coaches from Bournemouth West, at 9.50, 10.20, 10.45 and 11.45am. Other holiday trains included an 11.5am Bournemouth West–Burnham-on-Sea, and 11.35am return. One feature of the 1922 summer timetable had been a through coach from Manchester to Swanage, detached at Broadstone from the Manchester train. This was more successful than the MR's bid for some of the S&D trains to be diverted into Bournemouth Central station. In October 1922, the principal northbound morning express for Manchester and Bradford was made later and now left at 10.20am. Southbound, the 2.38pm from Bath regained its non-stop run to Poole, and reached Bournemouth West in 117min. By now, the competition offered by the through trains to Bournemouth via Oxford, from Birkenhead and Newcastle, was beginning to tell.

One chestnut in the history of train services was created by notes in the public timetable of Winter 1929/30 to the effect that there were daily slip coach workings on the S&D. This was misleading as in fact the 11.35am departures from Bath and from Bournemouth West alike came to a stand at Templecombe No. 2 signal box and in each case the vehicle was simply detached from each train and then worked to the Upper station. By this time, sets of Southern and LMS coaches were working over the S&D, and to Bristol.

Continuing losses signalled that the end was approaching for the S&D as a separate undertaking, and from 1930 the Southern took over maintenance of the track, the LMS assumed responsibility for motive power and for operating the line, and the two railways divided up the coaching stock. The realities of the S&D's altered circumstances were masked perhaps by the changes to the Bournemouth–Manchester trains. From 1927, their restaurant cars were diverted to Manchester London Road and the service was distinguished by the name of 'Pines Express'. In addition to the 'Pines', there was a regular 11.40am from Bournemouth West conveying through coaches to Bradford/York, worked to Mangotsfield and there attached to an express from Bristol. The balancing working for this train was the 4pm departure from Bath and in summer this started back from Gloucester where the through coaches had been detached from a Bristol-bound express.

By July 1938, the southbound 'Pines' was taking 137min from Bath to Bournemouth with four regular stops, and now ran into and out of Templecombe Upper. The northbound working, at 10.25am from Bournemouth West, did better in maintaining a 125min run to Bath despite six stops and avoided Templecombe Upper. One Bath–Bournemouth train of interest was the 10.20am down which included through coaches from Clifton Down and, with limited stops, took 155min, but like many others was slower on summer Saturdays. From the late spring of 1938 six LMS Class 5 4-6-0s had been allocated to Bath for work over the S&D and these were able to take 270tons unassisted over Masbury summit.

Midland & South Western Junction Railway

With the opening in 1891 of the railway's northern extension from Cirencester to Andoversford Junction came the opportunity to run through trains from Cheltenham to Andover, by virtue of running powers over the GWR's Banbury and Cheltenham line. As yet, the through trains were very slow, and improvements at first relied on the loan of locomotives and stock by the London & South Western.

From 1893, the MSWJR acquired a 4-4-0 and 2-4-0s capable of working faster trains, connecting at Cheltenham Lansdown with Midland Railway Birmingham–Bristol line expresses. The principal Cheltenham–Andover Junction workings were the 10.27am and 2.52pm, balanced by the 3pm from Andover. The afternoon trains conveyed through coaches from Sheffield to Southampton, these later running to/from Bradford, and in due course to/from York and Manchester. Other passenger services of interest at the turn of the century included special mails trains at 9pm from Southampton to Cheltenham and 6am return on Saturdays, run from July 1893 in connection with the sailings of South African and American steamers, and also conveying emigrant traffic; the northbound train seems to have been withdrawn before long. Between 1902 and 1913, the southbound 'American and Cape Lines Express' included a through coach leaving from Whitehaven or Carnforth on Friday nights, introduced during the period of acute depression in the iron trade which had led to emigration from West Cumberland. This coach was worked to Cheltenham on the 12.5am Leeds–Bristol which had connections from Glasgow (and at one time there was a through coach from St Enoch to Southampton) and Edinburgh.

The MSWJR relied heavily on Southampton Docks for its traffic, much of it in connection with military troop or stores movements, the War Office having developed its camps on the Salisbury Plain from the 1890s. Elsewhere on the line, milk and perishables consignments, and horseboxes, were probably more important to revenue than passengers. As Ahrons commented, 'The northern connection with the Midland was certainly the making of the railway . . .', the other catalyst being the appointment of Sam Fay as general manager in 1892. His efforts in boosting traffic receipts released the railway from receivership, and made it possible to offer more attractive services.

By 1910, the principal passenger trains were smartly timed, and comprised the 10.35am and 3.5pm from Cheltenham to Andover Junction, and 11.39am and 2.34pm return. The scheduled times from

Southampton West and Cheltenham were 150-180min for the 94¾ miles, the best trains being designated 'North Express' or 'South Express' in the timetable. The main connection southbound was from the Midland's 10.25am Bradford–Bristol, the through coaches being transferred to the 3.5pm from Cheltenham. With the introduction from October 1910 of the MR and LNWR's Manchester London Road–Bournemouth West train, emphasis shifted to that train, and a lunchtime connection at Cheltenham, and in May 1911 a through Manchester–Southampton coach was introduced, subsequently working to/from Liverpool. The LSWR certainly gave no quarter to the MSWJR as the Birkenhead–Bournemouth service jointly operated with the GWR was directly competitive with this through coach.

The MSWJR's fast trains were at their best in 1913/14 when the 1.10pm 'South Express' from Cheltenham was booked to Southampton West in 156min, including no more than 31min for the 21½ miles from Marlborough–Andover, including the stop at Ludgershall. The former 3.5pm fast train had by then become a slow train. The 1.45pm Southampton Town–Cheltenham 'North Express' called only at Southampton West, Redbridge, Andover Junction and Swindon Town, with a timing of 147min from Southampton West. There was even a Sunday morning

'North Express'. By virtue of good connections at Andover Junction to the LSWR and through ticketing, by using the afternoon 'North Express' it was possible to travel from Waterloo to Cheltenham Lansdown in 3hr 19min for the 135 miles, better than some GWR Paddington–Swindon–Cheltenham journeys.

During World War I the Railway was most important strategically and carried considerable traffic in ambulance trains from Southampton, usually hauled by London & South Western 4-4-0s. These military movements led to drastic reductions in the MSWJR's passenger services from which they never recovered and by the end of the war there were just five trains each way. The afternoon 'North Express' did not reappear but the through coaches between Southampton and Manchester London Road were restored in the summer of 1921, diverted to/from Liverpool Lime St. that autumn, and continued until the outbreak of World War II. In July 1922, the principal trains were the 1.35pm 'South Express' from Cheltenham Queens Rd to Southampton Town, and its untitled 10.16am counterpart from Southampton Town. The times between Cheltenham and Andover Junction were 133min southbound and 125min northbound.

With Grouping, the MSWJR passed to the Great

Into Andover Junction station comes the Midland & South Western Junction Railway's 1.52pm from Southampton to Cheltenham, Queen's Rd – the 'North Express'. The engine is 4-4-0 No. 8, its train comprising some of the handsome MSWJR coaches, with a through Midland brake at the rear, to Birmingham and Derby.

Western with effect from 1 July 1923. After completion of a programme of bridge strengthening and track relaying in the early 1930s larger engines, of GWR standard classes, took over train working and, in time, these included 'Manor' class 4-6-0s. From the Southern end, the usual choice for the Southampton– Cheltenham trains were Maunsell 2-6-0s. In 1938, the journey times of the two trains conveying the through coaches had been extended by the inclusion of additional stops.

Reductions in passenger services took effect from 30 June 1958 after which there was just one train each way between Cheltenham and Andover, with through coaches advertised in the down direction only to Southampton Terminus, a journey of 3hr 31min from Cheltenham Lansdown station. When it came to relaying Lansdown Junction in 1958/9, the connections from the Kingham and MSWJ line to Lansdown station were not renewed, and from 3 November 1958 the remaining pair of MSWJ line passenger trains were rerouted to Cheltenham St James station, as a prelude to the closure of the line to passenger traffic on and from 11 September 1961.

The Isle of Wight
The delightful island has been spared some of the ills of the mainland but it was always a desirable destination for the main line railways and was well-supplied, perhaps over-provided, with its own system of independent lines which even in the Edwardian heyday was just marginally profitable overall, despite rapidly growing traffic. Although the London & South Western and London, Brighton & South Coast Railway competed for access by ferry to the Island, the latter with the principal Portsmouth–Ryde service, the former with one from Stokes Bay (until 1913) and Lymington Pier–Yarmouth, they jointly owned Portsmouth Harbour station, and the pier and railway line at Ryde.

In 1901 a South Western & Isle of Wight Junction Railway was proposed with the aim of linking the LSWR's Lymington branch by a seven-mile railway including a tunnel under the Solent to the Freshwater, Yarmouth & Newport Railway. The plan was supported by the LSWR and Great Central, but opposed by the LBSCR. A Bill was more than once presented to Parliament. A revised scheme was resurrected in 1912, and was still being discussed in 1914. Another tunnel scheme was later proposed, to link the Newport–Cowes line with the Fawley branch.

In 1930, A. B. MacLeod was given control of the traffic and commercial departments of the Island's railways, and improved services greatly, including the innovation of tourist trains in summer. Notably, there was 'The Tourist' named train, at 9.55am from Ventnor to Freshwater (27 miles), arriving at 11.12am after non-stop runs from Sandown to Newport and from Newport to Freshwater. It returned at 5.20pm. Featuring two observation coaches, during one week in 1933 'The Tourist' carried 2,700 passengers.

London, Brighton & South Coast Railway
The pre-Grouping railways were particularly competitive in the south-east but this did not ensure that their services were either fast or frequent. Hastings was served by the LBSCR and South Eastern & Chatham Railway, but though the former had an easier graded if longer route from Victoria via Haywards Heath and Lewes, and its Hastings trains by-passed Eastbourne using the Polegate–Stobcross Junction spur, the best time in 1898 was 123min for the 76½-mile journey. This was achieved by the 3.27pm from Victoria and 5.5pm from London Bridge, the Hastings portion being detached at Lewes from that for Eastbourne. For travellers *to* London, the fastest time was 132min, and that meant a change at Eastbourne into the 8.30am to London Bridge which ran fairly smartly – non-stop to London Bridge in 90min for 65¾ miles. Sometimes, there were portions for both London termini, such as on the 9.55am ex-Eastbourne which covered the 55¼ miles to East Croydon – where the train divided – in 75min.

Much of the LBSCR's effort competitively speaking was engaged in a contest with the London & South Western for traffic to Portsmouth and the Isle of Wight. This was despite a route longer by 13 miles. While Portsmouth and Mid-Sussex stations are nowadays reached via Three Bridges and Horsham, in pre-Grouping days all Portsmouth expresses ran via Mitcham Junction, Sutton and Dorking. A time of 125min was made by the two crack trains of 1898, the 8.45am Portsmouth Harbour–London Bridge and 4.55pm return, each of which had three intermediate stops. Victoria was the terminus for the off-peak trains, such as the 11.35am and 3.37pm down, the latter running to Fratton in 128 miles for 84¼ miles, at the time the longest non-stop run in the south-east. From Portsmouth Harbour, the 9.40 and 11.35am to Victoria each had a journey time of 130min. The West Sussex resorts did not benefit from the Portsmouth service, and Littlehampton and Bognor's train service from London was poor, and usually included semi-fast connections from Arundel or Ford. Supplementing the London trains there were Brighton–Portsmouth semi-fasts such as the 9.40am westbound, taking 80min for the 45½ miles to the Harbour station.

The LBSCR's Newhaven–Dieppe steamer service was served by a daily boat train, at 10am from Victoria, running non-stop from East Croydon to Newhaven Harbour. The Lewes–Seaford line, part of which was traversed by the boat trains, incidentally featured an unusual through express to Victoria – the 3pm from Seaford, routed via the Bluebell Line north of Lewes, and calling at Horsted Keynes, East Grinstead and Oxted.

The LBSCR's prestige service linked Brighton and London. It was indeed prestige in more than one sense as most Brighton fast trains were originally restricted to first and second-class passengers. Travelling third-class the passenger could generally expect to take over 90min for the London–Brighton journey. The most important express in the service of 1898 was the 5pm from London Bridge, non-stop in 65min for the 50½ miles. Its up counterpart left at 8.45am and took 70min overall, as well as conveying a Victoria section which was slipped at East Croydon. Other non-stop trains were the 9.25 and 9.55am from Brighton, both for London Bridge, and taking 73 and 70min. The 2, 4 and 6pm stopped intermediately and spent 75-80min on their journeys.

As yet, the emphasis was on the City terminus: Victoria just had one non-stop ordinary train to Brighton, at 3.50pm daily and with a 75min timing. The best up train to Victoria took 80min. From 2 October 1898, there had also been the Sunday 'Brighton Limited' non-stop from Victoria in the hour, and returning at 9pm, also advertised to take an hour but actually booked in 59min. On Sundays, there were seven all-class trains. At the turn of the century, Brighton also boasted a late-night fast train from Victoria, setting out at 11.50pm ThSO, and reaching the town 70min later, including an East Croydon stop. Third-class passengers were admitted to the 11.50pm. Although there were a few through trains between London and Worthing, the best time for which was 95min each way for the 61 miles, the service mostly comprised through coaches detached at Haywards East or Preston Park.

Because the traffic between London and Brighton was self-evidently lucrative, more than once the LBSCR was threatened with competition from a new operator. In 1899, there was a plan for an electrically worked line to be devoid of intermediate stations but it failed to attract financial backing. At the time, the LBSCR's service was by no means brilliant but the opening of the Quarry line in April 1900, combined

with quadrupling from Earlswood to the north end of Balcombe Tunnel which was completed in 1910, made it possible to schedule faster trains. For the first time, the company had its own tracks independent of the South Eastern south from South Croydon, and they avoided Redhill into the bargain. Parliamentary powers in 1903 were secured for extension of the widening to Brighton but were never taken up.

To show what it could do as a counterblast to the proposed electric railway, at Christmas 1901 the LBSCR put on two fast runs with the 'Pullman Limited', out in just under 54min on 21 December, and in 51min on Christmas Day, no less. In both cases, the engines were B4 4-4-0s. But improvements to timetabled services were slow in coming, despite another flight of fancy in July 1903 when B4 No. 70 made a 48¾min sprint from Victoria to Brighton. In addition to its suburban electrification, the LBSCR also engaged a consultant who proposed electrification between London, Worthing and Portsmouth. Doubtless the resulting report was useful for the Brighton to keep in reserve, particularly as the company had obtained powers to work the whole of its system with electric traction.

The 1905 Victoria–Brighton service was at a two-hourly frequency, with trains timed in no better than about 80min, with the exception of the 'Pullman Limited' booked in 70min, and the 5pm from London Bridge, in 65min. From the coast there was nothing quicker than 70min, the time made by the 8.45am to Victoria, and 5.45pm up 'Pullman Limited'. Best up trains were the non-stop 7.15am to London Bridge in 67min and the 9.45pm, stopping only at East Croydon and reaching Victoria in 65min. Slip workings featured in the LBSCR timetables generally, and in 1906 there were five slips on weekdays. From July 1906 there was the novelty of a weekdays Brighton–Paddington and return train, up at 11.30am in 100min, back at 3.40pm in 3min less. Worked by a LBSCR locomotive at the head of a five-coach train of that company's stock, initial loadings were encouraging. The workings continued through the winter but soon they were carrying no more than a score of passengers and were withdrawn in July 1907.

A new set of Pullman cars entered service on 1 November 1908 on what became known as the 'Southern Belle'. This worked twice-daily to Victoria non-stop in 60min and was memorably described in Pullman Car Co. publicity as 'a chain of vestibuled luxury'. From 1 June 1909, the 'Belle' ran also on weekdays and from the start the train was associated with the Marsh Atlantics. When spare,

One of the London, Brighton & South Coast Railway's Mid-Sussex route expresses from Portsmouth is seen near Chichester on 15 April 1911. The engine is 4-4-0 No. 320, and its set train consists of Billinton non-gangwayed stock.

new Pullmans from the seven-car 'Belle' set were included in the 8.45am Brighton–London Bridge and 5pm return 'City Limiteds'. At East Croydon the 8.45am slipped a Victoria portion including a Pullman. In its official guide the LBSCR purred unctuously that the 'City Limited' 'conveys 300 merchant princes to and from their homes in Brighton'. The special set of coaches included elliptical-roofed 'balloon' coaches with gangways, otherwise rare on the LBSCR; not least, there was a brake coach furnished entirely with armchairs.

There was nothing in the way of a wholesale improvement to main line services on the LBSCR until the appointment in 1909 of F. Finlay Scott as Superintendent of the Line. Beginning with that summer's timetable, the train service was remodelled within a year or so and few trains remained unchanged. Generally, 60min timings were applied to the non-stop Victoria–Brighton workings and third-class passengers admitted to every train except the 'Southern Belle'. The railway discovered that the withdrawal of second-class was more than compensated by an increase in first and third-class travel. The London–Brighton service was also supplemented and the winter 1910 timetable, for instance, offered 25 down and 28 up trains, and there were first and second-class only, and first and third-class trains, as well as 'all-classes'. On weekdays the

down 'City Limited' remained first-class only and reached Brighton in 65min; it was 'all-classes' on Saturdays. Many of the best trains retained Worthing portions, detached at Preston Park, or slipped at Haywards Heath off the 3.40pm ex-Victoria; there was a Worthing slip at the same station off the 5.5pm London Bridge–Eastbourne.

Other developments on the Brighton service included the introduction of a 12.5am Victoria–Brighton in 1912, non-stop in 65min, and featuring a Pullman supper car in the ensuing year. By 1912, the Brighton and Worthing services were worked by the Marsh Atlantics and Pacific tanks, and time was kept with loads up to 325 tons or so. Reliability was excellent. Writing in 1923, one competent observer said that in over 25 years and 1,000-plus Brighton–London runs, on only 76 of these had the LBSCR engine 'failed to achieve what was demanded of it'. In March 1914 new Pullman cars were introduced on the Sunday 'Pullman Limited', and the weekday 8.45am and 1.20pm Brighton–Victoria.

By 1905, Portsmouth's services showed some improvement over those at the turn of the century. The 11.35am from Victoria, non-stop Clapham Junction–Fratton in 110min, reached Portsmouth Town in 121min, slightly faster than in 1898. The 4.55pm from London Bridge called at Arundel and

Chichester only, to Fratton and took 124min to Portsmouth Town. The counterparts to these trains, the 8.45am Portsmouth Town–London Bridge and 3pm to Victoria, took 125 and 133min overall respectively. The midday trains often loaded to no more than five coaches and, given the competence of engines such as the I3 class 4-4-2Ts, were not difficult to work despite the route's gradients and its permanent speed restrictions.

Eastbourne's best train in 1905 was the 8.30am, non-stop to London Bridge in 90min, and the 9.55am, also to London Bridge, in 93min and non-stop to East Croydon. By 1911, Eastbourne shed had two of the second batch of Atlantics for use on these trains. Off-peak services, such as by the 5.30pm from Eastbourne, involved a 138min journey to Victoria, but improvements came in June 1913 with the 9.35 and 11.45am and 6.15pm up, accelerated to an 85min journey and there was also a new 8.20am MX train. Similarly, to the same timing, were the non-stop 'Eastbourne Sunday Limited' Pullman trains in each direction for which day return fares were available, as indeed they were on the 'Southern Belle'. The best services to Hastings were by the 3.20pm and 5.20pm from Victoria, each with a portion slipped at Polegate, and these reached their destination in 120 and 118 min respectively.

Also improved from 1909 was the Newhaven–Dieppe route, with the new 24knot steamers of 1913 capable of making the crossing in 165min. Both day and night services were accelerated from June 1913 and, in 1914, Pullman cars were introduced on the day/night boat trains and there were plans to reduce the overall journey time to Paris by 30min the following year.

As late as 1910, the Uckfield line's weekday through services to/from London were restricted to coaches worked on the 8.3am Brighton–Tunbridge Wells, detached at Groombridge and then, with others coming from Eastbourne via the Cuckoo Line, attached to a train from Tunbridge Wells which was due in Victoria at 10.38am. The Uckfield line coaches returned in company with Eastbourne and Tunbridge Wells portions on the 3.45pm from Victoria which ran non-stop to Groombridge. With the opening in June 1914 of the Ashurst spur which avoided Groombridge through services between London and the Uckfield and Heathfield line stations were greatly improved. There was an 8.10am from Brighton, non-stop from Eridge to Victoria in 58min, but the best timing was made by the 3.45pm down which at one time reached Eridge in 53min for the 42¾ miles from Victoria.

By its Acts of Parliament of 1898 and 1899 the LBSCR gained powers to rebuild its side of Victoria station so as to improve passenger and operating facilities, and the formal reopening took place in July 1908. Although services were curtailed after the start of World War I, including suspension of the 'Southern Belle' during the first few weeks of hostilities, by 1922 they had returned to the equal of 1914, if not better. By now, the seven Baltic tanks were at work from Brighton shed and were establishing a reputation as good performers although on the 385ton trains such as the 'City Limited' they did not seem to have much in reserve. The Railway had officially bestowed the title 'City Limited' on the 5pm London Bridge–Brighton and up morning train with the acceleration of both trains in February 1921.

In the Summer 1923 service there were 31 down and 28 up trains between London and Brighton on weekdays, and 14 down and 16 up on Sundays – an increase on what had gone before. The 'Southern Belle' had reverted to a 60min timing both ways, and the 6.35pm to Victoria and 12.20pm from Brighton were non-stop in the same time while the 12.5am down called at Haywards Heath on two days of the week and took 65min. The 'City Limiteds' timings were 60min down and 62min up. The Sunday 4.55pm from Victoria and 11.30am ex-Brighton were composed solely of third-class Pullmans and ran non-stop in 65min. Over the Ashurst–Birchden spur there were now two through services each way, including a 6.6pm SX Victoria–Uckfield which slipped an Eridge coach at Ashurst.

East London Railway

Originally owned by the East London Railway, this link between the Great Eastern at East London Junction, near Shoreditch, and the London, Brighton & South Coast Railway was from 1882 leased to six railway companies and run by a joint committee. It deserves a footnote although it never saw a regular main line service in the 20th century. It was used by Croydon Central–Liverpool St. trains operated by the LBSCR, and 1876-83 by an underused return semi-fast service to Brighton. There were Richmond to New Cross through trains before the electrification of the Metropolitan and District Railways services through central London, but declining local traffic on the ELR led to realisation that electrification was its only salvation.

In March 1913, fourth-rail electrification of the East London was completed between the New Cross stations and Shoreditch and the running of the line was taken over by the Metropolitan Railway on behalf of the joint committee. By the 1930s its value as a link between the GE and the Southern lines was seldom exploited other than for parcels and freight trains, and excursions to the seaside and for football supporters. One excursion reported using the line on Whit-Monday 1936 was from Norwich to Eastbourne, and included a restaurant car.

The South Eastern & Chatham Railway

This railway invested heavily in its infrastructure during the immediate pre-World War I period, the weakness of the bridges having prevented the use of engines with an axle-loading of over 18 tons. The reconstruction of nearly 600 bridges and four tunnels, and relaying of the main lines with new rails and stone ballast was only completed in 1913, by which time Wainwright's L class 4-4-0s were being built, these being the first to take advantage of the increased axle-loading. The SECR also rebuilt Dover Admiralty Pier, built the fine station at Dover Marine, and improved its facilities at Folkestone. All told, the revitalisation of the SECR represented one of the largest investment programmes of the pre-Grouping railways but the immediate beneficiary was the military, and the movement of troops and stores to the Western Front. Yet, still more improvements were necessary after Grouping before the Southern Railway could operate 4-6-0s on its boat trains.

The deficiencies of the railways inherited by the SECR Managing Committee provide a perspective against which to review the services of 1898. On the London, Chatham & Dover, nearly all expresses were based on Victoria, generally calling at Herne Hill for connection with the City, but a few worked to Holborn Viaduct. On the Swanley–Maidstone–Ashford line there were just two trains, the 8.40am from Ashford and 4.12pm from Victoria, which were anything more than stopping trains, and these called at all stations beyond Maidstone in their 120min journey. The 9am Victoria–Dover was a Continental express but also conveyed portions for Canterbury and stations to Dover, and for stations to Margate and Ramsgate, both slipped at Faversham. There was a summer MSO relief at 9.2am from Victoria, reaching Margate at 10.53 and Ramsgate at 11.10am. Otherwise, the Thanet expresses took 120min or more for the 74 miles to Margate, with the exception of the 5.10pm from Holborn Viaduct which had a non-stop run from St Pauls (later Blackfriars) to Margate in 93min, and brought its passengers to Margate for 7pm. This train slipped two portions at Faversham, one for stations to Westgate-on-Sea, and the other for Dover.

Although ordinary passengers were much later

A down South Eastern & Chatham Railway boat train from Charing Cross to Dover approaches Grove Park on 6 May 1911 behind E class 4-4-0 No. 36 with a handsome train of Wainwright stock in tow, as well as a couple of Pullman cars.

precluded from using boat trains to the Channel ports, this was not the case before 1914 so that six down and five up Calais and Ostend boat trains served the needs of Dover's domestic passengers, as well as making intermediate calls. The fastest timing over the 78½ miles to Dover was 105min, but other than the boat trains Victoria–Dover services took over 120min for their journeys. Through coaches were provided for Walmer and Deal, running via Kearsney.

Apart from LCDR boat trains to serve that company's steamer sailings from Dover, the South Eastern also ran boat trains in connection. These were usually booked to leave Charing Cross simultaneously with the LCDR departures from Victoria, and to arrive at Dover Pier when they did. In 1898, the SER's 9am from Charing Cross ran via Cannon St. where it reversed, and then had a timing of 101min to Dover Pier. The 5.35pm from Charing Cross connected with a sailing to Ostend and also made a number of intermediate stops during its 132min journey.

Another LCDR boat train service was that to/from Queenborough Pier, to connect with the steamers to/from Flushing. Morning and evening boat trains were run over the 50¼ miles. The 8.30am from Victoria took 72min, stopping only at Herne Hill, and slipping a portion at Chatham for Faversham. In 1900 Queenborough Pier was destroyed by fire and, until it was rebuilt, the Flushing service was temporarily diverted to the former SER station at Port Victoria on the Isle of Grain which, until 1904, continued to be patronised by the night sailings. Competition from the Great Eastern Railway's Hook of Holland service influenced the transfer of the night sailings from Queenborough to Folkestone in 1911, and the day service was discontinued during World War I.

Other than the SER's boat trains to/from Dover, there were six down expresses from Charing Cross via Tonbridge and their time over the 69 miles to Folkestone Central was usually more than 120min, including several intermediate stops; the customary timing from Folkestone was around 150min. From October 1897, there had been the 'Folkestone Vestibuled Limited', at 4.28pm from Charing Cross to Folkestone Central, calling at Cannon St. and London Bridge, and running fast to Ashford. In the up direction, expresses included the 'Folkestone Vestibuled Limited', at 8.32am from Dover and 8.55am from Folkestone Central, then non-stop to Cannon St. in 95min. The 'Vestibuled Limited' was formed of British-built saloon cars to Pullman

specification and furnishings, and with accommodation for all three classes, as well as a buffet for the first-class. The cars were owned by the SER and passed to Pullman ownership at the end of World War I.

Folkestone Harbour was the SER's embarkation port for sailings to Boulogne, There were two regular boat trains in each direction, down at 10am and 2.45pm from Charing Cross, and at 4.10pm and 9.50pm from Folkestone Harbour. At the time, the latter included a portion for Reading and the GWR – see **Cross-Country services** – slipped at Tonbridge. The return working reached Tonbridge from Reading in time to be attached to the 2.45pm boat train from Charing Cross.

The cross-country boat train connections to/from the GWR comprised the only regular fast trains over the SER's Redhill–Reading line. There was a daily so-called express train in summer, leaving Reading at 8.40am, and getting the trippers to the coastal resorts for midday after having made stops at Wokingham, Ash, Guildford, Dorking, Redhill and Tonbridge. The return working got back to Reading at 9.18pm after a 127mile run from Folkestone.

The unremitting competition between the LCDR and the SER meant that the latter operated Thanet expresses via Ashford, Canterbury and Minster Junction to the SER stations of Ramsgate Town (85 miles from Cannon St.) and Margate Sands. A typical time was 130min to Ramsgate with three or four intermediate stops. Deal and Walmer were served by through coaches via Minster Junction.

The SER competed effectively with the London, Brighton & South Coast for traffic to Hastings, despite the disadvantages of its heavily graded and curvaceous route from Tonbridge via Tunbridge Wells. The best time of 99min to West St Leonards of the 3.45pm from Cannon St. was really creditable. This was by the 'Vestibuled Car Train' which was formed of Pullman-style saloon cars built for the SER in 1891 in the United States. They were remodelled in 1896 to provide accommodation for all three classes, and like the cars on the Folkestone service, had catering facilities. The return working of the 'Vestibuled Car Train' was at 8.40am from Hastings and, like one of the down evening trains, it was booked in 105min. The usual overall timing of the London–Hastings trains was 2hr or so.

The working union between the SE and LC&D railways came into operation on 1 January 1899 and resulted in simplified traffic working, as well as the introduction of services using both constituent railways, such as Victoria–Hastings via Sevenoaks.

Spurs were constructed at Bickley Junctions to link the South Eastern and Chatham lines, so allowing boat trains from Victoria to use the main line via Tonbridge rather than running on the heavily graded stretches of the Chatham route.

The widening of the South Eastern main line between London Bridge and New Cross, and between St Johns and Orpington, completed by 1905, greatly benefited train working. Until 1916, the majority of trains on the South Eastern reversed in Cannon St. before continuing to Charing Cross, and operating reliability was often poor. In 1904, for instance, 25 main line and local trains in each direction passed through London Bridge in the hour from 5pm, all but a couple reversing in Cannon St. Despite recent widening in the area a multitude of flat junctions remained and conflicting movements were unavoidable.

Within a few years measurable improvements had resulted from the working union of the former competitors. By 1905, Thanet was served by some excellent trains. The 10.45am from Victoria called at Herne Hill where a portion from Holborn Viaduct was attached and, after a non-stop run to Faversham, it reached Margate in 123min. The fastest train was the 'Granville Express', the 3.25pm from Victoria, non-stop from Herne Hill–Westgate-on-Sea and arriving at Margate at 5.13pm and Ramsgate Harbour at 5.30pm. By arrangement with the proprietors of Ramsgate's Granville Hotel (which boasted Turkish baths and scientific electric treatment), at weekends from 1877 the SER had run express trains to the resort, matched by competitive services from the LCDR.

Residential traffic between the Kent Coast and London was beginning to develop. The 'City Express', from Holborn Viaduct at 5.10pm, ran non-stop to Margate in 95min. The best up train from the coast was the 10.13am from Margate, reaching Victoria at noon. In 1911, the SECR reached agreement with the Association of Kent Coasters to attach saloons to certain workings, rather in the manner of the club saloons of the northern companies. At the Association's request, a train was introduced at 6.10pm from Victoria via the Catford loop, non-stop to Whitstable on its way to Ramsgate.

On the Tonbridge main line in 1905 the 'Folkestone Vestibuled Limited' departed from Cannon St. at 4.36pm and ran to Folkestone Central in 84min, continuing to Dover Town where it arrived at 6.15pm. A section was slipped at Ashford to serve intermediate stations to Dover. The return working of the 'Vestibuled Limited' was as the 8.5am from Dover Town, calling at Folkestone Central at 8.30am and then running non-stop to Cannon St. in 90min where it reversed for the trip to Charing Cross. Folkestone's other notable working was by a slip coach detached at Shorncliffe from the 9pm Ostend boat train, and arriving at Central station for 10.42pm.

Wainwright's D and E classes of 4-4-0 had been introduced from 1901, the last entering traffic in 1909. The class proved competent and fast runners for the express services of the SECR. From 1912 superheating was applied to a couple of the Es.

A major change to the SECR's operating came in October 1911 with the arrival from the London & North Western Railway of Francis Dent as General Manager. He was critical of the combination of responsibility for engineering and running matters under the Locomotive Superintendent. Despite subsequent managerial changes, reliability suffered as a consequence of increased traffic from 1910, combined with a failure to maintain locomotive renewals and effect repairs.

Not that the pace of change slackened. In 1911, there was a special 5.5pm Charing Cross–Folkestone Harbour boat train, non-stop from London Bridge to Folkestone Junction where the train reversed for the trip down the incline to the Harbour. Although the load of this train was often merely three coaches and a couple of vans, some boat trains loaded to 350tons or even more. Typical times were 92min for the 71 miles from Folkestone Junction to Charing Cross, such as was made by the 9.5pm from Folkestone Harbour.

By the outbreak of World War I there were down boat trains from Charing Cross at 9am (Dover, the morning mail), 10am (Folkestone, for Boulogne and Paris), 11am from Victoria for Dover via Chatham ('Calais Boat Express'), 2.20pm from Charing Cross for Folkestone (Paris service), the 4.30pm, and the 9pm night mail from Charing Cross to Dover. The 5.20pm from Dover was designated as a 'Royal Mail Express' and was non-stop to Herne Hill in 100min where it divided into sections for Victoria and Holborn Viaduct. The Continental rail/boat services were attracting particularly hostile comment at the time, but during May 1913 the *Railway Gazette* noted that on only three occasions was the 9am service from Charing Cross more than 10min late at Calais. The rolling stock was as good as any, SECR having built new coaches for the boat trains in 1905 (two sets); 1907/8 (three sets) and 1909 (one set). All were non-gangwayed. The new station at Dover Marine was not opened until December 1914.

The 5.5pm from Charing Cross earlier mentioned became the renowned 4.30pm boat train. This was timed to Dover Admiralty Pier in 90min, and in its early days might comprise no more than two Pullmans, three corridor coaches and a van. It had been introduced in July 1913 and, with a smart exchange of passengers at the Admiralty Pier, and at Calais, travellers reached Paris at 11.25pm, faster than anything previously available on any of the London–Paris service. The balancing working involved a night departure from Paris, and a breakfast-time arrival at Charing Cross. Initially intended to run during the summer only, from the end of October 1913 the 4.30pm and its return service became daily, the Paris arrival off the 4.30pm being brought forward to 11pm from 1 December. By now, the interval between the 4.30pm arriving at Dover and the steamer departing was no more than 5 minutes! The 4.30pm also offered excellent connections to Basle and Interlaken.

Thanet continued to enjoy improvements to its services. By 1912, the summer 9.10am and the 3.20pm FSO from Victoria were non-stop to Margate West in 90min, the 10.15am took 101min to Margate, non-stop to Westgate-on-Sea in 94min, and the 'City Express', at 5.10pm from Holborn Viaduct, ran non-stop from St Pauls to Margate West in 92min, having slipped a portion at Faversham for intermediate stations. The best up trains were the 7.50am from Ramsgate Harbour, fast from Margate West to Cannon St. (note that the down counterpart started from Holborn Viaduct) in 103min, and the 10.10am from Margate West, fast from Westgate-on-Sea to Victoria in 92min. There were two other 91min Margate West–Victoria timings.

Apart from the down 'Folkestone Vestibuled Limited' and its 84min timing from Cannon St. to Folkestone Central, the next fastest bookings of 1912 over the 69 miles from Cannon St. to Folkestone Central were 91min. On the Tonbridge main line, there were some sharp start-to-stop intermediate times by this time for some of the other trains, such as 23min for the 21¼ miles from Paddock Wood to Ashford, and 29min for Tonbridge–Ashford, 26½ miles.

There was a short-lived operation of through coaches from SECR stations via Ludgate Hill to King's Cross, there to connect into the afternoon express train departures. For an earlier and similar experiment, see earlier, under the **London & South Western Railway**. From July 1912, for the summer only, the 10.25am from Deal not only included through coaches to Manchester and Bradford, but

also conveyed coaches for King's Cross. These were detached at Ludgate Hill from the Midland portion, and reached their destination at 1.25pm. The return journey commenced at 2.40pm, from the York Road platform at King's Cross. This facility was reintroduced for the summer of 1913, when it was accompanied by through coaches leaving Ramsgate on the 9.45am to Victoria, detached at Herne Hill and travelling via Ludgate Hill to reach King's Cross at 12.10pm. The return working was at 2.55pm, with a Ramsgate arrival at 5.30pm. With changes, this service continued during the winter of 1913/14, and regained its former timings for the summer of 1914 when the Deal coaches reappeared. Through workings to King's Cross ceased after August 1914. For details of the coaches to destinations beyond London, see Chapter 8, **Cross-Country services**.

From its inception, the SECR made a major contribution to the development of cross-country expresses, the Birkenhead–Deal train being the principal service on the Redhill–Reading line. There had been earlier attempts to provide Reading–Redhill–Charing Cross residential services, and through trains ran in each direction, calling at most stations beyond Redhill.

Principal expresses were provided from 1910 with new Pullman cars, these being painted in SECR livery but lined out and lettered as Pullmans. Used initially on boat trains only, including the Queenborough service, from 1912 they were included in ordinary Charing Cross–Folkestone expresses. The new vehicles were an improvement on the Pullman-type cars introduced by the SER in the 1890s which at the time had been streets ahead of any other stock on either that railway or the LCDR. Even as late as 1910, a timetable note in *Bradshaw* had proclaimed: 'American Saloon Car Trains, 1st, 2nd and 3rd Class, warmed (IN WINTER) WITH HOT-WATER PIPES, AND LIGHTED BY ELECTRICITY, RUN BETWEEN LONDON, HASTINGS, FOLKESTONE and DOVER every Week-day'. These Hastings and Folkestone workings were withdrawn early in World War I, and the special train sets were not afterwards reinstated.

The volume of war traffic moving over the Railway to the Channel ports for dispatch to the Western Front resulted in severe cuts to passenger services. In 1917, the SE&CR's Board decided that postwar it would concentrate the whole of the Continental traffic at Victoria, but the problem was that the infrastructure of the former London, Chatham & Dover lines serving Victoria had not been strengthened to take heavier loads, as had the

The postwar SE&CR was somewhat austere in style, the locomotives in dull slate-grey and the coaches painted reddish maroon. This is the 'Thanet Pullman', actually in early Southern days, and here passing Birchington behind one of the excellent D1 class 4-4-0s, No. 747. The Pullmans in the train are a mixture. The first and sixth are of the type used on the South Eastern & Chatham after 1910, but the rest are from the 'Folkestone Vestibuled Limited'.

South Eastern line. That ruled out use of the L class 4-4-0s which had been delivered at the start of the war. Also, the SE&CR management wanted the boat trains to be increased to 300ton loadings. The result was that a new design had to be prepared and resources to hand meant that the only option was to rebuild existing types – the D1 and E1 4-4-0s – which were the heaviest class allowed on the Chatham lines. The first engines were ready during early 1919 when they went into service on boat trains from Victoria, at first timed in 103min from Victoria to Dover Marine. During 1921, the first train of a new design of boat train stock was put into service, notable for having end vestibule doors only and buckeye couplers and Pullman gangways. Further sets followed from 1923.

After World War I, the SE&CR was heavily engaged in drawing up electrification schemes for its suburban services which were intended to be energised at 3,000V. In addition, a complete recasting of all train movements into and out of Cannon St., Charing Cross and London Bridge was implemented in 1922. Meanwhile, improvements were in hand with the Folkestone/Dover expresses, and in 1921 the fastest service between Charing

Cross and Folkestone was the 4pm down, in 85min. In the summer timetable of 1922 there were one down and two up expresses booked to run non-stop to/from Folkestone Central in 80min. These trains included Pullman cars and were worked by the L 4-4-0s which did not prove entirely satisfactory on these trains and performed better on the Hastings line.

At the same time, the rebuilt D1 and E1 4-4-0s were used to speed up the Thanet coast expresses, notably the Sundays only first-class 'Thanet Pullman Limited' which was introduced from July 1921 and ran throughout the year at 10am from Victoria to Margate West in 90min, to terminate at Ramsgate Harbour. The return 'Thanet Pullman Limited' at 5.30pm also featured a 90min run from Margate West, with a Victoria arrival at 7.15pm. By summer 1923 the Pullman was running at 10.15am from Victoria and back at 7.5pm from Ramsgate Harbour, so as to give the rather superior daytrippers a longer day by the sea. Other expresses on this route were also accelerated in 1921 such as the 3.15pm down 'Granville Express', booked to Margate West in 92min and, in common with other expresses on the route, with a first-class Pullman car.

Chapter Three

The East Coast, Great Northern and North Eastern to 1922

East Coast Main Line services

The characteristics of the Anglo-Scottish services up to 1914, and even beyond, were the legacy of the two railway 'races' from London in the last two decades of the 19th century to Edinburgh in 1888, and to Aberdeen in 1895. The agreement of June 1896 between the East and West Coast companies fixed *daytime* Anglo-Scottish schedules at 8½ hours (later altered to 8¼ hours) as between London and Edinburgh and Glasgow. Overnight trains were not affected by the ruling. East and West Coast informed each other of changes to Anglo-Scottish services with the result that schedules and the pattern of services varied little for the next 35 years and until the agreement was rescinded.

The motivation for 'racing' had been commercial, in that the admission of third-class passengers to the best Anglo-Scottish trains had increased the market for long-distance traffic. There was a marked disparity in passenger carryings from London and Scotland as between winter and summer and, for some reason, down traffic was always heavier than up! During the grouse-shooting season which lasted three weeks from the last week in July, traffic doubled, and at times even tripled.

In 1898, the down day Anglo-Scottish expresses comprised the 10am 'Flying Scotsman' (the name by now being in general usage), the 11.20am in summer only and the 2.20pm. There was a corresponding pattern of morning and afternoon all-year trains departing at much the same times from Edinburgh, and a 12.25pm to King's Cross in summer. The East Coast summer workings began on 1 July and lasted

until the end of September, but some 'summer' arrangements continued into October. The down overnight trains were at 7.45pm, in summer only, 8.15pm (later 8pm) and 11.30pm. The last two took 7¾hr to Edinburgh, the 8pm reaching Aberdeen in 11hr 20min. The overnight trains were faster than the day services in view of their exclusion from the 1896/1900 agreement and took 3hr 35min to York. North of Aberdeen the 8pm from King's Cross retained much the same timings until 1914.

All these Anglo-Scottish trains usually made just a single stop between King's Cross and York, at Grantham where engines were changed. The 10am and 2.20pm down took 120/122min for the 105¾ miles from King's Cross–Grantham, and 98/97min respectively for the 82¾ miles on to York. The 11.20am down made its first stop at Newark where a connection was made from Nottingham. As yet, there was no separate service to Newcastle so that the north-east depended entirely on the Anglo-Scottish trains. In charge were the Stirling Singles probably putting up some of the best work of their lives. From 1896 12-wheeled clerestory stock had been introduced for the ECJS, and despite loads of 270tons or so the Singles coped well at speeds up to 70mph or over.

Minor change came during 1900 when, as a result of the Balfour ruling, the 'Flying Scotsman' and the other day trains were accelerated by 15min. The 'Flying Scotsman' received restaurant cars for the first time in August 1900, the afternoon pair of 'Scotsmen' having had them from 1893, and so rushed meal-stops at York became a thing of the past. After York, the 'Flying Scotsman' called at Newcastle

The down 'Flying Scotsman' waits at York on 7 August 1911, with North Eastern Atlantic No. 716 having taken over from GNR motive power. Next the engine is a postal sorting van which was diagrammed to work north of York on the down 'Scotsman' in those days.

and Berwick only, as did the 2.20pm. Both trains made the same stops in the up direction except that the 2.20pm additionally called at Darlington.

Until 1914, the basic train service of East Coast expresses hardly changed. The principal trains to Edinburgh remained the 10am – the 'Flying Scotsman' – and 2.20pm – the afternoon scotsman, with corresponding workings at the same times, and during the summer or at Christmas and Easter they were duplicated or triplicated. There was also the 'unbalanced' 7.45am from Edinburgh with through East Coast Joint Stock coaches, attached at Newcastle (previous to c1908, at York) to a train for King's Cross.

During the summer, there was a 9.50am to Edinburgh and 10.15am from Edinburgh; these were the relief workings to the 'Flying Scotsman' and were timed similarly, as indeed were the 11.20am down and 10.25am up seasonal trains. Other summer 'expresses' included the 10.35am King's Cross–Edinburgh and 2.30pm ex-Edinburgh, but these were even more

easily timed, taking 10¼hr each way for the 393 miles. While the basic service was between London and Edinburgh, the '10 o'clocks', as the railway managers tended to describe them, featured through carriages to/from Glasgow Queen St., Perth and Aberdeen. All of these trains provided dining cars. During the so-called 'Grouse Fortnight', any of all of these trains might spawn reliefs in the days before 12 August. The duplicate to the '10 o'clocks' was publicly advertised only from the summer of 1913.

Similarly, the overnight sleeping car expresses had a number of through sleeping and other carriages. From October 1909, the through coaches and sleeping cars between London and Inverness in winter were alternately provided by East and West Coast on their 8pm trains, returning on the 3.50pm ex-Inverness. Only the first-class offered sleeping berths, and third-class passengers were expected to travel sitting-up. The East and West Coast companies were unanimous that 'the undesirability of running third-class sleeping cars is still maintained', having first apparently discussed the subject in 1906.

In winter, the down East Coast sleeping car services were restricted to the 8 pm down to Aberdeen and 11.30 pm to Glasgow/Perth/Aberdeen, with up corresponding trains. Both workings would be duplicated at Christmas. The timings to Edinburgh were 7¾hr, and the fastest regular timing pre-1914 to Aberdeen was 11hr 7min. In summer, the 8pm divided into 7.55 and 8.15pm departures, and there was also an 11.45pm down, as explained below. There was also an 8.45pm to Edinburgh and Glasgow conveying TPO vans to Leeds and Newcastle, without sleeping cars in winter, and without a corresponding southbound train.

King's Cross to Newcastle traffic was separated from the Anglo-Scottish workings once the Great Northern and North Eastern railways decided early in 1899 to provide dining and sleeping cars between King's Cross and Newcastle only. The first such workings, using East Coast Joint Stock (ECJS) vehicles, included a dining car for Newcastle worked on the 6.15pm King's Cross–Wakefield and Bradford, to return the next day on the 12.20pm York to King's Cross which included the through carriages leaving Edinburgh at 7.45am. These arrangements applied from 1 October 1903 and meals were served south of York only. From 1 October 1904, a Newcastle portion, including the dining car from the 6.15pm, was conveyed on the 5.30pm King's Cross–Nottingham and detached at Grantham.

As the original ECJS agreement applied to trains running at least between King's Cross and Edinburgh, it was not surprising that the North British Railway objected to the use of ECJS vehicles on services running south of Newcastle. The first intention for new stock for the King's Cross–Newcastle service was that the GNR and NER should own the stock separately. But the companies concluded that a similar agreement should pertain as for the ECJS stock, with joint ownership, and these coaches were built at York. From 1 July 1905, the breakfast and luncheon cars were allocated to the retimed 8am from Newcastle (formerly the 7.40am) and the 5.30pm down.

Having detached a portion for Nottingham, from Grantham, the Newcastle portion of the 5.30pm down was worked to York by a GNR Atlantic or 4-4-0 or, even in the late 1900s, an Ivatt or Stirling Single, the last of which were only 15 years old. With a North Eastern Atlantic at its head, the 5.30pm had a 60mph timing over the 44 miles from York–Darlington, and arrived in Newcastle at 10.48pm. At first non-stop from Darlington, a call was soon inserted at Durham.

The 8am stopped at Durham, Darlington, York and Grantham, to reach King's Cross at 1.30pm, 70min faster than the 7.40am ex-Newcastle.

In time, GN/NE Joint Stock carriages formed part of the 10.28am from Newcastle–King's Cross train to which were attached the ECJS vehicles that had left Edinburgh at 7.45am. The overnight GN/NE trains were the 11.45pm King's Cross–Newcastle and 11.20pm return; in summer, these services also conveyed ECJS sleeping cars to Scottish stations, latterly including a sleeping car to North Berwick. Usually, the 11.45pm was withdrawn in winter and then the Newcastle sleeping cars were conveyed on the 11.30pm down.

There were other joint GNR/NER trains, operated with each company's own stock. The only early morning train from King's Cross in 1910 was the 7.15am, running through to Newcastle to arrive at 2.45pm, with a GNR restaurant car as far as York, and a North Eastern car beyond. In summer, there were holiday restaurant car trains at 11.25am from King's Cross to Scarborough and at 1.20pm to Scarborough, Whitby and West Hartlepool; in both cases the times quoted are for 1914. The latter train was alternately made up of GNR and NER stock. Both trains had corresponding up workings.

Special workings included trains formed of ECJS vehicles such as the regular summer Saturday-only King's Cross–Edinburgh and return 'guaranteed' trains operated for the Polytechnic Touring Association as part of an eight-day railway touring holiday on lines north of Edinburgh. At the height of the summer, nearly all carriages were hard at work. A census carried out of the ECJS in July/August 1913 showed that only seven out of 364 vehicles were not 'fully employed'.

From October 1912, all East Coast Joint Stock trains were worked on the vacuum brake only although some vehicles retained dual-braking a little longer for through workings. Elliptical roofed stock had been built for the ECJS from 1906, but discussion regarding the renewal of the sets forming the '10 o'clocks' began only in 1912. A year later, a mixture of clerestory and elliptical-roofed stock was being contemplated for the 'Flying Scotsman' sets. In the end, it was decided to form two ten-coach sets, of elliptical-roofed stock only, and comprising new and existing carriages, including locker composites. These were so-called because there was a locker-luggage compartment for passengers' belongings and such vehicles, as well as locker thirds, were a feature of East Coast trains.

The construction of 11 new carriages was put in

hand during 1913. Included were two three-car restaurant car sets, each comprising a first and third-class dining saloon, and an all-steel kitchen car. The separation of the kitchen facilities from the seated accommodation meant that the dining cars were lighter, and eight- rather than twelve-wheeled. More space was also available for meal preparation. The steel kitchen cars reflected public concern at the number of recent train fires and were the first of their kind. Gas cooking was the reason for the all-steel construction. The new 'Flying Scotsman' sets began work on 1 July 1914.

By October 1918, the '10 o'clocks' in each direction were taking 9hr 50min between King's Cross and Edinburgh. Their loadings had increased to 450/500 tons and that did not include the restaurant cars which had been discontinued and did not return until 1919. Between King's Cross and Grantham the running times had expanded to 150min for the 105½ miles although, unlike some railways, the Great Northern had not imposed a 60mph speed limit. The afternoon Scotsmen did not run at all in the last year of the war.

Recovery from World War I was not particularly fast, and as late as August 1920 the published best time from King's Cross to Edinburgh was 9hr, even though the working timetable showed 8hr 48min. It was not until the summer of 1923 that the timings of the day East Coast Edinburgh expresses had returned to the 8¼hr of the 1900 agreement.

By then, the best performer among the East Coast trains was the 5.30pm King's Cross–Newcastle which took 5hr 35min throughout as compared with 5hr 13min in 1914. This train no longer made a passenger stop at York station but engines were changed from GNR to NER at the north end of its platforms, and the train was then booked to Darlington in 47min, at an average speed of 55.9mph.

The main concern of the East Coast authorities was the state of the rolling stock. Just before Grouping, the case for the construction of new sleeping cars was made 'to compete more effectively with the West Coast, where it is stated that the sleeping car accommodation is now much better than the East Coast . . .' and the operating managers called for 'a thorough renovation of the East Coast Joint Stock which has been allowed to get in such a bad state that complaints are being received from the travelling public'.

Great Northern Railway

The GNR operated some of the fastest trains in Europe during the 1870s and 1880s. By 1898, over the 76¼ miles between King's Cross and Peterborough, ten down and eight up expresses, and even two on Sundays, had bookings of from 85-94min. To Grantham (105¼ miles) there were eight non-stop runs down, and four up in times of 117-125min. In general, the East Coast expresses were less speedy than those to Manchester, or some of the West Riding trains.

The West Riding expresses averaged about 4hr for the 185¾ miles from King's Cross–Leeds Central with four-six intermediate stops. Clerestoried 12-wheelers were being introduced, and dining car trains with third-class accommodation had been running to the West Riding from July 1896. The fastest train was the 9.45am down, taking exactly 120min to Grantham, 180min to Doncaster (156 miles), 3hr 28min to Wakefield Westgate (175¾ miles) and 3hr 49min to Leeds. A Bradford portion was detached at Wakefield and took 4hr 3min to Exchange station (193¼ miles). Up West Riding expresses maintained similar journey times. There were through coaches off the 9.45am from King's Cross for Huddersfield and for Blackburn. These were detached at Doncaster and then worked to Wakefield. Blackburn was reached via the Cleckheaton branch, the Low Moor fork and Halifax.

Nottingham and Lincoln were served by connections at Grantham, with best times in 155min and 165min respectively. There was just one through train to Hull from King's Cross, in 4hr 10min, and Grimsby was served only by changing at Peterborough and travelling over the East Lincs line; the fastest train was the 9.25am from Great Grimsby which reached Peterborough (78½ miles) in 2hr after several intermediate stops. There was also an evening Grimsby–Peterborough mail train.

Skegness (is So Bracing) had through trains in summer from King's Cross (131½ miles and 3¼hr distant), Leicester Belgrave Road and Derby Friargate. Similar workings appeared in the timetable over the years. The other seaside resort favoured by the GNR was Cromer, see **Midland & Great Northern Joint Railway**.

The GNR's expresses serving Sheffield were faster than the Midland Railway's and had given the latter stiff competition from their introduction in 1883 as through services to/from Manchester. Fifteen years later, the 2pm from King's Cross called at Grantham, slipped coaches at Retford and took 189min to Sheffield Victoria (161½ miles). An identical best time was offered in the up direction.

Traffic out of King's Cross increased rapidly from the 1890s, and by 1903 the station was reckoned to be the busiest of the northern lines' termini, largely on account of the suburban traffic although its main line services were extensive. In 1905, the principal down Leeds and Bradford expresses were at 7.15am (the Leeds Mail); 9.45am, non-stop to Doncaster in 169min, and reaching Leeds at 1.20pm; 1.30pm; 3.45pm to Leeds and Harrogate (via Knottingley and Church Fenton); 5.45pm to Leeds, and 6.15pm to Bradford. As in 1898, there was a service to L&Y stations, by now running independently at 3.25pm from King's Cross. This ran to Wakefield's Kirkgate station where an L&Y engine took charge for the journey via Todmorden and Burnley to Blackburn which was reached at 9.5pm. There was also the 1.40pm to York and Harrogate, its second portion routed via Knottingley and Church Fenton.

Up West Riding expresses included the 7.50am from Leeds, non-stop from Retford in 153min for 138½ miles and due in King's Cross at 11.30am; an arrival at 1.50pm from Leeds, and one at 2.10pm from Bradford and Harrogate. There was also the 'Leeds Special', leaving that city at 2pm, running non-stop from Wakefield, and arriving in King's Cross at 5.30pm. Loaded to no more than 200tons, this was a crack turn for the Ivatt Large Atlantics in their early days.

The Sheffield service comprised the 10.20am and 5.30pm from King's Cross via Nottingham, and the 2pm and 4.15pm from King's Cross via Retford. The 10.10am from Sheffield ran via Nottingham and was non-stop from there in 146min, to arrive at King's Cross for 1.30pm. In the early/mid-1900s Nottingham also had a breakfast car train to King's Cross at 7.50am, and a 12.30pm down from London.

The GNR speedily responded to the GCR's brilliant 1905 service of some 10 daily expresses each way between London, Sheffield and Manchester. That summer, it brought in a new Sheffield and Manchester express departing King's Cross at 6.10pm, and non-stop to Sheffield in 170min. A determined effort was made in 1906 to gain Sheffield and Manchester traffic for which three sets of elliptical-roofed corridor coaches were built. These made their debut in the winter service of 1906/7, one working down on the 6.5pm King's Cross–Manchester and 3.26pm return, the second used for the 6.35pm Sheffield–King's Cross, to return on the 10.20am King's Cross–Sheffield. The third set was spare. As with some of the other GNR expresses of the time, these were light formations of four carriages. The first-class seated two-a-side only. These were the first set trains to be built to the 'Gresley' general outline and features which become standardised for

Gresley GNR and LNER stock until 1941. The dining cars were 65ft 6in 12-wheelers, the other coaches of 58ft 6in length. At the same time, six composite dining cars were turned out for general service with all the general features of the Sheffield stock.

Despite the new rolling stock, the Sheffield/Manchester expresses of 1906 were gradually downgraded in the next few years, less because of the traffic offering than as a result of closer working with the Great Central such that the GNR Nottingham/Sheffield expresses gave ground to the service to/from Marylebone. By 1907, additional intermediate stops had been inserted in some schedules. The morning train was replaced by a 12.30pm King's Cross–Sheffield semi-fast whose restaurant car was worked on empty to Manchester for the next day's 3.40pm up to London. Yet the 6.5pm down retained a London–Sheffield timing of 180min which was as good as the Midland, and the 3.40pm ex-Manchester was faster with a time of 178min from Sheffield, and it spent no more than 110min between Grantham and King's Cross.

The 3.40pm up and the 6.5pm down were worked by a Great Central engine between Sheffield and Grantham and return, at first a Pollitt 4-4-0, later an Atlantic. By 1914, the Hull portion of the 6.5pm down was more important than the section for Sheffield and Manchester, and was detached during the additional stop at Retford.

The 5.30pm from King's Cross combined Newcastle and Nottingham portions, the former of Great Northern and North Eastern stock – see **East Coast services**. By 1909, this was the more important although a restaurant car still ran in the Nottingham section detached at Grantham. The next year, there was just a through coach which reached Nottingham Victoria at 8.6pm in a stopping train to Burton.

In June 1909, there was a locomotive exchange between the GNR and London & North Western involving the former's Ivatt Atlantic No. 1449 and the latter's 'Precursor' 4-4-0 No 412 *Marquis*. It lasted for a month, during which the 'Precursor' worked the 7.50am Leeds–King's Cross three days a week, returning with the 1.30pm West Riding express to Doncaster. The alternate turn was with the 12.19pm lightly loaded semi-fast from Doncaster and the 5.45pm King's Cross–Leeds 'Diner'. Both engines were well-matched and the results on coal consumption and average speed were close.

By 1910, the mid-morning Leeds express took up its time-honoured departure of 10.10am, and ran to Peterborough in 82min. With stops at Grantham,

Doncaster, Wakefield and Holbeck High Level it reached Leeds Central at 1.56pm. As with many other GNR trains of the time, the exacting sectional timing of 23min for the 17¾ miles to Hatfield was succeeded by a generous 28min over the easy grades from Hitchin to Huntingdon. In response to the competitive Midland Railway service to Bradford at 1.50pm from St Pancras, and routed via Thornhill, from 1 July 1910 the GNR responded with a pair of 'Bradford Specials' booked non-stop between King's Cross and Doncaster in 165min. The down 'Special' departed at 2.15pm, and took 3hr 40min to Bradford; the return working regained King Cross at 10.5pm. The load was usually no more than four coaches, one of which was detached at Wakefield for Leeds. The 2-2-2 or 4-2-2 often used on the 'Special' contrasted piquantly with the train's latest Gresley vestibuled stock including a composite dining-car. The trains were withdrawn for good during the 1912 miners' strike.

By contrast with the Singles, the series of Ivatt Large Atlantics equipped from the start with superheaters came into service in 1910, and showed the true potential of these capable engines, particularly when huge loads were handled during the 1912 coal strike. Unsuperheated, the Atlantics tended to be sluggish runners.

Elsewhere on the GNR in 1910, mention might be made of the service from Grantham to Nottingham, Derby and Uttoxeter, such as the 9.30am down semi-fast booked from Grantham–Uttoxeter in 130min, and the similarly timed 12.29pm up.

In 1913, the West Riding service comprised the well-established principal trains at 7.15am, 10.10am, 1.30pm and 5.45pm from King's Cross–Leeds. The 10.10am was prestigious but the 1.30pm was the fastest, in 3hr 42min to Leeds. Through coaches to Huddersfield were detached from the 1.30pm at Doncaster and, running via Wakefield Kirkgate and Mirfield, reached their destination at 5.34pm. Notable up workings included the 7.50am from Leeds, into King's Cross by 11.30am while the 2pm from Leeds was advertised as a 'Special Express'. A portion had left Bradford Exchange at 1.37pm and coaches from Huddersfield were attached to the main train at Wakefield. From there, and usually with a six-coach load of 200tons, the 2pm then embarked upon the longest non-stop run on the GNR of the time: 175¾ miles to King's Cross in 3hr 6min, at an average speed of 56.7mph. This train was worked by a King's Cross Atlantic which had gone down to Leeds on the 7.15am, so that its crew had an 11hr turn, the mileage payment for which was equal to a day's pay!

The 5.30pm from Leeds conveyed through carriages from Halifax. The 5.45pm down 'Diner' conveyed through carriages to Bradford, Halifax and Hull. There was also the 4pm down which was formed of Gresley non-vestibuled stock and included through carriages to Bradford, Sheffield and Grimsby. Those for the last-named were detached at Peterborough and their journey over the East Lincs line got their passengers to Grimsby Town for 7.29pm. The up working was the 9.15am from Grimsby Town, with a 3hr 50min journey for the 154½ miles

A little bit of a cheat as this is a post-Grouping view of Wood Green but it makes the point that the GNR Atlantics remained staple power on King's Cross expresses for a couple of decades. The engine is C1 class No. 1405 working the 5.30pm King's Cross–Newcastle. Pulling away from the station is an ex-North London Railway 4-4-0T on an up local for Broad Street.

to King's Cross. In view of all the changes that had gone before, perhaps it was unsurprising that no changes at all were made to GNR main line trains in the summer 1913 timetable.

While the Anglo-Scottish and Leeds/West Riding tended to attract more attention, the GNR also operated a service of main line fast/semi-fast trains to Doncaster and beyond. There was the 1.40pm down which ran to Doncaster, then proceeded to Harrogate via Knottingley and Church Fenton, and the 3.25pm down which was without catering vehicles but conveyed through carriages for Newcastle, Blackburn and Harrogate via Knottingley. The southbound counterparts of these trains included the 9.40am Ripon/10.10am Harrogate–King's Cross; the 12.25pm to King's Cross from York via Knottingley; and the 4.10pm York–King's Cross semi-fast, the last-mentioned taking just under 4½ hr for its journey. One important night train for postal traffic was the 9.50pm from York which reached London at 3.10am the next morning. The 3am King's Cross–York and Leeds was primarily a newspaper train but was described in *Bradshaw* as a 'Special Express', an epithet usually reserved for a crack working such as the 2pm Leeds–King's Cross.

The Cambridge service of 1914 was nothing like as good as in LNER interwar days, with the usual best timings being 79/80 min for the 58-mile journey. There were six down and eight up through trains, but on Sundays there were connections only, to/from Hitchin. Fastest timing in 1913 was by the 5pm down which split into three trains at Hitchin, fast for Cambridge in 75 min; for Stamford; and, lastly, all-stations to Cambridge. There was also the 3pm down from King's Cross which divided at Hitchin into a section non-stop for Cambridge, the rear carriages going forward to Peterborough and then to South Lynn and Cromer – see **Midland & Great Northern Railway**.

During summer peak Saturdays just before 1914 there might be 15-20 special and relief trains on the main line, but special workings were fairly numerous at other times, too. Some of these had dining cars and first-class accommodation and were run to race meetings or for liner sailings from Hull, Immingham or Tyne Dock. The GNR was no stranger to handling special traffic, notably at Doncaster in St Leger Week when something like 1,000 trains were dealt with, arriving from all over the country.

There were also the astoundingly cheap excursion trains to East Coast resorts such as Skegness: on

Similarly from the just post-Grouping period is this view of the down afternoon 'Scotsman', departing Grantham behind un-named A1 class Pacific No. 1479, ordered by the GNR but delivered after Grouping.

August Bank Holiday, 1913 no less than eight specials departed King's Cross for this resort during just 1½ hours. Suburban stock was used for such workings. Access to the resort from the West Riding was improved by the opening of the line through Stickney in June 1913. Suburban and six-wheeled stock was also worked on guaranteed excursion trains over the 187 miles from King's Cross to Yarmouth Beach via Peterborough and the Midland & Great Northern Joint line.

As World War I progressed, expresses were withdrawn, even the renowned 2pm Leeds–King's Cross which was discontinued during 1915. The loads of the remaining trains were accordingly increased by the combination of trains, such that the 10.10am King's Cross–Leeds and Bradford and down 'Flying Scotsman' were at one time running as a single train and another colossus was made up of the 5.30pm Newcastle, 5.45pm Leeds and Bradford and 6.5pm Sheffield. Restaurant cars had been withdrawn and non-gangwayed stock was used for the Leeds portions of some trains. Such was the weight of some expresses that a pilot locomotive was regularly provided between King's Cross and Potters Bar.

The Gresley quintuplet restaurant car set was one of the innovations of the early postwar period and from November 1921 entered traffic on the 10.10am King's Cross–Leeds and 5.30pm return. The large-boilered 2-6-0s, later LNER K3 class, were invaluable during the coal strike of 1921 when they were used on expresses loaded up to 20 coaches.

Just before Grouping major changes were made to the layout and signalling at King's Cross with the aims of reducing conflicting movements and to allow some up trains to use the departure platforms. A 70ft turntable was installed in the relocated station locomotive yard to turn the A1 Pacifics, the first of which were then in service.

North Eastern Railway
In pre-Grouping days a railway company could enter into agreements or obtain powers by Act of Parliament to provide it with the right to run over other Companies' lines, the authority to do so being known as 'running powers'. It provided a railway with a number of advantages, usually avoiding the need to construct new lines, and allowing it to improve its chances of competing for traffic over a fresh route, and to introduce through trains between important points. York provided the example of a station where no less than six companies provided services over track owned by the NER. The possession of running powers meant that the Lancashire & Yorkshire was able to offer through trains between Manchester and York, rather than making passengers change trains at Normanton, the limit of its own mileage. The running company paid the owning company a toll for use of the line of railway and so the arrangement was profitable to the owning company.

The NER provides an example where running powers were used to the full for through services which also benefited the company and ensured, for example, that traffic was encouraged to use the East Coast line north of York. The existence of running powers into York from the south is one reason why the services provided by the Great Central, Great Eastern, Midland and Lancashire & Yorkshire Railways are described under their own sections rather than here. From the south, access to York included the 16mile Swinton & Knottingley Joint line which had been promoted by the NER and MR with running powers granted to the GCR and GNR.

Apart from its contribution to running the East Coast expresses, the NER operated a limited number of its own fast trains and participated in cross-country services. Over the East Coast route one of the star trains operated with its own rolling stock in 1898 was the 9.5am Leeds New–Edinburgh Waverley, taking 6hr exactly for the 230½ miles with stops at York, Darlington, Gateshead West, Newcastle-upon-Tyne, Alnmouth and Berwick. This train competed for business between the West Riding and Scotland, and was a competitive response to Midland services routed via the Settle & Carlisle line. The Leeds–Edinburgh train was followed by a semi-fast to Edinburgh. There was also a 3.30pm York–Edinburgh, again making the principal stops en route. Southbound, there was the 9.15am Edinburgh–York, non-stop to Newcastle in 145min, then calling at Darlington and arriving in York at 1.25pm. All these trains had the opportunity to run fast over the easily graded 44 miles between York and Darlington, with bookings in 49-51min.

Towns and cities off the East Coast route were served by through coaches. As today, the best times to Teesside and the coast were achieved by changing at Darlington, but there were through coaches to/from West Hartlepool. By 1913, the down summer working was on the 1.5pm from King's Cross and, for a short while, up from Darlington on the afternoon 'Scotsman'. Trains between King's Cross, Darlington and Newcastle only were formed of Great Northern/North Eastern Joint Stock, but in summer Scarborough and Whitby were served by through trains formed of Great Northern or North Eastern stock – see **Great Northern Railway.** Some of the connections to/from Scarborough were made by trains of the Leeds–York–Scarborough service which in 1898 could boast 14 expresses in each direction between York and Scarborough, with a fastest timing of 1hr for the 42 miles.

Harrogate had direct GNR expresses from King's Cross reaching the town via the Church Fenton and Wetherby line, but otherwise changes were necessary at Holbeck between the GNR expresses to Leeds and the connecting NER trains. Harrogate's service northwards was catered for by the Leeds Northern line, but passengers travelled via York for Scarborough and Hull, and some of these semi-fast connections stopped only at Knaresborough. Until a connection was put in at Wetherby to allow through running between Leeds and Harrogate, all cross-country trains bound for west of Leeds had to reverse in Leeds New station. Hull was served by semi-fast and slow trains from Leeds and York although later there was a summer Liverpool–Hull through service to connect with the sailings of NER steamers to Zeebrugge.

In 1898, there were fast trains between Newcastle and Leeds New via Stockton and Harrogate, some of which were through workings to/from Liverpool – see **Cross-Country services,** Chapter 8 – and these were the three fastest workings, although through passengers between York and Newcastle could improve on the overall journey time by changing at York. There was only one through train each way between Leeds and Newcastle (94 miles) routed via

Harrogate and Darlington: this was the 9.47am, making three stops and taking 141min. Until 1905, and the opening of the new line between Seaham and Hart, there was no direct line between Sunderland and West Hartlepool, and through trains ran via Wellfield.

The remaining NER route with semi-fast or fast trains was that between Newcastle and Carlisle. 60¼ miles, the intention being to provide connections into West Coast trains. In 1898, no train made less than five stops and the best run was by the 3.5pm ex-Newcastle, in 100min. This had a through portion for Stranraer – see **Glasgow & South Western Railway**. Another NER cross-country route with limited through workings was that between Darlington and Kirkby Stephen. From 1905-11, there were through coaches, latterly in summer only, between Newcastle and Barrow-in-Furness Ramsden Dock (for the Isle of Man), and these were conveyed by a series of local trains but left Newcastle on the 9.30am Cardiff express. In the years to 1914, there were through coaches between York and Keswick, attached to a summer-only limited-stop train each way between Darlington and Penrith. The westbound of workings also featured a Newcastle–Keswick coach which returned from Penrith by stopping train.

The pattern of NER fast and semi-fast services was to change little in subsequent years up to and after Grouping. Improvements in operating came with the quadrupling from 1900 of the line between Church Fenton and Chaloner Whin Junction. From July 1902,

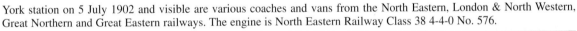

York station on 5 July 1902 and visible are various coaches and vans from the North Eastern, London & North Western, Great Northern and Great Eastern railways. The engine is North Eastern Railway Class 38 4-4-0 No. 576.

The 'Fastest Train in the British Empire' crosses over the Tyne on the King Edward VII Bridge on its opening day. The engine is North Eastern Railway Q class 4-4-0 No. 1877 and the formation of the 12.20pm from Newcastle includes the usual NER non-gangwayed stock at the front and rear, with Midland Railway through coaches amidships.

the railway made the most of its 12.20pm Newcastle–Sheffield train with a 43min run between Darlington and York at an average speed of 61.5mph. One timing of 39½min was recorded. Until interrupted by World War I, and afterwards until 1923, the 12.20pm basked in its reputation as the 'Fastest Train in the British Empire'. Yet the train itself was not particularly prestigious and comprised three or four NER non-gangwayed coaches for Sheffield and a couple of Midland gangwayed coaches for Bristol. This comprised a load of no more than 165tons gross for the Worsdell R 4-4-0 which usually hauled the 12.20pm whose schedule from Darlington to York required consistent running at 70mph for some 30 miles.

In 1905, a more exacting performance was probably required by the engine and men working 8.50am Leeds New–Edinburgh, the successor to the train earlier mentioned. It was booked to take just 82min for the 80 miles non-stop from York–Newcastle, including running through Gateshead and over the High Level bridge at Newcastle where the train had to reverse. The train lacked catering facilities until Newcastle where it gained the restaurant car that had come south on the 7.45am from Edinburgh Waverley. There was a corresponding up train from Edinburgh to Leeds in the evening. By April 1910, with an R1 4-4-0 at the head of a fine set of coaches built two years earlier, the down train set out from Leeds New

at 9am. Compared with 1905, the York–Newcastle non-stop timing was now 2min slower but the train benefited from the recent opening of the King Edward Bridge and ran directly into Central station. There the restaurant car was picked up to continue to Glasgow Queen St. where the train arrived at 3.25pm. The return working was at 5pm from Glasgow. A second NER restaurant car worked between York and Newcastle.

By 1910, Scarborough had a non-stop train each way from York in 50min, and others called only at Malton in 55-67min. As with other pre-Grouping railways, the NER worked hard to encourage businessmen to commute by train between the coastal resort where their families were staying during the summer, and their place of work. Such trains were first introduced in June 1900. One example was the 4.45pm Bradford Forster Square–Leeds New–Scarborough, booked non-stop from Leeds in 75min for the 67½ miles to Scarborough. The load was no more than three or so coaches, and the train was worked throughout by the NER engine. At one time in the early 1900s, the Bradford–Scarborough included a former Pullman sleeper which had been converted to a refreshment car. There was a similar train from Leeds–Bridlington via Selby, Market Weighton and Driffield. Again, it was lightly loaded, but the 73min schedule for the 63½ miles non-stop to Bridlington was no sinecure. For the 1913/14 seasons there was also a 7.55am Bridlington–Sheffield Midland (arr 9.53am), and 4.42pm return, due in Bridlington at 6.25pm. Calling only at Rotherham, these trains were routed via Gascoigne Wood, Milford Junction and the S&K line. Breakfast was served on the southbound journey, and tea going back. All three 'businessmen's specials' were worked by T. W. Worsdell J 4-2-2s which had been rebuilt as simples.

Hull was served by various semi-fast but few fast trains. On the line from York via Market Weighton, by April 1910 there were two semi-fasts in each direction, booked in 61-65min for the 42 miles. To and from Leeds there were through trains to Liverpool, Manchester and Halifax – see **Cross-Country services**. In competition with the Hull & Barnsley Railway, but to faster times, there were two trains each way to/from Sheffield Midland, at 9.38am and 3.20pm (splitting at Selby into Sheffield and Halifax sections), and from Sheffield at 9.42am and 5.10pm. Three of these trains took 105min for the 70-mile journey, the 3.20pm being slower.

Although the NER was an early user of bogie coaches, it was slower to introduce gangwayed vehicles and, apart from sets built from 1908 for the Leeds–Glasgow and Newcastle–Liverpool trains, they remained rare in general service.

By 1914, the Leeds–Glasgow express had been accelerated to reach Glasgow at 3.8pm, and was worked between Leeds and Newcastle by one of the R1 4-4-0s, and to and from Edinburgh by a NER Atlantic. In the summer 1913 timetable there were through coaches from Glasgow to Hull Riverside Quay, and between Newcastle and Scarborough. Attempts were made to improve the connections via Carlisle by the introduction in the summer 1914 timetable of experimental trains at 11.20am from Newcastle, booked in 93min to Carlisle, and eastbound from Carlisle at 11.55am.

The Railway's timings of summer 1920 were adversely affected by the stone ballasting of the main line between Ferryhill and Durham and between Morpeth and Alnmouth, a reminder that the reduced maintenance of British railways during World War I was at a cost, even with the general imposition of a 60mph limit. As late as 1917, the 'Fastest Train in the British Empire' had been running between Darlington and York in 45min start-to-stop, at an average speed of just under 59mph.

On the NER, the longest non-stop run of summer 1920 was made by the 8.55am Leeds–Glasgow express, booked to cover the 124½ miles from Newcastle–Edinburgh in 150min, at an average

speed of no more than 49mph. Reportedly, this service still retained non-gangwayed stock but a number of modern gangwayed coaches were built by the NER just before Grouping.

By the summer of 1922, matters had improved, and among the new services was a 7.20am Sunderland–York restaurant car train with through coaches to King's Cross from Sunderland and Middlesbrough. The prewar counterpart of this train had had no forward connection to King's Cross. The down through coach working was on the 5.35pm from King's Cross which split at York into a Sunderland portion, and one for intermediate stations to Newcastle. This train was additional to the 5.30pm King's Cross–Newcastle which made its first passenger stop at Darlington.

Hull & Barnsley Railway – to 1922

Primarily built to carry coal from South Yorkshire pits for export, surely there was no economic justification for the H&BR to run anything other than local passenger trains. From 1896, the Company operated an evening mail train between Hull Cannon St. and Cudworth, but attempts to introduce a through service to Sheffield were unsuccessful until the Midland Railway granted the H&BR running powers over its line between Cudworth and Sheffield Midland.

Through running to Sheffield Midland began in October 1905 with a service of four H&BR trains each way on weekdays, the best time for the 69½ miles being 98min with five conditional stops; one train each way ran via Chapeltown, the others via Rotherham. The Railway's 2-4-0s were used to work these trains with coaches borrowed from the MR. As early as July 1906, the Sheffield service was reduced to three trains each way and additional stops were added to their schedules. New semi-corridor coaches were delivered the following year to impart style to the Sheffield trains but their schedules were extended; at the same time, Sunday trains were introduced. Additional semi-corridor stock arrived in 1909, and the next year five J class 4-4-0s were built to work the principal trains. The usual load for the Sheffield trains was no more than three coaches, with a tail of fish vans on the afternoon working from Hull.

The Hull–Sheffield trains were suspended between January and October 1908, and again during the coal strike of 1912; after restoration, the Sheffield trains made extra stops and their fastest time was no better than 112min. When passenger services were cut severely throughout Britain in the later stages of World War I, through running to Sheffield ceased on and from 1 January 1917 and was not restored.

CHAPTER FOUR

THE GREAT EASTERN AND GREAT CENTRAL TO 1922

The Great Eastern Railway

The GER was the busiest passenger railway of the pre-Grouping companies, recording over 120 million passengers annually in the late 1900s. It was predominantly a workman's railway, and in 1902, for instance, some 91% of passengers using Liverpool St. travelled to/from stations less than 12 miles out. Somewhat gallingly, this tide of passengers was carried at a loss by 1899 as the GER was bound by law to carry workmen at a mere 2d a journey on its north-east London lines.

That was bad enough but, having built up the largest suburban traffic in the world, by 1913 the GER was all too aware of its depredation through competition with tramways and buses, and changes in local employment. To recoup the loss of revenue from suburban traffic, the GER paid close attention to improving its main line services, particularly after 1910, and benefited financially. In the autumn of 1914, the railway revamped its main line services, as described later in this chapter.

The territory served by the GER was badly affected by the agricultural depression induced from the late 1870s by the import of cheaper foodstuffs from abroad, one effect being to produce a drift from the land to the area's towns. The Eastern Counties were unpromising territory for main line services but the GER made the most of what was available.

Appreciating that its then Bishopsgate terminus was out on a limb for many passengers, with the opening of the Tottenham & Hampstead Junction line the GER announced that from its August 1870 timetable it would book passengers from St Pancras to Tottenham and places north. St Pancras was then advertised as the company's 'West End terminus'. Liverpool St. opened from 1874 in replacement of Bishopsgate. The GER boasted a third London terminus in Fenchurch St. but this was served only by suburban trains.

In 1898 the Cambridge line offered a service of a dozen expresses each way on weekdays, a few of which ran to and from St Pancras. The fastest times were by the 4.30pm from Liverpool St. to Cambridge, in 73min for the 55¾ miles, and the 5.8pm to the university city in 74 min, both trains running non-stop. Most other trains stopped at Bishops Stortford, and some at Broxbourne and Audley End. To Lynn (later King's Lynn) there was only one train each way booked in under 150min for the 97 miles.

The best time from London to Norwich via Thetford was achieved by the 11.50am from Liverpool St. and the 12.5pm from St Pancras: these trains combined at Ely (as did most portions from the two termini), and then there was a non-stop run in 62min for the 53½ miles to Norwich Thorpe which was reached at 3.10pm. The train continued via Reedham to Yarmouth Vauxhall where it arrived at 4.5pm. During the 19th century, the principal trains between London and Norwich ran via Ely, and the Colchester line's most important destinations were Yarmouth and Lowestoft. Operating difficulties and permanent speed restrictions did not help schedules on the Cambridge line, given the heavy London suburban traffic and the numerous coal and empty trains between the marshalling yards at Whitemoor (March) and Temple Mills. Early this century there were plans for quadrupling between Temple Mills and Broxbourne Junction but they could not be afforded.

Better times to Norwich were made by the Colchester line expresses. The fastest were the 1.35pm from Liverpool St, and 8.45am and 1.45pm from Norwich Thorpe; these took just over 150min for their 115mile journeys including a stop at Ipswich, and at Trowse in the case of the 8.45am up.

The GER set much store on its boat trains serving Harwich Parkeston Quay. In 1898, the best timings for the 68¾-mile journey were 85-90min. The fastest trains between Liverpool St. and Clacton-on-Sea – 69¾ miles – took 105 min in the down direction, and 110min coming up. Colchester's best trains took 70min for the 51¾-mile journey. On the Southend line, as yet no attempt was made to compete with the London Tilbury & Southend's fastest trains.

Indeed, at the turn of the century, the GER seemed to show more enterprise with its cross-country services than towards those serving coastal resorts. The 8.43am Ipswich–Peterborough via Soham made three stops in its 84¼-mile journey and there was a 1.20pm Yarmouth Vauxhall–Peterborough via Acle and Norwich, routed over the curve at Ely North Junction which permitted through running. This train took 168min for its 100-mile run, including five stops. Such trains to Peterborough called at the GER station before continuing to the GNR station where they connected into services to the North.

Sometimes referred to as the Cathedral Route, by 1882 the GER and GNR jointly-owned lines from Huntingdon and March to Lincoln and Doncaster had been completed to provide a through route, after which the Great Eastern ran trains to York from London and elsewhere on its territory. Pre-eminent in 1898 was the 7am from Harwich Town via Ipswich, Bury St Edmunds and Lincoln, and its balancing working at 3.50pm from York. These trains featured the GER's original restaurant car, as well as through coaches to and from the LNWR and GCR – see **Cross-Country services**. The objective of these trains, first run to Doncaster in 1885, and extended to/from York in 1892 was to feed traffic to the GER's Continental steamers. For the 218¾-mile journey each way the trains took from 5¾-6hr. New stock was provided for the York section in 1906, by which time it was worked by 'Clauds'. There was also a summer only Yarmouth Vauxhall–York train – see **Cross-Country services**.

Although the through expresses between Liverpool St. and York had lost some of the prestige of their early years, the fastest in 1898 was the 4.30pm up which arrived in Liverpool St at 9.50pm, a distance of 214½ miles compared with the East Coast route's 188 miles between London and York. The limited value of the Liverpool St.–York trains was that several useful connections were made, and Lincoln and Spalding enjoyed a direct service to/from London.

The service pattern on the GER's main lines was for up morning and down evening expresses, with little in the way of off-peak express trains. On the Colchester line, in 1905 the 3.20pm was the first down train of the day of any merit. Making a non-stop run to Ipswich in 90min, it took 157min overall to Norwich, a timing maintained in prewar years. The times to Yarmouth were 3hr 5min, and to Cromer, 3hr 35min. By now, there were other restaurant cars and these featured in the 4.55pm to Cromer and 5pm to Yarmouth. The 11.45am down was described in the April 1910 *Bradshaw* as the 'East Anglian' but its name and 'Luncheon Car' were the only evidence of distinction as it stopped at all stations from Marks Tey and only reached Yarmouth via Beccles at 4.12pm.

Catering vehicles were also provided on the 8.30pm Hook of Holland and 8.40pm Antwerp boat trains whose running times of 1905 had changed little from those of 1898. In 1904, the Hook train received a new, and heavier set of corridor coaches including restaurant cars and the timing to Parkeston Quay was slowed to 87min. Among the best up Colchester line expresses of the time was the 8am from Cromer, with restaurant cars throughout. It called at Norwich Thorpe, and at Trowse and ran the 45¼ miles to Ipswich in 51min, then the fastest point-to-point timing on the GER. With a non-stop run from Ipswich the 8am ex-Cromer reached Liverpool St. in 159min from Norwich Thorpe. The 8.20am express from Yarmouth South Town was routed via the East Suffolk line, and followed 10min behind the Cromer service south of Ipswich, its journey to London lasting 3¼hr.

Summer-only expresses had served Cromer from 1897, a major component in the GER's promotion of the locality as Poppyland, and several large hotels were built in the resort at the time. The two summer-only expresses each way from Liverpool St. to Cromer avoided Norwich Thorpe by taking the Wensum curve, and covered the 139 miles in around 180min. Of these, the star turns were the 'Cromer Express' at 1.30pm down and 1pm up, non-stop between Liverpool St. and North Walsham in 158min, and taking 175min overall. Non-stop runs such as these were possible by 1897 with the installation of water-troughs at Tivetshall and at Halifax Junction, Ipswich.

Neither Yarmouth nor Lowestoft had been previously served by through trains to/from Liverpool St. with journey times less than 3hr. Then, in the summer of 1900, new expresses were put on from Liverpool St. to both resorts, the 10.15am to Lowestoft running non-stop to Beccles. In 1904, Yarmouth and Lowestoft's summer only expresses became non-stop in 150min from Liverpool St. This demanded hard work on the part of the engine and men, given the sawtooth gradients and permanent speed restrictions of the East Suffolk line. Each season until 1914 the Yarmouth train continued virtually unchanged, but after the first summer the 10am Lowestoft train was combined with a Felixstowe portion detached or attached at Westerfield (from 1908-14, in no more than 1min!). Felixstowe was another resort nurtured by the GER, and in 1907 a through summer express was provided in each direction to a timing of 119min, at 4.10pm from Liverpool St. and 2.25pm return. Consequently, the up Lowestoft train now carried a portion for Aldeburgh instead, and ran non-stop from Saxmundham to Liverpool St.

At this stage, the 'Claud Hamilton' 4-4-0s were concentrated on the Colchester line (and gradually displaced 4-2-2s on the summer Cromer trains after 1900) but 2-4-0s were generally employed on Cambridge line trains.

For the Cromer service, a new set of 12 coaches was built in 1907 for what was now named the 'Norfolk Coast Express' which up to and including 1914 ran each season from July to September inclusive. Eight coaches including catering vehicles were run to Cromer, and two coaches for Sheringham and Mundesley alike. At peak times, though, the train might load to 13, 14 or even 15 coaches. With a 'Claud' this demanded superlative work from engine and men with the timings of 159min down, and 158min up. A second Cromer summer-only train followed in 1907. This departed Liverpool St. at 9.50am and ran 114 miles non-stop to Trowse in 137min where the portion for Norwich Thorpe was detached, the main train then proceeding to Cromer via the Wensum curve. The time to Thorpe was 146min, the fastest to date.

By 1905 or so, the Liverpool St.–York service comprised three down trains, at 8.40am, 11.5am and 4.30pm, the last two non-stop to Cambridge in 72min. From St Pancras, there were three fast trains, at 12.20pm, 2.40pm and 5.7pm, non-stop to Cambridge in 71-72min. At Ely they combined with the 12.7, 2.30 and 5.13pm from Liverpool St., and went forward to Norwich. At one stage, there was a separate 12.22pm summer only train from St Pancras through to Norwich in an overall time of 175min but the normal timing was 3½-3¾hr. Up from the varsity city there were three non-stop trains, at 11.20am, 1.33pm and 8.40pm, the last-mentioned being the 4.30pm from York. There was just one independent express from Ely to St Pancras, all other services to the terminus being by connections or slip coaches. The best times of 1905 declined in the years to 1914 by 5min or so.

The GER operated 25 slip coach workings in 1904, mostly at Tottenham, principally as through portions for St Pancras, and more than once daily there were slips at Broxbourne and Marks Tey. The GER was at that time second only to the GWR in its number of slip workings but by 1914 the total had declined to 14.

Improvements to year-round services to resorts commenced in 1910 with the introduction on 1 May of a 7.3am from Clacton-on-Sea, reaching Liverpool St. at 8.52am and conveying a Walton portion from Thorpe-le-Soken. The down working was at 5.6pm, with a 104min overall timing to Clacton. These trains were formed of a new set of coaches. At 6.20pm down, there was now a combined Clacton and Southend train, double-headed to Shenfield where the division was made. Previously, the best evening service to Clacton had been by coaches slipped from the 8.40pm Antwerp boat train, but now there was an independent 8.45pm train which itself slipped a Southend portion at Shenfield.

So far, Southend had not apparently been highly regarded by the GER but in November 1910 a trial was made to see if a 'Claud Hamilton' 4-4-0 loaded to six coaches would enable services to be accelerated. In place of a previous best time of 65min for the 41½ miles, from 1 May 1911 the series of new fast residential trains each way took 58-63min. New stock was provided including a restaurant car set which covered the 8.15am up and 5.3pm down, returned in the evening, and regained Southend at 1.10am as the midnight down supper train. The improved services quickly generated new business, particularly at Southend and Prittlewell where season-ticket-holders once numbered no more than 30 but had increased to 1,000 during 1913. What is more, the restaurant cars were profitable.

At the end of 1911, the first of the 1500 class 4-6-0s was completed and the next year these engines were used to work the 'Hook Continental' which was accelerated to a time of 82min between Liverpool St. and Harwich Parkeston Quay, despite a trailing load of some 400tons. By now, even in the winter timetable the GER boasted 13 expresses daily with restaurant car service.

The Great Eastern Railway put considerable effort into improving its Southend service from 1911. The month before new services were implemented in May 1911 'Claud Hamilton' 4-4-0 No. 1790 is working a down train approaching Southend with a lengthy set of non-bogie coaches in tow.

Pressure from the Norwich Chamber of Commerce resulted in the introduction of an early morning down express from May 1914. This was the 8.23am from Liverpool St., calling only at Colchester (connection to Clacton) and Ipswich, to arrive at Norwich at 11am. The train returned to London at 2.3pm. From 1 July 1914, there were improvements to the Cambridge line workings, with a new restaurant car express from Liverpool St. at 11.52am to Hunstanton (arr 2.45pm), leaving the resort at 5.37pm and reaching London at 8.33pm. To avoid overloading the 12noon down Norwich, previously catering services had been provided in winter only, but enquiry showed that this train had been duplicated on occasions in 1913. Pressure also came from Clacton interests for improvements in the town's service, so from 1 May 1914 the 1.30pm from Liverpool St. was altered to run daily instead of Saturdays only (except in summer, there had been no down through train between 11.40am and 3.25pm), and better connections were provided at Colchester into/out of Norwich expresses.

Encouragement for the GER's policy of improved services to the Eastern Counties' resorts came in 1913 with record sales of season tickets to London. Businessmen's season tickets were introduced in

1914 for those staying with their families at resorts during the summer and making a couple of trips to the London office in the week. There was also a drive to increase off-peak traffic to resorts to deflect holidaymakers from choosing the summer peak. From 5 July 1914, four additional fast trains were put on each way on Sundays between Liverpool St. and Southend, some timed in 60min. In April 1910, there had been no more than four Sunday trains each way between Liverpool St. and Southend.

Some of these innovations were attributable to one of the most interesting changes to affect the GER, once it had recovered from the disappointment of the Midland's acquisition of the LTSR in 1912. That was the appointment of Henry Thornton as General Manager in May 1914. He joined the GER from the Long Island Railroad, in the USA, and quickly set up a series of committees to review aspects of the GER's operation. Included was a timetable committee whose later objective was to draft an entirely new main line passenger service.

Surviving official papers demonstrate that piecemeal changes to services were time-consuming, and with the pressure for additional trains it made sense to recast the timetable entirely. What resulted was known as the 'Radical Alterations' timetable.

The Thornton 'Radical Alterations' timetable beginning on 5 October 1914 had as its ruling principles: that all main stations should benefit in equal proportion; that there should be a reduction in average journey time between all points on the GER; that the expresses should run at nearly even intervals; that semi-fast trains would provide connections at stations such as Cambridge and Colchester into and out of the expresses; that where possible, individual through coaches would be avoided, and conditional stops done away with. All these were to become routine tenets for modern railway timetables.

On the Colchester main line, there was a new residential express at 9.56am from Clacton-on-Sea to Liverpool St. booked in 95min, and returning at 5.30pm, running non-stop to Thorpe-le-Soken and slipping coaches at Colchester for Harwich. There was a later express for Ipswich and beyond at 7.45pm, into which a preceding semi-fast train fed in passengers at Colchester. The long-established 4.55pm Cromer and 5pm Great Yarmouth changed positions and left at 5.23 and 4.55pm respectively, and were substantially accelerated. The recently introduced 8.23am Liverpool St.–Norwich was retimed to leave at 8.30am, gained a portion for Yarmouth and was accelerated 9min. The 1.30pm Norwich was retimed to leave at 12.30pm. A new train was introduced at 11.33am from Norwich to Liverpool St., with connections from Yarmouth and Lowestoft. These two trains filled a previous gap in the Norwich service. Specified maximum loadings for classes of engine were laid down and there were standard schedules between principal stations. These were demanding, such that the fastest times from Liverpool St. to Colchester were reduced by 5min to 64min; to Clacton, by 8min to 95min; and to Norwich by 14min to 143min.

The Cambridge line service was similarly revolutionised, not least by the decision to separate the Liverpool St.–Cambridge service from that to/from St Pancras, so as to eliminate the time-wasting remarshalling of the two portions (typically 20min) at either Tottenham and Ely. Instead, just two fast services left St Pancras, at the new times of 10.30am and 3.55pm, for Norwich and Hunstanton. This allowed Liverpool St. expresses to be accelerated, and the previous 8.40am Liverpool St.–York was changed to leave 12min later and run fast to Cambridge. To King's Lynn the service was immeasurably improved, and not only was the average timing reduced to 135min daily from 151min on just three days a week, but the best train – the 3pm from Liverpool St. – was now 34min faster to King's Lynn.

The 'Radical Alterations' public timetable was backed up by improved working timetables and platform occupation diagrams for the principal stations, and facilitated by the adoption of modern timetable aids such as graphing. Complaints about the changes soon poured into the GER's Liverpool St. headquarters, and a few changes were effected with the new schedules. Still to be rehashed were Sunday main line services and the suburban lines and, although these were expected to change with the summer 1915 timetable, their postponement was inevitable. Despite the scale of the retimetabling process, official archives make only passing references to their introduction so that allegations that the Radical Alterations timetable proved a fiasco must be doubted.

Those Liverpool St.–York trains that had survived the October 1914 changes were withdrawn the next year, a report undertaken for Thornton having revealed that only 10% of passengers from GN/GE Joint line services were for or from London, the majority changing at March or Ely for the Eastern Counties, and that it would be better to recast the service to cater for them instead. Just one Liverpool St.–York train remained after July 1915 and this was cut back to Doncaster in January 1917, and withdrawn in May 1918. Until 1939, there was still a Sundays Doncaster–March–Liverpool St. train.

Another feature of the pre-1914 Great Eastern disappeared from 15 January 1917 when the Railway withdrew all its services to/from St Pancras. These were not to be reinstated, apart from a summer express between St Pancras and Hunstanton that was a feature of the 1923/24 timetables. The down train left at 11.20am and called only at Cambridge, King's Lynn and Heacham, to arrive in the Norfolk resort at 2.8pm. There was an up working from Hunstanton at 1.5pm, due in St Pancras at 4.2pm.

During 1920, ten new Pullman cars were introduced on some trains serving Cambridge, Clacton and Southend. From February 1921, they appeared in the Parkeston boat trains and in various expresses serving seaside resorts, and finally worked to/from Cromer in 1922. Gradually, Pullman operations on ordinary expresses were cut back, but cars were included in the boat trains until September 1939, and from 1929 featured in all-Pullman day excursions run by the LNER.

The summer 1920 timetable saw the resumption of many of the features of the 1914 service such as a successor to the 'Norfolk Coast Express' in the 12.25pm Liverpool St.–Cromer, once again non-stop to North Walsham but now taking 170min, or 12min more than prewar. On the Yarmouth service there was non-stop running again between Liverpool St. and Beccles; all round, though, the times were slower than in the October 1914 timetable.

The Midland & Great Northern Joint Railway

Cromer, Sheringham and their hinterland developed dramatically during the 1890s and 1900s as coy publicity extolled the virtues of Poppyland to holidaymakers. As compared with the Great Eastern Railway's 139 miles from Liverpool St, most of which involved main line running, passengers for Cromer from King's Cross faced a journey of 160¼ miles, further protracted on account of single-line working on the M&GN. During the Edwardian era, Lowestoft and Yarmouth were major holiday resorts and to both the M&GN could offer a competitive service to passengers from the Midlands and North.

The M&GN was managed locally by a Joint Committee, and served by through trains and coaches from both of its joint owners, the Great Northern and Midland Railways. From King's Cross, there were year-round through coaches to Cromer Beach, detached at Peterborough from the 3pm ex-King's Cross, and their overall journey expended 4½hr in 1899. On M&GN territory the through coaches were conveyed on the smartly-timed 4.40pm Peterborough–Cromer which ran to Melton

Constable in 110min, having made stops at Wisbech, Sutton Bridge, South Lynn, Melton Constable, Sheringham and West Runton.

In 1898, the GNR had reacted to the GER's 'Cromer Express' by introducing an alternative daily summer-only service, at 1.10pm from King's Cross. This had an enterprising non-stop timing of 95min for the 66 miles to Melton Constable, at an average speed of 43mph which was about the best that could be expected over the single-line sections. Once reached, the train reversed direction at Melton within 3min, another engine taking the train forward to Sheringham (arr 4.46pm), and to Cromer Beach where the train terminated at 4.55pm. But these timings were clearly too ambitious, and by 1901 the arrival at Cromer had been put back by 10min. The westbound working was at 12.55pm, the same station stops being made to Peterborough, and King's Cross was reached at 4.40pm. The up schedule was later eased, by 5min.

Considering that single track accounted for 60% of the system's mileage and at the time all single-line tablets were exchanged by hand, one of the up trains in 1898 timetable did well to run the 37½ miles between South Lynn and Peterborough in 62min and this included three stops and one 'by request' only. The need to eliminate the hand exchange of tablets was recognised by the Joint Committee which, from

It's 13 September 1910 and the Yarmouth Beach–Leicester London Road express has been photographed near South Lynn with Midland & Great Northern Railway 4-4-0 No. 53 at the head of an imposing set of the Midland Railway's clerestory stock.

16

KING'S LYNN, MELTON CONSTABLE
Single line Grimston Road to Raynham Park

DOWN WEEKDAYS

Notes and References. See also footnotes respecting underlined numbers.

Miles from South Lynn	Station		400	2	401	402	403	404	405	406	407	408	409	410	411	412	413
	Type		Gds.	Exp. Pass.	Pass.	Brkd. Gds.	Pass.	Gds.	Gds.	Gds.	H.B's	Pass.	Pass.	Eng.	Gds.	Gds.	Gds.
	Notes			12 m'ngt ex Manchester V	Not after 17th Sept.	To Norwich City.	Runs daily after 17th Sept.					9.23 a.m. ex Cromer Beach	6.50 a.m. ex P'boro' North	Eng of 7.50 a.m. ex Yarmouth		To Norwich City.	
			G			G		G	G	G						G	G
	See page			2									2				
	Class		D			No. 2		A	A	B						B	B
M. O.			SX	SO	80		SX				S0		Q	Q	SX ThO	SX	SX
			a.m.	a.m.	a.m.	a.m.	a.m.	a.m.	a.m.	a.m.	a.m.	a.m.	a.m.	a.m.		a.m.	a.m.
	King's Station dep. (1)		—										8 4				
	Lynn Exton Rd. " (2)		—										—				
	South Lynn arr. (3)		—										8 9				
	South Lynn arr. (4)		—	4 49									8 1				
	South Lynn dep. (5)		—	4 54									8 16			9 10	9 40
1 16	Hardwick Rd. Sdg. " (6)		—		5 50		6 18	7 30	7 46						**SUSPENDED**	9 10	9 40
3 53	Gayton Road arr. (7)		—						8 0								
4 53	Bawsey Siding " (9)		—										8 23				
6 40	Grimston Road arr. (10)		—										8 28			9 32	10 2
	Grimston Road dep. (11)		—	5 3	6 6		6 38	7 50					8 29			9 33	10 12
8 41	Hillington arr. (12)		—					7 57					8 33				10 20
	Hillington dep. (13)		—	5 6	6 10		6 43	8 6					8 34			9 40	10 30
13 20	Massingham arr. (14)		—										8 42				10 50
	Massingham dep. (15)		—	5 12	6 23		6 58	8 24					8 43			9 55	11 20
16 33	East Rudham arr. (16)		—					8 32					8 48				11 31
	East Rudham dep. (17)		—	5 16	6 29		7 5	8 54					8 49			10 2	11 58
18 30	Raynham Park arr. (18)		—										8 53				12 6
	Raynham Park dep. (19)		—	5 20	6 33		7 10	9 0					8 54			10 7	12 30
22 11	Fakenham arr. (20)		—	5 25		pass		9 10					9 0			pass	12 43
	Fakenham dep. (21)		—	5 26	6 40		7 18	9 25					9 2			10 17	1 0
25 10	Langor Bridge " (22)		—														
28 51	Thursford arr. (23)		—								9 0		9 13				1 23
	Thursford dep. (24)		—	5 41		pass		7 44	9 54		9 8		9 15				1 34
31 56	Melton Constable arr. (25)		—	5 41			7 2	7 18	8 10		9 8		9 21			10 48	1 50
	Melton Constable dep. (26)		5 0	5 46	7 10	7 2	7 18	8 10					9 35			10 45	11 0
35 33	Thurning Siding " (27)		—														
36 49	Corpusty arr. (28)		5 16		7 18		7 26					9 43					
	Corpusty dep. (29)		5 30	5 55	7 19		7 27	8 23				9 44		10 54			
43 20	Aylsham arr. (30)		5 31	6 4	7 31		7 39					9 56		11 12			
	Aylsham dep. (31)		6 5	6 5	7 32		7 40	8 38				10 0		11 18			
46 45	Felmingham (NB) " (32)		—									10 6					
48 69	Nth Walsham arr. (33)		6 27	6 15	7 42		7 50					10 0	10 11	11 40			
	Nth Walsham dep. (34)		6 50	6 16	7 43		7 56	8 55				10 2	10 13	10 23			
51 64	Honing arr. (35)		7 2		7 48		8 1					10 18					
	Honing dep. (36)		7 20	6 21	7 50		8 2	9 3				10 7	10 19	10 29			
55 51	Stalham arr. (37)		7 32	6 27	7 56		8 8					10 13	10 25	10 35			
	Stalham dep. (38)		9 35	6 28	7 57		8 9	9 11				10 14	10 26	11 8			
57 57	Catfield (NB) " (39)		10 0		8 2		8 14					10 31					
60 42	Potter Heigham arr. (40)		10 8	6 36	8 7		8 19	9 22				10 22	10 37	11 17			
	Potter Heigham dep. (41)		10 58	6 37	8 8		8 20	9 24				10 23	10 38	11 17			
63 22	Martham arr. (42)		See Col.		8 13		8 25					10 28	10 43	11 23			
	Martham dep. (43)			6 42	8 17		8 26	9 33				10 29	10 53				
66 7	Hemsby (NB) " (44)		415		8 23		8 32					10 34	10 59	11 23			
67 64	Great Ormesby arr. (45)		—		8 26		8 35	9 46				10 42	11 4				
	Great Ormesby dep. (46)		—	6 50	8 27		8 36	10 14				10 42		11 34			
70 44	Caister-on-Sea (NB) " (47)		—		8 32		8 41						11 10				
72 41	Salisbury Road " (48)		—	6 59	8 36		8 45	10 23				10 49	11 14	11 41			
73 15	Yarmouth Beach arr. (49)		—	7 0	8 37		8 46	10 26				10 50	11 15	11 42			

400   Catfield arr. 9.43.

⁓2   Not after 27th August.   Calls at Hemsby and Caister, if necessary, to set down passengers from Melton Constable and beyond.

404   Will not run on Saturdays between Melton Constable and Yarmouth Beach.

⁓408   Except Saturdays calls at Gt. Ormesby arr. 10.37 for crossing and loco purposes only.   On Saturdays Gt. Ormesby pass 10.37, Yarmouth Beach arr. 10.44 a.m.

⁓409   Will not convey Horse Boxes, Carriage Trucks, etc. between local stations.   Advertised to leave Martham 10.43, Hemsby 10.49, Gt. Ormesby 10.54, Caister 10.57 a.m., and on Saturdays to run at these times and cross No. 27 at Yarmouth.

411   Returns to Melton Constable as a special with cattle as required.

For additional trains between Potter Heigham and Yarmouth Beach, Saturdays excepted, 4th July to 9th September inclusive, see page 30.

Extract from the Midland & Great Northern section timetable for the 1938 summer service, showing some of the holiday trains.

17

AND YARMOUTH BEACH
and Corpusty to Salisbury Road

	414	415	4	5	416	6	7	417	8	418	419	420	10	421	11	11	422	423	12	424	425
	Gds.	Exp. Pass.	Exp. Pass.	Exp. Pass.	Gds.	Exp. Pass.	Exp. Pass.	Pass.	Exp. Pass.	Gds.	Pass.		Exp. Pass.		Exp. Pass.	Exp. Pass.	Gds.	Pass.	Exp. Pass.	Pass.	Pass.
	G	9.28 a.m. ex Peterboro' N.	8.37 a.m. ex Leicester		G	8.52 a.m. ex Leicester	8.30 a.m. ex Nottingham	Also on Sats. 17th, 24th Sept.	7.50 a.m. ex Derby.	G	Not after 10th Sept.		10.38 a.m. ex Nottingham		9.42 a.m. ex Birmingham	9.42 a.m. ex Birmingham	G	To Norwich City.	12.12 p.m. ex Derby	Also on Sats. 17th, 24th Sept	Not after 10th Sept.
		3	3		3	3		3					4		4	4		4	4		
		D			B					D							B				
	SX	SO	SO	SX	MFO	SO	SX	SO	SX	SO			SO		SX	SO	SX		SO	SX	SO
	a.m.	a.m.	a.m.	a.m.	a.m.	a.m.	a.m.	a.m.	a.m.	a.m.	a.m.		p.m.		p.m.	p.m.	p.m.	p.m.	p.m.	p.m.	p.m.
1		10 15			10 40		11 0								1 3	1 3			2 28		
2																					
3		10 22			10 45		11 5								1 8	1 8			2 33		
4		10 23	10 42		10 45	11 4		11 20			12 54			1 3	1 3			2 13	3 0		
5		10 30	10 49		10 50	11 10	11 17	11 26	11 35	11 44	1 0			1 12	1 12	1 25	2 38	3 6		
6																					
7							11 23			11 50								*		
8							11 24			11 51								2 45		
9																		2 50		
10		10 40	11 t 0		11 t 0		11 29			11 56				1 22	1 22	1 45	2 51	3 15		
11		10 40	11 4		11 4	11 22	11 30	11 36	11 55	11 57	1 9			1 26	1 26		2 55			
12			11 t 8				11 34	11 t40		12 1	1t12			1t26	1t26		3 55			
13		10 43	11 19		11 7	11 35	11 44	12 0	12 2	2 15			1 30	1 30	1 50	2 56	3 18			
14		10t49				11 44		12 17	12 10	1t22						3 4	3t24			
15		10 58	11 27		11 14	11 36	11 45	11 51	12 33	12 11	1 26			1 38	1 38	2 5	3 5	3 27		
16							11 51			12 17							3 10			
17		11 6	11 32		11 18	11 41	11 52	11 56	12 42	12 21	1 31			1 42	1 42	2 12	3 11	3 31		
18							11 56			12 25							3 15			
19		11 11	11 36		11 21	11 44	11 57	12 0	12 47	12 26	1 35			1 46	1 46	2 17	3 16	3 35		
20		11 16	11 41		11 26	11 49	12 3	12 5	12 57	12 31	1 40			1 51	1 51		3 22			
21		11 18	11 43		11 27	11 51	12 5	12 7	2 6	12 32	1 41			1 52	1 52		3 24			
22									*											
23							12 17		2 26	12 44							3 35			
24							12 18	B	2 40	12 45							3 36			
25		11 34	11 59		11 43	12 9	12 25	12 32	2 55	12 56	1 55			2 6	2 6	4 0	3 43	3 54		
26		11 40	12 6	11 20	11 48	12 16	12 40	12 40		1 10	2 0			2 12	2 12		3 48	4 0	4 10	4 10
27																					
28								12 48			1 18							4 18	4 20		
29			11 47	12 14	11 33		12 27	12 49	12 50		1 19			2 8	2 20	2 20			4 12	4 19	4 21
30			11 57	12 24	11 50		12 37	1 1	1 0		1 31			2 18	2 30	2 34			4 22	4 31	4 33
31			12 3	12 25	12 2		12 38	1 2	1 2		1 32			2 32	2 32	2 56				4 32	4 34
32								1 8			1 39								4 39	4 41
33			12 12	12 35	12 24		12 48	1 13	1 12		1 44			2 41	2 41	3 5			4t32	4 44	4 46
34			12 14	12 37	12 35		12 50	1 14	1 14		1 46			2 47	2 43	3 6			4 39	4 45	4 50
35								1 19			1 51								4 50	4 55
36		See	12 19	12 43	12 44		12 55	1 20	1 20		1 52			2 52	2 48	3 11			4 44	4 54	4 56
37		Col.	12 25	12 48	12 54		1 1	1 26	1 26		1 58			2 58	2 54	3 17			4 50	5 0	5 2
38		401	12 27	12 50	1 2		1 2	1 27	1 28		2 1			3 1	2 55	3 21			4 51	5 1	5 3
39								1 43			2 6								5 6	5 8
40		10 8	12 35	12 58			1 10	1 37	1 36		2 11								5 11	5 13
41		10 58	12 37	1 0	1 14		1 11	1 38	1 38		2 15			3 8	3 2	3 27			4 58	5 12	5 14
42		11 8						1 43			2 20								5 17	5 19
43		12 6	12 42	1 5	1 20		1 16	1 44	1 44		2 21			3 15	3 7	3 33			5 3	5 18	5 20
44		12 26	*	*			*	1 50	*		2 27				*	*			*	5 24	5 26
45		12 34			1 33		1t24	1 53			2 31			B	3t14	3t40				5 28	5 30
46		12 55	12 49	1 12	2 32		1 34	1 54	1 53		2 35			3 34	3 18	4 3			5 10	5 32	5 32
47		1 15						1 59	*		2 40								5 37	5 37
48		1 21	12 56	1 19	2 42		1 41	2 4	2 0		2 44			3 41	3 25	4 10			5 17	5 42	5 42
49		1 24	12 57	1 20	2 45		1t44	2 5	2 1		2 45			3 42	3 26	4 11			5 18	5 43	5 43

415 Hemsby arr. 12.16 p.m., Caister arr. 1.3 p.m.
=6 To Norwich and Cromer. Not after 16th September.
to set down passengers from Melton Constable and beyond.
to take up or set down passengers and runs thence 2 mins. later.
necessary to set down passengers from Melton Constable and beyond.
Rudham at 12.18, Potter Heigham 2.11 and Great Ormesby 2.32 p.m. and may so leave if necessary for crossing
purposes.   =11 Not after 17th September.   422 May call where required to detach or attach important traffic.

=4, 5, 7, 8, 10 & 12 Not after 10th September.
=5, 7, 8 & 12 Call at Hemsby if necessary
=417 Calls at Caister Camp Halt if necessary
=8 Calls at Caister Camp Halt if
=419 Advertised to leave East

1906, installed the Whitaker tablet exchange apparatus on its lines.

The Midland Railway's principal link with the M&GN in 1898 was by the weekdays and year-round 9.25am from Birmingham New St. which ran via Leicester and Bourne and used the avoiding line to by-pass Spalding. This service was inaugurated in 1894, and at first was summer-only. It ran from the Midland territory at Saxby to its destination at Cromer Beach (arr 2.35pm) in 3hr 20min, calling at Bourne, Holbeach, South Lynn, Hillington, Massingham, Fakenham Town, Melton Constable and then all stations. Connections were provided from Melton Constable to Norwich City, and to Yarmouth Beach. Westbound, the corresponding train took longer, despite making fewer stops. In the summer of 1902 Derby and Nottingham portions were added, and from that October the train ran year-round. At the same time, an M&GN 4-4-0 allocated to Yarmouth Beach depot began to work the 302 miles to Leicester and back with the Birmingham section of the train. Previously, MR engines had worked to and from Bourne, there to hand over to the Joint Committee's motive power.

With an eye to the competing Birmingham–Yarmouth (LNWR/GER) and Manchester–Yarmouth/Cromer (CLC/GCR/GER, dating from 1903) services, the Midland and M&GN responded with a Manchester Central–Yarmouth summer train for 1903. The following summer this blossomed into two services: Manchester Central–Yarmouth, and another conveying Liverpool–Yarmouth and Manchester–Cromer portions. With the opening of the Norfolk & Suffolk Joint line to Lowestoft, through coaches were also provided to serve this resort. A restaurant car was introduced from the summer of 1907, at first running between Manchester and Lowestoft, and returning to Derby only, but the next year provided between Nottingham and Cromer.

The GNR also instigated a cross-country train, and from July 1903 there was a summer only 'Tourist Express' from Leeds and Bradford to Cromer, Yarmouth and Lowestoft. This conveyed through coaches from Manchester Victoria to Cromer, one from Sheffield Victoria attached at Retford, and another from Nottingham Victoria which was added during the stop at Sleaford. The train's route was via Retford, Barkston North Junction and Sleaford and on the M&GN it ran the 56 miles non-stop from Spalding to Melton Constable in 81min. From 1909,

The early afternoon Cromer Beach–Peterborough train pauses at Wisbech behind Midland & Great Northern Railway Class C 4-4-0 No. 3. At the rear are three through coaches from Cromer to King's Cross.

a restaurant car was included between Bradford and Lowestoft, by which time the train also accommodated a short-lived through coach from Manchester London Road to Yarmouth. This was routed via Sheffield Victoria and Nottingham Victoria, where it joined the coaches originating there; the London Road coach was later cut back to run to/from Sheffield. On summer Saturdays in 1908, there was another GNR through service, also from the West Riding, Manchester and Derby but routed via Essendine and Bourne.

In 1906, the GER gained access to Sheringham by means of new junctions at Cromer and could now compete with the GNR and M&GN for London traffic. In reacting to its loss of monopoly at Sheringham, the M&GN took steps to accelerate the service to/from King's Cross. A 'Dining Car Trial Train' was run in December 1905 but, despite sprightly running from the M&GN 4-4-0 with a test load of five bogie coaches, the upshot was that over the 83¾ miles from Cromer to Peterborough only 3min could be shaved from the 128min running time of the existing 12.20pm service train.

Seemingly as a consequence of the trial run, in the summer 1906 timetable the GNR provided a restaurant car for the 1.10pm ex-King's Cross and return 12.50pm from Cromer Beach, and the overall time from London was reduced to 3hr 40min, the fastest ever by this route. There were also additional summer services from King's Cross: through coaches leaving at 10.35am (this was an Edinburgh train), and at 5.45pm on Fridays only. In the return direction, there were similarly four services from Cromer with through coaches to King's Cross: the 8am MTX, 7.45am MTO, its coaches conveyed from Peterborough on the 6.35am ex-York; the 9.50am, coaches from Peterborough on the 9.40am ex-Ripon; the 12.50pm, and 3.20pm whose through coaches were attached to the 4.15pm semi-fast from Doncaster at Peterborough. The first and third of these workings comprised GNR stock for London only, but the other pair of trains combined through GNR coaches and MR stock for Leicester and Birmingham. Indeed, during 1908 the 9.50am included a restaurant car for Nottingham.

With the opening of the Norfolk & Suffolk Joint line from Cromer to Mundesley, the earliest GNR departure from Cromer was altered to start at 7.15am from Mundesley which had received through coaches off the 3pm from King's Cross. The working of the 7.15am varied during the week. On Mondays and Tuesdays, west of Fakenham it called by request only at Massingham and Hillington, but otherwise

ran non-stop to Peterborough, with a King's Cross arrival at 11.50am. The rest of the week, the King's Cross coaches were attached to an all-stations train to South Lynn, and reached London an hour later than on Mondays and Tuesdays. From 1909, the summer 1.10pm from King's Cross was altered to a 1.5pm departure which also conveyed coaches for Scarborough and the north-east; the through timing to Cromer was slowed to 3hr 48min. The Friday afternoon through coach from King's Cross was discontinued after the 1909 season.

The effect of the through running of GER trains to Sheringham, and the advantage of that railway's shorter route to Cromer clearly had its effect, not surprisingly as there was almost an hour's less travelling for passengers to/from Liverpool St.

In wintertime up to and including 1914, the M&GN passenger service featured the midday through coaches from Cromer to King's Cross, and the return 3pm working from King's Cross, and the Leicester–Yarmouth train, with its through coaches from Birmingham (but returning to Leicester) and to Cromer. The remainder of the daily service mostly comprised stopping trains although, taking 1910 as an example, there were semi-fasts, at 6.55am from Peterborough to Lynn, 4.50pm from Lynn to Leicester, and at 5.10pm from South Lynn to Peterborough.

In March 1915 the King's Cross–Cromer service was reduced to one train each way and the Lowestoft through coaches were withdrawn from the 'Leicester'. From New Year's Day 1917 the 3pm from King's Cross and its return working also succumbed although the Leicester survived, if decelerated.

After World War I, the 3pm from King's Cross was restored in May 1919 but the return working was very slow until 1922. During the summers of 1923-32, the up train ran forward from Peterborough with the Grimsby coaches as an unadvertised relief to the 10.20am Newcastle–King's Cross, finally appearing in the timetable on its own account from 1932. By 1936, in winter the up working left Cromer at noon, made useful connections to the North at Peterborough, and came up to King's Cross on a mile-a-minute schedule to arrive at 4.20pm. The return working at 3pm got the traveller to Cromer for 7.48pm.

The GNR summer Saturdays train from the West Riding to Yarmouth was revived in 1921/22 as a through train from/to Leeds only and retained its routing of 1914 via the Barkston Junctions and Sleaford. Later, through LMS coaches from Leeds or Sheffield were provided on the Leicester–Yarmouth train.

The 4.5pm Spalding–Nottingham commenced running in 1921 and was worked throughout by one of the older 4-4-0s. The large-boilered 4-4-0s resumed their working to Leicester with the year-round through train, but the summer workings increasingly appeared at South Lynn behind Midland and later LMS 4-4-0s. By now, the 'Leicesters' made some reasonably fast runs such as Bourne–South Lynn in 50 min for the 34 miles. From the summer of 1924, the stock of the eastbound service started from Gloucester, and a restaurant car was provided from the summer of 1927.

One of the notable through summer trains after Grouping was the EWD Liverpool/Manchester–Yarmouth/Lowestoft/Cromer train – see **Cross-Country services**. This achieved one of the longest non-stop runs on the M&GN as the 41½ miles from Melton Constable were covered in 62min at an average speed of 40mph, good for a single-line railway such as this. The train's frequency was gradually reduced, at first to three days a week, then twice-weekly in 1932 and SO in 1934. This reflected the declining popularity of Poppyland for families although holiday camps grew up alongside the line to the north of Yarmouth and generated some alternative custom. There was also a summer Fridays train at midnight from Manchester Victoria, arriving at Yarmouth for 7am.

From October 1936, responsibility for working the M&GN passed from local management to the LNER which also took over the locomotive department. The LMS continued to provide rolling stock for the 'Leicesters' and other through trains. By this time, although local passenger traffic was being lost to road, the Railway continued to handle large flows of passenger-rated traffic at its western end, particularly soft-fruit, spring flowers and vegetables, much of it passing in special freight trains but also keeping passenger trains busy, too.

By 1936, the 'Leicesters' departed from Lowestoft at 8.18am, Yarmouth at 9am, Norwich at 9.35am and Cromer at 9.40am. The three trains were marshalled into one at Melton Constable, to run through to Leicester London Road where arrival was at 1.48pm. Stops were made only at Fakenham, South Lynn, Bourne and Melton Mowbray. The return working was at 3.22pm from Leicester, and once again the train was split three ways at Melton. A restaurant car worked between Yarmouth and Leicester in summer only but was discontinued after the 1937 season. In the 1937 timetable the long-standing practice of running the stock from Gloucester was advertised, with a departure from that city at 11.30am, then all-stations to Birmingham New St. and fast to Leicester. New motive power introduced by the LNER

included former Great Central D9 class 4-4-0s which replaced the indigenous engines on the 'Leicester'.

Once control had passed to the LNER, the search for economies began, with an eye to concentrating traffic on the former GER routes. From the summer of 1937 through coaches between Melton Constable and Liverpool St. were provided, attached/detached at Cromer High station to a London express. The summer through trains over the M&GN from LMS stations now ran on Saturdays only. With the outbreak of World War II, all through expresses were withdrawn, but although the 'Leicesters' reappeared in 1946 the noon Cromer–King's Cross and 3pm return through coaches were not reinstated.

Metropolitan Railway (and LPTB) to 1937
Under the chairmanship of Edward Watkin, the Metropolitan was an expansionist railway with main line ambitions. These never deserted the line, even after passing to the control of the London Passenger Transport Board after 1933, although the decision four years later to pass the working of its steam services north of Rickmansworth to the London & North Eastern signalled a change in the operation of the Metropolitan in advance of intended electrification to Amersham.

From 1906, all Met property north of Harrow was leased to the Metropolitan & Great Central Joint Committee. Steam working was progressively displaced north from London by electric locomotives or multiple-units, and after 1925 generally restricted north of Rickmansworth. The furthest point reached by Metropolitan trains running on Met & GC track was Verney Junction, 50½ miles from Baker St. The Metropolitan line north from Aylesbury had been incorporated in the main line forming the London Extension of the Manchester, Sheffield & Lincolnshire Railway, and thereafter Quainton Road to Verney Junction effectively became a branch line.

Emphasising the main line character of the Metropolitan, from 1 July 1910 the Pullman Car Co. provided two Pullman cars which were put into service between the City or Baker St. and Aylesbury or Chesham, making several journeys daily – with some inebriated patronage on the late-evening runs! Some workings took the sets of Met Dreadnought coaches with Pullman car from the City to Verney Junction. An example in the July 1922 timetable was the weekdays 10.2am from Liverpool St. whose overall journey time was 134min. LPTB trains ceased running north of Aylesbury with the withdrawal of the Quainton Road–Verney Junction passenger service after 4 July 1936. The Pullman

The Metropolitan Railway, and its inheritor, maintained a main line style until 1937. An up Pullman car train is unusually headed by a Class E 0-4-4T. Note the shoe beam fitted to the leading brake third of Met 'Dreadnought' stock.

cars last operated on the Met on 7 October 1939, latterly having been restricted to peak-hour trains.

Perhaps the only Met train to have carried Class 'A' headlamps was the 9.45am Aylesbury–Baker St. The working began in 1932 when changes in LNER GC main line services resulted in the loss of Aylesbury's morning fast train to London, and so the Met put on the 9.45am in compensation. It was hauled by a Met 4-4-4T and stopped only at Wendover, Great Missenden and Harrow-on-the-Hill. The non-stop run between the last two stations was 19½ miles, the longest ever scheduled on the Met. Although a stop was later inserted at Rickmansworth, the change to an electric locomotive continued to be made – exceptionally – at Harrow.

The Metropolitan handled through trains from other railways, nearly all suburban workings. Before closure in 1904, an Aylesbury–Yarmouth excursion formed of Met stock worked over the spur between its line at Liverpool St. and the Great Eastern

Railway. The Railway also owned the Widened Lines between King's Cross and Moorgate and these were used by the main line railways' suburban services and some longer-distance through workings, see **London & South Western** and **South Eastern & Chatham railways**.

The Great Western Railway offered a service from various stations via Paddington and over the Circle Line tracks to Liverpool Street. After 1900, there were through workings from/to Oxford, Reading, High Wycombe via Maidenhead, Windsor, and from stations nearer London. With electrification of the Circle Line in 1907, the GWR trains were hauled from Bishops Road station by Met electric locomotives. The service reached its maximum in 1914, but by 1922 there were seven up and nine down trains to/from Liverpool St., Windsor being the furthest-out point served. The number of through GWR trains to/from the City had declined by 1938, and all were withdrawn on and from 16 September 1939.

The 8.45am Marylebone–Manchester, one of the Great Central's light, fast restaurant car expresses, passes Whetstone on 26 March 1910 behind GCR Compound Atlantic No. 259.

Great Central Railway

With the opening of its London Extension, the Manchester, Sheffield & Lincolnshire Railway had moved from its status of a provincial system with a main line from Manchester London Road to Cleethorpes via Sheffield and Retford, and an alternative route via Doncaster, to a trunk railway with the title of Great Central.

The London Extension began with a weekday service of expresses from Manchester London Road to Marylebone on and from 15 March 1899, at 10am, 2pm, 5pm and 7.30pm, and in reverse direction at 9.15am, 1.15pm, 5.15pm and 10.15pm. All these had first and third-class dining cars except the midday workings which had the innovation of buffet cars and which put up the best time of 5hr over the distance of 206 miles. There were other through trains at 2.15am down from Manchester, and 5.15am from Marylebone, the latter becoming a newspaper train to Leicester later in 1899. More significant in this role was the 2.30am newspaper train from Marylebone which began running that October and quickly became one of the star turns on the main line. Both newspaper trains also had accommodation for bleary-eyed travellers. In the early days of the London Extension, there were just two through passenger trains each way on Sundays.

From 1 May 1900, weekday dining car trains were introduced between Marylebone and Huddersfield, Halifax and Bradford. With the appointment in January 1902 of Sam Fay as General Manager the GCR embarked upon its expansionist phase. As yet, longer non-stop runs were not possible as water-troughs had not been available, but once these were installed at Charwelton in July 1903, and then at Killamarsh, an express ran non-stop each way over the 164¾ miles between Marylebone and Sheffield, from Marylebone in 190min, and southbound in 2min less, at an average speed of over 52mph. This was the celebrated 'Sheffield Special' which ran first on 1 July 1903.

The southbound 'Special' left Wakefield at 8.2am, slipped a coach at Nottingham, and took 4hr 20min overall. The northbound train to Sheffield was the 3.25pm from Marylebone and this slipped a coach at Leicester for a service to Nottingham and Grimsby. At this stage, the 'non-stops' comprised no more than four coaches, and one of these was slipped en route. From October 1903, the 3.25pm down was accelerated by 8min, and extended to Leeds, and the up morning service speeded up by 10min to produce schedules of exactly 3hr to/from Sheffield. Then, in July 1904, Fay made further changes to the main line expresses. The 3.25pm was accelerated by 3min to

Sheffield, and diverted from Leeds to Manchester, which journey took 3hr 50min from Marylebone. The previous 5.40pm down was altered to 6.20pm and ran non-stop to Nottingham in 133min (126 miles), and arrived in Manchester at 10.35pm. There was a new train, at 11.25am from Manchester, stopping at Sheffield, Nottingham and Leicester, with a brisk non-stop run to Marylebone in 105min for the 103 miles.

From the summer of 1902 the GCR had made a bid for traffic between London and Stratford-upon-Avon, via Woodford Halse and the Stratford-upon-Avon & Midland Junction Railway. The summer 1904 timetable saw the best time to Stratford reduced to 125min for the 93¼-mile journey which, even after the opening of the GWR's Bicester line, provided the shortest rail route to the town. While all these changes were implemented, equally praiseworthy services were being set up to link the North with the East Coast, West Country and Wales – see **Cross-Country services**, and all the GCR's initiatives were vigorously promoted by Fay's newly established publicity department.

More accelerations were to come in the summer of 1905 when the 3.25pm 'Sheffield Special' was timed in just 170min non-stop from Marylebone. By now, the Sheffield non-stops were loading to five or six coaches. The 3.20pm was retimed to leave 5min earlier in July 1907, and at about this time the timing to Sheffield was eased by 7min; the 170min schedule had been too demanding. The train was altered again in July 1909, to leave at 3.15pm and to terminate instead at Manchester Central (for forward connections by the CLC), as well as conveying a slip coach slipped at Penistone for Huddersfield and Bradford. The existing Leicester slip coach was worked forward to Nottingham and Lincoln via Edwinstowe in a Cleethorpes train.

At times between 1904 and 1906, another travel opportunity was offered to travellers on the 3.25pm when it called by request at Darnall where they could alight to join the following Bournemouth–Newcastle train which avoided Sheffield on its trip to York and beyond. In its early days as the Great Central the railway had indicated its keenness to create a route for traffic to the north-east. Through coaches from Marylebone to Scarborough were also offered during the summers of 1904-6.

The 1905 timetable reveals how the original pattern of expresses introduced on the opening of the London Extension had changed. There was now an 8.45am down semi-fast to Manchester; a 10am semi-fast to Bradford; 12.15pm semi-fast to Manchester;

1.40pm Manchester, non-stop Aylesbury to Leicester, then calling at Nottingham and Sheffield and into Manchester for 6.15pm; the 3.25pm already mentioned; 4pm semi-fast to Nottingham; 4.35pm to Manchester, similar in calling pattern to the 1.40pm and both allowed 201/205min to Sheffield; 5.25pm semi-fast to Manchester; the 6.20pm Bradford, and the 10pm to Manchester. The 'semi-fasts' were smartly timed and took from 3½-3¾hr to Sheffield. There was a similar service pattern in the up direction. The expresses to/from Bradford Exchange were routed via Penistone, Huddersfield, the Anchor Pit Junction–Wyke Junction line, and Low Moor. For some time, and as late as 1910, the 6.20pm down was routed via Halifax. Apart from the through trains, there were two through coach workings each way between Marylebone and Bradford.

In the earliest days the expresses were worked by the Pollitt 4-4-0s, as well as the designer's 4-2-2s, but from 1904/5 the Robinson Atlantics took charge. The loads were light, reflecting limited patronage for this excellent, almost lavish service of trains, all formed of modern gangwayed stock and with catering vehicles.

Away from the London Extension and the Marylebone–Sheffield/Manchester expresses, fast running was largely confined to the Manchester–Retford section, and principally involved the through expresses to/from King's Cross – see **Great Northern Railway**. Another cross-country facility of 1898 was offered by the 3pm from Manchester London Road–Lincoln which took the through coaches to Harwich Parkeston Quay which in the reverse direction travelled from Lincoln to Retford, there to be attached to the 10.15am King's Cross–Manchester.

The trains over the lines from Cleethorpes via Retford or Doncaster were at best semi-fast, but, by 1910, *Bradshaw* described as 'Express' those to Sheffield, at 6.30am and taking 121min for 71¼miles; to Leeds, at 8.43am and 4.5pm via Frodingham, Applehurst Junction and the West Riding line, and the 1.13pm to Nottingham 109½ miles in 162min. The westbound afternoon trains tended to comprise a handful of coaches and a tail of fish-vans.

Some of these cross-country trains connected with the sailings of GCR steamers from/to Grimsby, and on summer Saturdays there were one or two faster workings. In 1898, the 2pm Cleethorpes–Manchester London Road ran the 109½ miles from Great Grimsby in 175min with calls at Brigg, Gainsborough, Retford, Sheffield, Penistone and Guide Bridge. Faster was the 5.10pm Cleethorpes–Manchester introduced in the summer of 1905 which reached its destination in 201min. Better still was the 10am from Manchester, as accelerated in July 1911 to reach Grimsby Town in 164min after a non-stop run from Sheffield. Summer trains were introduced in 1908 from Leicester and Nottingham to Cleethorpes, routed over the Lancashire, Derbyshire & East Coast line by means of the recently installed junctions at Duckmanton.

The LD&ECR had amalgamated with the GCR as from January 1907. From 1904 until June 1905, the LD&ECR had operated a fast service between Lincoln and Sheffield Midland taking 75min for the 51¼ miles, and this conveyed a through coach to Manchester via the Hope Valley line, connecting out of the GER's Harwich–York train. After its opening in September 1907, the connection between the two railways at Duckmanton also featured fast trains each way between Lincoln and Nottingham, there to connect into Marylebone expresses.

A longer established cross-country service was that operated in competition with the Lancashire & Yorkshire between Liverpool and Hull. The GCR trains used the Cheshire Lines' Liverpool Central station – or ran to/from Manchester only – and worked over the North Eastern Railway's line from Thorne Junction into Hull. At the turn of the century there were four trains each way and they covered the 136¼ miles in 4hr or so. Best was the 3.25pm from Hull which reached Liverpool at 7.5pm. By 1910, this had been brought forward to a 2.55pm departure, and a 7.15pm arrival at Liverpool. There were better trains at 10.40am and 7pm from Hull, booked in 4hr 5min overall, and best of all was the 3hr 29min of the 2pm from Liverpool Central and the 8.30am from Liverpool took 2min under 4hr.

In the early years, one of the difficulties faced by the GCR London expresses was congestion on the Met & GC line north of Harrow. With the opening of the GW & GC Joint line through High Wycombe, from the summer of 1906 three weekday trains each way between Marylebone and Manchester, and one to/from Bradford, were re-routed to the new line and via Ashendon Junction and Grendon Junction. From 1 July 1907, the GCR set its sights on Stratford-upon-Avon with a through coach on the 6.20pm ex-Marylebone slipped at Woodford Halse. By 1910, there were through coaches to Stratford on the 10am, 4.30 and 6.20pm down.

An up breakfast express from Sheffield to Marylebone was introduced in July 1911, at 7.20am, with stops at Chesterfield, Nottingham and Leicester. There were seven non-stop runs (including one to Leicester by the slip coach off the 3.15pm down) of 100 miles or more by 1914, some of these requiring

an average speed of 55mph or so. The fastest start to stop run was made by the early morning newspaper train from Marylebone, booked to take 22min for the 22½ miles between Leicester and Nottingham.

By 1914, the GCR was operating slips at four locations: two from the 6.20pm Marylebone–Bradford, at Woodford Halse for Stratford-upon-Avon, and at Heath for Chesterfield; at Leicester from the 3.15pm down, and at Penistone, for Bradford, off the 6.17pm Sheffield–Manchester. From the summer 1913 timetable new sets of elliptical roofed stock had entered service on the Marylebone–Manchester expresses, at which time the famed 'Director' 4-4-0s were newly built and displacing the Atlantics on the principal turns. Despite such enterprise, the GCR had to fight hard to win passengers for its fast trains, with their comprehensive range of through coaches and cross-country connections.

During World War I, the GCR managed to avoid slowing its best expresses too drastically, as well as continuing to operate restaurant cars, and for a time offered the fastest service between London and Manchester. GCR enginemen also seem to have taken a liberal view of the prevailing 60mph limit.

Paradoxically, the GCR took longer than other railways to recover from the slowest schedules as applying in October 1918 and, apart from the acceleration in May 1920 of the 6.10pm from Marylebone to reach Sheffield at 9.37pm, achieved largely by cutting out stops at Brackley and Woodford Halse, the inflated schedules were maintained through 1919/20. The GCR's best time from Marylebone to Manchester of 4hr 45min compared unfavourably with the Midland – 4½hr – and with the London & North Western – 4hr 23min. Between Marylebone and Leicester via Aylesbury the best time was 116min.

One of the features of the restored services from 1919 was a slip at Brackley off the 6.10pm Marylebone–Bradford, and for some time the sole slip coach operation on the GCR. The Brackley slip coach continued to Stratford-upon-Avon but was withdrawn in September 1921. Only a month passed before slipping was revived and the former 6.10, retimed to 6.20pm, now slipped at Woodford Halse, for Stratford-upon-Avon, as it had in prewar days. The third GC line slip was not inaugurated until the first day of Grouping and was at Finmere, south of Brackley, also off the 6.20pm down.

By 1921, nearly all the cross-country inter-Railway expresses had been reinstated with the notable addition of the Aberdeen–Penzance whose introduction was largely instigated by the Railway –

see **Cross-Country services**. In the summer 1922 timetable, there was a new 8.12am Mansfield–Marylebone and 4.55pm return, giving overall journey times of 178min in each direction for the 144¾ miles. Between the autumn of 1921 and the next following summer, the prewar times of the crack trains had been largely replicated, even if non-stop runs were now shorter as slip coaches had almost been discontinued. A good performance was put up by the 3.20pm down non-stop in 109min to Leicester, and reaching Sheffield in 3hr 6min, and Manchester Central at 7.45pm – but 15min slower than in the heyday of the 'Sheffield Special'. The fastest up express from Sheffield was no longer one of the morning trains which now made additional stops but the 2.15pm Manchester London Rd–Marylebone (due 6.38pm), with a time of 3hr 14min. This train conveyed a through coach at 2.40pm from Barnsley Court House via Chapeltown, with a return working on the 6.20pm Bradford train. This working dated from April 1922.

Cheshire Lines Committee – to 1949

As incorporated by the Cheshire Lines Act, 1867, the CLC system was a separate undertaking operated under the direction of a board of directors appointed by the Great Central, Great Northern and Midland railways (later the LMS and LNER). Its system included main lines from Manchester to Liverpool and Chester, and the CLC also worked the line between Aintree and Southport. Motive power was supplied by the Manchester, Sheffield & Lincolnshire Railway (later the Great Central and, in due course, the LNER) but the parent companies' engines worked through trains over the line although CLC-based engines also worked through trains off their native territory. The undertaking owned its passenger rolling stock which was maintained by the MS&LR (later GCR and GNR, and eventually the LNER). The CLC remained in being at Nationalisation. From its headquarters at Liverpool Central it continued to be worked separately within the London Midland Region, and was not incorporated under Regional management until 1 December 1948.

The principal service operated by the CLC remained largely unchanged for nearly a century. An hourly express service between Manchester Central and Liverpool Central was introduced soon after the direct line was completed between the cities, and with the opening in 1877 of the temporary Manchester Central station. By 1898, the CLC offered an hourly service between Manchester

The through coaches from Marylebone to Stratford-upon-Avon lasted until 1936. This May 1904 view shows one of the GCR slip coaches at Stratford in the company of East & West Junction Railway 0-6-0ST No. 1.

Central and Liverpool Central between 8.30am and 8.30pm inclusive, with extras from Liverpool Central at 11am and 9.30pm, and from Manchester Central at 9am (summer only), 10am and 10pm. Two trains each way covered the 34 miles in 40min non-stop (these non-stop trains having been introduced in 1883), but the standard timing was 45min with a stop at Warrington Central. This station was on a loop line ¼ mile longer than the avoiding line. On Sundays there were two 45min trains in each direction. Until the 1900s the inter-city CLC expresses were worked by MS&LR Sacré 2-2-2s dating from 1882, but from the mid-1900s they were displaced by Pollitt 4-2-2s.

In addition to the Manchester–Liverpool service operated by the CLC alone, there were the Liverpool–Hull through trains, see **Great Central Railway**, the Midland's various through expresses to Liverpool, see **Midland Railway**, and the Harwich–Liverpool boat train, see **Cross-Country services**.

Over the Southport branch, in 1898 the 8.50am from Southport Lord Street was allowed 65min for the 49½ miles to Manchester Central calling regularly at Birkdale Palace, and conditionally at Gateacre; the return train at 5.10pm needed only 1hr. Some residential trains on the Manchester Central–Northwich–Chester line were at least semi-fast such as the 4.33pm from Manchester Central which reached Chester Northgate, 38¾ miles, in 63min with four intermediate stops. This was some 3min slower than in 1890.

During World War I, the Manchester–Liverpool fast services were not decelerated until January 1918 when their time became 50min. These weekdays trains regained their 45min one-stop timings by 1922, and were usually no heavier than 200tons. By now, only the Harwich–Liverpool boat train and the 10.5am ex-Manchester were non-stop, in 40min. From 1917-19 the regular passenger service over the Southport Extension from Aintree was withdrawn, and this line entered a long decline with closure coming in 1952. In July 1922, its best trains were the 4.30pm ex-Manchester Central, in 100min, and the 9pm up in 85min. Fastest workings on the Chester line were by the 4.32pm semi-fast ex-Manchester in 73min, and the 9.25am return, in 83min.

From about 1930, an extra stop at Farnworth (on the outskirts of Widnes) was included in the schedules of some 45min Manchester–Liverpool trains, but without an increase in overall time. The non-stop 40min trains had disappeared and the best time in the service was by the Harwich trains, in 43min with a Warrington stop. The through trains from Liverpool and elsewhere loaded more heavily

than the Manchester–Liverpool trains and sometimes had slower timings. That said, the 4pm Liverpool–Hull of the late 1920s was booked in 42min only, including a conditional stop at Hunt's Cross. One of the long-established through workings was a portion of the overnight mail train between Marylebone and Liverpool Central, detached from the Manchester section at Godley Junction and running via Stockport Tiviot Dale. By July 1938, the Southport line retained residential trains at 5pm SX to Southport, in 102min, and 7.58am return EWD in 79min, as well as summer Saturday semi-fast workings. The Manchester–Chester trains showed no real change over 1922.

For almost 40 years the customary engines at the head of the Manchester–Liverpool fast trains were the Pollitt LNER D6 class 4-4-0s, first transferred to CLC sheds in the 1900s, and only gradually displaced from 1933 by D9s. By this time, ex-GNR Atlantics allocated to Sheffield Neepsend shed were diagrammed to cover some of the fast trains, but the D6s did not disappear from the service until after World War II.

The rolling stock used on the fast trains had been renewed before World War I, in particular by six-coach sets of non-gangwayed stock built at Doncaster by the GNR from 1911, and five-coach sets supplied by the GCR in 1914. From 1937, eight-coach trains of twin-articulated sets built to Gresley's LNER designs were put into service, and these were the most modern vehicles in the CLC fleet, apart from a limited number of some late 1920s/early 1930s non-gangwayed coaches.

In the early days of Nationalisation, the Manchester–Liverpool trains at first retained their wartime timing of 55min with two stops. The Pollitt D9s were soon replaced by Robinson 'Director' 4-4-0s but, once the LMR took control, a mixture of types worked the fast trains including LMS 4-4-0s and ex-Great Eastern D16/3 4-4-0s. In the winter of 1949/50 the best timing for the fast trains with Warrington and Farnworth stops was 52min, but the 10.5am ex-Manchester ran non-stop in 44min, and the westbound Harwich train took 45min, eastbound in 44min.

The final steam motive power comprised LMS Class 5 4-6-0s and 2-6-4Ts, hauling mostly LMS-design non-gangwayed stock. Immediately before diesel multiple-units were introduced – from June 1960 – the best inter-city times were again 45min with two stops, 38min non-stop for the 10.8am ex-Manchester and 41min non-stop for the 4.50pm Liverpool–Hull. The diesel service retained the best steam timings, and in due course the through trains from beyond Manchester were withdrawn.

CHAPTER FIVE

THE WEST COAST SERVICES AND LONDON & NORTH WESTERN RAILWAY TO 1922

West Coast Main Line services

The Races to Aberdeen of 1895 established record times on both routes but the consequence was to be the imposition of a standard time which, with one alteration, was to last until 1932. The fastest scheduled times by either route until the late 1930s were those operated in the summer of 1896 when the 8pm Euston–Aberdeen was allowed only 10hr 25min overall and the 10.15pm to Aberdeen 10hr 35min – the East Coast's 8.15pm 15min less. But in June 1896 the East and West Coast companies agreed to run the day London–Edinburgh and Glasgow expresses in a minimum time of 8½hr.

Operated as the West Coast Joint Stock (WCJS), all passenger vehicles were designed, built and maintained by the London & North Western Railway's Wolverton Works. The Joint Stock fleet had been set up in 1863, and the design of its vehicles remained somewhat backward until the early 1890s, but then so did the East Coast Joint Stock although the archaic survivals differed! In 1893 the WCJS inaugurated the first all-gangwayed dining car train in Britain, put into service on the 2pm from Euston and from Glasgow which then became known as the 'Corridor'. These arc-roofed vehicles had first-class and third-class accommodation only, and included coaches necessary for through workings conveyed on the 2pm, such as between Lancashire and Scotland; additional examples had to be built later.

In 1895 it was decided to replace nearly all the older WCJS coaches, particularly the non-bogie radial coaches, and new non-gangwayed stock was built, the decision being reached two years later that only gangwayed stock would be used for the WCJS. The 1897 stock was built for a new 11.30am Euston–Glasgow–Edinburgh restaurant car express and comprised 65ft dining cars and 50ft other coaches.

The timings of Anglo-Scottish expresses were changed as from December 1900. This arose from a decision the previous year by the North Eastern Railway to reduce the meal-stop at York by 10min, thereby reducing the London–Edinburgh time to 8¼hr, in contradiction of the West/East Coast agreement to maintain times at a minimum of 8½hr. In those days disputes between railway companies went to arbitration, and in this case Lord Balfour of Burleigh was appointed by the Board of Trade who regulated the affairs of the industry. Balfour upheld the NER's position, and the decision was associated with his name. From December 1900, therefore, the mutually agreed timing of London–Scotland day trains was reduced to 8¼hr. Departure times from either of the Scottish terminals were identical on both routes, and of course so were the corresponding arrivals. One belated innovation was that restaurant cars were introduced on the morning 10 o'clock expresses on the East Coast route, having run on both routes' afternoon trains somewhat earlier and on the West Coast's 10 o'clocks from 1898.

From the Balfour decision until 1914, the West Coast Anglo-Scottish expresses saw relatively few changes, and were slower than other expresses over both routes. An exception came in 1901 when the Midland, unfettered by the Balfour ruling, accelerated its 9.30am St Pancras–Edinburgh, and

West and East Coast alike responded by running their 10 o'clocks to reach Edinburgh before time.

There was no doubt that the provision of services on the three Anglo–Scottish routes exceeded demand in the 1900s. In 1908, quite apart from what was taking place in Scotland – see **Caledonian Railway** – the LNWR and MR reached an agreement to pool all competitive traffic including that to/from Scotland. The result was to bring a reduction in some seasonal services, such as running the midday West Coast Anglo-Scottish at the height of the summer only.

By the winter of 1913/4, there were four day and four night services between Euston and both Edinburgh and Glasgow, with average journey times to both cities of 8hr 25min or so for the day trains, and just over 8½hr at night. Aberdeen was served by a total of four day and three night trains, with average times of 12hr 41min and 11hr 53min respectively. The East Coast was faster to Aberdeen by day or night.

In 1898 there were seven through expresses daily in winter between London and Scotland by the West Coast route. Departures from Euston were at 5.15, 7.15 and 10am and 2, 8, 8.50 and 11.50pm. Apart from the 8pm which was primarily for passengers travelling beyond Stirling, the others served Edinburgh and Glasgow.

The 5.15 and 7.15am were much slower than the other trains, the former being described as a newspaper train, and made about a dozen stops between Euston and Carlisle. The 5.15am eventually reached Glasgow at 3.30pm, and the later train arrived there at 6pm. By winter 1900/1, the 5.15am was running through to Aberdeen.

Even the best daytime expresses of 1898 took about 30min more than the overnight trains. The night trains remained faster in the years to come as they were not covered by the agreement between East and West Coast companies on minimum journey times. As an example, the 11.50pm down called at Crewe only, and reached Carlisle, 299 miles, in 5hr 50min, Edinburgh in 7hr 55min, Glasgow in 8hr, and Perth in 9hr 20min. Two night expresses took 6hr 10min between Euston and Carlisle and all stopped only at Crewe and Willesden Junction. Over the 141-mile Crewe–Carlisle section, there were non-stop runs between both points in 160-168min, and between Preston and Carlisle, 90 miles, the best times were 102-106min.

The sleeping car trains in the Summer 1900 timetable included the 7.45pm Euston–Perth for the Highland line which ran from mid-July until end of August. The 8pm down was the main year-round train with coaches for Perth, and Aberdeen and, except when the 7.45pm was running, for the Highland line. The 8pm conveyed a portion for Stranraer in winter – see **Glasgow & South Western Railway** – which between July and September inclusive during the early 1900s became a separate train to Carlisle, at 8.10pm from Euston. In the summers of 1913/4 there was an additional 8.5pm from Euston which conveyed coaches for Oban, and for intermediate stations between Perth and Aberdeen, and in 1914, included a sleeper composite for Inverness.

The other trains in the 1898 timetable were to be found in those for 1900. The 8.50pm was for Glasgow only in winter, but was split during summer into a Glasgow via Birmingham New St. working and a second part following at 9pm comprising the Edinburgh coaches, others for the North and a residual section for Glasgow. The 11.50pm continued unchanged in summer with an Aberdeen arrival at 11.25am the next morning. The 11.50pm was supplemented by a summer midnight departure for Aberdeen via Birmingham New St. From the summer of 1905, the 11.50pm's Edinburgh coaches ran as a separate train, departing Euston at 11.35pm.

The principal up overnight trains were the 9.5pm Glasgow–Euston, due 6.35am; the 5.40pm Aberdeen–Euston, due 7.30am; the 7.10pm from Aberdeen with a section for Euston (arr 7.10am), and with through coaches to Manchester Exchange and Liverpool Lime St. which were detached at Carlisle. In summer, and often until the end of October, the 7.10pm ex-Aberdeen ran separately from the Glasgow–Euston coaches which formed a separate train departing at 10.45pm. There was also an 8pm Aberdeen–Euston which, until December 1904, detached a Liverpool/Manchester portion at Carlisle, thereafter at Wigan. By 1908/9 sleeping cars were run year-round to Stranraer, Perth and Aberdeen in the 8pm from Euston, to Glasgow on the 8.50pm, and to Edinburgh and Glasgow on the 11.50pm down.

The Anglo-Scottish trains originally combined portions from Euston, Birmingham and Manchester and Liverpool. For instance, the 10am from Glasgow and 10.15am from Edinburgh were independent trains as far as Crewe where they remarshalled as departures for London and Birmingham. With a connection at Crewe from Bristol, in summer 1898 the 11.30am from Birmingham reached Carlisle (193¾ miles) in 4hr 25min after three stops. At Preston, it had received through Lancashire & Yorkshire coaches from Manchester Victoria (dep 12.50pm) and Liverpool Exchange (1.5pm). The return workings for these coaches were on the

10.5am from Glasgow and 10.20am from Edinburgh. In the Summer 1900 timetable, the Liverpool and Manchester departures were altered to 2.45pm and 3.5pm respectively, to keep the Birmingham train out of the way of the 11.30am ex-Euston. Further changes saw the through coach departures changed to 3.20pm ex-Liverpool and 3pm ex-Manchester as from the Winter 1905/6 timetable.

The West Coast recorded an increase in Anglo-Scottish traffic between 1899 and 1900 but most of this was on the daytime trains. From 1900 until the summer of 1905, during July and August the 10am down comprised only through coaches between Euston and Glasgow, and Edinburgh, and there was a 10.5am down, with the Aberdeen coaches normally on the 10am, and also those for the Highland line. From 1905, there was a separate 9.55am Euston–Edinburgh in high summer which made a connection at Crewe with a train from Bristol. In the up direction, until the winter 1904/5 timetable, the 10.15am ex-Edinburgh and 10am ex-Glasgow combined at Symington and took 8½ and 8¾hr to Euston respectively but, from then onwards, the 10am ex-Glasgow and the now 10.15am ex-Edinburgh ran independently as far as Crewe where they combined, to arrive at Euston 6.20pm.

The late running of the Birmingham–Glasgow express tended to delay the 10am ex-Euston, and to improve matters changes were made to both trains from the winter 1907/8 timetable. The 10am now divided at Crewe and the Glasgow portion departed first, non-stop to Carlisle, then Symington only. The Edinburgh and Aberdeen portion was then attached to the Birmingham train which went forward shortly afterwards, also non-stop to Carlisle and after slipping a coach at Lockerbie, calling also at Symington. Here the train divided into Edinburgh and Aberdeen sections. During the summer peak of 1913 and 1914, the 10am down included through coaches for Gourock.

The principal train from the North of Scotland was the 6.45am Aberdeen–Euston which made a number of important connections on its journey south, and reached Euston at 7.10pm. There was also a 10.5am from Aberdeen, making a midday departure from Perth, which combined with the 2pm from Edinburgh at Symington, called at Carlisle and proceeded to Preston. Here there was a grand remarshalling with the arrival of the 2pm from Glasgow, as noted below. Finally, there was the 'Scotch Mail' at 1.10pm from Aberdeen and this made its weary entrance to Euston at 3.50am the next morning. Up trains had slower schedules than down

workings perhaps because this gave a little leeway when late handovers from the North would otherwise have affected pathing over the heavily used sections of the LNWR.

Catering for the seasonal increase in daytime travel to Edinburgh, Glasgow and further north, a summer 11.30am Euston–Glasgow/Edinburgh had been introduced in 1897. Both cities were reached at 7.55pm. The corresponding up service was the 11.30am Glasgow and 11.35am Edinburgh–Euston, and had a 6hr 5min schedule from Carlisle. From the summer of 1903 the up train was retimed to leave both cities 30min later, with connections provided from Oban and Crieff; in summer 1912, the down train was retimed to 11.25am. In 1906 both trains ran during October and November, and began running as early as May the following year, this arrangement being repeated in 1907/8.

Moving to the late 1900s, in winter the 2pm from Euston featured a six-coach portion with restaurant car for Glasgow, and other coaches for Edinburgh and Aberdeen. The train stopped at Crewe, then Preston where it was remarshalled. Detached were the Edinburgh and Aberdeen portions, to be replaced by others for Glasgow, from Liverpool Lime St. and Manchester Exchange which had arrived at Preston by the 5.45pm departures from both these stations which also brought coaches for Edinburgh. These latter were attached to the Euston–Edinburgh and Aberdeen coaches to form a train leaving Preston at 6.53pm, 8min behind the Euston–Glasgow service. In the up direction, the 2pm departures from Glasgow and Edinburgh ran separately to Preston, each conveying Liverpool and Manchester portions of LNWR stock which were detached at Preston. The train was then made up into a combined Euston train of Glasgow and Edinburgh portions, to which was added the through coach from Whitehaven.

In summer, the Euston and Lancashire trains ran independently north of Preston and there was also a morning Liverpool Exchange and Manchester Victoria–Aberdeen train. A new 4.35pm Glasgow–Manchester and Liverpool was introduced in the Summer 1903 timetable.

The 2pm from Euston also included a LNWR brake composite for Whitehaven, detached at Preston, and a brake tri-composite for Altrincham – see **London & North Western Railway**. For the summer of 1913, the Aberdeen coach was detached at Preston and worked forward on a Liverpool/Manchester train, and replaced by a LNWR Blackpool–Glasgow through coach.

The 10am from Euston received all-gangwayed

The glory of the pre-Grouping West Coast services: the up 2pm 'Corridor' from Glasgow Central, formed of the handsome West Coast Joint Stock of 1909, approaches Carlisle on 31 July 1912 behind the famous Caledonian 4-6-0 No. 903 *Cardean* which will then return north with the down 'Corridor'.

stock in 1900 but it was well into the new century before all the West Coast Scottish expresses were rid of non-gangwayed stock. Typical loadings of the day expresses between Preston and Carlisle were 225-375 tons although when trains such as the 10am down were run in separate portions in summer there were some lighter formations. These trains were supplemented from time to time with family saloons, carriage trucks and other passenger-rated vehicles.

In 1902, it was decided to build 15 new 65ft sleeping cars, with the intention that as many as possible would be ready for the following summer's services but the batch was not completed until 1904. In July 1906 it was agreed that the Highland Railway could provide a sleeper composite to alternate with a West Coast vehicle on the Inverness service.

Until 1909, the most modern WCJS coaches were arc-roofed, gangwayed vehicles which compared unfavourably with the modern-looking elliptical roofed stock built from 1906 for the East Coast Joint Stock. But the 18 65ft 6in long by 9ft wide twelve-wheeled coaches turned out at a cost of £33,000 by Wolverton Works in 1909 for the 2pm 'Corridor' were superior to anything on the East Coast. Entrance to all coaches was by the end vestibules only, and there were no outside doors to the compartments. The stock was used to form two

eight-coach sets, each including four coaches for Glasgow with dining car, three coaches with dining car for Edinburgh, and a brake composite for Aberdeen. The dining cars were earlier, clerestory-roofed stock. New elliptical-roofed 57ft stock was built in 1913 for the 10 o'clock and other sets, including brake composites for through coach workings such as Liverpool Exchange–Edinburgh. Despite the new vehicles, the majority of WCJS fleet at Grouping comprised arc-roofed vehicles dating from 1897-1903.

During World War I journey times and facilities were increasingly affected for the worst, and delays resulted from the running of ambulance trains and freight services loaded with war supplies. In 1915-17, the summer services were generally the same as for the previous winter timetable, but the late night sleeping car trains were decelerated appreciably. In time, there was pooling of services so that the West Coast provided an afternoon day train, and the East Coast the morning service; there was a morning day train on the Midland route. Restaurant cars were withdrawn on all WCJS services after 30 April 1916 and the rates for sleeping berths were increased to discourage traffic.

Although operating conditions had improved from early 1918, by that October the midday express from

Euston did not reach Glasgow Central at 11.10pm. Some improvements in timings materialised in March 1919 at which time restaurant cars were restored to some trains. At this stage, the former 10 o'clocks left at 9.15am northbound, and 10am southbound, and were composed of through coaches between Euston and Scottish destinations as well as Manchester–Glasgow sections. The former 2pm departures had been advanced to 1pm and, similarly, there were Manchester and Euston sections in each train. March 1919 also saw the acceleration of the overnight services, and a separate Inverness sleeping car train was run from July to October 1919.

Further acceleration of services came in early 1922 when the pattern of services began to approach prewar standards. The down daytime trains from Euston were the 5am, 6.45am (with through coaches and restaurant car Liverpool Exchange–Glasgow), 10am, a summer 10.30am to Edinburgh and Glasgow conveying through coaches from Liverpool Exchange and Manchester Victoria, and the 1.30pm, in place of the honoured 2pm departure. There was also a 9.40am Manchester Victoria/9.47am from Liverpool Exchange to Edinburgh/Glasgow. Night trains included the 7.30pm Euston–Oban and Inverness, 9.20pm Euston–Glasgow, 11pm Euston–Perth and Aberdeen. Southbound there were mostly familiar trains such as the 6.30 and 9.30am ex-Aberdeen (former 6.45 and 10.5am), 10am ex-Glasgow/Edinburgh with through coaches for Birmingham, Manchester and Liverpool, and the 4.10pm Glasgow/Edinburgh–Liverpool/Manchester. The long-suffering lunchtime departure from Aberdeen was leaving at 12.30pm but now had a more important role as a cross-country service. The times of the day trains were not reduced to the agreed 8¼hr until the summer of 1923.

Overnight trains comprised the 9.30, 10.30 and 11.10pm Glasgow Central–Euston (sleeping car Glasgow–Liverpool), 9.10pm from Perth with through sleeping car Inverness–Euston, and 7.30pm Aberdeen–Euston.

No mention of West Coast Main Line services can afford to ignore the 'Up' and 'Down Special Mails' between Euston (dep 8.30pm) and Glasgow and Aberdeen and return. Introduced in 1885, they carried no passenger coaches, except between Perth and Aberdeen on the down train. Arrival at Aberdeen was at 7.35am the next morning.

London & North Western Railway

At the turn of the century, probably the most important services on the LNWR were those to and from Scotland, and those serving the ports for steamer sailings to Ireland. Belfast was reached by sailings from Stranraer to Larne (for the Stranraer boat trains see **West Coast Main Line**), and a rail connection, by steamers from Fleetwood operated jointly with the Lancashire & Yorkshire Railway, and from Holyhead, by way of Greenore and Dundalk. There were two sailings daily from Holyhead to Kingstown (now Dun Laoghaire), and two to Dublin North Wall. The Irish mail steamer contract was held not by the LNWR but until 1920 by the City of Dublin Steam Packet Co. Its ships used the Admiralty Pier at Holyhead, and the 'Irish Mail' trains were worked to and from Holyhead station by 0-6-0STs.

Fleetwood was reached by a Belfast boat express from Crewe which left at 9pm, having made connection with the 5.30pm from Euston, a Liverpool (and Manchester) express. The fastest of the Euston–Holyhead expresses was the 10.15pm (for Dublin North Wall) which called only at Crewe and took 5¼hr for the 263¾ miles. The 6.30pm connected with the Greenore sailing and made eight intermediate stops and took 95min longer. The 'Irish Mail' trains left Euston and Holyhead at 7.15am and 8.45pm, and 11.15am and before midnight respectively. The up Holyhead boat trains were timed in 5¾hr or so and their timings along the Chester & Holyhead line included some fairly smart bookings between stations. All these boat trains included restaurant or sleeping cars, and most had connections at Chester General on to Manchester Exchange. The night sailing from Dublin North Wall had a boat train connection direct to Manchester in 3¼hr for the 124½ miles with no more than three stops. Other Holyhead expresses also served the resorts along the North Wales coast, such as the 9.30am from Euston which also featured through coaches for Pwllheli detached at Bangor.

The Euston–Liverpool service of 1898 had five or so trains each way, and the fastest time was made by the 10.15am down, 2.15 and 5.30pm which needed 4¼hr for the 193½ miles, but the 12.15 and 4.15pm made seven stops en route and required 4hr 35min. The fastest time was achieved by the noon Euston–Liverpool Riverside American boat special in making the longest non-stop run on the LNWR, to Edge Hill where engines were changed for the descent to the dockside. The overall time was 4hr, with about 3¾hr to Edge Hill. As late as 1907, Rous-Marten travelled on this train which was worked by a 'Precedent' 2-4-0 at the head of a 200-ton load; Edge Hill was reached early in 3hr 33min.

The 10.15am, 2.15 and 5.30pm Euston–Liverpool all had portions for Manchester London Road, detached at Crewe and with an overall journey of 4¼hr. The same overall time from Manchester via Crewe was made by four up services, two being through portions attached to Liverpool expresses. Apart from the portions worked on the Euston–Liverpool expresses, Manchester had two down and three up expresses each way routed over the North Staffordshire Railway's more heavily graded line from Colwich–Macclesfield, at noon and 4pm from Euston, in 4hr 20min and 4¼hr respectively, and 8.30am, noon and 6.15pm up. Each made six or so intermediate stops.

In 1898, Birmingham was served by a number of through Wolverhampton High Level expresses from/to Euston, but there were some workings with portions detached at Rugby from expresses routed via the Trent Valley main line. The fastest time was made by the 9.20am from Euston, in 140min for the 112¾ miles to Birmingham New St., and stopping only at Willesden and Coventry. The 8.45am up stopped also at Rugby and took 5min longer while the 7.30am called also at Stechford and Hampton-in-Arden. The 10am from New St. and 4.30pm down ran via Northampton. Wolverhampton was about 30min further from Euston, and the expresses generally stopped also at Dudley Port. There were through coaches between Birmingham New St., Kensington Addison Road and the Brighton side of Victoria station.

The LNWR worked hard to develop traffic between Euston and the Lake District and to Furness. There were through coaches to Windermere off the 10pm from Euston, and off the 2.15pm from Euston which connected with the 5.40pm Crewe–Windermere, and by connection from Crewe to Kendal off the 5.30pm from Euston. Through coaches were provided twice daily to Keswick although fastest times from Euston were achieved by changing trains. From the winter 1902/03 timetable, Windermere was given a through coach working from Euston on the 10.15am down, the train later being retimed to 10.10am when it conveyed a through coach for Whitehaven detached at Carnforth – see **Furness Railway**. From the early 1900s, the 11.30am summer Scotch express conveyed through coaches for Keswick, Windermere and Whitehaven, a restaurant car working throughout in the Windermere portion.

The Lake District towns were adequately served by through trains to Manchester Exchange, notably the summer 8.30am from Windermere and 4.15pm return, booked in 125/130min. As elsewhere, these were originally seen as services for businessmen staying with their holidaying families, and travelling each day to work in the city. From 1899/1900, the down train left at 5.2pm and, from winter 1911/12, the train became year-round SX and included a Club saloon, the down train now departing 5min later. Keswick had no through year-round trains but, with the best connections, the town was no more than 3½hr from Manchester. In 1904, the LNWR introduced a summer 8.15am Morecambe Euston Road– Manchester Exchange which ran non-stop from Preston via Standish Junction and Tyldesley.

From the turn of the century, the L&YR began to work more closely with the LNWR, resulting as from Summer 1901 in a Preston–Morecambe Euston Road train which was worked with L&YR engine and coaches. Before long, a through summer season working was inaugurated between Manchester Victoria and Windermere. From the summer of 1905, there was the Preston–Windermere train, and the Manchester–Windermere service with through coaches from Liverpool Exchange.

The resorts along the North Wales coast were served by Euston–Holyhead trains and there were through trains between Llandudno and Liverpool Lime St., Manchester Exchange and Birmingham New St., but none was particularly fast. The principal residential train was the 8.10am from Llandudno–Manchester Exchange, timed in 120min for 86¾ miles, and conveying also a Liverpool portion. In due course, the Llandudno train also included a Club saloon. The LNWR's Central Wales line was reached via Stafford and Shrewsbury, the principal trains of 1898 being the 10.25am from Euston which reached Llandrindod Wells in 5½hr, with the return working starting from Llandovery.

For the Liverpool Lime St.–Newcastle service jointly operated with the North Eastern Railway – see **Cross-Country services**. The Manchester–Leeds main line included other fast and semi-fast trains but the usual timing over the 43 miles was at best 63-67min, and sometimes up to 90min with six or so stops. The best timing of the early 1900s was by the 3.20pm Leeds New–Liverpool Lime St., booked non-stop to Manchester Exchange in 60min, the train comprising four coaches worked by a 'Jumbo' 2-4-0. Connections were provided with Manchester expresses at Stockport Edgeley by trains via Stalybridge which gave through Euston–Huddersfield times of around 5hr. Between Manchester Exchange and Liverpool Lime St., the LNWR offered an hourly interval service timed in

Doubtless motivated to compete with the improved GWR Paddington–Birmingham service and to offer a departure from a city terminus, the LNWR put on the 'City to City' express in 1910. The inaugural 5.25pm from Broad St. is ready to depart on 1 February 1910 behind LNWR 'Renown' class 4-4-0 No. 1918 *Renown*.

40min with a stop at Edge Hill in each direction from 9am to 7pm. This service, like that of the Cheshire Lines Committee, changed little over the years.

At the turn of the century, the LNWR faced something of a motive power crisis when it came to its main line expresses, and double-heading became unavoidable. The situation was hardly improved by the disappointing new 'Jubilee' 4-4-0s but matters recovered somewhat with the introduction of the 'Alfred the Great' 4-4-0s in 1901. At first, like many engines of their time, they were intensively diagrammed, some working six days a week on daily turns of over 300 miles. But then the general manager introduced a rule that any train of over 17 coaches (270 tons) must be piloted so that the demands on motive power were again increased.

After appointment as CME in 1904, Whale set about scrapping the Webb 2-2-2-0 compounds in favour of larger, new engines such as his 'Experiment' 4-6-0s. At a time when traffic was increasing, the process of renewal was undertaken at such a rate that the number of locomotives declined and reliability suffered.

By 1905, the emphasis was already switching to expresses serving the major industrial cities. In 1902, the LNWR had introduced non-stop trains between Euston and Birmingham, one each way being booked in 125min, the 5pm up being accelerated by 5min in August that year, when other trains on the service were also speeded-up. This initiative was somewhat misplaced because, unless piloted, the Webb 'Jubilee' compound 4-4-0s used on these expresses were unable to keep time.

The Euston–Birmingham–Wolverhampton express service of 1905 featured four 2hr trains non-stop each way to/from Birmingham, at 11.50am, 2.30, 4.45 and 6.55pm down, and 8.40, 11.25am, 2.45 and 5pm up. Coventry was served by slip coaches, detached from the 8.40am and 6.55pm down: in 1914, two vestibuled slip coaches were built for this working so that Coventry passengers could have access to the restaurant car en route. In advance of the opening of the GWR's Bicester new line, Leamington and Warwick Milverton (98¼ miles) were served by coaches slipped at Rugby from the 11.50am and 4.45pm 2hr trains, and they reached their destination in just under 120min from Euston.

In part-answer to the improved GWR Paddington–Birmingham service, the LNWR introduced the 'City-to-City' express in February 1910, leaving New St. at 8.20am, calling at Coventry, and arriving in London Broad St. at 10.35am. The trains were worked throughout by a LNWR 'Renown' 4-4-0 at the head of a four-coach restaurant car set. The return working to New St. was at 5.25pm, calling at Willesden Junction and Coventry, again with a timing of 135min. A typewriting compartment with secretary was provided on this train, and also on the 4.45pm ex-Euston and 8.40am return from New St. The down 'City-to-City' express was withdrawn in the summer of 1914, and the up train the next year. In 1913, the LNWR moved to counter competition from the GWR for Birmingham traffic. New restaurant car trains were introduced on 1 July 1913, at 12.30pm down, and at 6pm from Wolverhampton, and also an 8.10pm 2hr train from New St. which was put on to take traffic from the GWR's 8pm from Snow Hill, due to commence running a fortnight later. The Euston–Wolverhampton expresses tended to be formed from what the LNWR termed 'Inter Corridor Sets' of four coaches with a restaurant car inserted in their midst, and strengthened by other vehicles.

In 1905, the Euston–Liverpool service featured five trains each way, down at 10.45am, 12.10, 2.40, 4.15 and 5.30pm, up at 8, 11am, 2, 4.5 and 5.20pm. The last-mentioned took 3¾hr but otherwise the times were 4-4¼hr. On one run in 1902, the 5.20pm up was recorded to take just 169½min from Crewe with 320tons double-headed by a 'Lady of the Lake' 2-2-2 and a 'Jumbo' 2-4-0. Equally good in 1904 was a run timed by Rous-Marten when a 'Precursor' gained 3½min to Stafford on the 10.45am, despite a load of 350tons. The 12.10 and 2.40pm also included through Manchester portions.

The 5.30pm from Euston had been sufficient previously for evening traffic to the North-West – to Manchester, Liverpool and Fleetwood but matters changed rapidly. The first change was that the 5.30pm had portions only for Liverpool and Fleetwood (for the Belfast boat connection) and the 6.5pm Manchester was introduced. Then came the 5.55pm for Liverpool only, running non-stop to

Mossley Hill, and booked in 3hr 35min overall. This was described as a Belfast Boat Express and had bus connections at Lime St. for the Belfast Steam Ship Co. sailing from Prince's Dock. Similarly, the 5.20pm Liverpool–Euston was run separately from the up Manchester working after May 1905, and given a non-stop booking from Edge Hill. By 1909, the then 2.40pm down Liverpool not only included a Manchester portion but also through coaches for Colne and Windermere and a Welshpool coach slipped at Rugeley. The 4.10pm from Euston conveyed through coaches for Llandudno and Blackpool Central, the latter returning at 8.55am. At Edge Hill, through coaches between Euston and Southport were attached to or detached from four Liverpool expresses each way.

The Liverpool Special boat train received a special set of stock in 1908, comparable only with those built the next year for the 2pm 'Corridor' – see **West Coast Main Line**. These 15 65ft vehicles were normally made up into eight-coach sets with restaurant cars, a kitchen car and a couple of brake vans.

Between Euston and Manchester there were two 3½hr expresses in 1905 running via Crewe, down at 10.35am and 6pm, and up at 10.20am and 4.10pm. These ran non-stop between Euston and Stockport Edgeley in 198min for the 183miles, at an average speed of 55.5mph. At Stockport, the coaches for Colne and Rochdale were detached. The 6pm was later retimed to 6.5pm, and with the opening in 1909 of the Wilmslow–Levenshulme line avoiding Stockport, it was re-routed this way. The Colne portion was then detached at Wilmslow, reached non-stop from Euston. The expresses via Stoke and Macclesfield took 3hr 40-50min, and the fastest were the 8.30am and 12.10pm up.

The through service from Euston to Dublin via Holyhead offered journey times of 9hr or so, such as by the day Kingstown sailing for which the connecting boat train was the 8.30am from Euston, designated as 'Irish Mail' in the timetable. The second day service from Euston was marginally faster, by the 1.20pm ('Irish Day Express') which connected with the Kingstown sailing and gave an arrival at Dublin Westland Row station of 10.25pm. The evening boat trains from Euston–Holyhead were at 7.30pm (for Belfast via Greenore), the 8.45pm 'Irish Mail' via Kingstown, and the 10.15pm 'Irish Night Express' with a connection with the North Wall steamer. In all, there were five daily through services between Euston, Holyhead and Ireland. The up boat trains reached Euston at 6.10am ('Irish Mail'), off the night sailing from Kingstown;

7.30am, connecting with steamers from Greenore and North Wall, the principal 'Irish Mail' day service at 5.40pm, having left Holyhead at noon, and the 11pm arrival at Euston, the 'Irish Day Express' connecting with the 1.40pm sailing from Kingstown.

In 1905 there were 16 slip coach workings on the LNWR, mostly at Nuneaton (5), Bletchley (3) and Blisworth (3), and at Leighton Buzzard, Rugby and Rugeley. One of the Bletchley slips was off the 4.5pm to Manchester and was worked via Buckingham to Banbury Merton St. station (arr 6.32pm).

By 1910, the Liverpool/Manchester expresses were being hauled by 'Precursor' 4-4-0s and loaded to 390tons or so. The performance required from the engines was typified by the 10.30am down, with its booking of 171min for the 158 miles from Euston to Crewe. The 'Precursors' were good performers but even better standards were set with the entry into service of the superheated 'George Vs'. The Manchester expresses included through L&YR coaches from Colne (dep 8.15 and 10am and 4.20pm) to Euston, worked via Blackburn and Bolton to Manchester by L&YR engines. With the diversion of the 6.5pm down via Levenshulme, its East Lancs portion was detached at Wilmslow.

Manchester Oxford Road was the terminus of two daily trains from Crewe via Northwich and Altrincham, and from 1900 one of these conveyed a through coach from Euston, detached at Crewe from the 2pm 'Corridor', and worked round into London Road station for 6.45pm. By 1910, the return working by this route was at 10.37am from Oxford Road, to arrive in Euston at 3.15pm. There was a through coach from Bolton Great Moor St (dep 11.20am) – Euston (arr 4pm), via Eccles and Knott Mill but not in the down direction. Other through coach workings to the North-West in these years – the timings are for April 1910 – included those to/from Buxton, one detached at Nuneaton from the 10.37am down North Wales express, and the other slipped from the 5.30pm Liverpool express, to arrive in Buxton (169 miles) at 9.55pm. The up workings were at 7.50am and 12.45pm from Buxton. The route followed by these through coaches was via Shackerstone, Burton-on-Trent, the North Staffordshire line to Uttoxeter, and on through Ashbourne to Buxton. The timings did not present much of a competitive threat to the Midland with its 4hr services to the town.

At Coventry, the LNWR maintained its monopoly despite attempts to challenge its position and, other than to Euston and Birmingham, through services were restricted to twice-daily through trains introduced in 1908 from Leamington, or Coventry via Nuneaton to Leicester and Nottingham Midland. The Great Northern and London & North Western Railway Joint Line included six Northampton–Market Harborough–Nottingham London Road Low Level trains daily each way at the turn of the century, of which the 9am ex-Nottingham received a through coach to Euston attached at Melton Mowbray. This vehicle returned to Northampton on the 4.30pm Birmingham express, and worked forward on the 6pm to Melton where it arrived at 7.13pm. From 1900-14, there was a weekdays Northampton–Newark GNR and return train, to connect into Doncaster semi-fasts.

The Peterborough–Rugby line seldom saw any fast trains with the exception of those run in connection with the Great Eastern Railway's Harwich Parkeston Quay–York boat train. Through coaches for Rugby and Birmingham New St. were detached from the train at March, and the train ran non-stop from Peterborough GE to Rugby, 50¾ miles in 66min. The return train, at 4pm from New St. made more intermediate stops. The other (relatively) fast trains on this line comprised the 8pm Rugby mail from Peterborough and 2.40am return.

By April 1910, there was an express leaving Euston at 10.37am for the Central Wales line, the Cambrian Coast and North Wales. At Stafford, the train divided into North Wales portions – and the rest! The latter were routed via Shrewsbury and on departure from Stafford included portions for Shrewsbury, Barmouth and Aberystwyth, the tri-composites in each being Cambrian Railways' vehicles, as well as LNWR coaches for Swansea Victoria (arr 6.15pm). The corresponding up workings were on the 8am from Swansea Victoria, the Euston coaches being attached at Stafford to the 11am from Liverpool, in company with those from Aberystwyth and Shrewsbury. The 11am also conveyed through coaches from Birkenhead Woodside and Manchester London Road via Altrincham. In summer, there were additional through trains between Euston and the Cambrian Coast, sometimes running non-stop between Wellington and Welshpool by using the Abbey Foregate curve to by-pass Shrewsbury.

There was the EWD 'York Mail' in each direction between Swansea and York, with coach and van dual-fitted to work over the North Eastern Railway. In 1910, the 12.40am from Crewe – the down York Mail – comprised a sorting van from Shrewsbury, and a coach and a van from Swansea Victoria–York as well as GWR coaches and a TPO from Cardiff–Newcastle.

Most of the North Wales coastal towns benefited by connections at Chester into/out of Holyhead boat trains. Through workings were restricted, but there was the 10.37am from Euston with restaurant car to Chester and through coaches for Pwllheli via Bangor and Afon Wen, and Llandudno. There was a through coach working from Llandudno at 8.55am to Euston (arr 2.10pm), conveyed from the Junction station on the 7.40am from Holyhead, this effectively being the counterpart to the 10.37 down. The return through working was by the 4.10pm Liverpool train to Crewe, then by a semi-fast, and giving the through traveller to Llandudno an overall journey of 4hr 55min. In the summer of 1914, there was a summer restaurant car express to North Wales, at 11.10am from Euston, and running non-stop to Rhyl. A short-lived residential train had been introduced the previous June, at 7.40am from Llandudno to Birkenhead Woodside, and 4.5pm return. Another facility for holidaymakers in that fateful summer of 1914 came with through coaches from Euston to Fleetwood which were conveyed for the first stage of their journey on the 10.5am Scotch train. They connected at the port not with a Belfast sailing but with one for the Isle of Man.

As an example of the sort of working that might be expected from LNWR express engines, the first 'Claughton 4-6-0, No. 2222 *Sir Gilbert Claughton*, was put on to an experimental diagram in May/June 1913, involving a mileage of 2,000 weekly. It worked the down 'Corridor', the 5.19pm Crewe–Carlisle, returning with a sleeping car express at 1am the next morning, then the 5.5pm to Euston on Sundays with the return to Crewe on the Monday 8.30am 'Irish Mail'. From October 1913, the old system of calculating passenger train weights as equivalent to a number of coaches was replaced by a tonnage-based system, such that 420tons (15 coaches) was fixed as the maximum weight for a passenger train, for a 'Claughton', or a superheated 'George V' or 'Precursor' on the down 'Corridor' and 7.32pm ex-Crewe only. The Euston–Wolverhampton expresses were limited to 350tons for a superheated 'George V' or 'Precursor'.

The LNWR invested heavily in additional running lines before 1914, including the New Lines between Kensal Green Tunnel, Harrow and Watford Junction, not only to develop suburban traffic but ease operating congestion, a process later completed by a third Primrose Hill Tunnel and associated burrowing junctions at Chalk Farm. That was not all. Quadrupling was carried out from the 1890s, particularly in the Wigan area, from Milford to Stafford, through Preston, after 1900 between

In the Wirral the Great Western & London North Western Railways' Birkenhead Joint line from Chester saw a surprising number of Class 'A' trains, even if like this example, the main part of the train was formed of local stock. The engine is LNWR 0-6-0 No. 1355, departing from Rock Ferry.

Tamworth and Atherstone, Colwich and Rugeley, north of Preston to Barton, and through Crewe including burrowing junctions to keep freight workings clear of passenger services.

As with many railways, although express schedules were lengthened in the early years of the war, the standard of running remained high until the mechanical condition of the locomotives deteriorated. Writing in February 1915 Cecil J. Allen was to say: ' . . . it seems almost impossible to travel on the North Western without a substantial gain accruing to the locomotive at the close of the run.'

During World War I, the slowest times were in 1918 when the Euston–Birmingham time was 155min, and Euston–Liverpool 4hr 45min, no less than 70min more than in 1914. Some of the Liverpool and Manchester expresses included portions for Wolverhampton, and loads of 450-500tons were not unusual.

In the Summer 1920 timetable there was a 10.40am Euston–North and Central Wales express routed via Northampton and this was leapfrogged by a 10.55am down, also to North Wales but running non-stop to Crewe. By July 1922, the Swansea Victoria and Aberystwyth portions were conveyed on the faster train which now left at 11am and ran non-stop to Stafford where the Central Wales and Aberystwyth portions was detached, to run via Shrewsbury.

The 11.5am Euston–Manchester of Summer 1920 carried a Windermere portion and, after stopping at Bletchley where connections were made from Oxford and Cambridge, the train ran non-stop to Crewe. The usual timing in 1920 between Euston and Crewe was 193min for the 158 miles, at an average speed of 49mph. Some of the apparently non-stop runs from Euston–Crewe and Crewe–Carlisle actually included intermediate stops for crew relief. The very best that the LNWR could show in terms of speed was a 52mph run from Blisworth to Willesden. Unlike some other railways, by 1920 the LNWR had nowhere regained the number of restaurant car workings offered in 1914, but was however making use of newly built tea cars, in which light refreshments were served from a galley inserted in an otherwise ordinary gangwayed thirds.

By July 1922, 2hr timings had been resumed for the Euston–Birmingham expresses, with departures at 11.30am, 1.15, 2.20, 4.35 and 6pm, the majority of trains calling at Coventry, and all going on to Wolverhampton. There was also a slower 9.15am. Up trains were at 8.40, 11.15, 1pm, 2.30 and 3.25 (125/130min respectively), 4.50 and 6.20pm. The majority of these expresses either had restaurant cars or, as noted in the timetable, it was a case of 'Teas served on this Train'. The usual motive power for these trains were 'George V' 4-4-0s displaced from longer distance expresses by the recently built 'Claughtons' and 'Prince of Wales' 4-6-0s.

In the Summer 1922 timetable, the best times to Liverpool were 4hr, still 25min slower than in 1914 while the Manchester expresses at 4pm and 5.35pm from Euston were timed in 4hr and 4hr 5min respectively, again taking 30 or more minutes longer than in 1914. As an example of the complexity of some LNWR expresses, the 10.35am MFSO 'Luncheon & Tea Car Express' from Euston to Penrith had through coaches for Blackpool (Central) – 3.45pm – detached at Preston; for Barrow/Whitehaven (6.10pm) and Morecambe (FSO), detached at Lancaster; for Windermere (4.35pm), detached at Oxenholme, and for Keswick (5.45pm).

North London Railway

From February 1909 the North London Railway was worked by the London & North Western but remained independent, a move induced by the loss of traffic to trams and buses. Other than the 'City-to-City' express introduced by the LNWR, the NLR saw little other than local trains. From 1907 to 1914 the NL and London, Tilbury & Southend Railways operated a regular summer service from Chalk Farm to Southend, the smaller company's engines being used only at bank holidays.

The Stratford-upon-Avon & Midland Junction Railway

After a shaky history, not least receivership, a clutch of railways, including the East & West Junction Railway, combined to form the SMJ as from January 1909. The principal route was from Stratford-upon-Avon to Towcester. Spurs linked the E&WJR at Byfield with the London Extension of the Manchester, Sheffield & Lincolnshire Railway, and through coaches between Marylebone and Stratford-upon-Avon operated from the summer of 1902 – see **Great Central Railway –** and until 1936.

Connections for Stratford-upon-Avon were also made at Blisworth with expresses to/from Euston: the best, in the summer of 1924 only, offered a 145min journey to London. For the opening in 1931 of the London Midland & Scottish Railway's Welcombe Hotel at Stratford, an evening express was run between that town and Blisworth and return, with journey times of 62-70min. It was repeated the next summer. In the intervening period, the SMJ saw

The Cambrian Railways' 9.5am Aberystwyth–Whitchurch gathers speed out of Machynlleth on 15 August 1913 behind 4-4-0 No. 95, with a banker pushing hard at the rear. Visible are Cambrian and LNWR through coaches. This locomotive was to be destroyed in the Abermule crash of 1921.

the experimental Karrier 'Ro-Railer' road-to-rail convertible bus which from April to July 1932 worked between the Welcombe Hotel (some way from the station) and Blisworth. On Easter Mondays only, a through excursion was run from 1927 until 1939 between St Pancras and Towcester on the occasion of the Grafton Hunt steeplechases. In the 1930s, the LMS ran some long-distance evening excursions to Stratford-upon-Avon.

Cambrian Railways
With its incorporation into the Great Western Railway at Grouping, the Cambrian lines increasingly became associated with connecting services from GWR territory whereas their earlier affinities had been with the London & North Western Railway, traffic passing via the Stafford–Shrewsbury–Welshpool lines or via Whitchurch and Crewe.

At the turn of the century, traffic was increasing on the Cambrian and there were five through trains each way between Whitchurch and Aberystwyth. The delivery of new 4-4-0s had allowed schedules to be cut appreciably in 1898. The summer 12.20pm North Express from Whitchurch covered the 95¾ miles between the towns in 3¼hr, and through coaches from Manchester London Road took 4hr

50min to reach the coast; there were also coaches from Liverpool. The time from Manchester was bettered by a coach from/to Manchester Central, routed via Chester, Connah's Quay, Wrexham Central, and a spur on to the Cambrian line via Ellesmere. In 1899, the 12.20pm was accelerated by 10min, to take 3hr 5min from Whitchurch.

Two Aberystwyth trains each way conveyed through coaches to Euston, the best time being made by the 1.50pm from Whitchurch. There were connections at Shrewsbury to/from GWR services, the line between Shrewsbury and Welshpool being LNWR & GWR Joint, and most of its trains were all-stations. Trains to/from Pwllheli on the Coast line were often limited-stop, and the 3.42pm from Machynlleth took 123min for the 57¾ miles. By this service, the journey time by the 8.30am service from Euston was 9¼hr, but it was 60min less by using the 9.30am ex-Paddington. Passengers for Barmouth could improve on this further by travelling via the GWR's Ruabon–Dolgelley line. During the 1900s, the best up fast trains from Aberystwyth were the 8.45am, and the 12.5pm 'North Express'.

The other through service was that to/from Cardiff and Newport which was introduced in 1891 – see **South Wales companies**. From 1900, the GWR began to improve its through services to the

Cambrian coast, by introducing summer trains routed over the joint line to Welshpool to the Cambrian, and to Barmouth via Dolgelley. They were further improved after the opening of the direct line to Birmingham in 1910 when there was a summer 9.50am Paddington to Aberystwyth and Pwllheli. Other through trains came from Leicester (Central) – see **Cross-Country services** – and from Stoke, see **North Staffordshire Railway**. For the numerous through coach workings off its territory, from 1905 the Cambrian Railways built vestibuled stock, mostly tri-composite brakes.

The other limited-stop services were the mail trains at 2.25am from Whitchurch, and 6.35pm return from Aberystwyth. In the April 1910 timetable, the other principal trains were the 1.50pm ex-Whitchurch, with several stops 'by request' west of Welshpool and taking 3hr 50min to Aberystwyth, and the 1pm from there to Whitchurch which provided a connection via Crewe into the 5.25pm Liverpool express. This made its Euston arrival at 9.15pm.

In the Summer 1920 timetable, the tilt towards the Great Western was apparent with the introduction of through restaurant car trains at 9.50am from Paddington to Aberystwyth (arr 4.15pm), the return train leaving at noon, and due into Paddington at 6.30pm. The latter left Dovey Junction at 12.45pm and made the longest regular non-stop run on the Cambrian's system – the 45 miles to Welshpool in 83min, at an average speed of 32.5mph. These trains involved the Cambrian engines working into Shrewsbury. At the same time, the through GWR coaches from Paddington to Barmouth and Pwllheli were re-routed via Welshpool instead of via Ruabon and Dolgelley. By now, there were four Cambrian trains with 'teas' service from a pantry in the guard's van of four gangwayed composites and brake composites. The GWR restaurant cars were the first such to work over the Cambrian.

In the Summer 1922 timetable the Paddington train operated between mid-July and mid-September and was retimed to leave at 10.15am. It included through coaches for Aberystwyth and Pwllheli, and the up working left from Pwllheli at 10.15am and from Aberystwyth at noon. The service was unusually routed via Ealing Broadway and Greenford and the down train was booked to Birmingham New St. in no more than 125min. The trains do not appear to have been a success because in the following summer's timetable there were no through workings, and passengers changed from the 10.20am down Birkenhead at Birmingham Snow Hill where a through train ran via the Abbey Foregate

curve to avoid reversal at Shrewsbury, and there was a similar connection into the 2.5pm Birkenhead–Paddington.

The premier motive power at Grouping comprised the final class of Cambrian 4-4-0s built in 1904. Until the late 1920s when they were finally supplanted by standard GWR classes, these five engines continued on the heaviest duties such as the 8am (later 7.50) Aberystwyth–Whitchurch and 1.50pm return. These two trains conveyed the through coaches to/from Euston, while the 1.50pm down started from Birkenhead Woodside and included through coaches from Manchester and Liverpool.

Furness Railway

The Furness principally exchanged through traffic at the joint station at Carnforth where the layout was particularly awkward, and the transfer of through vehicles caused delay to operations on the West Coast Main Line. Where possible, connections were made with the LNWR at Preston, such as in 1898 by the 11.30am from Whitehaven which gave passengers a 6hr 5min journey between Barrow-in-Furness and Euston, and 7hr 40min from Whitehaven. The return connection was off the 2pm 'Corridor' from Euston. On the Furness metals, some trains made limited stops between Carnforth and Barrow, with times of 50min or so for the 28½ miles. The 6.30am MO from Whitehaven Bransty ran to Barrow in just 77min for 46 miles, again with limited stops, but otherwise the time allowed over this partly single line was around 90min. This train connected at Lancaster with the 8.30am from Windermere–Manchester and though the overall time from Whitehaven was 4hr 5min this was considerably better than by other trains.

Carnforth was the exchange point for Midland traffic routed over the Furness & Midland Joint line from Wennington, and the layout at Carnforth station meant that it was preferable to stop trains at Carnforth East Junction to attach/detach vehicles, such as the boat train through coaches for Barrow's Ramsden Dock, leaving Leeds at 6.33pm. In 1897, the Midland had started running through coaches between St Pancras and Barrow, the 7.58am departure getting to St Pancras for 3.30pm. In 1903, boat passengers from St Pancras travelled in a through coach conveyed as far as Leeds on the 1.30pm Scotch express, and it arrived at Ramsden Dock for 8.25pm. The 10.30am from St Pancras had through coaches for Whitehaven and Windermere, the latter detached at Ulverston.

During the 1900s, the Furness improved its locomotive stock and coaching fleet, following the appointment of a progressive general manager. The Railway proceeded to promote tourist facilities in Lakeland, and this included the running of combined rail/coach tours of the Lakes, rail/Lake Windermere steamer excursions, and the availability of area cheap weekly tickets. In summer, there were through workings by its engines and stock from Barrow and Grange-over-Sands to Morecambe Euston Road, running via Hest Bank. By 1910, there were through coaches from the Furness to Euston and Manchester, and to Southampton – see **Midland & South Western Junction Railway**. There was a small fleet of gangwayed coaches for the through coach workings, just four being built 1904-14. Furness trains worked through between Grange-over-Sands and Kendal via the Arnside–Hincaster Junction line, with through workings in summer to/from Windermere. This route saw the limited operation of through coach workings from Newcastle-upon-Tyne – see **North Eastern Railway** – run to connect with sailings between Barrow and the Isle of Man.

Major improvements to the Railway's infrastructure were carried out during the late 1900s, with track relaying, and the renewal of bridges and viaducts on the main line. Accelerated services followed in 1911 such as the summer 4.43pm from Carnforth which now arrived at Whitehaven at 7.10pm, and conveyed the through coaches leaving Euston at 11.25am. The year-round service from London was on the 2pm 'Corridor', with the Whitehaven coach being detached at Preston with the Aberdeen section. It worked forward from Carnforth on the 7.23pm so-called 'Belfast Boat Express' which got to Whitehaven at 9.55pm. This train slipped at Grange-over-Sands, apparently employing a MR coach as the Furness had none of its own. Through coach workings to Euston were on Mondays only, at 7.45am, and EWD from Whitehaven at 11.30am, attached at Preston to the 6.45am from Aberdeen. One curious working was a through coach in summer only from Cambridge to Whitehaven.

In 1903, there were three through coach services from Leeds to Whitehaven, as well as a 2pm train with through coaches to Windermere Lakeside and Coniston. By then, all timetabled trains off the F&M Joint line ran into and out of Carnforth station. With the opening by the Midland in 1904 of its new port at Heysham, sailings were gradually transferred there from Ramsden Dock, and most of its boat train workings to Barrow had ceased. By 1911, through coach workings between St Pancras and the Furness

district had come to an end but not through services from the West Riding, and two years later these comprised the 6.30am Leeds–Barrow, the 10.5am and 1.55pm Leeds–Whitehaven trains, and four or so corresponding return workings from Whitehaven and Barrow.

In the 1922 timetable the first down train was the 4.40am mail from Carnforth to Whitehaven, and this called at principal stations only on its 2¾hr journey. Other down trains were all-stations but the 1.30pm from Carnforth conveyed the through coaches off the 6.55am from Euston. The last two through trains of the day to Whitehaven were the 4.20pm and 7.10pm from Carnforth, the former semi-fast between Ulverston and Millom, then all-stations, and the latter providing the fastest service of the day, including seven mandatory and four conditional stops, to arrive at Whitehaven at 9.35pm. In summer, there were through coaches from Manchester Victoria to Barrow conveyed on the 9.53am to Whitehaven which was semi-fast Carnforth to Foxfield and 3.43pm Carnforth–Whitehaven which took the through coaches detached from the summer mid-morning Euston–Windermere express.

Of the up trains, the 6.35am from Whitehaven called at nearly all-stations and included a through coach for Euston while the 11.35am from Whitehaven was the best train of the day in winter and called only at St Bees, Seascale, Millom, Barrow and Ulverston to Carnforth; it had through coaches for Euston and Leeds. The 1.50pm from Whitehaven also had a through coach for Euston (and in summer for Manchester Victoria), and was semi-fast from Millom. The last principal train of the day was the 7pm mail from Whitehaven which was the counterpart to the early morning down train. In addition, there were Carnforth–Barrow workings, including the 11.5pm with the through coaches off the 5.20pm from Euston. In summer, there was a 9.25am from Whitehaven semi-fast to Carnforth with through coaches to Manchester Victoria and Liverpool Exchange. On Sundays there were just two through Carnforth–Whitehaven trains each way. In summer there were Lancaster–Lakeside trains which operated in conjunction with sailings on Lake Windermere, and used the Leven curve to avoid the need for reversal at Ulverston.

The five big 4-6-4Ts, based at Barrow and dating from 1920/1, included among their seven passenger turns the morning mail train north to Whitehaven and the 3.5pm Barrow–Lancaster, and shared the principal Furness passenger duties with 4-4-0s based at Carnforth. At the time of Grouping, through trains

Maryport & Carlisle Railway 2-4-0 No. 10 arrives at Carlisle Citadel station on 31 July 1921 with the 1.25pm from Whitehaven Bransty.

were running between Carlisle and Carnforth via Workington – see **Maryport & Carlisle Railway**.

The Maryport & Carlisle Railway

The West Cumberland iron ore industry declined during the last decades of the 19th century, with marked effect on the economics of the Maryport & Carlisle and the Furness railways. With some success, the latter developed passenger traffic to compensate but the M&C, in Ahrons' words, was 'like Peter Pan, and had never grown up'. Early in 1914, its staff were on short-time due to the reduced iron traffic. The principal passenger service at the turn of the century comprised five all-stations trains over the 28 miles between Carlisle Citadel and Maryport, with one each way omitting some station calls. Some trains ran through to Whitehaven, usually worked by a M&C engine but otherwise a change was made at Maryport to London & North Western motive power.

By April 1910, there were seven trains each way between Carlisle and Maryport, and they included a 'fast' train at 4pm from Carlisle, making limited stops and taking 50min, the similar 11am from Maryport, just 2min slower. Two trains ran through

between Carlisle and Whitehaven, worked by LNWR engines.

Towards the end of World War I, the Furness Railway was short of motive power and stock and the M&C engine on the 4.20pm from Carlisle worked through to Millom on the 7pm mail from Whitehaven, returning with a train reaching Whitehaven at 9.20pm. Two other passenger trains worked through to Workington with M&C engines. To balance these workings, LNWR engines were used for Whitehaven–Carlisle trains, and that Railway's coaches appeared on a return working to Carlisle. One set of Furness coaches ran to Carlisle and back.

After World War I, there was a return Keswick–Bullgill–Carlisle through coach (a vehicle on loan to the M&C from the LNWR) which worked out from Carlisle via Bullgill at 6.30am, departed from Keswick at 9.35am and reached Carlisle at 11.45am. The latter manoeuvre involved a reversal at Brigham on the Cockermouth, Keswick and Penrith line, and the coach then traversed the M&C Derwent branch to Bullgill where it was attached to a through train which had left Carnforth at 6.55am. The return through coach working to Keswick was at 4.20pm; once there, it departed for Carlisle at 6.30pm.

The North Stafford Railway's favoured passenger workings were through to Llandudno where NSR 4-4-0 No. 86 is standing on 29 July 1920.

North Staffordshire Railway

The North Staffordshire Railway enjoyed extensive running powers, including being able to run its own passenger and freight trains over the London & North Western Railway from Macclesfield through Stockport, and to Manchester London Road. It also had powers to run trains over the Midland Railway from Willington Junction into Derby Midland, into Burton Midland and, south of its territory, to Walsall and Birmingham.

From at least the 1880s, the London & North Western Railway routed some Euston–Manchester express via Stoke-on-Trent, in so doing creating the impression that Colwich–Macclesfield was the North Staffordshire's main line. That company nevertheless regarded the Derby–Crewe service as its principal passenger operation. The Euston expresses were however the fastest trains over the NSR, and the 12.10pm ex-Manchester was booked in 27min for the 19¾ miles between Macclesfield and Stoke-on-Trent. This train of 350tons tare was usually worked by a NSR 0-6-2T, or 4-4-2T, for the first 37½ miles of its journey to Stoke. There, an LNWR express engine took over, and the portion for Birmingham New St. was detached. The express presented a hard task for

the NSR engine, for after a stop at Stockport it faced a stiff climb from Cheadle Hulme to the next stop at Macclesfield Hibel Road station. From there, the train was banked to the summit beyond.

There were only five through trains each way between Derby and Crewe at the turn of the century, at best taking 105min for the 51 miles. In April 1910, the 1.30pm from Crewe was the fastest train, booked in 100min for the journey to Derby, with eight intermediate stops. Most Crewe–Derby trains had connections to/from Burton. Schedules hardly changed by 1914, and up until the Grouping. Uttoxeter was also served by through LNWR coaches between Euston and Buxton – see **London & North Western Railway**.

In summer, there were through trains between Derby Midland and Llandudno. These were worked by NSR engines, at first 2-4-0s. With the introduction of bogie stock, something more powerful was required, such as the Class G 4-4-0s of 1910 which were otherwise employed on Derby–Crewe trains. In this period, the 11am Derby–Llandudno ran daily in summer and conveyed through NSR coaches from Derby, one from Nottingham MR, another from Nottingham GNR, one from Burton-on-Trent added at Uttoxeter, and a coach for the Cambrian Coast detached at Stoke, to run forward via Whitchurch. The main train passed Crewe without stopping and was scheduled to continue over the 52½ miles to Rhyl non-stop in 62min, and to arrive at Llandudno for 2.50pm. The return train from the resort left at 4.10pm. The working was balanced by an LNWR run from Derby to Llandudno.

In the summer service of 1908 there were through coaches from Stoke to Liverpool – for the Isle of Man steamers – and to Blackpool Talbot Road, both conveyed by the 9.45am Stoke–Crewe. On weekdays in the 1900s, there were three fast summer workings each way (and two extra on Saturdays) between Macclesfield and Buxton via the Great Central/NS joint line and the Middlewood curve. Their journey took 40min and some trains included through coaches from/to Stoke. The service ceased with the outbreak of World War I.

Semi-corridor non-gangwayed coaches with lavatories were built from 1906, these being the Railway's first bogie stock, other than on the narrow gauge Leek & Manifold line. In winter, they were used in Derby–Stoke trains, but worked in summer to/from Llandudno. Composite brakes were built for the through workings to Llandudno from Nottingham MR and GNR stations, and Burton. The New F class 0-6-4Ts built 1916-9 took over haulage of the 12.5pm Manchester London Road–Euston as far as Stoke, and also worked Derby–Crewe trains.

By the summer of 1922, the through trains to Llandudno were running on weekdays at 11am from Derby, with a Burton portion attached at Uttoxeter. Stops were now being made at Crewe, and at Chester and Prestatyn. The return weekdays train left Llandudno at 1.25pm for Derby. There was also a summer MSO 8.45am Stoke–Llandudno, and through coaches on two services from Holyhead. The Euston–Burton–Buxton service had not reappeared after World War I.

---

8   A.B.C. GUIDE TO THE HIGHLANDS, via THE HIGHLAND RAILWAY.

Notes on The Train Service to and in The Highlands.

FROM London passengers have the choice of three different routes to Perth and the Highlands—the East Coast Route from King's Cross Station, the Midland Route from St. Pancras Station, and the West Coast Route from Euston Station. Splendidly equipped sleeping cars are run from London through to Inverness by all these routes, and it would be impossible to increase the standard of public convenience and comfort reached by each of the Companies interested in the various routes. Passengers travelling in third class compartments will also find through carriages awaiting them, and as they can obtain the use of a pillow and rug for a very small charge, a very comfortable journey may be made to the far north at a low cost; pillows and rugs are supplied to those who wish them on the platform before the train starts.

The journey from London to Inverness is too long to be comfortably made by day, and the through service is therefore a night one. The train from King's Cross is generally timed to leave at 7.55 p.m. (but any times quoted here should be verified by reference to the official time-table, as alterations may be made) in summer, and 8.15 p.m. during the winter and spring, and reaches Inverness shortly after 9 a.m. next morning (9.30 a.m. in winter).

The train from Euston leaves at 7.45 p.m. in summer, and 8 p.m. in winter and spring, arriving at Inverness about the same time; sometimes these trains are joined together at Perth and run to Inverness as one train; at other times they run separately, and no one can say which will arrive first; in the busiest times (between July 20th and August 20th) each train may be in several portions, and it is most important that passengers should be at the stations in London whence they depart in ample time to allow of their luggage being properly labelled and placed in the proper van; great delays are frequently caused at Inverness to the north-going trains in the morning by the almost inextricable muddle of luggage, some with labels and some with none, which is entirely due to a host of passengers arriving at the

CHAPTER SIX

THE MIDLAND AND LANCASHIRE & YORKSHIRE RAILWAYS TO 1922

Midland and Scottish Joint services

With the completion of the Settle & Carlisle line in 1876, the Midland Railway combined with the North British and Glasgow & South Western railways to provide a third Anglo-Scottish route. In similar style to the West and East Coast companies, a joint passenger stock fleet was set up in 1876, and for some 20 years vehicles were lettered 'Midland Scottish Joint Stock'. From 1897, this arrangement came to an end with the formation of separate fleets, designated and lettered: 'Midland & G.S.W', and 'Midland & N.B'.

A summary of the principal Anglo-Scottish services in the MR public timetable spoke of the allure of the 'Valley of the Eden, Land of Burns, Home & Haunts of Scott, Forth Bridge, &c'. But scenic and historical attractions could not counter the major disadvantage of the Midland Scottish route which was its greater distances. From St Pancras to Glasgow St Enoch was 424½ miles, as against 401½ by the West Coast, and St Pancras to Edinburgh Waverley was 407¼ miles compared with the 393 miles from King's Cross. But not all passengers wanted to travel to the main centres, and the MR and its partners served the Border towns, and the south-west of Scotland.

In 1898, the Anglo-Scottish services were the most important trains on MR lines north of Sheffield. The fastest was the 10.30am St Pancras–Glasgow St Enoch which by-passed both Sheffield and Leeds, using the direct Staveley line and the curve at Leeds' Whitehall Junction. Calling at Leicester, Trent, Chesterfield and Skipton, it reached Carlisle (308½ miles) in 6½hr, and Glasgow in 9hr 5min. Motive power for these trains south of Leicester was usually a Midland Single, and a 4-4-0 northwards, a new class of which was built for Settle & Carlisle duties from 1900. North of Carlisle, the timings of 150min for the 115½ miles from Carlisle to Glasgow, including stops at Dumfries and Kilmarnock, represented hard work for the G&SWR Manson 4-4-0s.

The 10.30am was followed closely by the 10.35am St Pancras–Edinburgh Waverley which stopped at Bedford, Nottingham, Chesterfield, Sheffield, Leeds Wellington, Skipton, Hellifield, Appleby (by request), Lazonby and Carlisle, by which time the train had been running for 7hr 10min. The 2.10pm from St Pancras took only 6¾hr with four stops to Carlisle, and 9¼hr to Glasgow. The Hellifield–Carlisle run over the 'Long Drag' took 92min for the 76¾ miles.

At night, there were sleeping car trains, from St Pancras to Edinburgh, and to Glasgow. The Edinburgh sleeper of the late 1890s was the fastest train over the Waverley Route, but not as fast as it had been 20 years earlier. With two conditional stops, it ran the 98¼ miles Carlisle–Edinburgh in 144min. The usual formation was a sleeper composite for Inverness and for Aberdeen, and coaches for Perth, Aberdeen and Fort William. Pullman sleeping cars had been used on the Glasgow service, and these were replaced by new examples built from 1900 to Pullman specification but owned by the MR. There were also through coaches from Bristol to Glasgow. Connecting trains of MR coaches ran from Liverpool and Manchester via Blackburn and Hellifield and were worked to exacting timings over the Lancashire & Yorkshire metals by Midland engines. The best Manchester–Glasgow time was 5hr 40min.

In the up direction, there were easier schedules, as seemed to be the case on other lines, too, and the 10am from Glasgow St Enoch took 6hr 40min from Carlisle to St Pancras, with stops at Kirkby Stephen, Skipton, Leeds and Leicester. There was a fast time of 4hr 5min for the 196¼ miles from Leeds. The fastest up train over the Waverley Route was the 10.5am from Edinburgh which with three stops reached Carlisle in 153min, and by July 1900 it was 10min quicker to Carlisle. The engines used north of Carlisle were the NBR 729 class 4-4-0s which in due course were supplanted by the Reid Atlantics.

In July 1901, the MR attempted to poach traffic from the competing Anglo-Scottish routes, and with its partners revised the services and introduced gangwayed stock. There were then through trains from St Pancras at 5.15am, 9.30, 10.30, 11.30am and 1.30pm. Most divided at Carlisle into Glasgow and Edinburgh sections. There were sleeping car trains at 7.20pm for Inverness, 9.30pm for Glasgow, 10.30pm for Edinburgh, and 11.55pm for Glasgow. Several trains called at Hellifield to make connections from Liverpool or Manchester or to attach through coaches. By 1903, the midnight St Pancras–Glasgow sleeping car train was provided with a restaurant car north of Carlisle, and its arrival at Glasgow St Enoch at 9am compared to the weekdays 7.5am arrival of the earlier train from St Pancras.

The 1901 timetables included the acceleration of the 9.30am from St Pancras to reach Edinburgh Waverley at 6.5pm. Its timekeeping proved problematic, and the West Coast companies put on a special effort to reach Edinburgh Princes St. earlier with their 10am down from Euston. The first down Midland Scottish express was the 5.15am from St Pancras which divided at Sheffield into Edinburgh and Glasgow portions. The first called at Leeds, and by 1907 the through train was altered to a 10am express starting from Leeds Wellington, with through coaches from Manchester to Edinburgh (connecting into an NBR express for Aberdeen), and combining at Hellifield with through coaches from Liverpool and Manchester. But the majority of traffic on the Midland trains was from London and, despite good connecting services, not enough business was generated outside the summer peak to make the trains a paying proposition north of Leeds.

From the summer of 1903, two new down expresses were put on, at 7.30pm for Edinburgh and the Highlands with sleeping cars for Edinburgh,

Perth and Inverness, and at 8.30pm for Glasgow and for Stranraer Harbour (including sleeping car), with restaurant cars as far as Leeds. There were return workings at 11pm from Glasgow and 11.30pm from Edinburgh. Both overnight expresses were retained for the winter of 1903/4. Although Johnson Compound 4-4-0s had already made their appearance north of Leeds, Deeley's 990 class were specifically introduced for the route in 1907.

The July 1905 timetable saw the debut of newly built restaurant cars on the 1.30pm departures from St Pancras and Glasgow, and similarly new sleeping cars on the Stranraer service. All this new stock was clerestory roofed. For some time the 1.30pm called only at Leicester on the way to Leeds but later a Sheffield stop was included, and both gave a useful late afternoon service from metropolitan Yorkshire to Scotland. The following year, a new Glasgow/ Edinburgh express was introduced from Leeds, departing at 8.40am, to arrive in Edinburgh at 1.35pm, and Glasgow at 1.45pm. It lasted only for the 1906 season, and was aimed at attracting traffic from the North Eastern Railway's Leeds–Glasgow train. A 'Cheap Third-class Scotch Corridor Express' was an innovation on peak Saturdays, at 11am from St Pancras, stopping only at Nottingham (also, at Leeds Engine Shed Junction, to change engines) with journey times of 8¼hr to Glasgow and Edinburgh alike. Such trains loaded to capacity but the year-round service was another matter.

By the late 1900s there were nine daily Scottish expresses from St Pancras in summer, and seven in winter, the up service being similarly lavish. Before 1914, the Midland Anglo-Scottish expresses also included several through coaches to other destinations. For instance, the 9.30am to Edinburgh and Glasgow had through coaches for Perth and Aberdeen, as did the Edinburgh sleeper. In 1905, there was a 7.15pm from St Pancras with sleeping cars for Edinburgh, Aberdeen and Inverness and a through coach to Fort William (circuitously routed from Carlisle via Edinburgh and Glasgow!). Through coaches leaving Bristol at 10.45am were worked north of Leeds on the 11.30am from St Pancras, and the 7.55pm Bristol–Leeds conveyed through coaches for Edinburgh, Glasgow (and sometimes Aberdeen, a 580-mile through journey) which were attached at Leeds to the 9.30pm from St Pancras.

The timings for some of the trains over the Settle & Carlisle were demanding, and there were some fast bookings on the downhill stretches, such as south of Hawes Junction, and between Appleby and Carlisle. The fastest train in 1905 was the midnight

A glowing example of Midland pre-1914 standards at St Pancras on 2 September 1901. Proudly heading the 1.30pm to Glasgow St Enoch is Johnson Single No. 2601 *Princess of Wales* (No. 685 from 1907).

sleeping car express from St Pancras, the 4am departure from Leeds which ran to Carlisle in 127min for the 113 miles, at an average speed of 53mph.

The July 1908 timetable featured what was to be the last real initiative in the Midland Anglo-Scottish services. This involved running the 11.30am from St Pancras as a Glasgow express only which en route to Carlisle made just one intermediate stop – on Shipley curve where the engine was changed. This was the longest non-stop run on the MR, at 206 miles. The 11.30's overall time to Carlisle was 5hr 59min, and the train then continued non-stop in 2hr 25min to Glasgow St Enoch, to arrive at 8pm in the public book, but 5min earlier in the working timetable. Such runs were made practicable following the provision of water-troughs at Garsdale in 1907, but the train also loaded to no more than five coaches, two of them diners. Before long, stops 'by request' at Dumfries and Kilmarnock were inserted in the schedule.

The potential for continued development of the Midland Anglo-Scottish services can only be conjecture for, in the summer of 1908, the LNWR and MR entered into a working agreement with the aim of pooling all competitive traffic, including that to/from Scotland. The LNWR expressed unease at the coincidental acceleration of the 11.30am from St Pancras but this had predated the agreement, and was

not expected to recur. Consequences of the agreement were deceleration of the Anglo-Scottish expresses, a reduction in through coaches to Inverness, and the restriction of the midday (and some overnight) summer trains to operate between July and September only.

With the hope of attracting traffic between Scotland and Bradford, from the Autumn 1908 timetable through coaches to Market St. (later Forster Square) were slipped at Saltaire South from the 1.30pm from Glasgow, and the 2.20pm ex-Edinburgh. Reflecting the terms of the 1908 pooling agreement, in the following summer's timetable there was a combined Glasgow/Edinburgh express departing St Pancras at 11.50am. This was publicly advertised as 'first-stop Carlisle' but engines were changed at Shipley and the train ran to slower timings than in 1908. Running just ahead of this train was an 11.30am St Pancras–Carlisle which made several intermediate stops in order to provide connections from Cambridge, the Midland & Great Northern, Bournemouth and Bristol. Such an arrangement was expensive, just to preserve a lengthy non-stop run for the Anglo-Scottish express. But there were other non-stop runs from Leeds to St Pancras, notably by an Edinburgh train which, in 1910, was timed in 3hr 36min, and at one stage 3min

Away from Carlisle Citadel station in early LMS days comes a southbound Midland Anglo-Scottish express including through coaches from Aberdeen–St Pancras. The engine is Deeley 990 class 4-4-0 No. 992.

faster. Later, the MR route north of Sheffield was bedevilled by mining subsidence, and such timings could not be repeated.

From July 1910, a first portion of the 10am from Leeds was detached at Skipton, and diverted to run via Clapham and the Ingleton–Low Gill line to the West Coast Main Line. In the timetables the train was styled 'Lake District Express' and it ran non-stop to Penrith where there was a connection to Keswick. A similar route was followed by the 10.30am Edinburgh Waverley–St Pancras, in both cases just for the holiday season and these arrangements were repeated in the summers of 1911/12.

There were few changes to the Anglo-Scottish expresses up until 1914. In August 1913 an additional third-class special was run on Saturdays, at 11.33am from St Pancras, routed between Leeds and Skipton to call at Ilkley, and arriving at Edinburgh at 9.58pm. The Highland sleeper now ran via Derby where it picked up through coaches from Bristol.

With the outbreak of World War I, the MR speedily cut back the Scottish services to their winter level but, apart from the withdrawal in February 1915 of the 1.30pm from St Pancras, major reductions were not implemented until the timetable introduced in January 1917.

The casualties included the MR's connecting services between Liverpool, Manchester and Hellifield which were withdrawn at the end of 1916. By direction of the Railway Executive, from January 1917 the Midland Anglo-Scottish services comprised only the 9.15am St Pancras to Glasgow whose journey was inflated to 10hr 5min. This was the replacement not only for the former 9.30, but also the 11.30am. There was no morning train by the West Coast route to either Edinburgh or Glasgow, and the Midland trains were the only ones with restaurant cars. By January 1918, the Scottish express was retimed to an 8.50am departure and arrived in Glasgow after a lengthened journey of 10hr 40min.

With the ending of hostilities, a 10.45am St Pancras–Glasgow was introduced in March 1919. From October 1921, through coaches were reintroduced to the day Scottish trains, and from February 1922 the 9am St Pancras was extended to Carlisle conveying an Edinburgh portion, and with a through coach for Aberdeen. By that year's July timetable, there were seven daily Scottish expresses each way, three of them for Edinburgh only, at 9 and 11.30am, and the 9.15pm overnight train. But loadings were often poor, and some expresses north of Leeds had no more than 30 passengers.

Midland Railway

The Midland was provincial in the sense that it retained its headquarters and heart at Derby, despite its aspirations as an Anglo-Scottish railway with a showy London terminus, and a multitude of connections using its own and jointly-owned lines which took its rolling stock to Yarmouth, Bournemouth, Swansea and York. The main passenger services overlapped on the stretch between Derby and Sheffield which had advantages when it came to the operation of through coaches, and at this the MR excelled.

Next to the Anglo-Scottish services which are separately described, the MR was proudest of its St Pancras–Manchester trains. In 1898, there were six expresses each way on this 191½-mile route and they took from 4hr 20-25min with four or five intermediate stops. Down departures were at 10.5am, noon, 2, 4, 5 and 6.45pm from St Pancras, and 9.10, 10.30am, noon, 1.30, 4.10 and 5.35pm up. Some conveyed through coaches from Bristol or Nottingham via Butterley, but there were also through portions for Liverpool detached at Marple, or Stockport Tiviot Dale, and for Manchester Victoria and Blackburn, also handled at Marple. Until completion of the New Mills–Heaton Mersey cut-off in 1903, all trains for Manchester had to travel via Marple. To or from Liverpool, the best timings were 5hr 5-10min. Buxton was also served by through coaches detached at Derby from the 2pm down, and these arrived in the spa town at 5.50pm. A 4hr timing to Buxton was achieved by the 12.10pm St Pancras–Liverpool.

From Sheffield to Manchester via the Hope Valley line, there were no principal trains, let alone St Pancras expresses, the service aspiring only to semi-fasts which made four or five intermediate stops. An exception came later, from October 1911 until 1915 when the 8.30am Manchester–St Pancras took the Hope Valley route in order to call at Nottingham. Previously, Manchester trains had served Nottingham by running via Radford, Codnor Park and Ambergate.

The St Pancras to Leeds/Bradford expresses of 1898 were generally not as fast as the Anglo-Scottish trains, and the best of them, the 5.40pm from Bradford, ran via Sheffield and Nottingham, made six stops and took 4hr 35min overall. Most expresses between the West Riding or Sheffield and London were routed via Nottingham, so that the 158½ miles from Sheffield–St Pancras was a 3½-4hr journey. The routing adopted meant that Leicester was principally served by Manchester expresses, and to/from St Pancras the non-stop timings were usually 2-2¼hr for 99 miles.

The West of England line from Derby to Birmingham, and south via the Lickey Incline, Gloucester and Mangotsfield had four or five fast trains each way in 1898, the best of which was the 9.45am from Bristol which called only at Cheltenham Queens Road (later Lansdown) during its 117min run for the 89 miles to Birmingham. Others needed longer – typically, 140min. Down trains had similar timings, and the slow exit from Birmingham and cautious descent of the Lickey Incline meant that the Birmingham–Cheltenham timings were 58-65min for 45½ miles; a minority of trains ran via Worcester Shrub Hill. Through coaches for Bournemouth – see the **Somerset & Dorset Joint** – were detached at Gloucester or Mangotsfield, as at this time there were no regular through trains to the south coast.

Some West of England expresses ran to York, and from Sheffield were routed over the Swinton & Knottingley joint line. The 12.35pm from Bristol, with through coaches to Newcastle, required 115min for the 80¼ miles between Derby and York, and stopped at Chesterfield and Milford (now Monk Fryston). Its southbound counterpart was non-stop between York and Sheffield.

Morecambe was a far-flung post of the MR empire, and had some smartly-timed residential trains to/from Leeds and Bradford. The 8.5am from Morecambe Promenade was non-stop to Skipton in 53min for 42¼ miles, and ran to Bradford for a 9.30am arrival; Leeds passengers changed at Shipley. There was a corresponding westbound evening train. Other trains to/from Morecambe were slower, and made several stops but the service with the West Riding was expanded in summer. The other traffic flow from Leeds was to/from Ramsden Dock, Barrow – see **Furness Railway**.

The MR had running powers to Harrogate over the North Eastern's line from Holbeck, and began to exercise them in 1902 with the introduction of through expresses between St Pancras and Harrogate. These were worked throughout by MR engines, the trains having to reverse direction in Leeds Wellington station. By the summer of 1903, there were four up and three down expresses, with journey times of around 4½hr, the 10.27am from Harrogate and the 5pm ex-St Pancras having restaurant cars. By 1910, the service had reduced in status to through coaches only.

In September 1904, Heysham Harbour was opened and the MR used agents to operate a steamer service to/from Belfast. From the start, a boat train was run, at first leaving St Pancras at 5pm and due at Heysham at 10.45pm, with return from Heysham at 5.20am and an arrival 6hr later in London. In July 1906, the down train was retimed to 6pm and stopped only at Sheffield before Leeds, getting to Heysham in 5½hr. A summer FSO train in the same timetable was intended for those holidaymakers joining a sailing from Heysham to the Isle of Man, and it left St Pancras at 8.30am. There was also a corresponding Monday morning train from Heysham to St Pancras. One of the up expresses from Heysham was unusually routed from Sheffield via Beighton Junction, Langwith Junction and Shirebrook Junction before rejoining the main line at Nottingham. There were also Sheffield–Heysham and return trains which connected with the Isle of Man sailing.

In 1904, there was fierce competition with the LNWR for the London–Manchester traffic, the Great Northern soon joining in again for good measure. The previous year, the MR had opened its line from New Mills to Heaton Mersey and the Railway's best St Pancras–Manchester time came down to 3hr 50min, reducing in summer 1904 to 3hr 35min, only

5min longer than by the easier and shorter routes from Euston. Despite the change to routing, in the 1905 timetable the best trains from St Pancras to Manchester left at much the same intervals as seven years earlier – 10am, noon, 2, 4.30, 5.35 and 6.45pm. Of these, the first two as well as the 5.35pm by-passed Derby station by taking the Chaddesden line and saved nearly a mile's travelling by doing so. All three trains ran the difficult 90 miles between Leicester and Manchester non-stop in 105min, as did the noon and 4.15pm departures from Manchester and the 10.30am Cheadle Heath–Leicester. Schedules were later eased and, by 1914, 3hr 40min was the fastest overall timing, by the 10am from St Pancras, and 4.15pm from Manchester. From 1912-14, there were through coaches for Liverpool Central on the 10am, worked forward on their own non-stop from Manchester Central by a Johnson Single, and offering a 4hr 25min timing between St Pancras and Liverpool.

Competition for London–Sheffield traffic was also intense during the early/mid-1900s and, running either via Leicester or Nottingham, the MR was hard-pressed to maintain a 3hr timing which was

Up through Blackwell comes Johnson Class 3 4-4-0 No. 776 with a Derby–Bristol Temple Meads express.

achieved only by one down, and two up expresses. Other fast times ranged from 3hr 3-12min. The principal Scottish expresses avoided Sheffield altogether by running via the 'Old Road' from Tapton Junction, north of Chesterfield, to Rotherham. The MR also faced competition with the Great Central for London–Leicester traffic, and set its stall with an impressive total of 15 trains non-stop between St Pancras and the city, six in as little as 105min. Similarly, Nottingham demanded a good service to counter the GCR's efforts, and the MR expresses running non-stop via Manton and Melton Mowbray did well to require no more than 132-135min for the 123½ miles. In all, 15 EWD expresses each way from St Pancras had restaurant cars.

Between Bristol and Derby, six expresses in the 1905 timetable had an average time of 3hr 16min for the 130miles, and the fastest took just 177min: just 13min quicker than the best of 1900. The 10.55am from Leeds ran non-stop to Derby, and reached Bristol at 3.57pm. During the Derby stop, it gained a restaurant car and through coaches from Newcastle and Liverpool for Bristol while, at Cheltenham Queens Road, the 10.55 shed a coach for Southampton via the Midland & South Western Junction line. The Bournemouth portion was detached at Gloucester, and finally a through coach was handed over at Temple Meads for Kingswear. This train was not surprisingly a poor timekeeper, but matters were made easier with the introduction in 1910 of the Manchester–Bournemouth train.

From the summer of 1905, a morning express was run from Bournemouth at 8.40am as far as Cheltenham, there to connect into the 10.55am ex-Bristol. That train unusually ran non-stop between Derby and Leeds where it connected into the 11.30am Scottish express from St Pancras. The 3.25pm from Bristol had so many through coaches that *Bradshaw* referred the inquirer to the Notes for the MR's West of England service where it proclaimed: 'Through Carriages, Bristol to Great Malvern, Manchester (Cen,), Halifax (L. & Y.), Heysham and York; also Bournemouth to York, and Southampton to Derby.' No wonder that an observer of those times was to comment: 'To step into a Midland express at Birmingham was practically to receive an open sesame to the British Isles.'

Most of these cross-country expresses made several intermediate stops but there were a couple of non-stop workings between Bristol and Birmingham over the years, notably during 1908 when the initiative was to divert attention from the GWR's new Birmingham–Bristol route. Three expresses

each way between Derby and Bristol had restaurant cars and the trains usually loaded to no more than six or seven coaches. The 700 class 4-4-0s allocated to Derby shed were the largest engines used for these workings. Until just before World War I, the other depot involved in express working over this route was Bristol whose largest engines were rebuilt Johnson 4-4-0s. From 1909, the West of England expresses benefited from two developments: the opening of the direct line between Kingsbury and Water Orton which by-passed the speed-restricted curve at Whitacre, and the installation in the previous year of water-troughs at Haselour, north of Tamworth. A major development for the West of England route came in October 1910 with the joint introduction by the MR and LNWR of the Manchester–Bournemouth through trains – see **Cross-Country services**.

There were daily through MR coaches between Birmingham New St. and Brecon or Swansea, worked on Great Western trains from Worcester to Hereford where they regained MR metals, before passing to the Cambrian at Three Cocks Junction. From there the route was over the Brecon & Merthyr between Talyllyn Junction and Brecon, and then over the Neath & Brecon Railway before the MR's Swansea Vale line was reached at Ynys-y-Geinon Jct. Worked by MR 0-4-4Ts, there were three through workings each way but their appeal for long-distance travellers was limited as the trains called at nearly all stations between Hereford and Swansea. The through coaches to/from Birmingham survived until the end of 1916.

Despite the MR's impressive array of express services and fast timings, their punctuality was not particularly good in the early years of the century. From 1907, the MR became the first major British railway to introduce the centralised traffic control of freight trains, involving a central office at Derby and district controls linked by telephone. The control system was extended from 1917 to passenger train working and became the pattern for the train control system used by the LMS.

Integral to the system was the production of working timetables in which each train had its 'path'. Meanwhile, all passenger trains were assessed on the basis of their loading, and schedules were prepared according to point-to-point timings calculated on the basis of the power classification of the engine type diagrammed to the train. The fastest MR expresses were limited to a maximum load of 240tons (tare) for a Compound, 200 for a Class 3 4-4-0 and 180tons for a Class 2 4-4-0.

The results of this radical approach were incorporated into the timetables introduced in April 1908 but relatively few timings were changed. The new timetables did reveal a better spacing of expresses in particular services, and had involved the cancellation of some superfluous semi-fast workings. Punctuality was greatly improved, such that the MR soon established an enviable record for timekeeping. During the last few prewar summers, the number of summer Saturday timetabled and relief trains had increased to the extent that the Railway cut back on some business workings – on Saturday homeward residential trains generally left at lunchtime – and the more complicated through coach workings were curtailed to simplify train working.

The MR's more professional approach to train operation was symptomatic of the changes that affected British railways immediately before World War I. Not least, there was a growing realisation that the productivity of engines and rolling stock needed to be improved, something that was given impetus post-1918 by a rapid increase in costs, including the introduction of the 8hr day for railwaymen.

Traversing the Royston–Thornhill line which had been constructed as recently as 1905/6, three through trains daily were introduced in July 1909 between Sheffield, Bradford Exchange, Halifax and Huddersfield. This was a jointly worked operation by the MR and L&YR who each used their own engines and coaches, and all trains conveyed through coaches to/from St Pancras. By October 1909, the service via Thornhill had increased to five trains each way, the next step being in July 1910 with the introduction of a through 1.50pm St Pancras–Bradford express. The response from King's Cross was to put on its 'Bradford Specials' – see **Great Northern Railway**.

A major user of slip coaches, from 1910 the MR began building gangwayed vehicles so that during their journey passengers might have access to the restaurant car. The only example on the Railway of two slips being made off one train occurred after October 1911 when the 4.55pm from St Pancras, already 'slipping' at Melton Mowbray, now made an additional slip at Oakham.

In **Midland and Scottish Joint services**, mention was made of the diversion from the summer of 1910 of a couple of expresses via Penrith, in order to tap traffic to the Lake District. These workings ceased with the 1912 summer timetable but, during the next two summer peak periods, there was a 9.35am MTFSO Leeds–Keswick train routed via Ingleton, and a return working at 12.35pm. Also, in 1913, the

North Eastern and MR co-operated in the operation of a Harrogate–Otley–Ilkley–Skipton–Heysham train which connected with a sailing to the Isle of Man.

During 1913, the MR opened the Adelphi Hotel in Liverpool. In those days, the Cunarders sailed from Liverpool on Saturday afternoons. To attract Cunard Line's transatlantic passengers to stay at the Adelphi overnight rather than patronise the LNWR boat trains from Euston, from May 1914 the MR put on a Fridays-only train from St Pancras at 6.10pm, booked to run non-stop over the 217¾ miles to Liverpool Central in 250min. This wrested from the 11.30am Scottish express its previously record-breaking non-stop run to Shipley. The Liverpool train was routed via Cheadle Heath, West Timperley and Glazebrook and its first run coincided with the maiden voyage of the *Aquitania*. The train was made up of seven coaches and was always hauled by a Compound. A best time of 3hr 52min was recorded.

The first wartime timetable, effective from 1 October 1914, included almost all the normal winter services and, with few changes to the main line services, it remained in force until February 1915 when a number of expresses were withdrawn, principally between St Pancras and Manchester, and the West Riding. From March 1916, the Heysham–Belfast passenger sailings were withdrawn, not to be restored until May 1920, but otherwise trains continued more or less at prewar speeds, if more heavily loaded, until the big cut-back of services which came into force in January 1917. From this date, all the fastest timings were discontinued, and many through coaches and all slip workings were axed. By now there were only 15 main line departures from St Pancras daily.

From the autumn of 1917 the MR followed other railways with the imposition of a maximum line speed of 60mph and to 40mph, no less, between Ambergate and Cheadle Heath. Yet the MR managed to maintain its excellent restaurant car services, even if in 1918 only 20 were operating out of a prewar winter total of 55.

Towards the end of the war, the MR planned for the full restoration of passenger services over a period of three years or so, and among the noteworthy – but unrealised – proposals were a regular interval service between St Pancras and Manchester, all running via Derby station, and to Yorkshire. The 25min past Manchester departures from St Pancras that were to endure for so long were instituted from the autumn of 1921. In May 1919, two 4¼hr St Pancras–Manchester expresses were introduced, as well as new services to Liverpool and Leeds, and between Bristol and Sheffield. May 1920 saw the reinstatement of the St Pancras–Heysham boat train, and two Manchester, Blackburn and Hellifield trains, and two from Sheffield over the Thornhill route (trains over the latter had been suspended in 1917). That July, the MR and Lancashire & Yorkshire introduced one of the few new services of the period, a 1.30pm (later 1.25pm) restaurant car express from St Pancras to Hellifield via Manchester Victoria, returning at 11.5am. Both trains were worked by L&YR engines north of Manchester. But non-stop runs on the MR did not repeat those of prewar years and the longest in 1920 were from St Pancras to Nottingham, the faster of the two by the 9.15am down, in 146min. The fastest run on the MR was over the 31miles from Appleby to Carlisle, in 34min – an average speed of just 54mph.

During World War I, most of the MR's West of England line expresses had remained when many other cross-country trains had been withdrawn. In March 1919, a 10.15am Bristol–Leeds and 3.15pm return were put on, and new Bristol–Sheffield trains followed in May 1919, while that October the GWR connection at Bristol into the 2.10pm to Leeds was again made off the 10.25 ex-Plymouth.

One other innovation of the postwar years was a summer 12.48pm WThX train from Leeds via Bradford to Carnforth, with through coaches for Whitehaven, Windermere Lakeside and Keswick; there was a corresponding return working. In the Summer 1923 timetable, the Keswick portion was rerouted to run via Ingleton and the Low Gill line and continued in various forms until 1939.

One characteristic feature of MR expresses had changed during the war as in October 1915 the board of directors had approved the adoption of elliptical roofs for all future main line coaches, and some entered service during 1917.

London, Tilbury & Southend Railway

The acquisition of the LT&SR by the Midland delivered a shock to the Great Eastern which fondly thought that its own secret negotiations for merger were secure. But the MR offered both a better price and an attractive deal for shareholders. Whether the MR made the most of the Tilbury is another matter. The Bill for acquisition included an undertaking to electrify the line but the First World War intervened.

In 1898, the principal residential trains took 50min for the 35¾ miles from Fenchurch St to Southend, calling only at Westcliff-on-Sea. Gradients were negligible, apart from the climb in both directions at

1 in 100 or so to a summit at Laindon Hills. From Fenchurch St., to which GER terminus the LT&SR had perpetual running powers, the first 2¾ miles were largely on viaduct before Tilbury metals were gained at Gas Factory Junction, and were slow-going on account of speed restrictions. The LT&SR ran 14 weekday morning trains from Southend between 5.40 and 9.35am, including two to Ealing and one to St Pancras. Yet punctuality was excellent. A major problem for the Railway was that it was able to use only *one* face of the two island platforms at Fenchurch St. for all but two of the morning peak trains, some of which comprised 12 or 13 coaches packed with 900-1,000 passengers.

In October 1911, a new residential train was introduced with an overall timing of 50min to Southend-on-Sea, but including stops at Stepney and Westcliff-on-Sea. Another difficult booking was 46min for the 33 miles between Leigh-on-Sea and Fenchurch St. By now, the GER was competing strongly for the Southend traffic with the blandishments of gangwayed stock and on-train catering, particularly for regular travellers – see **Great Eastern Railway**.

In the April 1910 timetable were three through trains each way between Southend-on-Sea and St Pancras via the Tottenham & Forest Gate, and Tottenham & Hampstead lines, and the best time for the 52-mile journey was 94min. Such trains were worked by LT&S engines by this time, previously the MR had out-stationed at engine at Shoeburyness. A boat train was run EWD from Fenchurch St. at 4.48pm to Tilbury to connect with the Batavier Line sailing to Rotterdam. In later days, boat trains to Tilbury would start from St Pancras and run over the T&H line but the port did not develop generally until just before World War I.

With the opening of the Whitechapel & Bow line, and subsequent electrification to Barking worked by District Railway trains, the LT&SR appreciated the value of a cross-London connection, and on 1 June 1910 a through service was introduced between Ealing Broadway and Southend-on-Sea. At first, existing LT&SR coaches were used, hauled by pairs of District electric locomotives as far as Barking where steam took over. The service was increased in 1912 to four trains on weekdays and six on Sundays, and new stock was provided in the shape of two eight-coach trains built for the LT&SR by Birmingham RCW. These distinctive vehicles had sliding entrance doors, a centre corridor layout and gangways. The heating was electric, the current being supplied from dynamos mounted on the

One of the imposing London, Tilbury & Southend Railway 4-6-4Ts, carrying Midland livery and No. 2104, makes its way past Cranham with the 9.34am Ealing Broadway–Southend of 26 May 1913.

underframes. The coaches had Westinghouse air braking which was anyway used by the LT&SR. The Ealing services were withdrawn in September 1939, and most of the coaches then passed to War Department use.

The LT&SR relied on various classes of 4-4-2T for its passenger services, and on the busiest trains they had no problem with trailing loads grossing 360-380tons. Eight 4-6-4Ts were delivered in 1912 to work the residential trains between Fenchurch St. and Southend, but they were soon found to be too heavy for the bridges west of Barking, and were restricted to working the Ealing trains to the east, and between Southend and St Pancras. On the hardest train of the day from Fenchurch St. in 1913/4 a 4-6-4T took over at Barking from a 4-4-2T.

The Midland Railway took over the operation of the LT&SR as from the start of 1912 (and totally from that August), and soon the locally managed organisation was changed to one run by remote control from Derby. Reliability suffered as a result of changes made to the design features of the indigenous locomotives, and the quality of coal they used.

By late 1913 the MR announced its intention to invest heavily in its recent acquisition, including electrification of all 70 route-miles and the provision of new lines between Gas Factory Junctiom and Bromley. The Midland Bill to facilitate the project had its third reading in Parliament in July 1914, but the plans for electrification had been put on ice earlier pending receipt of the consultant engineer's report.

Lancashire & Yorkshire Railway

Over 70 years after it ceased its independent existence, the L&YR is perhaps one of the most elusive companies to recall but it was a giant among Britain's railways. Until 1914, of all the British railways, the L&YR turned in the highest gross earnings per route-mile and per track-mile, and net earnings per passenger train-mile, and accordingly spent more than any other on maintenance per mile of track. Perhaps these were unsurprising statistics given that, on average, there was a large town at intervals every six miles on the L&YR's routes. It was among the first of the British railways to install block system on its main lines and recorded a number of other firsts. The lingering impression is of bustling short-distance expresses, rather overpowering and sombre stations, and engines and coaches that were sometimes wilfully ugly. As

Hamilton Ellis put it: 'How different a thing was a Midland train from one on, say, the Lancashire & Yorkshire, with its grim horsehair seats in the third-class and its pompous frightfulness in the first!'

The Railway styled itself as The Business Line and it made much of its status as the largest railway steamship operator. By 1914, the L&YR advertised through services from Colne to Euston; Bradford and Hailfax to St Pancras; Bradford and Huddersfield to Marylebone; Manchester and Liverpool to Scotland via Hellifield, and via the West Coast; Liverpool–York–Newcastle/Hull, and from several Lancashire and Yorkshire towns to the south coast. All these were run with the co-operation of other companies which meant that the L&YR extended its reach from its traditional area of operations in a way that was not immediately obvious.

From 1888, the L&YR had operated an hourly interval service between Liverpool Exchange and Manchester Victoria. Departure times were at 8.30am to 9.30pm from Liverpool, and 8.30am to 6.30pm from Manchester. For 36 miles non-stop, the allowance was 45min, including occasionally, a conditional stop at Sandhills. The 8.30am westbound ran via Wigan and took longer, and there were also a few additional fast trains outside the 30min past pattern. Counting up the number of fast trains between Liverpool and Manchester by the three competing routes, the total was a staggering 45 on a summer weekday. Of the three, the L&YR route was the most difficult with some stiff climbs and slacks imposed for mining subsidence.

Most of the Liverpool–Manchester fast trains were part of an hourly trans-Pennine service to Bradford and Leeds over the Calder Valley main line, and calls were made at Rochdale, Todmorden, Hebden Bridge and Sowerby Bridge. All trains stopped at Halifax and either divided there, or at Low Moor, into Bradford and Leeds portions. Journey times between Manchester and Bradford (40½ miles) and Leeds (48¾ miles) were 75 and 80min respectively. Other trans-Pennine trains ran to York via Normanton, one each way being booked non-stop over the 48 miles between Manchester and Wakefield in 58min, to reach York in 75min.

From Manchester, the L&YR served the various residential satellites of the city, with ten down and eight up trains on the Southport line. A morning express from Southport Chapel St. took 45min including a non-stop sprint over the 34 miles from St Luke's Road to Salford in 39min, at an average speed of over 51mph. Between Manchester and Blackpool Central the residential expresses usually ran via

Atherton so as to bypass Bolton and followed the coast line via Lytham. They were allowed 80min or so for the 50 miles. One exception was a train which ran to Blackpool Talbot Rd in 70min for the 46¾ miles. For the rest of the day, Manchester–Blackpool trains ran via Bolton Trinity St., a route longer by 2 miles, and their journey times were 90-108min. There were also expresses between Blackpool and Rochdale via Bolton and Bury, and from the West Riding.

The residential trains between Manchester and Southport and Blackpool were regarded as the most prestigious on the Railway, and from 1902 had almost entirely comprised gangwayed stock. The Blackpool residential trains included Club saloons on three workings in each direction. These vehicles were exclusive to Club members who paid a fee to use them, and they were served cups of tea en route.

There were also residential trains between Colne and Manchester. The best-known was the 4.25pm down which started from Salford. In April 1910, this train and the 6pm, both SX, ran non-stop over the 22¾ miles to Accrington, as did the 9.5am Colne–Manchester Victoria. The three down and four up trains each way that conveyed through coaches from/to Euston were routed from Manchester via Bolton and Blackburn. There were MR expresses between Manchester and Hellifield via Darwen, as well as L&YR slow trains.

In May 1901, the L&YR put into service its first gangwayed restaurant car train between Fleetwood and Leeds. The restaurant car-cum-brake was a unique vehicle in more ways than one with its six-wheel bogie at the kitchen end and part-clerestory roof. The boat train connected out of the sailing from Belfast and left at 6.15am (later 5.55am) with its return working departing from Leeds at 8.20pm. This train was worked to Leeds by a Fleetwood Atlantic which next worked west to Manchester, and then home with the 1.40pm from Victoria. Another of the shed's Atlantics worked to Manchester, then to Leeds, in order to return home with the westbound boat train.

Until 1912, the Fleetwood–Leeds boat trains followed a route via Todmorden, Burnley and Blackburn, after which they were re-routed via Manchester. This was one of the changes to services as a consequence of the coal strike of that year. The boat train set fitted in a return trip to Liverpool from Leeds in-between the runs from/to Fleetwood, and the westbound 1.2pm from Leeds included through coaches for Southport which were detached at Low Moor. There was also a Southport section on the 5.6pm Bradford–Liverpool.

York – and the Lancashire & Yorkshire Railway's 4.25pm to Liverpool Exchange departs on 7 August 1911 behind Aspinall 'Highflyer' Atlantic No. 1413.

When accelerated to 40min only in 1901, the non-stop trains from Manchester to Liverpool became a testing proposition, even allowing for the light loads, and timekeeping required the locomotive to be in tip-top condition and an absence of signal checks. At first, only a handful of trains ran to the 40min schedule but by the end of 1902 there were 29. The following summer, express timings between Southport, Manchester and Harrogate were accelerated, and there were summer-only workings between Manchester and Scarborough. The last-named continued until Grouping and the trains were worked throughout by an L&YR engine – usually an 0-6-0 – as L&YR stock was vacuum-fitted and most NER engines were Westinghouse only.

In October 1910, the 5.10 and 5.55pm Manchester–Blackpool, both routed via Lytham, were given slip coaches, detached at Kirkham. The slip coach off the 5.10pm was worked to Blackpool Central by the New Line, and that from the second train travelled to Poulton-le-Fylde and Blackpool Talbot Road. In the same timetable there was a new 7.32am Blackpool Central–Manchester Victoria, non-stop from South Shore to Salford. The daytrippers' 8.45am Manchester Victoria–Blackpool Central via the Coast line was allowed 68min to Lytham inclusive of a 3min stop at Preston. This was a regular turn for many years of one of Newton Heath shed's Atlantics.

Apart from the Manchester trains there was a 7.35am Blackpool–Colne which ran non-stop from Lytham to Rose Grove. Three coaches were slipped at Blackburn for Accrington as the main train was routed via Great Harwood. Its Blackpool engine then worked to Manchester, regaining its home town on the 4.26pm from Victoria. This was one of the residential trains which took the Bolton avoiding line from Dobbs Brow Jct to Horwich Fork Junction in the course of its non-stop run to Lytham in 64min, inclusive of a 3min stop at Preston. A summer season express between Liverpool Exchange and Blackpool Central via Ormskirk and the West Lancashire line was put on in 1911. There was also a residential express from Blackpool Central via Lytham to Liverpool Exchange, returning at 4.45pm; at one stage this train slipped an East Lancashire portion at Midge Hall.

In the late 1900s the Liverpool–Bradford/Leeds trains received new elliptical roofed stock, made up into two three-coach sets. One served each destination, and often the trains comprised just one set west of Manchester. Such three-coach sets became known as LBL sets. Typical timings for these trains were the 4.40pm from Liverpool, into Bradford at 6.39 and Leeds at 6.48pm. Some of the trans-Pennine trains featured slip coaches, such as the 9.40 and 11.10am from Bradford which slipped at Rochdale for Southport via Bury and Bolton.

By 1907 there were the 9.5am Hull–Liverpool and 2.10pm return expresses which ran from/to Riverside Quay in summer to provide the connection with the steamer service to Zeebrugge; in winter, the train ran from/to Hull Paragon station. For a while this train also had through coaches to Harwich Parkeston Quay. This was another turn for an Aspinall Atlantic, a Hull-based engine working to/from Leeds. In the 1905 timetable the eastbound train was booked to cover the 48 miles from Manchester to Wakefield in 60min including a stop at Brighouse. The 12.13pm York–Manchester express conveyed the Parkeston Quay–Liverpool Exchange through coaches but these reached their destination some 25min later than those travelling via Sheffield.

Until the late 1900s, L&YR passenger stock had been flat-roofed and of rather dour appearance, with horsehair covered seats. Elliptical-roofed stock was then built which stood comparison with any other company, and included a proportion of open layout vehicles. An impressive 12-wheeled restaurant car was built in 1908 for the 10.55am Liverpool–York express. *The* train of the day on the Calder Valley route was the 12.35pm Newcastle–Liverpool – see **Cross-Country services**. At the end of 1913, a claimedly fireproof set of eight open layout coaches with steel panelling and gas lighting was put into service between Manchester and Southport.

L&YR engines worked Bradford Exchange–Marylebone expresses to/from Sheffield Victoria via Penistone, and they formed one of the turns for the new Hughes 4-6-0s in 1908.

One of the major interruptions to services during World War I had nothing to do with hostilities but to the failure of a span of Penistone Viaduct in February 1916. The viaduct was reopened that August and the through West Riding–Marylebone expresses were reinstated with one additional working each way.

During the war, the L&YR and North Eastern Railway Liverpool–Newcastle service was cut back to York, and only extended again to Tyneside in the Summer 1920 timetable when the outward train was accelerated to run non-stop over the 47¾ miles from Manchester to Wakefield in 70min. The return working now left Newcastle at 4.55pm, but was semi-fast from Normanton and included through coaches from Hull. The 2.35pm departure from York of the prewar Newcastle train was now taken by a Manchester train, leaving at 2.40pm and booked in 120min to Manchester. Its counterpart was effectively the 2pm Liverpool–Hull boat train which carried a through portion for York, detached at Wakefield and taking 115min overall from Manchester. The westbound boat train left Hull Riverside Quay at 8.45am and ran to Liverpool, and like the eastbound train had a through coach from Preston. The through coaches between Liverpool Exchange and Harwich Parkeston Quay via the Calder Valley line and Doncaster had not been reinstated.

In the early 1920s, the 4.25pm Salford–Colne residential train ran non-stop over the 27¾ miles to Burnley Barracks and, three days a week, slipped a portion for Accrington. The 10-coach train was usually worked by a superheated 2-4-2T which had to tackle a nine-mile climb of 1 in 132/78 to the summit at Baxenden, to the south of Accrington. This was probably the hardest task undertaken by a 2-4-2T in the British Isles and such engines proved superior to the LNWR 'Prince of Wales' which was tried on this working in 1922. In time, they were replaced by the Hughes 4-6-4Ts.

The L&YR and LNWR amalgamated as from January 1922. One of the last major tasks for the L&YR had been the rebuilding of all but five of the 20 Hughes 4-6-0s as virtually new engines. They re-entered service in 1920/1, and from the summer of 1921 were joined by new examples, some of which, with rebuilt engines, too, were transferred to work over the West Coast Main Line between Crewe and Carlisle. One feature of the amalgamation was the promotion of through trains between Euston and Huddersfield and Halifax via Stockport and Stalybridge, at 10.30am and 4pm down, and 8.20am and 1.5pm from Halifax.

CHAPTER SEVEN

THE SCOTTISH COMPANIES TO 1922

Caledonian Railway

Passenger services on the CR were dominated by the Anglo-Scottish day and night expresses, described under **West Coast Main Line services**. Of these, the 'Tourist', the 'Postal', and later the 'Corridor', were the CR's star trains. As to purely internal workings in Scotland, pre-eminent were Edinburgh Princes St–Glasgow Central and the combined Glasgow Buchanan St/Edinburgh Princes St Dundee/Aberdeen operations. The Edinburgh–Glasgow service via Shotts was frequent and in 1898 some half-dozen fast trains each way needed only 65min for the 46 miles, with perhaps two or three stops. By 1910, there were eight westbound fasts, and six eastbound, in 65-75 min. Ahrons considered that 1896 was the high-water mark of CR express schedules in the 19th century, and that subsequently there was a process of 'letting-out' timings.

The Northern Section main line generally offered disappointing journey times at the beginning of the century, this despite the celebrated Forfar–Perth timings mentioned in **West Coast Main Line services**. From Buchanan St. to Aberdeen (153 miles), the 10am down offered the fastest time of 4hr with seven intermediate stops on this line of junction stations – it fed 12 branches north of Stanley Junction. The 10.5am up from Aberdeen managed a 5min faster journey, including a 37min timing from Forfar to Perth.

One reason for the relatively slow overall timings of the Glasgow–Aberdeen services was the customary and lengthy stop at Perth General, sometimes for 15 min or so. Edinburgh and Glasgow sections were usually combined at Perth (or Stirling), where the trains were remarshalled into Dundee and Aberdeen workings. Trains such as the 6.45am and 10.5am from Aberdeen, and 10pm ex-Glasgow were integral to West Coast timetables and conveyed through sections attached/detached at Perth, sometimes for the Highland Railway, to those to/from Buchanan St. Although there were some reasonably smart times over the Perth–Dundee line, the remarshalling affected overall timings, and the best Glasgow–Dundee time in 1898 was as much as 130min for 84 miles.

As an instance of the status of particular trains on the route, after their introduction in 1896, two of the 'Dunalastair 1' 4-4-0s based at Perth worked the principal expresses at 9.10am and 12.6pm from Perth to Buchanan St., (the Glasgow section of the 6.45am and 10.5am ex-Aberdeen respectively), returning with the 5.30pm for Aberdeen as far as Perth, and the 5pm to Dundee respectively.

For a through train over the Callander & Oban line, in 1898 the best time was made by a seasonal Glasgow–Oban working which, with a dozen intermediate stops, achieved an overall journey of 4hr. The seasonal trains greatly expanded the service. New trains in the summer 1908 timetable were the 7.55am and 7pm Oban–Glasgow. Fastest times in April 1910 were 4hr 15min, by the 4.45pm ex-Buchanan St, and 6am ex-Oban. At that time, the C&O's service comprised five down and four up trains, the 11.50 pm ex-Stirling connecting out of the Aberdeen section of the down 'Corridor' from Euston. From 1 July 1908, the 10.38am from

Callander conveyed through coaches from Oban, attached at Carstairs to the 12noon ex-Glasgow Central – see **West Coast Main Line services**.

The CR competed energetically with the Glasgow & South Western Railway for the custom of Glasgow businessmen who spent the summer, and sometimes the winter, domiciled at Clyde coast and island resorts. Both railways offered a combined train/steamer service, and one of the best-known trains was the CR's 4.13pm Glasgow Central–Gourock which connected for the steamer to Rothesay – journey time from Glasgow a little over 105min – and beyond. This was the cream of the traffic in Glaswegians going 'doon the watter'.

The CR introduced its first modern passenger stock in 1902, in the shape of 50ft centre-corridor third-class coaches, with hot and cold water supplies and a high-specification interior. Competition with the North British Railway was intensifying, and not merely with scheduled services. Notable was a train put on for the Dundee *Evening Telegraph* to take excursionists to an international soccer match held at Parkhead on 9 April 1904, booked to run non-stop over the 83 miles between both points in 97min, and hauled by newish 4-6-0 No. 49.

Boldest bid in the CR/NBR competitive stakes came on 10 April 1905 when the Caley introduced the 'Grampian Corridor Express', at 10am from Buchanan St. to Aberdeen. This was formed of a 'block train' of new 68ft, twelve-wheeled corridor stock, the intention being to compete with the NBR, not least by offering superior accommodation. The four coaches from Buchanan St. combined at Perth with a section of the same stock departing Princes St. at 9.25am, the train, now also with restaurant car, going forward to Aberdeen, to arrive after taking a not too impressive 3hr 50min from Glasgow. The return working was at 5.25pm, again non-stop from Perth and with the restaurant car working throughout, but this completed the 153 mile journey in 3hr 35min. These trains were later joined by another named train – the 'Granite City Express' – at 5pm from Buchanan St., and 4.25pm from Princes St. Both titles were used with variations for the next 60 years or so. Hamilton Ellis pointed out that the chosen Grampian title was somewhat curious as the train was never really in sight of the main range of these mountains!

The new expresses were heavily promoted by the CR which during the Edwardian era built its publicity image around a golfing theme, its posters carrying the slogan The True Line of Way, and often featuring a coy-looking Golfing Girl. Advertising

campaigns became muted after 1908 when the CR and NBR toned down their competitive instincts.

The appearance of the 'Cardean' 4-6-0s, and the allocation of a pair to Perth further enhanced the status of the Glasgow–Aberdeen route. There could have been few grander spectacles than the Prussian blue of the engine and the stately dark chocolate and cream painted coaches. One of the 4-6-0s worked the down 'Grampian Corridor' forward from Perth to Aberdeen, returning with the up working, while its companion covered the 2pm ex-Buchanan St., and the 7.50pm from Aberdeen, the latter being a combined train for the South, and for Glasgow Central, dividing at Perth.

A major change came to passenger services in 1908 as a result of an agreement between the Caledonian, North British and Glasgow & South Western railways to cut out wasteful competition, and needlessly fast schedules, the clampdown also being influenced by the CR's Tannochside accident of 1906 and concern at excessive coal consumption. From 1 October 1908, a number of CR and NBR trains were decelerated on the Glasgow–Aberdeen, Edinbugh–Aberdeen and Edinburgh–Glasgow services, and speed limits imposed between Kinnaber Junctiom and Aberdeen. There had been also a reduction in the number of competitive Clyde steamer sailings in the spring and summer of 1908, and connecting boat trains on the Glasgow–Greenock/Gourock/ Ardrossan services were decelerated.

Another result was to cut the number of through portions conveyed on Glasgow/Edinburgh–Aberdeen expresses by both routes. By April 1910, the service between Glasgow and Aberdeen comprised six down and five up expresses, the majority with sections to/from the South. Earlier mention of the 2pm from Buchanan St. is a reminder that the CR was a user of slip coaches for this train slipped at Coupar Angus. By 1914, north of the Border only the CR and the Great North of Scotland were still operating slip coaches. In that year, there were ten slip coach workings on the Caley, at widely separated locations on its main lines. All these workings were withdrawn during World War I, and not reinstated.

Immediately before World War I, the CR had established a fine reputation as one of Britain's leading companies for the standard of passenger facilities on its trains and at stations. Early in 1914, the directors made it clear that they were impressed with the popularity of Pullman cars on English lines, and had decided to introduce 'dining and drawing room cars' between Glasgow and Aberdeen, buffet cars between Glasgow and Edinburgh, and on

It's 3 August 1921 and, despite the number of 4-6-0s on the Caledonian Railway, the 1.30pm to Aberdeen is waiting at Glasgow Buchanan St. behind Pickersgill 4-4-0 No. 76, with one of the typically smart CR elliptical-roofed coaches behind the tender.

residential expresses to Strathearn, and an observation car to/from Oban. The company talked of Pullman cars as being included in trains serving what it termed its 'Delightful Districts'. Most of the Pullmans were in service by the late summer of 1914. Passengers using the composite dining cars for a meal and then returning to their seats elsewhere did not have have to pay a supplementary charge. *Maid of Morven* was the celebrated buffet/observation car, and in September 1914 it was announced that 'it will be shortly introduced between Glasgow and Oban', and it ran also in the summer of 1915.

The Railway purchased six of the 'River' class 4-6-0s which had been ordered by the Highland Railway but not accepted for traffic. Although they were eminently capable of working express passenger turns, and reputedly so used between Perth and Glasgow and Aberdeen after acquisition by the CR in 1917, the management seems to have decreed that they should be used only on fitted freight trains. By then, the Railway's own outside-cylinder 60 class 4-6-0s had appeared and, from 1917, were appearing on the vestigial Anglo-Scottish services, where they were faced with loads of up to 500tons or so.

One notable train of the early 1920s was the unofficially titled 'Tinto Express' from Moffat,

calling at Beattock to reverse, then all-stations to Carstairs and calling at Motherwell only before arrival at Glasgow Central. It was made up of twelve-wheeled stock and returned at 4.45pm SX, and 12.45pm SO, from Glasgow Central. The predecessor of this working had been allocated a Pullman car in 1914.

The Pullman cars delivered just before World War I were soon withdrawn from service and not reintroduced until March 1919. They were then employed on a variety of workings, including expresses between Edinburgh Princes St. and Glasgow Central which were booked in 70min for the 46miles, including a stop at Holytown. There were as many as seven or eight Pullman workings each way on this route; such trains loaded to no more than six or seven coaches. More Pullman cars had been delivered in 1922/3 and were used between Glasgow and Aberdeen, and to Perth and Dundee, to the Highland section, and as restaurant cars on overnight and day West Coast expresses.

On the Northern section, the principal Glasgow–Aberdeen services in 1922 were at 4.15am from Central, arriving 7.52am; 7.15am (this and all succeeding departures were from Buchanan St.) with Pullman car, taking 4hr 35min to Aberdeen; 10am, with Pullman car in 4hr 5min, with TC in summer for Elgin via Aberdeen; 1.30pm, with Pullman car, in 4½hr; 5pm with Pullman car, in 4hr 5min, with TC to Dundee and in summer to Crieff; 6.10pm, with TC for Dundee and Callander, and combining at Perth with the Aberdeen section of the 10am from Euston; and the 10pm to Inverness which included through coaches for Aberdeen detached at Perth where they were attached to the Aberdeen portion of the 1.30pm from Euston. In summer, there were additional workings between Glasgow and Aberdeen, and seasonal through coaches between Buchanan St. and Crieff via Gleneagles.

The postwar Aberdeen–Glasgow expresses followed much the same pattern as in 1914 with departures at 6.50am, the Glasgow portion being detached at Perth from the train for Euston; at 9.30am, the Glasgow portion being detached at Perth from the train for Euston (but gaining a Pullman car); 12.30pm Glasgow portion detached at Perth from the train for the South; at 3.25pm, Pullman car from Perth only; at 5.30pm for Glasgow Central and with Pullman car throughout. As in the down direction, none of the timings was particularly exacting.

The Highland line services included the 10pm from Glasgow Buchanan St., with sleeping car for Inverness and through coaches also for Aberdeen, the train awaiting a connection at Perth off the 2pm ex-Euston; the 10.10am from Buchanan St. with Pullman car to Inverness; a 1.30pm from Buchanan St. with portions for Inverness by both routes from Aviemore; from Inverness at 8.10am; at 10.30am, combining at Perth with a Dundee portion; at 3.30pm, Pullman car to Buchanan St., and the 11.20pm, with sleeping car to Buchanan St., and later with a Pullman breakfast car from Perth. In summer, there were through coaches between Glasgow and Aberfeldy.

Perth retained its prewar reputation for remarshalling trains into combined portions from Dundee and Aberdeen, or for Edinburgh and Glasgow, and from/to the Highland line and the South, and from the South and from Glasgow – not to mention the detaching and attaching of Pullman and restaurant cars! Not surprisingly, the process of shunting required the constant services of three locomotives.

The Callander & Oban line had departures from Buchanan St. at 7.40am; 10.10am, including the observation car *Maid of Morven* and TC to Loch Tay

The massive 956 class 4-6-0s were a disappointment, to put it mildly, and here the first of the class is raising the echoes on 9 August 1922 as it works hard up the 1 in 98 past Milton Junction, on the exit from Glasgow, at the head of the 5pm Buchanan St.–Aberdeen Pullman car express.

in summer; noon, also with through coaches for Crieff, and at 5.10pm, this train later featuring a Pullman car. From Oban there were trains at 5.40, 8.45, combining with a train from Dundee at Stirling; 11.45am, for Edinburgh; 3.50pm, the return working for *Maid of Morven*, and 5.30pm, with sleeping car for Euston which had worked to Oban on the 6am from Stirling.

Between Perth and Glasgow, and supplementing these Aberdeen, Oban and Highland line services, were various independent trains to/from Dundee.

Glasgow & South Western Railway

As with the Caledonian, passenger services on the G&SWR (usually referred to as the Sou'West) were dominated by the Anglo-Scottish day and night expresses, in its case operated in conjunction with the Midland Railway, see **Midland and Scottish Joint services**. From Kilmarnock, there were connections out of these trains to the coastal towns.

The Sou'West was proud of its boat trains. Longest distance of these were the Glasgow St Enoch–Stranraer connections for the sailings to Larne. These boat trains was known to railwaymen as the 'Paddy', in 1900 at 5 pm from St Enoch, and 8.30pm return. Worked by Manson's Class 8 4-4-0s, the Glasgow-bound 'Paddy' was given no more than 67min to Girvan (38 miles) despite three stops, the fearsome gradients, and the single line with eight tablet exchanges by hand, and seven passing loops dictating severe speed restrictions. The Sou'West's timetable clerks tended to schedule almost impossible point-to-point timings over uphill sections, and comparatively easy ones downhill. Yet, on one occasion, a driver managed to get the up 'Paddy' to Girvan in 59min. In 1904, this train was altered to leave Stranraer at 9.55pm, and to run the 59 miles to Ayr non-stop in 83min, with just 55min allowed to passing Girvan. The load was usually no more than three coaches weighing just 88tons. Two years later the schedule was slowed by 8min to passing Girvan. The down train was by then leaving St Enoch at 4.15pm, and was less hectically timed. During the winter service, passengers for Northern Ireland spent the night on the steamer which sailed at 6am, after the transfer of travellers from the boat train from Carlisle. In summer, there were day sailings between Stranraer and Larne.

The early days of the century saw spirited rivalry between the Caledonian, G&SWR and North British for Clyde Coast passenger business. All offered combined train/steamer services, their boat trains having some very sharp timings, with sometimes no more than two minutes between arrival of the train,

and departure of the steamer! Greenock Princes Pier station of the Sou'West had attracted the bulk of the steamer traffic until the CR opened its Greenock–Gourock line in 1889, after which competition intensified, and the Sou'West opened a new station/pier at Princes Pier in 1894. Demanding timings were scheduled over the steeply graded line from Elderslie to Kilmacolm and Princes Pier, notably 34min from St Enoch to quayside in 1900 by the 4.3pm from St Enoch ('no heavy luggage allowed'), and a tough timing for the 9am up – by April 1910, the 8.25 am was the 'flyer'. In addition to the boat trains, there were 'residentials' to Glasgow serving Kilmacolm and Bridge of Weir. Other boat train services included those to Ardrossan for the Arran steamer, and to Fairlie Pier for Campbeltown. All such services were affected by the agreement reached in 1908 by the CR, G&SWR and North British Railways to cut down on inter-company competition – see **Caledonian Railway**.

Residential traffic from the Ayrshire Coast to Glasgow was assiduously fostered by the Sou'West, the services to Ayr and Largs being expanded in summer for day-trippers. By the early years of this century, pride of place was accorded to the 8am ex-Ayr and 5.15pm from St Enoch, and from 1 June 1905 these became non-stop, in 50min for the 41miles, despite routeing via the longer, curved Canal line. The up train was then the 8.25am from Ayr (7.30am ex-Girvan), and the homebound one the famed 5.10pm which ran through to Girvan.

If the Glasgow boat train from Stranraer was the 'Paddy', that to/from Carlisle was referred to as the 'Irishman'. From Challoch Junction eastwards, the Carlisle trains ran over the metals of the Portpatrick & Wigtownshire Joint Railways, until regaining the Sou'West's mileage at Castle Douglas. From 1885, four railways (LNWR, Midland, CR and G&SWR) had owned this joint line which was operated by both Scottish participants, equally sharing the daily locomotive mileage, and both providing rolling stock. The CR had running powers from Dumfries to Castle Douglas. With three or four stops, the boat trains at 3.10am from Carlisle, and 10.3pm from Stranraer Harbour, were allowed 160 min up, and 180min down, for the 105 miles from Carlisle to Stranraer Harbour, passing over a single-track line through the wildly beautiful country of Galloway. These trains conveyed a section to/from St Pancras, and a through North Eastern Railway coach departing Newcastle at 1.10am in April 1910, arriving back at 2.30am The three other through trains on this line called at almost all stations.

Glasgow & South Western 4-4-0 No. 190 sets off from Carlisle on 3 June 1911 with an express that includes through coaches from the Midland Railway.

The Railway was probably most affected in the postwar period by the revival of the Anglo-Scottish services as from May 1919, the chairman of the G&SWR having earlier suggested that an early improvement in the train service was desirable. Generally referred to as 'The Pullman', although such vehicles had not been used on them for 40 years, all fast Carlisle–Glasgow trains were through from the Midland, with the exception of the 1pm from Carlisle and 5.30pm from Glasgow (later extended to Leeds). The running times were usually 2¾hr or just under for the 115½ miles, the longest non-stop run being Kilmarnock–Carlisle in 113min for the 91 miles. The same year – 1919 – saw the restoration of the Railway's fastest workings – the 50min trains between Glasgow St Enoch and Ayr, at 5.10pm down and 8.25am up. The set used for both trains loaded to just over 220tons tare and featured a restaurant car while a note in the timetable warned 'No luggage allowed'.

After the appointment of R. H. Whitelegg as Locomotive Superintendent in 1918, a number of locomotive classes were re-boilered or otherwise altered, usually to the detriment of their performance. On the Carlisle–Glasgow main line, the loads of the expresses were usually no more than 175-250tons tare and, yet, reporting on the running with the

Manson 4-6-0s as rebuilt by Whitelegg, Cecil J. Allen summed up his experience as 'a tendency to loss of time rather than its recovery'. The 5.10pm Glasgow–Ayr was regularly worked by a Whitelegg 4-6-4T which engines were also used on trains to Ardrossan.

North British Railway

Any review of the NBR in 1900 must take account of events affecting the railway in the previous decade. The Forth Bridge opened in 1890, before which the journey from Edinburgh to Dundee took over 2hr, including a ferry crossing of the Firth of Forth. Indeed, the second Tay Bridge had been completed only three years earlier, since when the NBR had offered a train service between Burntisland and Aberdeen via Dundee. Trains comprised Burntisland (Edinburgh) and Glasgow sections, dividing at Thornton Junction, the Glasgow section running via Dunfermline and Alloa. Punctuality was not of the best. Next had come the opening, in 1894, of the West Highland Railway, the line staffed and worked by the NBR. It challenged the duopoly in the Highlands of the Highland Railway and Callander & Oban line.

The NBR had also inflicted injury on itself. About 1894, the company decided it wished to end a working arrangement of some 30 years, by which

North Eastern Railway motive power had handled all through trains between Newcastle and Edinburgh. The North Eastern Railway was given six months to quit. The matter went to law, then arbitration but, before a judgement was reached, the NBR informed the NER that from 14 January 1897 a train destined for north of Berwick would stop there, and the NER engine would be replaced by a North British one; the latter company rashly guaranteed that existing timetables would be kept, even for non-stop workings. To seek redress, the NER went to the House of Lords, and to the Railway Commissioners, the NBR meanwhile finding it necessary to double-head most trains for timekeeping. Early in 1898, the NBR decided to eat humble pie, and concluded an agreement for the companies to share haulage over the main line north of Berwick.

What of the NBR's main lines and passenger services? Edinburgh–Glasgow was straightforward, with the exception of Cowlairs Incline which until 1901 trains ascended by cable, or descended by gravity. By 1898, ten expresses in each direction averaged about 70min in journey time, the fast trains making up to four stops. Five Edinburgh–Perth expresses in each direction needed 65-70 min for the 48-mile run, beset with speed restrictions, and the steep climb south from Perth up Glenfarg bank.

The Waverley Route was no bagatelle either, not having been constructed as a main line but fashioned from a local railway south to Hawick, to which was grafted the Border Union line to Carlisle. Curvature and gradients abounded, and so when joint Midland and North British Anglo-Scottish services began running over the line from 1876, engines and men faced a real challenge; the non-stop timing of 140 min of 1881 remained an unbeatable schedule for many years. In addition to the Anglo-Scottish trains, there were two or three purely NBR expresses over the route, taking 150 min or so for the 98 miles. With never less than four stops, the Edinburgh–Aberdeen expresses took at best 3hr 10min northbound, and 3hr 17min going south, but those not making connections with East Coast services stopped more frequently and their journey time was over 4hr.

On the West Highland Line, the Mallaig Extension on from Fort William had opened in 1901. Before then, there had been three trains each way from Glasgow Queen St. to Fort William and, during summer months only, through coaches from King's Cross on one train each way. From 1895-99, there had also been a seasonal Edinburgh–Fort William working. When the Mallaig Extension opened, services were increased over the WHR proper:

through coaches provided from King's Cross to Mallaig (sleeping cars from 1901); three down and three up (four, from 1913) through trains operated each way from Glasgow–Mallaig, and two down and two up (one only from 1904) between Fort William and Glasgow. Most of the rolling stock included saloon/compartment coaches built specially for the WHR's opening. In 1914, there was even an attempt to encourage residential traffic from Crianlarich to Glasgow and Springburn and back, but it did not survive the war.

With all these events under its belt, and more forceful directors on the board, the NBR was stung to counter competition from the Caledonian. The 1905 introduction of the 'Grampian Corridor' Express had diverted custom from the NBR's Edinburgh–Aberdeen trains. The solution was to be found in greatly accelerated trains over the company's routes, to start in the summer of 1906. There were to be big, new Atlantic engines, top-rate coaches, and associated cascading of existing power to speed-up Edinburgh–Glasgow, and Fife Coast trains. But the Atlantics were not ready in time, although the suitably embarrassing publicity was, and only some of the new coaches; in any case, facilities to turn the Atlantics at Aberdeen and Carlisle alike were lacking.

Originally planned for introduction in May 1906, neither engines nor coaches were ready. The new timetable was deferred until 2 July when the Edinburgh–Aberdeen trains were advertised to 3hr schedules, including a stop at Dalmeny to attach/detach the Glasgow section, and at Dundee. At the same time, Atlantic-worked Edinburgh–Perth trains were to make the journey in 60min, and 4-4-0s displaced by the Atlantics would also permit 60min timings between Edinburgh and Glasgow. On the appointed day, a press trip was run from Edinburgh to Aberdeen with the one set of coaches to hand, but the Atlantic was still in works grey and was quietly removed soon after the start – it had made its first trial run only the previous day. Yet a service of 3hr trains was advertised from 10 July but worked by 4-4-0s, and also without the second set train. The trains were the 11am and 3.20pm from Edinburgh Waverley, and the 9.30am and 6.55pm from Aberdeen. A timing of 95min applied north of Dundee, non-stop southbound, but a Stonehaven stop included northbound; at that time, the line was single between Arbroath and Montrose. It was not until the winter of 1906/7 that the Atlantics were in charge of the Edinburgh–Aberdeen trains.

The coaches for the Edinburgh–Aberdeen set trains were built at Cowlairs by the NBR. Compared

The 1 in 70 gradient up though North Queensferry station is telling on North British Reid Atlantic No. 868 *Aberdonian* at the head of the 12.25pm Perth–Edinburgh Waverley on 21 September 1910. Three of the coaches in the centre of the train are Midland vehicles, and at the front of the train is what appears to be a Great Northern saloon.

with the Caley's 'Grampian' stock, they were 58ft long and eight-wheeled. With elliptical roofs, steam heating and electric lighting, they were streets ahead of existing NBR coaches, and their general pattern was adopted for all vestibuled stock – which was limited in number – built up to Grouping.

On the Waverley Route, the intention was not to use the Atlantics to accelerate timings, but to obviate double-heading as trains had become heavier. The best Edinburgh–Carlisle times were 2hr 11min down, and 2hr 17min up.

The ambitious plans of 1906 for accelerated trains were an influence on the series of meetings between the general managers of the Caledonian and North British railways during 1908 with the aim of cutting down wasteful competition – see **Caledonian Railway**. The result was an agreement in May 1908 for the introduction of decelerated timings, by up to 30min, and a reduced number of through coaches on the Edinburgh/Glasgow–Aberdeen services in particular, and slower schedules, too, on the Edinburgh–Glasgow, Edinburgh–Perth and Waverley Route expresses.

By April 1910, the schedules of the four original North British Edinburgh–Aberdeen 3hr trains averaged 3hr 17min. Between Edinburgh and

Glasgow, 65min were allowed for the best trains in April 1910, with 53min from Haymarket to Cowlairs. The 1908 inter-railway agreement had seen 5min added to schedules. 'Scott' 4-4-0s were the usual power for the NBR's expresses on this route but, despite level track, speeds of much over 60mph were rare. A 60min timing between Edinburgh and Perth had been advertised in 1906 for the 10.35am and 3pm down, and 71min for the 3.45pm and 7.20pm up. This route was also covered by the agreement and so by 1910 the timing for the down trains had been eased by 5min. The Atlantics had been blamed for spreading the track, particularly on the Waverley Route, but were in time vindicated, and more were delivered in 1911.

In 1912, the 'Lothian Coast Express' was introduced between Glasgow, Edinburgh, North Berwick, Gullane and Dunbar, another of the Scottish companies' initiatives to attract the businessman staying with his family by the sea during the summer, and travelling into work in the city. A section from Dunbar attached coaches from North Berwick at Drem, and those from Gullane at Longniddry Junction. Arrival at Glasgow Queen Street was 9.49am, and the businessmen threw off their cares to rejoin the train at 3.50pm (12.30pm

The 'Lothian Coast Express' residential train waits at Edinburgh Waverley behind the first of the North British 'Scott' 4-4-0s, No. 895 *Rob Roy*.

Saturdays), to arrive at Dunbar at 5.45pm in time for high tea, or lunch on Saturdays.

New stock was ordered by the NBR in 1913/14: four sets of 52ft non-vestibuled coaches for the West Highland line, and five all-steel dining cars, these not delivered until after World War I. The competitive fervour between the NBR and CR had abated, NBR General Manager, Jackson commenting in 1914 that; 'competition . . . has resulted in considerable diminution of the net revenues of the companies without adding anything like an equivalent advantage to passengers . . .' It was not his attitude in 1906.

During World War I, the West Highland services were thinned out, the 12.45pm Glasgow–Mallaig being withdrawn in 1915, and the 6.25am Mallaig–Glasgow cut back to Fort William in 1916 which year also saw the withdrawal of the sleeping cars from/to King's Cross. By 1923, the year-round Glasgow–Fort William service comprised a working each way conveying the through sleeping cars from/to King's Cross, and an up morning train to Glasgow and the 3.46pm down. An additional train each way ran in summer between Glasgow and Fort William. The sleeping cars only ran daily in summer at this stage, and the rest of the year were restricted to Fridays in the down direction, up on Mondays.

The summer 'Lothian Coast Express' was reinstated in 1921. One difference with the prewar working was that the Dunbar portion was withdrawn. The North Berwick (dep 8.5am) and Gullane (dep 8am) portions were combined at Longniddry, the former in due course including one of the pantry cars which had been built in 1907 for the Edinburgh–Aberdeen 3hr expresses. The return workings were at 12.25pm SO and 3.50pm SX from Glasgow Queen St. The 'Lothian Coast', the Leeds–Glasgow train – see **North Eastern Railway** – and the King's Cross sleeping car services were the star workings between Edinburgh and Glasgow, the other Edinburgh–Glasgow expresses numbering seven or so each way. The fastest took 60min, and some of the trains in 1922 were advertised as running from/to Leith.

On the Edinburgh–Aberdeen route, the heaviest express in the summer 1922 timetable was the 7.40am down with its through sleepers and coaches from King's Cross, and coaches only from St Pancras. This train featured one of the six NBR all-steel restaurant cars which had been built in 1919 for the Edinburgh–Aberdeen and Glasgow services. But the principal East Coast Aberdeen sleeping car train was the 4.12am from Waverley which also included the through coach from Penzance – see **Cross-**

Country services. The 10.25am down included a through coach for Elgin, alternately provided by the NBR and Great North of Scotland Railway. Then there was the 2.20pm, the fastest down express at 3hr 26min to Aberdeen; a 4.25pm semi-fast, and the 6.35pm, with the through coaches off the 10am from King's Cross which arrived in Aberdeen at 10.26pm. Southbound, the 6.15am from Aberdeen had through coaches for King's Cross for the 10am up from Edinburgh; the 9.45am had the coach for Penzance and the 12.50pm, the through coach from Elgin. The 3.40pm semi-fast was devoid of a catering vehicle as was the 4.25pm down, and both in contrast to the other principal trains on the route. The 5.45pm from Aberdeen had the through Midland & North British coaches to St Pancras, and the main sleeping car train to King's Cross was the 7.15pm departure, also the fastest up express in 3hr 14min to Waverley. From the introduction of the 8hr day for railwaymen in 1919, all Aberdeen expresses had changed engines at Dundee in each direction.

On the Perth service, the principal trains connected with the up and down 10 o'clocks on the East Coast route and with the East Coast sleeping car trains. One short-lived working introduced before Grouping comprised through coaches between Perth and York, out on the 7.50am from Edinburgh, and back at 11.45am from Perth.

Over the Waverley Route in 1922 there were four expresses each way with through coaches from the Midland. These included a through coach from Bristol to Edinburgh which travelled on the 4.33am from Carlisle in company with the sleeping cars from St Pancras to Edinburgh and the through coaches to Aberdeen. There remained two day expresses each way between St Pancras and Edinburgh, supplemented by other so-called 'Expresses', at 9am and 1.5pm from Carlisle and 6pm up from Edinburgh, the last-mentioned conveying the through coach to Bristol. The best times between Carlisle and Edinburgh were made by the 4.7pm down in 147min, and the 10.40am up which was 1min slower.

The Reid Atlantics were greatly improved by superheating from 1915, and two were built new with superheaters in 1921. All 20 original engines were not fitted with superheated boilers until 1925.

Great North of Scotland Railway

The train service of today often provides no guide to that of the past, and this is particularly true of the Great North of Scotland Railway. While the first railway link to Inverness was by way of Aberdeen, via Keith and Elgin, with the opening in 1863 of the Highland Railway's direct main line from Forres to Perth, that became the north to south artery instead, and the GNoS concentrated on developing traffic between Speyside and the Moray Firth ports through Aberdeen. As to the traffic to/from Inverness, the GNoS attempted to keep as much as possible on its own routes to Elgin, via Buckie and via Craigellachie. Today, the only surviving passenger service is Aberdeen–Inverness and this uses a combined ex-GNoS and Highland route.

Much has been made elsewhere of the GNoS's unfriendliness with its neighbours, but its care to keep traffic on its own lines as much as possible was both a reflection of the motivation of the pre-1923 railways, and the problems it faced from the available business in its territory. Of the 2.5 million engine-miles run by its engines, passenger workings accounted for some 60 per cent. Unusually, the GNoS lacked 0-6-0 tender engines, and the prevailing 4-4-0s dealt with passenger and freight working, the latter dominated by fish, loaded on special trains during the summer when the herrings were landed, and in winter mostly conveyed by passenger trains. The whisky distilleries were an important source of traffic when that precious liquid was in demand; when the market fluctuated, the fortunes of the GNoS suffered.

From Aberdeen, the principal lines were the Deeside line to Ballater; to Keith, by both routes, and the Buchan line, serving the fishing ports of Fraserburgh and Peterhead. The Aberdeen–Keith workings were handled by engines based at Kittybrewster (outside Aberdeen), Keith and Elgin.

The Races to the North in 1895 by the East and West Coast companies seemingly had their effect on the GNoS. Late that year, the company first took delivery of a batch of the Pickersgill T class 4-4-0s, and their arrival was followed by acceleration of passenger services by the Autumn 1896 timetable. Star working was the 6.45am Aberdeen–Elgin, allowed only 123min by the 87 mile coast route, despite five stops and, by 8.48am, getting the overnight traveller off the competitive 8pm sleeping car trains into Elgin, in just 12hr 45min from London. Such smart running was possible with the use of the Manson automatic tablet exchanger which enabled tablets to be exchanged at speed on single lines. The 336-mile network was primarily single-track, little more than 60 track-miles being double.

Such enterprise was short-lived, and by 1898 the four composite expresses from Aberdeen to Elgin, dividing at the Exchange Platform of Cairnie Junction for the Buckie and Craigellachie routes;

featured a best time of 135 min, and 5min longer for the remainder with eight to ten intermediate stops. The 3.30am mail reached Keith in 105min with six stops via the coast line. The up trains needed more time for their journeys, and the through Inverness–Aberdeen journey could be a weary business. Best time was provided by the 3pm departure from Inverness, routed from Elgin over the Highland line via Mulben, and offering an overall time of 3hr 5min for the 108 miles. On the Deeside line, there were residentials at 8.30am from Ballater, and 4.35pm from Aberdeen; each with four intermediate stops took 70/75min respectively for the 43 miles. From 1904, there were railway-run motorbuses connecting Ballater and Braemar. Passenger stock was improved, with the first corridor coaches in 1896, and bogie corridor coaches entering service in 1898/99.

The GNoS suffered financial troubles in 1899, as a result of which it could not take delivery of five new 4-4-0s which were then acquired by the South Eastern & Chatham Railway. There were also cuts in services, the result being that fast trains such as the 6.45am had additional stops inserted to cover for the withdrawal of stopping services. On the other hand, the GNoS pressed ahead with its Cruden Bay hotel and golf course development, described as a 'disastrous undertaking' by the line's best-known

historian. Despite the undoubted attractions at Cruden Bay, the season was too short for profitability. The Speyside line also featured in the GNoS's tourist promotions although its usual train service was limited. Express half-day excursions offering cheap fares, were operated from Aberdeen to Boat of Garten and back. Sometimes they were duplicated, and they continued to be run until at least the late 1920s.

Up until 1914, the pattern of passenger services remained stable as regards times and the number of trains, but they were generally slower than those in the last years of the 19th century. Our friend the 6.45am was retired to depart at 6am and, although running every day in summer, from 1902 was restricted to Mondays only in winter. From 1906 the Railway began through coach workings from Elgin to Glasgow and Edinburgh in conjunction with the CR and NBR and for which some smart brake composites were built at Inverurie. In May 1909, the Scottish companies agreed to improve connections at Aberdeen between the Anglo-Scottish trains and GNoS services, with the result that the connection into the 6am ex-Aberdeen was made more generous while the mid-afternoon train from Elgin due in Aberdeen at 7.27pm was altered to arrive 11min earlier, and the East/West Coast sleepers retired to depart 25/30min later.

At the south end of Aberdeen Joint station, a Great North of Scotland M class 4-4-0 pulls out with a train for Ballater on 4 August 1911.

From April 1908, and for the next few years, engines and stock of the GNoS and HR worked through on Aberdeen–Inverness services, the former covering the 3.30am and 9.40am ex-Aberdeen and 11.5am and 3.20pm return. The GNoS used its V class 4-4-0s and the HR 'Small' and 'Large Ben' 4-4-0s. In April 1910, the 8.5am from Aberdeen was into Inverness at 12.5pm, while the best timing in the reverse direction was offered by the 9.8am departure, giving an Aberdeen arrival at 12.55pm; also important was the 2.40pm from Elgin, into Aberdeen at 5.10pm. Most of the faster trains on this route had conditional stops at stations such as Dyce and Fochabers. The Buchan line maintained a service of five trains in each direction, usually all stations for the 44 miles Aberdeen–Peterhead, but in April 1910 there were semi-fasts at 8.10am down, and 3.40pm up.

One innovation came in the last summer before World War I. As a result of an agreement by which Sir Thomas Burnett waived the right to stop any train at Crathes on the Ballater line, the 4.45pm from Aberdeen – the 'Deeside Express' – was retimed to run the 23 miles from Aberdeen to Torphins non-stop in 33min, and the 19 miles on to Ballater in 32min with a stop at Aboyne. Banchory was served by a slip coach, the first – and only – to be operated by the GNoS. The up morning train called additionally at Banchory but its overall journey time Ballater to Aberdeen was just 66min for 43 miles – 30min quicker than the all-stations run. These fast trains, and the slip coach working, lasted just for summer 1914. Hamilton Ellis reckoned the pre-1914 GNoS had the 'smartest, cleanest and most comfortable trains', on what was the smallest of the main line Scottish companies.

Soon after the outbreak of war, it was agreed with the Highland that the GNoS would work all trains between Aberdeen and Inverness. Passenger services were drastically curtailed and decelerated in 1915, and did not recover to prewar levels before Grouping, one other casualty being the withdrawal of the mail sorting and TPO facilities.

Generally speaking, the service offered after 1916 was inferior both in terms of connections with the South and through journeys within the GNoS territory. An example of the decelerated timings was provided by the 10am Aberdeen–Elgin which left 25min earlier and arrived 10min later. By the summer of 1922, the service from Aberdeen started with the 4.35am which reached Keith at 6.23am, and continued to Elgin via the HR line. The 8.5am to Inverness took 3hr 50min overall, and the balancing working was the 12.50pm from Inverness, taking no

less than 4hr 24min to Aberdeen. The fastest down train was the 2.30pm from Aberdeen with its through coach from Edinburgh. The 3.30pm down was the last train with connections to anywhere north of Elgin. It divided at Cairnie Junction into Coast and via Craigellachie portions, and called at almost all stations.

The best up trains in the summer 1922 timetable were the 9.28am from Elgin (TC to Edinburgh), not stopping after Huntly, and arriving in Aberdeen at 12.16pm, and the 2.25pm from Elgin via Buckie (and 2.20pm via Craigellachie) which was due in Aberdeen at 5.14pm. Trains such as the 'Ballater Express' were fated not to reappear although limited-stop residential trains remained at 8.30am from Ballater (67min to Aberdeen) and at 4.40pm SX from Aberdeen.

Other than cold meals served to travellers on the Aberdeen–Speyside excursions there was no on-train catering on the GNoS until the last six months of its existence when a restaurant car was hired from the NBR for use on the Aberdeen–Inverness through workings. Some of the later gangwayed coaches built at the Railway's Inverurie Works stood comparison with any other and were used for the through Elgin–Aberdeen–Edinburgh workings – see **North British Railway**. Although a larger 4-4-0 had been contemplated before 1914, the last passenger engines delivered in 1920, the F class, were superheated versions of the 1899 V 4-4-0s.

One of the most notable features of the period was the completion of the fine station at Aberdeen jointly owned with the Caledonian and comprising 13 platforms.

Highland Railway

The challenges faced by this railway need some explanation before reviewing its passenger services which at first glance appear slow and unadventurous. Running through some mountainous country, the Highland was primarily a single-track railway, replete with steep gradients. By the turn of the century, automatic tablet exchangers were being installed and crossing loops realigned to permit faster running while, from 1900 and 1909, the main line was doubled in stages between Blair Atholl and Dalwhinnie. Yet such improvements could not overcome the reality of the Highland's operations, that its network was at the extremity of what at one time were three competitive Anglo-Scottish routes, each extending over 400 miles and open to a variety of their own operating delays. To cap it all, winter frequently brought the HR appalling problems with snow. The upshot of all this was that its operators were not predisposed to experimentation in favour of hard-won experience!

The Highland faced another challenge with the tremendous disparity in passenger traffic levels as between summer and winter. In particular, the shooting season lasted for three weeks, from the last week in July, during which the principal Anglo-Scottish services might be regularly duplicated, even triplicated. To the Highlands came not only the ordinary coaches and sleeping cars of the three Anglo-Scottish joint stock operators, but a multitude of family saloons, horseboxes, and vans for luggage, not to mention accommodation for dogs. What went north then had to return south, as empty stock, then back north again – empty – in September to collect holidaymakers.

In winter, the competing Anglo-Scottish operators duplicated accommodation, needing considerable pleading from the HR to desist, and so avoid the haulage of unnecessary tonnage over the main line north from Perth. An informal agreement between East and West Coast to discontinue through sleeping cars to Inverness in winter had existed in 1903 but the East Coast was accused of disregarding it. In April 1908, it was the East Coast companies who requested a meeting of all parties to Anglo-Scottish passenger traffic to see if economies could be made in operations, with a conclusion that cuts should be made in the number of through coaches to the Highland Railway. Beginning in the period November 1909 to May 1910, the East and West Coast companies agreed that the through coaches and sleeping cars for Inverness would run alternately from Euston (MWFO) and King's Cross (TThSO).

With the first year of the new century, the HR had had only one season of operating the direct line to Inverness via Carr Bridge, as opposed to running trains via Forres and Nairn. The opening of the new line in November 1898 had changed markedly the pattern of operations while a route from Perth shorter by 26 miles brought appreciable accelerations to and the retiming of trains, not only to Inverness but also to the Far North. The HR's principal services were dependent on the times when the through coaches off day and night services from London and the South presented themselves at Perth, and also by the requirements for postal traffic.

From Perth northwards, there was a night train with sleeping cars, later running through from Glasgow Buchanan Street; the summer connection from the West Coast Tourist express; the morning 'Limited Mail', connecting out of the overnight

Postal and the 8pm from Euston; and two other Perth–Inverness workings. All five trains took from 3hr 15min to 4hr 20min. Southbound, there were the corresponding services. Previous traffic flows were catered for by running the up night train via Forres and Nairn.

From the summer of 1900, the through coaches off the 10am trains from Euston and King's Cross were worked on a new 8.15pm from Perth, balanced by an 8.50am from Inverness which brought the through coaches into Perth for the midday Caley and North British departures southwards. The down train was continued for the summer only, but the up train continued through the year, with a fast booking from Blair Atholl to Perth. The summer timetable was usually more expansive than those for the rest of the year, but the appearance of a train one season was no guarantee that it might continue thereafter. So, for summer 1902, the down 8.15pm was diverted via Forres, and, as with some other Perth–Inverness trains, slowed by the inclusion of additional stops; train mileage was also reduced at the time. By summer 1904, it was retimed to leave Perth earlier, and so missed the 10 o'clock Anglo-Scottish trains, reportedly because the HR was not prepared to maintain the connection when the trains from the South were badly late – as so often they were.

By April 1910, the basic pattern of service north from Perth comprised trains at 6.15am – with sleeping cars from Euston or King's Cross, as earlier noted; at 9.30am, with early morning connections from the Lowlands, but destined to become summer-only from the 1911/12 winter; at 11.50am, with through coaches off the 10am ex-Glasgow Buchanan St., and the 3.55pm, connecting out of the 2pm ex-Buchanan St., and 1.45pm ex-Edinburgh Waverley. Principal up trains from Inverness were the 8.40am – the fastest train, in 3hr 16min for the 118miles to Perth, and with connections culminating with arrivals at the London termini in late evening; the 11.5am, with a through coach for Glasgow Buchanan St., and the 3.50pm, with the through sleeping cars and coaches alternately provided by East and West Coast joint stock. There were other through Anglo-Scottish trains, such as guaranteed excursions organised by the Polytechnic Touring Association which ran on summer Fridays from King's Cross to the Highlands.

The Aberdeen–Inverness service is described under **Great North of Scotland Railway**. Through passengers for the HR lines north of Inverness were able to use through coaches conveyed from/to Perth on the mail trains; in 1898, the extension of the down

An official photograph of what is described as 'Royal Mail, London to Inverness and the Highlands, approaching Culloden Moor'. This was the morning train from Perth, leaving there at 6.15am in April 1910. The engine in the photograph is HR 'Castle' 4-6-0 No. 148 *Cawdor Castle*, built in 1902.

'Limited Mail' got the traveller into Wick at 4.35pm after a 6hr hike over the 161 miles from Inverness. This was the latest departure from there to stations north of Helmsdale. Otherwise, passengers had to change at Inverness for the Far North, with the exception of the 'Strathpeffer Express' mentioned below. There was tourist potential, of course, and on summer Fridays in 1906 the 'Further North Express' left Inverness at 4.30pm for Dornoch, connecting out of the forenoon train from Perth–Inverness. For the 1906/7 winter, the 'Further North Express' was extended to Wick, taking 5hr 5min, and retimed to leave Inverness at 2.20pm, having connected with the morning train from Perth; its counterpart was a Thursdays only un-named express, at 10.35am from Wick. For summer 1907, the train regained an Inverness departure at 4.30pm but ran through to Wick. This and the up train continued as

year-round workings until withdrawn for autumn 1912; in the summers of 1913/4 the northbound train ran on Wednesdays and Fridays, the southbound train, on Thursdays and Saturdays.

The line to Kyle of Lochalsh had three/four trains each way initially, calling at all stations. An additional and unbalanced semi-fast working featured in the summer timetables for 1901-3, at 10.36am from Dingwall where it connected out of the down morning Far North train. With just three intermediate calls, the semi-fast reached Kyle of Lochalsh at 1pm. In the April 1910 timetable, there were no more than two down, and three up trains over the line.

The spa town of Strathpeffer was normally served by connecting trains from Dingwall, but on Saturdays there was a return Inverness–Strathpeffer

The picture was taken before there was a restriction on through sleeping cars from the three Anglo-Scottish routes. Behind the HR sorting van is a West Coast Joint Stock sleeping composite coach, then two Highland coaches, a Midland Scottish Joint Stock sleeping car, an East Coast Joint Stock sleeping car and finally a brake van.

train. With the opening of the HR hotel at Strathpeffer in 1911, and in succeeding summers to 1915 inclusive, the 'Strathpeffer Express' was run through from Aviemore on Tuesdays, connecting out of the forenoon Perth–Inverness working. It passed Inverness station without stopping, a distinction achieved by no other HR train. In 1909, the East and West Coast companies agreed that the East Coast would advertise that its Inverness coach off the 7.55pm from King's Cross would be extended to Strathpeffer if required; whether this was done is unknown.

With the outbreak of World War I, naval requirements dictated that the north of Scotland assumed strategic importance, and the HR was in the front line of supplying the bases at Invergordon and Scapa Flow and to the major naval distribution centre

set up at Inverness. There were numerous troop specials over the HR and after 1917 regular leave trains were run between Euston and Thurso for naval personnel. The HR's locomotives became rundown through intensive use, and stock was borrowed from other companies.

Regular passenger services were not greatly changed until the end of 1916 although the previous years' summer services had been virtually identical to winter. One curiosity was the 9.30am slow from Perth to Blair Atholl which from the winter of 1915 to late 1916 was extended to Inverness, calling only at Kingussie. From the start of 1917, the night trains from the South were considerably slowed and through sleeping cars suspended, thereby affecting Perth–Inverness workings which were accordingly thinned out and decelerated.

For some years before World War I, there was through working of HR and GNoSR engines and coaches between Inverness and Aberdeen. This is the 2.20pm Aberdeen Joint–Inverness adding to the drama of the occasion as it starts its journey on 3 August 1911 behind Highland 'Small Ben' 4-4-0 No. 2 *Ben Alder*, its train mostly comprising GNoSR stock.

Through sleeping car services to/from London were restored in 1919, but a daytime journey between Inverness and London was not possible until the 8.40am Inverness–Perth was restored in the summer of 1921. Even then, services were still not the equal of prewar years. In the summer of 1920, the through journey from London to Inverness by the West Coast route took 14¾hr at best, nearly 2hr longer than in 1914. The fastest run was with the 3.30pm from Inverness, booked non-stop over the 35 miles between Blair Atholl and Perth in 50min, a marginally quicker timing than in 1914. During 1919 and in 1921 the HR took delivery of the 'Clan' 4-6-0s for main line duties but the earlier series were soon unserviceable, and in general the HR locomotive department seemed in rather poor order.

One area where there had been an improvement in passenger services was in the introduction to the HR of on-train catering. From June 1922, one of the Pullman cars in the CR allocation worked through from Glasgow (dep 10.10am) to Aviemore on the midday train from Perth, accompanied by HR gangwayed stock which alternated with a CR set on this Glasgow–Inverness service. The car returned on the 3.30pm Inverness–Glasgow. In 1921, a short-lived restaurant car service had been provided as far north as Blair Atholl using a former ECJS car by now in NBR stock. This worked out on the 2.5pm from Edinburgh which provided through coaches for the 3.50pm Perth–Inverness. The car was detached at Blair Atholl and returned to Edinburgh in the later afternoon train from Inverness which had the West and East Coast sleepers, and then on the 8.5pm from Perth.

When, in 1920 the Postmaster-General suspended the Sunday delivery of letters throughout the country, the Sunday service between Perth and Inverness was withdrawn, as were those further north so that at Grouping passenger services were restricted to weekdays only.

Elsewhere on the HR passenger services were gradually restored to winter prewar levels but many of the special facilities enjoyed before 1914 had gone for good.

CHAPTER EIGHT

CROSS-COUNTRY INTER-RAILWAY SERVICES TO 1922

Cross-Country Services 1900-1914

North West to South West/South Wales
North and West via the Severn Tunnel

Soon after the opening of the Severn Tunnel in 1886, the Great Western and London & North Western Railway introduced a 'North and West' express service between Bristol and Crewe which challenged the Midland Railway's previous monopoly of North to West Country traffic. In Ahrons' memorable phrase: 'The trains were heavy, for they consisted of a profusion of through coaches from everywhere to everywhere else'. The North and West expresses constituted one of the most important cross-country services, comparable to those on the Midland's Leeds–Bristol axis which similarly competed for traffic between Glasgow/Edinburgh and Manchester and the south-west.

The abolition of the broad gauge in 1892 allowed through coaches to be run to Devon and Cornwall and, by 1898, there were half a dozen expresses between Bristol (or beyond) and the North of England via the Severn Tunnel and Shrewsbury, usually to Birkenhead and Manchester but also for Liverpool. Some conveyed portions to/from South Wales, attached or detached at Pontypool Road, but there were also separate expresses for Cardiff.

One of the principal trains over the North and West Route was the 10.45am from Manchester London Rd–Plymouth which called at Stockport, Crewe, Shrewsbury, Hereford, Pontypool Road, Bristol, Taunton, Exeter and principal stations, taking 8hr 29min for the 311¼ miles. Most of these cross-country trains stopped for 10min at intermediate stations and for 15min or so at Bristol. Most were timed to provide connections at Crewe to Scotland: for example, the 9am Bristol connected into the 10am from Euston which got passengers into Edinburgh at 6.30 and Glasgow at 6.45pm.

Although some of the through services were seasonal, by 1898/99 one of the principal through trains was the 1.20am Crewe–Plymouth with through coaches from Glasgow (dep 5.55pm), Liverpool and Manchester to Penzance. The train reached Bristol at 5.15am, and Plymouth at 10.50am. Just 10min later from Shrewsbury there was a Cardiff train; going north, there was a similar pattern of Bristol and South Wales trains in the small hours. The corresponding working of this night train was the 7.40pm Bristol–Crewe which from Bristol conveyed through coaches from Penzance to Manchester and Liverpool and Glasgow. Torbay's through coaches from the North were conveyed on the 11.40am Crewe–Bristol and returned north on a Paddington express to Bristol, then by a Weston-super-Mare–North of England working. From summer 1899, there was a new train from Bristol–Crewe which connected into the West Coast's 11.25am Birmingham–Glasgow.

The service over the North and West Route was improved in 1906, to compete with the MR expresses to/from Bristol. Northbound, the principal train was the 9am Bristol–Crewe. This train connected into the 10am Euston–Glasgow, or its relief in summer, and in due course conveyed a Bristol–Glasgow through coach which was taken forward from Crewe on the 10am ex-Euston, and through coaches from Cardiff.

From Bristol to Crewe took 3hr 38min for the 153 miles. The 9am ex-Bristol was followed closely by the 9.30am Bristol–Shrewsbury. A restaurant car featured on the 12.45pm Bristol–Liverpool (arr 5.25pm) with similar timings to the 9am ex-Bristol. The 12.32pm Plymouth Millbay–Liverpool Lime St. (arr 9.10pm)/Manchester had a restaurant car throughout to Liverpool, TCs from Cardiff, Plymouth and Kingswear to Manchester; TCs from Plymouth–Leeds and Liverpool and TC from Penzance–Liverpool and, for good measure, combined with a Cardiff portion at Pontypool Road! The 7.40pm mail from Bristol included a through coach from Cardiff to Newcastle, and one Bristol–Newcastle.

Southbound there was a 1.25am from Crewe with through coaches from Glasgow to Bristol, and Liverpool–Plymouth. The principal morning West of England service was at 9.10am from Liverpool, forward from Crewe at 10.17am. The main portion with restaurant car ran from Liverpool to Plymouth Millbay (arr 5.43pm), and there were TCs at 9.25am from Manchester (for Plymouth and Cardiff, the latter detached at Hereford). Just over an hour later from Crewe there was a 10.30am Liverpool Lime St.–Bristol, also with restaurant car. At midday there was yet another service from Liverpool, with through coaches to Bristol and Cardiff. The 10 o'clock Glasgow–Euston brought a Glasgow–Bristol through coach, worked forward from Crewe on the 3.55pm departure which connected at Temple Meads into the 6.30pm Paddington–Plymouth. The last of the southbound workings on the route was the 8.15pm from Crewe, with through coaches from Liverpool to Bristol (arr 12.35am) and Cardiff (arr 12.10am).

Manchester/Halifax/Leeds–Bristol/Ilfracombe
On 1 July 1904, the Great Western and Great Central launched a through express from Leeds, Halifax, Huddersfield and Sheffield to Bristol via Swindon and Bath, and it was later extended to Torquay and Kingswear.

In winter, the service was reduced to through coaches only, at 7.47am from Halifax to Bristol. The northbound departure from Bristol was at 3.56pm, the coach going forward from Woodford Halse on a semi-fast, to be attached at Leicester to the 6.20pm Marylebone–Bradford express which was diverted to run via Halifax where the Bristol coach was detached. From summer 1911, the coach was extended to run to/from Ilfracombe via Taunton and Barnstaple. There was already an evening Bristol–Leicester train and, from July 1913, this 7.50pm

departure was extended to York, arr 2.43am, with a return working at 10pm ex-York which arrived at Bristol at 5.5am. The intention was to feed Scottish and West of England traffic to the East Coast route, and connections were made into the last of the night's down sleeping car trains at York.

South Coast to South Wales
Portsmouth–Cardiff
Through workings were introduced in 1896, and two years later there were through trains at 8.15am and 5pm from Portsmouth Town to Salisbury, Bath and Bristol Stapleton Road and Cardiff, with return workings at 10.15am and 4.20pm. Over Great Western metals the best time for the 91¼ miles from Salisbury–Cardiff was 162min including four intermediate stops, a time that seems pedestrian until the reader appreciates that the fastest train of the late 1950s took 5min longer! One of the more sprightly runs in 1898 was made by the 4.20pm from Cardiff which ran fast from Salisbury to Southampton West in 36min for 24¾ miles. Early in the 1900s two services were introduced between Bristol Temple Meads and Portsmouth which called at most stations en route.

Associated with these services are the other through coaches from Brighton, such as a summer working to Bournemouth which first started in 1908. The coaches were detached at Southampton West from the summer-only 11.20am Brighton–Salisbury/Plymouth which changed engines at Cosham and avoided Portsmouth. In the eastbound direction the coaches were attached to the Brighton train at Eastleigh. By the summer of 1914 there was a through Brighton–Bournemouth train on weekdays July-September.

North East to South West/Wales
Newcastle–Bristol
Through coaches had been provided by the Midland Railway as early as 1880, and later they were conveyed on the 8am and the famed 12.20pm from Newcastle – see **North Eastern Railway** – and at 9.45am from Bristol. There was also the night mail in each direction, with 7pm departures from Newcastle and Bristol alike and these featured sorting coaches provided by the joint Midland & North Eastern Joint Postal Service.

Newcastle–Barry
The train was introduced on 1 May 1906 by the Great Central, North Eastern and Great Western railways, and was worked by the Great Central Railway from

York to Banbury. From there, it travelled over the Banbury and Cheltenham Direct Railway via Chipping Norton and Andoversford, this having been instituted as a through route that same year by virtue of a bridge spanning the Oxford–Worcester line to bypass Kingham Junction, and by the installation of the Hatherley curve which avoided reversal at Cheltenham; the train called at Cheltenham South & Leckhampton station. The service was provided with a restaurant car and was composed of Great Western and Great Central Railway stock on alternate days.

Many of the train's passengers were ships' crews bound either for South Wales or Tyneside and, as much of this traffic originated at Barry, the Barry Railway persuaded the GWR to extend the service to Barry, as from August 1906. Not surprisingly, the train became known popularly as the 'Ports-to-Ports Express'.

Initially worked by GWR 'Barnum' 2-4-0s west of Banbury, the 'Ports-to-Ports Express' settled down to haulage from Banbury to Barry by 'Bulldog' 4-4-0s, or by 'Aberdare' 2-6-0s which were suitable for the route through the Cotswolds. Barry motive power was used to/from Barry – see **Barry Railway**.

From July 1909, a through coach between Hull and Barry, and return was included. The GCR built a new set of coaches for the service in 1911.

North West and West Midlands to Channel Ports
Birkenhead–Dover

Once standard gauge track was available on the Great Western Railway as far south as Reading, through coach workings were introduced between Birkenhead and Dover and Hastings as early as 1863 but they lasted only three years. They worked over a link line between the GWR and South Eastern Railway to the east of Reading station, but a more practical connection was completed in 1899.

In the summer of 1897, the South Eastern and Great Western Railways combined to reintroduce through coaches between Birkenhead and a Channel port, this time to Folkestone Harbour. The specially constructed GWR slip coaches were attached to an early train from Birkenhead, and slipped at Reading, to be worked on stopping services to Tonbridge where they were attached to the afternoon boat train from Charing Cross to Folkestone Harbour. There they connected with a Boulogne sailing which offered the opportunity for a late evening arrival in Paris. In the reverse direction, there was a connection off the evening sailing from Boulogne, the coaches being attached at Reading to the midnight express from Paddington which arrived at Birkenhead at 6.30am.

More remarkably, this summer-only working was changed in July 1898 by starting it back at Liverpool Central at 8am. This indicated that the coaches had to travel over the Mersey Railway, and were attached at Rock Ferry to an up express from Birkenhead Woodside. Northbound, the GWR coaches were slipped at Paddock Wood, and again were worked from Reading on the midnight Birkenhead express. For these workings unusually short length slip coaches were built at Swindon, but what was described on the roof-boards of the coaches as 'Continental service through carriage between Great Western and South Eastern Railways via Reading' lasted only for the summers of 1898-1900.

In the summer of 1903, a new 9.25am Birkenhead–Reading–Dover Harbour through train was introduced, and extended to/from Deal the following October. Also, at the same time the train gained a short-lived portion from Manchester London Road–Deal – qv. The Birkenhead–Deal operated until 1916, and in 1904 left Birkenhead at 9.25am, arriving at Deal at 6.27pm. The northbound train departed at 10.52am from Deal, with arrival at Birkenhead at 9.15pm.

Over much of its route the southbound train formed part of other trains, and in 1905/6 the Deal coaches were combined with those between Birkenhead and Bournemouth qv, being transferred at Wolverhampton to a Paddington express and slipped from this at Reading. From the summer of 1906 they formed a separate train between Banbury and Reading, but with the winter timetable reverted to through coaches slipped at Reading. The Birkenhead–Deal service treated its passengers to lengthy station stops en route, particularly at Oxford and Reading, a reversal of direction at Chester and Redhill (where it was combined with an SE&CR stopping train), and several engine changes. The stock used included a GWR slip coach (those dating from 1897), and new SE&CR brake composites.

With the opening of the shortened route to Birmingham in 1910, the Deal coaches ran no further than Leamington on a Birkenhead–Paddington express, going forward separately to Oxford, there to be attached to the rear of another Paddington express (!), from which they were slipped at Reading. The slip was replaced by a station stop in February 1914.

With the formation of the SE&CR, spur lines were constructed at Bickley Junctions which enabled a through train to run from July 1905 between Deal (dep 10.25am) and Victoria, via Folkestone and Ashford. This train stopped at Herne Hill where through coaches for Birkenhead (GWR), Liverpool

(LNWR), Manchester Central and Bradford (MR) were detached and, from 1911, the through coaches to King's Cross – see **South Eastern & Chatham Railway**. The Birkenhead coaches seem to have run through to/from Dover but the working survived until 1908 only. Northbound, the coach ran via Uxbridge Road Junction and Latimer Road to Paddington where it was attached to a down express. Southbound, the through coach was detached at Southall, and worked via Kensington Addison Road to Herne Hill.

West Midlands to Channel Ports via Victoria
After the opening of the Bicester New line, in October 1910 the GWR launched a new initiative in the shape of trains at 6.30am from Wolverhampton to Victoria, running non-stop between Banbury and Kensington Addison Road, with though coaches for Queenborough Pier (for the day sailing to Flushing) and for Ramsgate Harbour, the latter attached to the 10.45am ex-Victoria. In the return direction, the through coaches from Queenborough and Ramsgate Harbour were worked to Victoria, to run forward as a separate train to Wolverhampton which was reached at 11.7pm.

There was also a 5.20pm Wolverhampton–Paddington which, at Ealing Broadway, detached a portion for Victoria consisting of through coaches for Folkestone Harbour. These worked forward from Victoria on the 8.45pm boat train. Their return was on the 6am from Folkestone Harbour, departing Victoria at 8.15am and running first to Paddington, to become part of an express for Wolverhampton which arrived there at 11.34am.

GWR engines, including even the occasional 'Star' 4-6-0, worked the trains to/from Victoria but the workings were to be short-lived. At the time of the 1912 miners' strike they were reduced to a morning departure from Wolverhampton and an evening train from Victoria, and these were withdrawn with the start of the Summer 1912 timetables.

Cross-country to East Anglia
Harwich–York/Liverpool
This train was the doyen of through workings to/from East Anglia and has been referred to in the **Great Eastern Railway** section as for the majority of its journey it ran from Harwich Town to York over GER or GN/GE Joint Line metals. It was one of the principal cross-country trains throughout the period, and in 1898 carried through coaches for Birmingham New St. – see **London & North Western Railway** – and Liverpool Central – see **Great Central** and

Cheshire Lines Committee. Later two coaches ran to/from Liverpool Exchange – see **Lancashire & Yorkshire Railway**. These were detached/attached at Doncaster, to be worked forward via Knottingley and Wakefield.

Manchester/Liverpool and York–Lowestoft GC/GE
In 1898 there was a summer-only 10.12am York–Yarmouth express which took 5½hr for the 216½ miles, timed to arrive at its destination for 3.40pm. In various forms this was to prove a long-lived service. In April 1910 there were through coaches from Yarmouth at 7.33am, arriving York at 2.10pm in the formation of the 8.40am ex-Liverpool St. The return working was at 12.50pm from York.

From July 1902 a summer express was introduced by the Great Central and Great Eastern Railways between Liverpool and Manchester and Yarmouth, Lowestoft and Cromer, and from Birmingham, in association with the London & North Western Railway. The 1903 timings were 11.5 from Liverpool Central and 11.40am from Manchester Central, with the return from East Anglia at midday. Early in 1914, when reviewing the service, the GER's traffic committee noted that passenger receipts did not cover running expenses but that 'indirectly the service has been of some benefit to the company and should be continued in summer 1914' – a candid insight into the operation of trains such as this.

Cardiff–Yarmouth/Lowestoft
With the opening of the Cheltenham–Honeybourne–Stratford route in 1908, new cross-country expresses were introduced – see **Great Western Railway** – but there was one inter-railway working, too. From 10 July 1908, there operated a summer Cardiff–Yarmouth and Lowestoft train, with through coaches for each destination conveyed as far as Gloucester on the 10.20am Cardiff–Newcastle train – qv. From Gloucester, the two coaches formed a lightweight train which travelled via Stratford, Hatton and traversed a new connection put in at Leamington. From there it was worked by an LNWR engine non-stop to Wansford, and handed over to the Great Eastern Railway at Peterborough East. From there the coaches went forward to Ely where they were attached to a London–Yarmouth/Lowestoft express. Westbound, as far as March the coaches worked with those to York – see above – and then made up a separate train to Gloucester, to be attached there to the Newcastle–Barry train. The service reappeared for just the Summer 1909 timetable.

North West to South Coast

The 'Sunny South Special'

This train was inaugurated on 1 March 1905 by the London & North Western and London, Brighton & South Coast railways, and followed a successful operation in 1904 when a couple of coaches had been run to Brighton and Eastbourne from Liverpool Lime St., having been detached at Willesden Junction from a Euston-bound express. In charge of an LBSCR engine they had run over the West London and West London Extension lines to Clapham Junction, and down the main line to Brighton.

The new train operated EWD year-round and the LNWR provided it with gangwayed sets including restaurant cars which ran in the Manchester London Road portion departing at 11.20am. At Crewe this section combined with coaches from Liverpool Lime St. which had left at 11am. A through portion from Birmingham New St. (dep 1pm) was attached to the train at Rugby. Stops were made at Willesden Junction and Clapham Junction but not at Kensington Addison Road. Arrival time at Brighton was 5.5pm, the train reversing there for the run to Lewes and Eastbourne. The up train left Eastbourne at 11.35am, Brighton, 12.25pm, and in this direction was routed via the Quarry Line rather than via Redhill. At Willesden Junction, connection was made into the 2pm 'Corridor' from Euston, and during the Rugby stop the Birmingham coaches were detached. The train became known as the 'Sunny South Special' during 1905, a name adopted by the LBSCR and by *Bradshaw* but not by the LNWR. The train's prestige – and level of patronage – was such that the LNWR provided new elliptical-roofed coaches in 1907 for the Liverpool/Manchester portions, these being of special 8ft 6in width to suit the Southern companies' loading gauges.

From 1905-7 there was a through coach to/from Leamington (Avenue) and, as from the summer 1905 timetable, north of Willesden Junction the 'Sunny South' had acquired two 'foreign' through coaches to Liverpool: a SE&CR vehicle from Deal and a LSWR coach from Bournemouth; both were altered by July 1908 to run to/from Manchester London Road. In the up direction, these two coaches first worked from London Road in a train featuring through coaches for the North & West Route to which at Stockport were attached through coaches from Colne to Euston. The Deal and Bournemouth coaches were then transferred at Crewe to an up North Wales express from which they were detached at Willesden Junction! The Deal coach was worked to Herne Hill to join Manchester/Bradford–Deal coaches on the MR service – qv.

Comparative trials were staged with the 'Sunny South' in October 1909 pitting an LBSC superheated I3 4-4-2T against an LNWR unsuperheated 'Precursor' 4-4-0. During the trials the engines worked out and back over the 264 miles between Brighton and Rugby and return, and the favourable showing of the 4-4-2T demonstrated the superiority of the superheated engine in terms of water and coal consumption. Normally engines were changed at Willesden Junction.

The 'Sunny South' continued running until March 1915.

Manchester and Bradford–Deal, Portsmouth and Southampton

From July 1905, the Midland and London & South Western railways co-operated to provide a rival to the Manchester–Kensington–South Coast workings known as the 'Sunny South Special'. A train was made up at Leicester, comprising a Deal coach brought that far in a Manchester–St Pancras express, with one for Deal and one for Portsmouth that had arrived on an express from Bradford, and a third contribution from Nottingham in through coaches for Southampton Town. Made up from these three sources, the train ran non-stop to Hendon. There, the Portsmouth and Southampton coaches set out behind an LSWR engine for their next stop at Richmond via the Dudding Hill line and the line from Bollo Lane to Kew Old Junction. Next calls were at Staines, Woking and Basingstoke to Eastleigh where the train split into Portsmouth and Southampton sections. The journey from Hendon to Portsmouth took 4hr.

The Deal coaches were worked from Hendon via the Widened Lines to Herne Hill and there joined the LNWR vehicles forming the Deal portion of the 'Sunny South' and those from Birkenhead (GWR), the combined train going forward at 3.2pm for Deal. Northbound, the general procedure was the same, and at Hendon the train was made up for a non-stop run to Leicester where the Manchester, Bradford and Nottingham coaches went their ways. Hendon was an awkward station at which to re-marshal trains, and the process seems to have delayed expresses from/to St Pancras.

In its next form, after July 1907 the train included a restaurant brake car, and at 11.15am departed Manchester Central for Portsmouth and the Kent Coast, running as before to Hendon. The Portsmouth/Southampton section of the train was withdrawn in October 1908, after which the Deal coaches continued in their Bradford–St Pancras express as far as Kentish Town. The Manchester–Deal coach went through to St Pancras, to be tripped to Kentish Town to join the Bradford section, and combined the coaches were worked to Herne Hill over the Widened Lines. In the reverse direction, the Midland coaches came up in a Victoria train as far as Herne Hill with an LNWR coach for Manchester London Road, and were then worked separately to Kentish Town. There the Bradford section was picked up by a down express, but that for Manchester Central was worked into St Pancras to be attached at the front of the 2.30pm express. This reached Manchester Central at the same time as the LNWR Deal coach was due to arrive at London Road! The through workings to Deal continued until the timetable cuts of February 1915 and did not reappear.

Midlands to North West
Leicester/Sheffield–Llandudno/Blackpool
The Great Central worked hard to promote travel from the Midlands and South Yorkshire by means of summer through expresses. From 1901, there had been a Leicester–Blackpool/Fleetwood train while in 1905 it was joined by one from Sheffield to Llandudno. From 1904 until 1912, a through coach was run to Aberystwyth from Leicester, Nottingham and Sheffield to connect with the Cheshire Lines' summer train from Manchester Central – see the **Cambrian Railways**.

The Midland Railway seemed less enterprising when it came to running similar holiday trains but a Sheffield–Llandudno summer service was introduced in 1910. For some reason this was not routed, as might be expected, via Marple and Manchester Victoria, but from the Hope Valley line turned south at the Chinley junctions to Buxton, there to be routed over the LNWR via Northenden and Warrington Arpley to the Chester line.

North East to South Coast
Oxford–Leicester/Newcastle–Bournemouth
The key to the cross-country trains jointly promoted by the Great Central Railway was the opening in August 1900 of the Culworth Junction (south of Woodford Halse)–Banbury Junction line. The first cross-country service over this link comprised two return workings between Oxford and Leicester which were usually worked by a Great Western engine and coaches.

Two years later – July 1902 – the Newcastle–Bournemouth train began life put on with the co-operation of the North Eastern, Great Western and London & South Western railways. It was difficult to find a suitable path for the train, particularly south of Oxford, but from 1891 the GWR had been running an

Oxford–Basingstoke train in early afternoon and its timings were appropriated. The main portion of the new express was formed of GCR coaches, and one of the gangwayed composites had a galley from which meals were served to adjoining compartments. There were also through coaches from Manchester London Road (later switched to Central station, and subsequently from Liverpool) and Bradford Exchange. At first, the GWR through coaches from Birkenhead to Bournemouth were attached south of Oxford which was the furthest point reached by GCR engines.

From 1902 until the service was withdrawn in 1916, the train ran both ways north of York via Sunderland and Stockton. In both directions, from 1905 the train by-passed Sheffield using the direct line from Rotherham to Darnall. The train was accelerated by an hour overall in July 1903, and further acceleration followed in the summer 1905 timetable. Use of the Scours Lane Junction–Reading South Junction link meant that the train was unable to serve Reading until 1906 when Reading West station was opened, largely for the benefit of cross-country travellers.

From October 1903 and up to and including the summer of 1906, south of Nottingham Victoria the southbound train included a through portion from Manchester London Road, dep 9.5am, to Deal. This was detached at Banbury, to be worked forward on the Birkenhead–Deal – qv. Northbound, the Deal coaches were taken forward to Woodford Halse by local train, there to be attached to the 4.35pm Marylebone–Manchester where they arrived at 9.40pm.

In 1911, the GCR built two 12-coach sets for the Newcastle/Manchester–Bournemouth workings.

York–Southampton
From October 1902, a Leicester–Southampton Town service was introduced, taking the Didcot, Newbury & Southampton line from Didcot and advertised as a connection for the evening sailings of the LSWR steamers to/from France. The next development, from July 1903, was to extend the usefulness of the trains by starting and terminating them at York. They now comprised sets of gangwayed GCR coaches including restaurant cars, departing at 7.5am from Southampton Town to Didcot and then running to Oxford and Banbury. In subsequent summers, the train was extended to Scarborough but in winter it terminated at Woodford where there was a connection into the 10am express from Marylebone to the North. In the reverse direction the coaches came from York at 2.47pm (Scarborough in summer), and arrived at Southampton in time for the

The earliest cross-country trains to work over the Great Central main line were those between Oxford and Leicester. This is a later, but nevertheless a rare view of the 9am Oxford–York, effectively a semi-fast train, due in York at 1.32pm and photographed on 15 April 1911 near Ashby Magna on the approaches to Leicester. The engine is Dean Single No. 3073 *Princess Royal* at the head of a rake of GWR non-gangwayed coaches, and horse-box.

steamer sailings but after an almost all-stations run from Didcot – 56¾ miles in 136min!

North West to Bournemouth
Manchester and Yorkshire–Bath–Bournemouth
Through coaches to/from Birmingham were introduced with the opening in 1874 of the Somerset & Dorset line from Evercreech through to Bath and two years later there were also through coaches between Bournemouth and Bradford, Leeds and Newcastle. These were conveyed on the Bath–Bournemouth fast trains, see **Somerset & Dorset**. During the 1900s there were other through coaches, at least in summer, between Bournemouth and Harrogate, Manchester and Southport via Derby. Four or so trains each way over the S&D featured year-round long-distance through coaches.

In April 1910 there was the 'North and Scotch Corridor Express', at 8.37am from Bournemouth West which advertised through coaches to Leeds and Bradford, to Birmingham and Bristol Temple Meads and a restaurant car to Derby. This train ran to Gloucester where the through coaches to the Midlands and North were attached to the 10.45am

Bristol–Leeds/Bradford, itself featuring through coaches to Glasgow. By moving down the train after Gloucester, Bournemouth passengers could ensconce themselves in the Glasgow coach which would reach its destination at 8.25pm. The 9.40am 'North Express' from Bournemouth conveyed through coaches from Bournemouth to Birmingham and Leeds, and ran to Cheltenham Queens Road where it combined with the 12.20pm from Bristol. In summer there was a faster 10.40am from Bournemouth which was non-stop from Poole to Bath, avoided Sheffield and connected at York for Edinburgh. Southbound, the principal express was the 2.13pm from Bath, non-stop from Bath to Poole, and with a restaurant car from Derby and through coaches from York. Through coaches from Bradford, Leeds and York were conveyed on the 4.4pm ex-Bath–Bournemouth while Newcastle coaches came from Bath on the 6.7pm down, a semi-fast train.

A major development came to the S&D from 1 October 1910 when the MR and LNWR co-operated in running a year-round service between Manchester London Road and Bournemouth West which was their response to the Birkenhead–Bournemouth train introduced that summer by the GWR and LSWR (with its through coaches from/to Manchester). That service had exposed the slowness of the MR route between Manchester, Derby and Birmingham used by the previous through coaches to Bournemouth, and so the new service ran over the LNWR between Manchester and Birmingham New St via Crewe. In spending no more than 105min for the 83½ miles it turned in the fastest yet scheduled time between the cities.

At New St, an MR engine came on to the train to run through to/from Bath Queen Square. The southbound train avoided reversal at New St. by continuing eastwards and travelling via Camp Hill to Kings Norton while the northbound train adopted a different manoeuvre to achieve the same end – but at the cost of by-passing Wolverhampton – in setting out eastwards by way of the Aston and Bescot loops, and rejoining the main line at Bushbury Junction.

Manchester–Southampton
Through coaches between Southampton and Bradford and Derby were worked over the **Midland & South Western Junction** and, with the introduction in October 1910 of the Manchester–Bournemouth service, this included a coach to/from Southampton.

Birkenhead–Oxford–Bournemouth
GWR through coaches between Birkenhead and Bournemouth were initially attached south of Oxford to the Newcastle–Bournemouth train, but in July 1910 they blossomed into a separate train which ran ahead of the Newcastle service. The initiative came as a result of the working agreement between the GWR and LSWR which had been signed in May 1910.

Two sets of coaches worked the train alternately, one GWR, the other LSWR. The Birkenhead–Bournemouth also conveyed GWR through coaches from Manchester to Bournemouth, routed via Crewe, Market Drayton and Wellington. These coaches provided a Manchester–Bournemouth journey some 40min faster than by the Midland/S&D route, and resulted in the LNWR and MR combining to introduce the Manchester–Birmingham–Bournemouth train – qv. The Birkenhead–Bournemouth was booked to run non-stop between Eastleigh and Oxford and over this section was worked each way by an LSWR T9 4-4-0.

North East to North West
Newcastle–Leeds–Liverpool
From 1883, a service between Liverpool Lime St and Newcastle was jointly operated by the London & North Western and North Eastern Railways via Stockton, Harrogate, Leeds New and Manchester. The through journey times were 5hr 10-30min. By 1898, there were trains leaving Newcastle in the early morning, 10am and midday, running non-stop between Leeds and Manchester. The 10am to Liverpool called at Sunderland, Wellfield, Stockton, Northallerton, Ripon, Harrogate, Holbeck, Leeds and Manchester, and reached Liverpool at 3.10pm. There was also a night mail from Liverpool to Newcastle routed via Warrington and Stockport.

In the April 1910 timetable there were Newcastle–Liverpool expresses at 7.30am, 10.8am, and 4.20pm (refreshment car to Leeds), and trains from Hull to Liverpool at 8.20am and 4.3pm. From Liverpool the times were 8.35am, 11am (also to Hull), 2pm, 4pm to Hull, 6pm, and 7pm to Hull. All Newcastle trains were routed from Leeds via Wetherby, Harrogate, Ripon and Stockton and journey times throughout were usually over 5hr. *Bradshaw* indicated that 30min could be saved if through passengers from/to Newcastle changed at York and Leeds.

Newcastle–Wakefield–Liverpool
An express each way between Newcastle and Liverpool was operated by the NER and Lancashire & Yorkshire Railway. These were routed via York, Normanton and the Calder Valley main line. In April 1910, the down train was the 10.55am from Liverpool, and the up working was the 12.35pm Newcastle–Liverpool, both conveying restaurant cars and using the East Coast Main Line via Durham and Darlington. The L&YR supplied one train set, and the NER the other. Journey time throughout was 4hr 53min northbound, 4hr 40min southbound, some 40min faster than by the NER/LNWR Newcastle–Liverpool expresses – qv. At York, where the engine changed from L&YR to NER and vice versa, the station stop usually occupied 20min, and it was arranged to give a connection into the 10am ex-King's Cross–Edinburgh, and out of the 10am ex-Edinburgh respectively.

Cross-Country Services 1914-23

Aberdeen–Penzance – East and West Coast
This service was one of the highlights of the dreary postwar period and followed the reinstatement in the summer of 1921 of the cross–country services using the Great Central's Woodford–Banbury line. The Aberdeen–Penzance train began on 3 October 1921, press trips having taken place over the previous couple of days, the Eastern group managers subsequently reporting that the press trip 'went off

well!' The service was jointly operated by the North British, North Eastern, Great Central and Great Western railways and was offered on weekdays only, over the 792¾ miles between the two terminals.

The Aberdeen–Penzance service did not run as an independent train for most of its journey but comprised through coaches which were worked on a series of trains in each direction, the only additional mileage being York–Swindon southbound, and Westbury–York northbound. To publicise the service, the Eastern group of companies paid for posters in red and green proclaiming the 'new through service Scotland to Cornwall', and promoted it along with the Edinburgh/Newcastle–Southampton/Bournemouth and Newcastle–Swansea services. The notes in the public timetable suggested that restaurant and sleeping cars were available throughout. This was not so. Southbound, 'by notifying any station master en route' before 3pm on the day of travel, sleeping car accommodation was available to passengers beyond Swindon on the 11pm Paddington–Penzance, to which the Aberdeen coaches were attached at Swindon. Northbound, a similar procedure had to be followed for the reservation of sleeping berths from York on the 7.30pm King's Cross–Aberdeen. On the sleeping car portions of the journey restaurant cars were not available.

The throughout journey time southbound was 21hr 55min, with departure from Aberdeen at 9.45am, then via to York, over the GCR main line to Woodford Halse and on to Banbury, Oxford and Swindon. From there the southbound coaches worked to Bristol Temple Meads, Taunton and Plymouth, and arrived at Penzance at 7.40am. The northbound working which was speedier, departed from Penzance at 11am, and differed by travelling as far as Westbury in a Paddington express. The coaches left there at 5.20pm for Swindon, the route onwards being as southbound, with arrival in Aberdeen at 7.40am the next day. In the northbound direction, from July 1922 an ingenious connection was provided by slipping a coach at Swindon from the 5pm Bristol–Paddington 2hr train which gave a faster journey time from Bristol to Leicester and Nottingham than by the Midland's West of England main line.

Passenger stock comprised a gangwayed brake composite working between Aberdeen and Penzance and vice versa, alternately a North British and Great Western vehicle; a gangwayed brake third York–Penzance and vice versa (GCR) and a restaurant car set and brake between York and Swindon, alternately North Eastern and GWR. The NBR built coaches specially for the service which were so used into the

Splendid spectacle as one of the Lancashire & Yorkshire Railway Hughes 4-6-0s, No. 1506, brings its company's prestige 11.5am Liverpool Exchange–Newcastle into York on 7 August 1911.

late 1930s. Their roofboards proclaimed: 'Aberdeen and Penzance via Edinburgh York Sheffield Leicester Swindon and Plymouth'. A through coach from/to Glasgow was later provided. Early in 1923, the London & North Eastern Railway agreed to build first-class sleeping cars for the working.

The publicity attracted by the East Coast and GWR service must have stung the West Coast to a reply for a new Penzance–Aberdeen service was advertised in the July 1923 timetable. Effectively this was an extension of the existing Aberdeen–Plymouth and Exeter–Glasgow through coaches. The northbound through coach departed on the noon train from Penzance to Bristol and Crewe via the Severn Tunnel and the North & West Route and was partnered by the existing coach for Glasgow. At Crewe, the Aberdeen coach was attached to the 7.40pm Euston–Aberdeen sleeping car express. The return working was on the 12.30pm from Aberdeen, the route being the same as northbound, with arrival at Penzance at 1.20pm (later on Sunday mornings). The value of the West Coast service came in connections made possible to/from Inverness, and to/from South Wales.

North West to South West/South Wales
North and West via the Severn Tunnel
By the summer of 1922, the number of through expresses remained at half a dozen each way between Bristol (or beyond) and the North of England via the Severn Tunnel and Shrewsbury, These usually ran to Manchester and Liverpool and there were additional services to/from South Wales. During World War I, the North & West services had not been greatly reduced until May 1918 when the 9.30am from Bristol and 11.40am from Crewe were withdrawn.

Among the principal trains over the North & West route in the 1922 timetable, as compared with 1914 there remained the mid-morning train from Liverpool (dep 9.10am) and Manchester London Rd–Plymouth, and the 1.25am from Crewe with its through coaches from Aberdeen to Plymouth. As in 1914, the 9.10am was followed just over 1hr later by another West of England service, the 10.35am Liverpool Lime St.–Plymouth, also with restaurant car. At midday, there was a third service from Liverpool, with through coaches to Taunton, and from Manchester and Birkenhead to Swansea. The 10 o'clock Glasgow–Euston brought a Glasgow–Plymouth through coach which was taken forward from Crewe on the 4pm departure which connected at Temple Meads into the 6.30pm Paddington–

Plymouth. As in 1914, the last of the southbound departures on the working on the route was the 8.17pm from Crewe, with through coaches to Bristol, and between Manchester and Cardiff.

Northbound, apart from the night mail, the first principal North & West train was now from Cardiff at 9.25am, with through coaches for Birkenhead and Manchester. This train was followed closely by the 9.45am from Bristol to Shrewsbury which took 2hr 56min for the 153 miles. There was then another South Wales/Bristol train, combining at Pontypool Road and going forward at 12.15pm to Manchester. The lunchtime Bristol–Liverpool train now departed at 12.32pm, and also gained a South Wales portion at Pontypool Road. There was now a 2.25pm from Bristol and Cardiff to Manchester and Birkenhead to emphasise the growth in services from South Wales. The midday service from Plymouth in the Summer 1922 timetable had through coaches from Truro and Newquay to Liverpool Lime St., and Truro–Birkenhead, with a restaurant car between Plymouth and Liverpool. The 7.20pm mail from Bristol included through coaches from Exeter to Glasgow, and a portion from Cardiff to Liverpool.

Although operating solely within GWR territory it makes sense to include another service using the North & West line. For the summer of 1922, and in contrast to what had been offered in 1914, the service between Birmingham and South Wales was strengthened and accelerated in each direction, the majority of trains routed not over the Honeybourne line, but via Worcester, Hereford and Pontypool Road. From Snow Hill, there were departures at 8am, 9.45am, and 5pm, the quickest of these trains taking 3¼hr for the 118 miles to Cardiff, and compared with the 164min journey time of the 9.20am to Cardiff via Honeybourne. From South Wales, the three trains routed via Pontypool Road were less speedy than westbound, but the 8.15am from Cardiff was advertised as an 'Irish and South Wales Express' and connected out of the early morning boat train from Fishguard. The GWR managers considered the results good enough for the summer 1922 trains to be continued in the winter timetable.

Sheffield–Bristol/Weston-super-Mare
In place of the GCR/GWR express from Leeds and Manchester to Bristol and the West Country, from July 1922 there was a summer restaurant car train at 8.55am from Sheffield Victoria via Oxford and Swindon to Weston-super-Mare (arr 3.10pm). It returned at 8.48am to reach Sheffield at 3.34pm.

An evening service from Bristol to GC main line

services was catered for by the slip coach connecting with the Penzance–Aberdeen – qv, and there were night trains between Swindon/Bristol and York – qv.

South Coast to South Wales
Portsmouth–Cardiff
After World War I the service was improved until there were two trains each way to/from Cardiff, and three to/from Bristol Temple Meads. Overall times were not impressive: the best Bristol–Portsmouth timing was 4hr 5min – by the 7.35am Portsmouth–Bristol–Bridgwater – but more usually entailed 4½hr journeys. The 5.25pm Portsmouth–Cardiff took 4hr 50min overall, but the other trains took up to 5½hr.

From the July 1922 timetable, the 11.30am from Cardiff was given a restaurant car and extended to Brighton (arr 5.42pm). At Salisbury it picked up coaches from Ilfracombe and then ran from Romsey via Eastleigh to Portsmouth & Southsea where it gained through coaches from Bournemouth West to Brighton. The combined train then set out for Brighton and there were stops to set down at Chichester, Barnham, Ford and Worthing. The return working for Cardiff was at 11.20am from Brighton with through coaches for Bournemouth West which were detached at Portsmouth & Southsea to run as a separate train from there. Routed via Eastleigh, the Cardiff train detached its Brighton–Ilfracombe coaches at Salisbury, and reached Cardiff at 5.45pm.

North East to South West/Wales
Newcastle/West Riding–Bristol/Torbay
Through trains were restricted to the night mail in each direction, with 7pm departures from Newcastle and 7.20pm from Bristol, going forward on the Leeds and Newcastle Mail from Birmingham New St. From October 1921, through coaches were worked on the 7.35am Newcastle–Sheffield, then on the Bradford–Torquay/Paignton train – qv. On the return, departing at 2pm from Bristol, the Newcastle coaches travelled to Chesterfield on a Bradford train and ran separately from there over the 'Old Road' to Rotherham and York.

In July 1920, the MR and GWR jointly introduced a Bradford–Torquay/Paignton through train, with MR restaurant cars in each direction although the other stock was alternately provided by the MR and GWR. This train became the 'Devonian' in later years. In the Summer 1922 timetable it left Bradford Market St. at 10.12am with through coaches for Bournemouth, and ran via Leeds to Sheffield Midland where it divided. The first section called only at Derby, Birmingham New St., Cheltenham

and Gloucester and reached Bristol at 3.40pm. From there, the Bradford coaches were attached to the 10.20am Liverpool Lime St.–Plymouth which had come over the North & West route.

The second section left Sheffield with the Bournemouth coaches, shed at Gloucester, made more stops and eventually reached Bristol at 4.52pm. Northbound, the express left Paignton at 9.25am and ran independently to Bristol. From there to Leeds, the only intermediate calls were at Gloucester, Cheltenham, Birmingham, Derby and Sheffield. Bradford was reached at 6.35pm, after a journey of 322½ miles which was scheduled to take 9hr 10min, only 44min slower than the 'Devonian's' best (southbound) time of the late 1930s.

Newcastle–Barry
Reintroduced as from July 1920, the service retained its prewar routing via Banbury and Cheltenham. Charlewood said that there had been a proposal to re-route the train via Birmingham and Gloucester by the Midland route but that the GCR had fought to retain the train on the grounds that the company had built new stock for the service before 1914.

Compared with 1914, intermediate timings were slower, particularly north of York. The service was provided with a restaurant car and Great Western and Great Central Railway sets of coaches alternated. As noted in **South Wales railways**, the train was later extended to/from Swansea via the Vale of Glamorgan line and, by July 1922, was leaving Newcastle at 9.30am, and arriving at Cardiff at 6.40pm, and Swansea at 8.45pm. The northbound times were Swansea 7.30am and Newcastle, 6.45pm. The Hull portion of prewar days was not reinstated but in both directions the train now conveyed coaches between Newcastle and Bristol. Early in 1923, the south and northbound trains were being worked by a GWR Mogul between Swindon and Leicester and return.

Other through trains between the West Country and the GC main line included the 9.5pm Swindon–York (arr 2.40am) and the 10.3pm York–Bristol, the latter avoiding Sheffield Victoria by way of the Darnall curve and then following the usual route via Leicester and Oxford with arrival at Bristol Temple Meads for 5.52am. At Grouping, both trains were worked out and back between Swindon and Leicester by a 'County' 4-4-0.

North West and West Midlands to Channel Ports
Birkenhead–Dover
By October 1916, the Birkenhead–Deal service had been withdrawn. It reappeared on 10 July 1922, this

time as a full train with restaurant car and another distinction, as its sets of seven GWR coaches were among the first to be painted in chocolate and cream livery, which had been abandoned in 1909 in favour of a single-colour scheme. Also seat reservations were available. The GWR's Passenger Train Services Committee commented: 'It is proposed to reinstate the service between Birkenhead and Dover via Reading. This service was popular in 1914 and it is confidently expected that it will again be successful.'

Departing from Birkenhead at 8am, and Birmingham Snow Hill at 11am, four coaches including the restaurant car went through to Dover Marine, arr 4.30pm (rather than Priory station, in order to connect with cross-Channel steamers) and the remainder were detached at Ashford and worked through to Canterbury West and Ramsgate Town where there was a reversal, to reach Margate Sands at 4.54pm. The northbound journeys started from Dover at 9.45am and Margate Sands at 9.25am, the coaches in that portion being attached at Ashford. Birkenhead was reached at 6.20pm. To and from Guildford the train carried a through coach from Bournemouth to Dover – see **London & South Western Railway**. On the SE&CR, the engine taking over from the GWR at Reading General was usually a Stirling F1 4-4-0.

Cross-country to East Anglia
Harwich–York/Liverpool
On revival after World War I, the train's working was changed. Instead of working to/from York, the main section with Great Eastern Railway restaurant cars ran to and from Manchester Central and Liverpool Central. The through coaches for Liverpool Exchange via the Calder Valley line were discontinued.

Leaving Harwich Parkeston Quay at 8.2am, the coaches for Birmingham New St. were detached at March. From there, the train called only at Spalding before Lincoln, reached at 11.58am. With reversal at Manchester Central, the train terminated at Liverpool Central at 3.20pm. The eastbound journey started from that station at 2.30pm and, with the same calls as the outward working and the addition of the Birmingham coaches at March, Harwich Town was the destination, reached at 9.51pm. At this stage, the train's operation involved an inordinate amount of engine changing which was to be amended just before Grouping when a portion for York was introduced, with a through coach for Glasgow. At first, the York portion was worked to Sheffield in the down direction but this was soon altered, such that

the coaches were detached at Sleaford and worked to Grantham where they were attached to a down East Coast express. The up York portion ran via Sheffield, to be joined there to the main part of the train.

York–Lowestoft and Manchester/Liverpool to Lowestoft GC/GE
The York–Lowestoft Central through coaches of prewar days had developed into a through restaurant car train leaving at 10.25am, and arriving at its destination at 4.46pm. It was now worked on the first stage of its journey by a North Eastern engine as earlier in 1922 the allocation of a Great Eastern engine to York had ceased. The return train, also with restaurant car throughout, left Lowestoft at 10.5am and arrived in York at 4.33pm. Both trains had their origins in Liverpool St.–York trains withdrawn during World War I.

In the summer 1922 timetable, the seasonal Liverpool Central–Yarmouth Vauxhall and Lowestoft Central restaurant car train reappeared and in much the same timings as those of 1914: 11.5am from Liverpool, and 11.30am from Manchester, with return at 12.10pm from Yarmouth and noon from Lowestoft. The booked time at Manchester London Road was 6.12pm, and for Liverpool, 7.15pm.

North West to South Coast
The 'Sunny South Special'
The first manifestation of the service after World War I came in December 1921 when through coaches from Liverpool and Manchester were attached at Crewe to a Holyhead–Euston express, to which also had been added a restaurant car which travelled from Crewe to Eastbourne. At Rugby, coaches from Birmingham were attached and the train ran to Willesden Junction where it was remarshalled. The London coaches went forward on their own, and the rest of the train departed for Kensington, East Croydon, Brighton and Eastbourne which was reached at 4.50pm.

In the northbound direction, the prewar departure times from the South Coast resorts were adhered to. Having reached Willesden Junction, the train departed independently for Rugby. After cooling their heels for 30min, the Liverpool coaches went forward on the 2.30pm Euston–Liverpool, but that was nothing compared to the Manchester coaches which contemplated Rugby for an hour before going north on the 2.55pm Euston–Manchester via Stoke. The restaurant car was advertised between Eastbourne and Rugby only.

On 15 March 1922, the 'Sunny South' reappeared

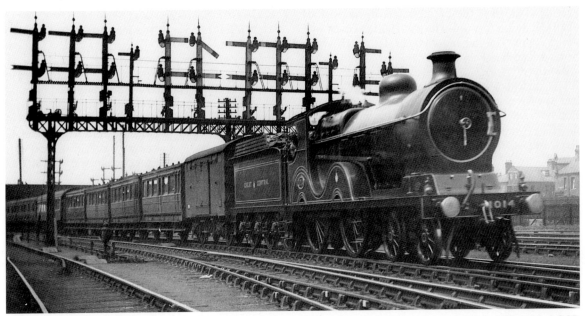

Great Central cross-country: the 9.25am to Manchester London Road leaves Hull Paragon on 22 June 1920 behind GCR 4-4-0 No. 1014. At the front of the train are four GCR saloon coaches, no doubt used for a special party, but behind them is a GCR elliptical-roofed coach.

in something like its old form (except that it would not regain through coaches to/from Bournemouth) becoming a separate train south of Crewe where the through coaches from Liverpool and Manchester had been combined. From 12 June 1922, the 'Sunny South' gained through coaches for Whitstable and Ramsgate Harbour via Chatham. In this summer service the train no longer called at Rugby but took the Northampton line. Meanwhile, the Birmingham coaches had left New St. at 12.30pm with a restaurant car for Ramsgate Town, and called at Rugby before reaching Northampton Castle where the two trains were remarshalled, the SE&CR line coaches being placed at the rear. With a load of 13 coaches including two restaurant cars, the 'Sunny South' set out for Willesden Junction where it split into two sections – Brighton/Eastbourne and Ramsgate.

In the northbound direction, the Ramsgate section (dep 11am) was first to reach Willesden Junction and ran forward separately to Northampton. The Eastbourne train kept to its original departure times and arrived at Northampton 14min behind the Ramsgate section. There the trains were reformed into a Liverpool/Manchester train, and one for Birmingham New St. At Crewe, the respective portions for Liverpool and Manchester were then added to expresses from Euston for the final leg of their journey. Despite its complexity and expense,

this pattern of operation was carried forward into Grouping.

North East to South Coast

Newcastle–Bournemouth

The first revival of the Newcastle–Bournemouth service came in the 1921 timetable when there was a peak summer 11.50am Bournemouth–Sheffield via Oxford and return working. That October, the service was extended to run to/from Newcastle. The Manchester coach of prewar days had been discontinued and instead there was one from/to Bradford Exchange, worked to Sheffield on the 9.55am Marylebone express. The GCR restaurant car set alternated with one supplied by the LSWR.

From Newcastle, the Bournemouth coaches formed part of the 8am to King's Cross and so avoided the time-consuming detour of prewar days via the Durham coast. Having gained a restaurant car, the train ran separately south of York which was left at 10.13am. It took the East Coast Main Line and called at Selby on its run to Sheffield Victoria. From there, and over the GC main line and from Oxford southwards, the train followed the pattern of prewar working and arrived at Bournemouth West at 6.28pm. Departing from there at 11.50am, the train followed the route and calling stations of the southbound working but ran direct from Sheffield over the S&K line. The Bradford coach came off at Sheffield, to go forward with the Halifax coach off the 3.20pm Marylebone–Manchester, both then being detached at Penistone.

North of York, the Newcastle section were combined with Midland coaches from Bristol (which had spent most of their journey on a train with Bournemouth–Bradford coaches!), to travel along the East Coast Main Line and to an arrival in Newcastle at 10.5pm.

York–Southampton

This GCR/GWR service was reinstated in 1921, the innovation being through coaches to/from Edinburgh and Glasgow. As before, the main objective was to make connection with steamer sailings from Southampton to Le Havre and the Channel Islands.

Leaving Southampton Town at 7.35am with through coaches for Scarborough and Glasgow Queen St., the northbound train was once again routed over the Didcot, Newbury & Southampton line, calling at all stations to Didcot and Oxford where at last it became something like an express and a restaurant car was added. Over the GCR main line and to York it remained a separate train but there the Glasgow coach was attached to the 11.20am King's Cross–Glasgow. In winter, the service was cut back to York only.

The southbound train left York at 3pm. It consisted of coaches for Southampton, a restaurant car as far as Oxford, a Glasgow coach which had got to York on the 8.40am Glasgow Queen St.–King's Cross, and one from Scarborough. From Oxford, the train was routed via Reading West and Basingstoke, and arrived at Southampton Town at 10.46pm, the journey from Oxford having taken 30min less than the DN&S route used by the northbound train.

At Grouping, in both directions the train was worked between Banbury and Sheffield by one of the recently built GCR 9Q 4-6-0s.

North West to Bournemouth

Manchester and Yorkshire–Bath–Bournemouth
Although the full express service was still running over the Somerset & Dorset in December 1914, the through services were gradually withdrawn during the war such that only the through coaches to/from Bradford were continued, conveyed on the 9am from Bournemouth and the 2.50pm from Bath. In May 1919, a 11.5am Derby–Bournemouth through train was introduced. As related in **Somerset & Dorset**, the pattern of through trains was well-established before Grouping.

Manchester–Southampton

See **Midland & South Western Junction Railway**.

Birkenhead–Oxford–Bournemouth

Withdrawn in October 1915, the train was restored in May 1919 (the restaurant car was reinstated the next month throughout between Birkenhead and Bournemouth), and for a while ran non-stop – as it had done in 1914 – between Oxford and Eastleigh, but a stop at Winchester was substituted for Eastleigh. The Manchester portion was not at first included.

In the Summer 1922 timetable the train left Birkenhead Woodside at 7.35am and, after reversal at Chester, called at Wrexham, Shrewsbury and Wellington before Wolverhampton Low Level. There, the portion from Manchester London Road (dep 10.15am) was attached and the train went forward on its prewar route to Bournemouth West, to arrive at 5.30pm. Northbound, the train left at 9.45am and, after calling at Boscombe, Christchurch and Southampton West, ran non-stop, if not very speedily, from Winchester to Oxford, in 91min for 58 miles. At Wolverhampton, the train split into Birkenhead (arr 5.27pm) and Manchester (arr 6.25 pm) portions. One curiosity was that at Crewe the Manchester portion was attached to the Bournemouth/Swanage–Manchester coaches which had travelled by the S&D and whose throughout journey was 40min faster!

Calls were later added at Reading West and Basingstoke.

North East to North West

Newcastle–Leeds–Liverpool
As in 1914, all postwar Newcastle–Leeds–Liverpool trains ran via Harrogate, Stockton and Sunderland. Somewhat surprisingly, the service received new rolling stock in 1917 when the London & North Western built two six-coach sets, the coaches being to 52ft 6in length and 8ft 6in width to suit North Eastern requirements and they were also dual-fitted for haulage by NER locomotives. In the Summer 1922 timetable, there were through trains from Liverpool Lime St. at 8.35am – in 5hr 48min – and at 2.10pm – 1min faster – and from Newcastle at 10am – 5hr 15min overall – and at 4.17pm – taking no less than 6hr 26min. None of these trains conveyed restaurant cars. They were supplemented by three Hull/Leeds–Liverpool trains in each direction.

Newcastle–Wakefield–Liverpool
See **Lancashire & Yorkshire Railway**.

CHAPTER NINE

THE GREAT WESTERN RAILWAY FROM 1923

Through 1923 and 1924 traffic generally improved, the Railway having extended its winter train service as late as July in 1922 because of the 'prevailing depression in trade'. The main improvements in the Summer 1923 timetable had been to Paddington–West of England and Paddington–Birmingham–Birkenhead expresses, the latter having been accelerated by cutting out some of the station stops north of Wolverhampton. But the masterstroke of publicity was the decision to accelerate the 2.30pm Cheltenham St James–Paddington to cover the 77¼miles from Swindon in 75min, at an average speed of 61.8mph. This gave the GWR the fastest train in Britain. On the inaugural working of 9 July 1923 'Saint' No. 2915 loaded to nine coaches reached Paddington 3min early.

The major development in the early years of Grouping came with the July 1924 timetable for which the timing and diagramming sections of the passenger manager's office had combined to achieve more intensive diagramming of engines and rolling stock which had resulted in a 'saving' of 35 locomotives and 79 coaches. One aspect of these changes was that longer through workings by engines were introduced, such as Paddington–Carmarthen and Paddington–Chester. The standardisation of starting times from London and from provincial centres was a major feature of the recast express services. 'Numerous complaints' at the altered train timings were anticipated by the passenger train services' committee who noted that 'satisfactory compensatory services have been arranged wherever possible'.

From July 1924, Birmingham and the North trains left Paddington at 10min past the hour (9.10, 10.10, 11.10am, 2.10, 4.10pm, 12.10am, also 7.45pm); Bristol trains at 15min past (7.15, 9.15, 11.15am, 1.15, 5.15pm, but there were also Paddington–West of England services at 30min past, eg 4.30 and 6.30pm and slip coaches off Fishguard trains); West of England (or Weymouth) via Westbury trains at 30min past (5.30, 9.30, the 10.30am 'Cornish Riviera', 12.30, 1.30, 3.30pm and 12.30am, also the 'Torquay Limited' at noon); West Midlands and Worcester line at 45min past (9.45am, 12.45, 1.45, 4.45, 7.45pm); South and West Wales at 55min past (8.55, 11.55am, 1.55, 3.55, 4.55, 5.55, 7.55pm and 9.15pm, also 12.55am). From the 'provinces', the Birmingham departures of Birkenhead/Wolverhampton expresses were on the hour; from Bristol to Paddington at 15min past, but with several additions such as the 7.45am business express, and West of England–Bristol–Paddington trains; lastly, the departures from Cardiff of West/South Wales–Paddington expresses were at 15min past, eg 6.15, 8.15, 10.15, 11.15am, 1.15, 3.15, 5.15pm, and 6.35 and 10.42pm). Sunday services were not generally included in the scheme but the 10min past and 30min past departures from Paddington held good.

Over the years, these times were generally held to but by 1939 there were some noticeable exceptions to the so-called clockface departures. One influence was the uncertain demand for passenger services during the period. This ensured that new services introduced for the summer service and which might have been expected to continue into the winter often

Holiday traffic grew on the Cambrian lines in GWR days. This shows an up train with a mixture of GWR and LMS coaches, no doubt bound for Paddington and Manchester London Road. The engines are 4575 class 2-6-2T No. 5541 and a 'Dukedog' 4-4-0 in this late 1930s' scene.

fell by the wayside. Even the 'Cheltenham Flyer' was withdrawn during the 1928/9 winter timetable.

In addition, there were numerous special and excursion trains. Pride of place went to the boat trains connecting with transatlantic liners which ran from Plymouth Millbay to Paddington. Fast runs were made in 4hr or less from 1924 or so, and the trains became more prestigious still when some fine new first-class 'Super Saloon' coaches were built in 1929/31. By contrast, although continuing to be served by boat trains for the Rosslare and Waterford sailings, Fishguard had been shunned by the transatlantic liners and the Irish traffic was adversely affected by the Troubles.

Whereas the other Big Four companies were content to let slip coach workings decline and did not bother to build new vehicles the GWR not only maintained its services but built new stock, particularly for prestige workings such as the Weymouth slip off the 'Cornish Riviera'. In 1914 there had been no less than 70 slips on the GWR, but there was still the respectable total of 44 in 1927, the majority made at Reading and Westbury. Some slips gave a wide range of connections to wayside stations and country branch termini as they were worked from the point where they were slipped to a convenient destination, typified by the slip

introduced in 1927 at Didcot off the 11.15am Paddington–Bristol, and which provided a fast service to Oxford, and connections to a handful of branch lines.

The GWR made much of the 'Cornish Riviera' which was afforded attention and publicity which exceeded that for all the other services combined. With the advent of the powerful 'King' 4-6-0s, the non-stop run from Paddington to Plymouth was reduced to the level 4hr from September 1927, and the new class was strongly promoted in all GWR publicity. Yet the record for the longest regular non-stop run in Britain, as made by the 'Cornish Riviera', passed to the LNER in the same year. Generally speaking, the GWR was not unusual among the Big Four in having shown little improvement in the journey times between Paddington and the main cities and towns when comparing 1927 with 1914. Only to Chester and Cardiff was there any measurable reduction in the *fastest* times made but on the GWR there remained an appreciable disparity between the principal trains and the 'also-rans', even on the Paddington–Bristol service.

As with the other companies, the GWR also went in for naming its trains during 1927, including the title 'Belfast Boat Express', at first sight inexplicably bestowed on the 4.10pm Paddington–Birkenhead

An up Torbay express passes Taunton in 1930 behind 'King' 4-6-0 No. *6014 King Henry VII*. The rake of coaches looks smart and is composed of the GWR's 57ft 'bow-ended' stock, with one of the company's articulated triplet restaurant car sets as fourth, fifth and sixth coaches in the formation.

Woodside and 9.5am return but both trains were advertised as convenient for the Belfast sailings to/from Liverpool. Named at the same time was the summer 10.10am from Paddington to Pwllheli and Aberystwyth which became the 'Cambrian Coast Express' and at this stage ran FSO. Other namings were straightforwardly publicity-seeking such as the 'Shakespeare Express' which was one component of an 11hr rail/road excursion from Paddington to Stratford-upon-Avon and back in the summer of 1928; it was repeated in 1931, at least, when special luggage labels were part of the attraction of travelling on the 9.25am from Paddington. In the winter of 1928/9 third-class sleeping cars were introduced on the Paddington–Penzance and West Wales overnight trains.

The preferential status of principal trains received special attention in the Summer 1929 timetables when the 'Torbay Limited' made the fastest time from Paddington to Exeter, just 173min, and reached Torquay in 3hr 30min. Newly equipped with 60ft coaches, and celebrating its silver jubilee, the down 'Cornish Riviera' now took 6hr 20min to Penzance, and included coaches for Falmouth and St Ives. The up 'Riviera's' timings were unaltered. One innovation was an all-Pullman express to Torquay and Paignton on Mondays and Fridays only, leaving

Paddington at 11am but slower by 10min than the 'Torquay Limited'. The service proved disappointing and perhaps gave the GWR an opportunity to demonstrate to Pullman that there was no real market for supplementary fare travel on its territory.

But grabbling the headlines that July was the acceleration of the 'Cheltenham Flyer' to run from Swindon to Paddington in 70min, at an average speed of 66mph, thereby becoming the world's current fastest start to stop train schedule. The 8am Cheltenham–Paddington had been introduced as a new service the previous year, but in the July timetable was booked for a smart daily run non-stop to town from Kemble in 89min for the 91 miles.

All the Big Four offered something in the way of worthwhile improvements in the Summer 1929 timetables but it was the GWR which boasted the biggest reduction in its fastest times as compared with 1914. But these were by crack trains only. In some cases, longer non-stop runs had been discontinued in favour of additional stops, some in place of slip workings, but the train's overall schedule was unaltered. In this way, the last Birmingham Snow Hill–Paddington non-stop run was eliminated with the Summer 1929 timetable. On the harder duties of the times the 'Stars' were hard-put to keep time for, as yet, sufficient 'Castles' were unavailable and, when they were, at holiday times they were often worked to their limit on West of England trains that frequently loaded to 500tons. The additional power of the 'Kings' was essential for such workings.

But the international economy was to take a nosedive shortly, and to relieve growing unemployment the Government introduced the Loans and Guarantees (1929) Act by which the railways could take advantage of the state paying the interest due on capital expended on development schemes. The GWR reacted swiftly and produced an impressive shopping-list including improvements to principal stations, quadrupling in the Taunton area and in the Birmingham suburbs, and the construction of cut-offs at Westbury and Frome to speed holiday expresses to the West. The last-named projects combined with the remodelling of Aller Junction, the provision of additional block sections west of Exeter and the completion of doubling the Cornish main line (except over Saltash bridge) to smooth the passage of trains, to which traffic was attracted by midweek excursion fares introduced in 1929. By the mid-1930s, summer Saturday train loadings were

burgeoning. There was a group of six West of England trains which set out from Paddington within the space of 45min, all booked to run non-stop to Newton Abbot. There was heavy traffic elsewhere, too, on high summer Saturdays such that the Wolverhampton–Penzance sometimes ran in four parts.

Whatever the peak summer traffic, passenger receipts as a whole were falling and in 1931 were 9% below those of the previous year. The only solution was to make the main line expresses more attractive and their acceleration continued. By the Summer 1931 timetable the GWR had more trains than any of the other Big Four companies operating to mile-a-minute timings and 73 daily runs, totalling 5,820 miles, booked at 55mph or over, all distributed over the main express services. From September 1931, the 'Cheltenham Flyer' was further accelerated, and now took 67min from Swindon, at an average speed of 69mph, and once more justified its self-proclamation as 'The World's Fastest Train.' Record runs followed, culminating during June 1932 in *Tregenna Castle's* 56¾min sprint to Paddington. In September 1932 the 'Flyer's' schedule was cut to 65min, for a

The 'Torquay Pullman Limited' lasted only for one season as an all-Pullman car train, and the following summer – 1930 – just five cars were run, attached to through Paddington–Kingsbridge coaches. The down train is seen here at Powderham, with 'Castle' 4-6-0 No. 4075 *Cardiff Castle* at the front end.

train that usually loaded to six or seven coaches. Sometimes extra coaches might be attached for parties that had toured Swindon Works and than timekeeping could be problematic.

Probably more testing for the locomotive and crew was the retimed 3.30pm Paddington–Plymouth which, from September 1932, took 150min for the 142¾ miles to Taunton including a 3min stop at Westbury. Accelerations continued through the worst of the Depression, and by the winter of 1934 there were three trains with mile-a-minute schedules (or better) between Swindon and Paddington. The 8.55am Worcester–Paddington featured two 60mph timings (between Moreton-in-Marsh and Oxford, and from there to Paddington) and as such was unique when first introduced during 1934. For some time longer this train was worked by one of Worcester shed's 'Stars'.

Signs of economic recovery included the retention in the winter 1934 timetable of the 9.40am Paddington–Cheltenham and 4.20pm return, first introduced that summer. Indications of increasing traffic had begun the previous year when, for the first time in the 1930s, there had been an increase in booked passenger train-miles over the year before.

The much lower operating costs of diesel railcars allowed the introduction of experimental services such as the two workings each way between Birmingham Snow Hill and Cardiff which started in July 1934. They were retained during the succeeding winter and new services were introduced between Bristol and Cardiff from the winter of 1936. But overall prospects were still uncertain and, although services were expanded in the Winter 1935/6 timetable, the tide changed again the following year when some fledgling trains were again withdrawn after the summer.

With the centenary of the GWR came the introduction of the 'Bristolian', and the provision of the splendid 'Centenary' stock for the 'Cornish Riviera Limited' which, from the Summer 1935 timetable, reverted to its old title and ran in two parts. The first of these made no passenger stop before Truro (engines were changed at Devonport) and reached Penzance in 6¼hr, the fastest timing on record. The second part assumed the historic title of 'Cornishman' and was non-stop to Plymouth in 4hr 1min. It conveyed the Weymouth slip portion and arrived at Penzance 20min after the 'Limited'. A similar arrangement – without the slips – applied for the up workings. Also notable in the new timetable were the 25min acceleration of the 7am from Weston-super-Mare to Paddington, 30min saved on

the schedule of the 9.45am Paddington–Worcester, and a 145min timing for the new 4.10pm Worcester–Paddington buffet car express.

The 'Bristolian' began running Mondays–Fridays only from 9 September 1935, at 10am from Paddington to Bristol Temple Meads via Bath in 105min, and 4.30pm return, routed via Badminton in this direction. At first hauled by a 'King' and with no more than standard gangwayed stock, the next year the 'Bristolian' moved to 'Castle' haulage and the GWR's latest 'Sunshine' coaches. But time was not always kept. The same timetable brought a 120min timing via Badminton for the 5.5pm Paddington–Bristol–Plymouth, and a new 9am Penzance–Paddington. Out went the 'Cornishman', for the second part of the 'Cornish Riviera Limited' now became a Torquay and Kingsbridge train with the usual Ilfracombe, Minehead and Weymouth portions of the old 10.30am down.

This burst of improvements was not sustained up until the outbreak of World War II. For instance, the only significant change in the Summer 1937 timetable was a new express at 6.55pm from Paddington to Cardiff, booked over the 133½ miles to Newport in 137min, the fastest yet by a passenger train but equalled by a newspaper train, some of those on the GWR being notably speedy. The 6.55pm was extended to Fishguard Harbour in the Summer 1938 timetable and with just the Newport and Cardiff stops was booked in the record timing of 3hr 45min for the 191 miles to Swansea High St. In the Winter 1937/8 timetable the 8.55am Paddington–Fishguard Harbour was accelerated by 31min, largely by cutting out intermediate stops.

More tightening-up of timings was repeated in the same timetable, particularly on the Birmingham line, but it was nothing exceptional. In reply to criticism, the GWR argued that if a 105min schedule were introduced between Paddington and Birmingham the load of the train would have to be restricted to 300tons and left it at that, forgetting perhaps that the 'Bristolian' loaded to 220tons only. That seemed to point to some limitations to steam performance, and coincidentally the GWR commissioned a report into the case for electrifying all lines west of Taunton; the basis of its estimates was considered unsound and the study was pigeon-holed. Operating costs were a matter of concern as freight traffic declined, and the Winter 1938/9 timetable brought retrenchment with the cancellation of the 6.55pm Paddington–Fishguard Harbour (but restored the next summer), of the 4.25pm Cheltenham–Paddington (which had disappeared briefly from the scene a couple of years

'Saint' 4-6-0 No. 2903 *Lady of Lyons* works an up express past Taplow in 1938, and its train includes some of the GWR's 'Sunshine' stock.

earlier, but had also reappeared in Summer 1938), of cross-country trains between Swansea and Manchester, and two out of the three West of England expresses each way over the Honeybourne route, leaving only the Wolverhampton–Penzance. That line retained its Birmingham–Cardiff diesel railcar expresses. Had war not intervened it seems likely that operating economies would have been made by a wider substitution of diesel railcars for steam workings, particularly as an order for 20 railcars had been placed in 1938.

World War II brought a number of changes to operations, one minor development being the cessation of GWR engine workings from Chester via Warrington to Manchester Exchange, various classes including 'Halls' and 'Saints' having made regular appearances on this jointly-worked service. From late August 1939, a major programme for the evacuation of schoolchildren from urban areas went ahead, and over the next month the normal public services were greatly reduced. From 25 September 1939, the GWR brought in its first wartime

timetable, with widespread curtailments and those that remained were decelerated as all expresses were restricted to a start-to-stop average speed of 45mph. At first, all West of England trains were diverted via Bristol, the 10.30am, for instance, being expected to cater for traffic which had been accommodated on three former departures. The Wolverhampton–Penzance and return expresses were discontinued. Withdrawn at the start of war, a limited number of restaurant cars were restored in October, and shortly afterwards the Westbury route was opened to the West of England expresses.

Once the prospect of invasion had receded, some main line services were reinstated during the summer of 1941, particularly to/from the West Country, and speed limits were relaxed. But the need to free the South Wales main lines for additional coal trains meant that trains from Paddington and Bristol–South Wales were temporarily suspended. A number of other withdrawals came with the winter 1941/2 timetable although the 'Cornish Riviera' now ran in two parts, the second being a Torbay train, and

A Birmingham–West of England express leaves Wickwar Tunnel behind 'Castle' 4-6-0 No. 4032 *Queen Alexandra* on 14 April 1938. The distinctive train reporting numbers had become a familiar sight in the last summer Saturdays before the war, and interchangeable metal plates were carried in a frame affixed to the locomotive's smokebox. Main trains, such as this one, had numbers ending in '0' or '5'.

generally the Bristol line and West of England services were kept independent. Wartime passenger timetables were somewhat inconsistent in that services were inexplicably unbalanced, for example, the up service from Oxford to Paddington was much more frequent and faster than on the down line. Also the up service to Paddington from Exeter was much the better.

During the spring and summer of 1946 there were improvements to GWR main line services. Through express trains over the Honeybourne line were restored after a gap of almost seven years, and the Paddington–Bristol service included three expresses non-stop to Bath in 115min for the 107 miles (not unconnected with the naval presence there) and slip workings recommenced. From Paddington to Plymouth, the 10.30am was running non-stop in 4hr 30min and the noon Torbay express from Paddington was booked in 3hr 10min to Exeter. Altogether there were 21 weekday non-stop runs of 100 miles or over.

CHAPTER TEN

THE SOUTHERN RAILWAY

The newly formed company faced numerous problems in trying to weld a unified system from individualistic constituents. Possibly the 1923 summer timetable had been largely planned before Grouping, but there were a number of touches that owed something to the new management. Some noticeable accelerations came to the Waterloo–West of England services, the 3pm down being retimed to arrive in Plymouth 30min earlier, and through journeys by this and other trains to elsewhere in Devon, and to Cornish destinations, were made faster. The Portsmouth line gained additional expresses, apart from the usual seasonal trains, and on the Isle of Wight the train service was remodelled to provide even-interval workings on the main routes. On the Brighton section, again there were new trains to Brighton, Eastbourne and the West Sussex resorts, in addition to seasonal additions. On the Eastern section, a new residential train came into Cannon St at 8.36am from Ramsgate Harbour (dep 6.35am) thereby relieving the existing train which was retimed to leave Margate at 6.56am. Additional expresses to Dover and Folkestone were accompanied by a new 80min train to Folkestone at 1pm from Charing Cross. One aspect of Grouping was the appearance of two trains each way on weekdays (and one on Sundays) between Folkestone, Margate and Brighton.

The process of integrating facilities increased, and the facilities were improved within the Brighton and Chatham sides of Victoria station which came under unified management during 1924. In October 1924, the London–Paris services formerly operated by all three constituents were co-ordinated to give the best results. The Summer 1924 timetable was the first produced under the new Chief Operating Superintendent and had two main features: all fast London–Portsmouth services now worked from/to Waterloo, and the best London–Hastings trains ran via Tonbridge and Tunbridge Wells. The downgrading of the former Brighton route services via the Mid-Sussex to Portsmouth and to Bexhill and Hastings aroused a storm of protest and better services returned to both lines with the Winter 1924/5 timetable.

Some practices of the former constituents persisted for although the last three slip workings on the Chatham lines disappeared during 1924, those on the Brighton line at Horley (for stations to Forest Row) and at Haywards Heath (for stations to Brighton) were retained on two residential trains from London Bridge until 30 April 1932, just before the Three Bridges electrification. Apart from an established pattern of main line, residential and suburban services, the Southern inherited a wide range of other workings: boat trains to Dover, Folkestone, Gravesend, Newhaven and Southampton to connect with sailings to French ports, Ostend and Rotterdam; ocean liner specials to Southampton Docks, and a variety of occasional workings to the 23 racecourses served by the Railway.

Before more could be done to make the most of the network, physical unity had to be achieved, notably by eliminating awkward features of the once competitive lines in Thanet, in particular rationalising the four stations in Ramsgate and

Non-gangwayed stock forms this Saturday Waterloo–Portsmouth train approaching Surbiton on 28 August 1926 behind LSWR T14 class 4-6-0 No. 460.

Margate. In July 1926, a new connecting line was opened, just under 1½ miles in length, joining the former South Eastern and Chatham lines, and accompanied by a new station at Ramsgate, an improved station at Margate and new locomotive and rolling stock depots at the former. Apart from modern and larger stations, fast services were reorganised so that the basic services ran from Victoria to Ramsgate via Chatham and Margate, and the existing Charing Cross–Dover trains were extended to Margate via Deal; there were other workings from Ashford via Canterbury. In summer, there were even some trains which ran through from one London termini to another via Thanet. A smaller rationalisation scheme at Dover concentrated non-boat train traffic at a rebuilt Priory station.

Less dramatic at first sight was the bridge-strengthening programme, authorised in 1924 and which saw over 100 underline bridges renewed over a period of three years to permit use of 4-6-0s, particularly on boat trains. Work was concentrated first on the Victoria–Bickley loops–Tonbridge–Dover line, completed by July 1925; then on the Catford loop, and via Swanley, Maidstone and Ashford, finished by the end of the next year, while the most expensive part of the programme featured the line via Swanley, Chatham and Canterbury, dealt with by Summer 1927. This led to the use of the new 'King Arthur' 4-6-0s on the boat trains, the new L1 4-4-0s meanwhile having displaced the SE&CR Ls on the Charing Cross–Folkestone 80min expresses, these being the 4.15 and 7.15pm from Charing Cross, and the 11am and 5.10pm up from Folkestone Central.

During 1926, similar bridge-strengthening on the Brighton main line meant that 'King Arthurs' were also passed to work to Brighton, Eastbourne, Newhaven and Worthing. Unhappily, the scale of the full bridge renewal programme was such that resources were diverted from track maintenance as the Sevenoaks accident of 1927 made all too apparent, largely because both the South Eastern and Brighton had used shingle rather than rock ballast and, in any case, laid their track on an inadequate formation. An extensive programme of reballasting was necessary to rectify matters. All told, though, the Southern had achieved its aim to bring all three constituents' main lines to something approaching a common standard.

Some of the operating problems at the London termini were mitigated by the resignalling in 1926 of Charing Cross, in the London Bridge area and at

The Southern Railway built 2-6-4Ts for main line passenger work, such as 'River' No. A797 *River Mole,* seen passing Merstham on 27 August 1926 with a Victoria–Eastbourne express. The train consists of non-gangwayed ex-LBSCR coaches, and two Pullman cars.

In due course, the 'Rivers' found out the weak spots in the track, with tragic results and loss of life, as seen here near Sevenoaks on 24 August 1927. The accident forced the SR to undertake improvements on its permanent way. Wrecked beneath the overbridge is Pullman car *Carmen,* rebuilt in 1920 from one of the 'American' cars built for the SER in 1891.

Charing Cross station with E class 4-4-0 No. 1176 departing with a Pullman car train for Ashford on 14 July 1937.

Cannon St. As a consequence of all this activity improvements to main line services were held back until the various components had been completed and new motive power was delivered. On the Brighton line, the arrival of the newly named 'King Arthurs' and also the 'River' 2-6-4Ts saw the transfer from Brighton of the Marsh Atlantics, to work the London expresses from Eastbourne and Bognor. A larger engine was in prospect, the SR's traffic manager having decided that there was a requirement to haul 500 tons at an average speed of 55mph. As events turned out, the target was unrealistic, and in any case the resultant 'Lord Nelson' 4-6-0s were unable to meet it consistently. The new engines were concentrated on the Eastern Section for the boat trains, with two only initially used on Waterloo–West of England services. When the boat traffic declined during the Depression, the Western Section's allocation was made up to six.

The pride of the Western Section was the 'Atlantic Coast Express', so named as from 19 July 1926. The train was duplicated on summer weekdays, except on Saturdays when during the 1920s the total increased to five or six trains. The 10-coach formation in winter comprised three coaches for Ilfracombe (two brake thirds and a composite), a brake composite each for Torrington, Plymouth, Padstow and Bude, the restaurant cars going to Exeter Central, and a brake composite each for Exmouth and Sidmouth. Hauled usually by a 'King Arthur', and more rarely by a 'Nelson', the 11am 'ACE' was booked to Salisbury in 90min, then non-stop in 87min over the 75¼ miles to Sidmouth Junction (where the Exmouth and Sidmouth coaches were detached), to arrive at Exeter Central for 2.22pm. There the train split into two sections: for Ilfracombe/Torrington, and to Okehampton where the Plymouth and North Cornwall portions divided. By the winter of 1928/9, the 'ACE' had also gained a coach for Honiton, detached at Salisbury and taken on by a semi-fast train and so providing a service for intermediate stations. This made the 'ACE' the most 'multi-portioned' train in Great Britain.

From November 1924, the Dover Continental boat trains had included an all-first-class Pullman car express at 10.45am from Victoria, known by no more exalted title than the 'Continental Express'. Its coaches wore the Pullman umber and cream livery at a time when all other cars on the South Eastern Section retained their crimson-lake paintwork. The normal load of the 10.45am was nine cars, and two vans and two flat-trucks loaded with containers, all conveying registered luggage. In the 'low season' the formation included non-Pullman stock, the second part of the train otherwise having the ordinary first and second-class accommodation – the SR having retained the latter for boat train services – and its own Pullman cars. For the 78 miles to Dover Marine the schedule was 98min, the 'King Arthur' normally diagrammed to this working being cleared to take a 425-ton load.

On the French side of the Channel, a new Pullman car service had been introduced in 1926, known as the 'Flèche d'Or' (Golden Arrow). With the delivery in 1929 of the ss *Canterbury,* a new SR steamer designed for first-class passengers only, a through 'Golden Arrow' service was inaugurated on 15 May 1929. Departure from Victoria was now 11am, and the schedule to Dover still 98min but smart work thereafter and the French customs inspection on the train got the luxury travellers to Paris Gare du Nord for 5.35pm. With the decline in Continental travel after the onset of the Depression, the luxury overland service lasted only a short time in its original exclusive form. In the winter of 1931/32, the *Canterbury* became a two-class ship and third-class accommodation was included in the 'Golden Arrow'.

The SR then turned its attention to the Bournemouth/Weymouth line, still much as it had been in 1921. With the Summer 1929 timetable, four 2hr expresses were reinstated for the first time since 1914, and the whole service was overhauled. The standard non-stop time from Waterloo to Southampton West became 89min, and 90-92min in the up direction while the overall time to Bournemouth Central by these one-stop trains was 130-135min. All express trains had a restaurant car attached – 26 in all, as compared with six in 1914 – and new gangwayed stock was introduced.

The flagship of the new service was the 2hr 'Bournemouth Limited' which ran first on 8 July 1929 when it was worked by 'Lord Nelson' No. E860 *Lord Hawke*. The usual engines working the accelerated Bournemouth trains were 'King Arthurs'. The Bournemouth line services were worked by the so-called 'Ironclad' gangwayed stock delivered from 1921, and increased in number in 1924/5. Apart from the addition of some new open third coaches from 1930, the Bournemouth sets changed little. In the

previous few years new gangwayed stock had been built for the Eastern Section's Thanet services (1924/25); West of England expresses (1926/28); the 'City Limited' (1925); for Worthing/Eastbourne services and the Newhaven boat set (1927); Folkestone (1929/31) and Hastings services (1929/31); and principal workings to Portsmouth and to Littlehampton (both 1930).

New rolling stock and locomotives revolutionised the style of the SR's principal passenger services even though timings were largely unaltered. In April 1930, 'Schools' class 4-4-0s began to take over the Charing Cross–Folkestone/Dover expresses from L1 4-4-0s, and made their debut on the London–Eastbourne trains to join a variety of ex-LBSCR express engines. By late 1931, the easing of curves and reballasting of track between Tunbridge Wells and Hastings allowed 'Schools' to work on this line.

The SR was also gearing itself up for main line electrification, and in 1930 General Manager, Sir Herbert Walker, presented the Coulsdon–Brighton/Worthing scheme to the SR Board, the plans providing for a 150% increase in train-miles operated. Also included was the largest colour-light signalling installation so far envisaged in Britain.

Pullman services returned to the former South Western lines early in 1931 on the Waterloo–Southampton Docks ocean liner boat trains, the cars having been transferred from ·the unsuccessful 'Torquay Pullman' – see **Great Western Railway**. A regular Pullman service followed on 5 July 1931 with the introduction of the 'Bournemouth Belle' at first daily in summer only, from Waterloo at 10.30am and non-stop to Bournemouth Central in 129min. It terminated at West station, from where the return journey started at 6.8pm, the Waterloo arrival being 8.30pm. In its first summer, except on Sundays the 'Belle' ran through to Weymouth where it arrived at 1.45pm, and departed at 4pm. Before long, a stop was inserted in the schedule at Southampton Central. In its first winters, the 'Belle' ran on Sundays only but, from 1 January 1936 became a daily year-long service, and the return journey was advanced to a 4.35pm departure from Bournemouth West.

Attempts to develop new sources of traffic were not always successful. The opening in May 1932 of the Allhallows-on-Sea branch from Middle Stoke Junction, east of Gravesend, at first looked promising and through coaches were run from London, but traffic declined quickly although through excursion trains ran as late as the 1950s. In contrast, the electrification to Three Bridges, the first stage in the electrification to Brighton, was

The Southern Railway ran a vast number of special trains every year. This is the 11.45am departure from Waterloo for Southampton Docks on 13 September 1931, to take passengers to join the SS *Leviathan*. Motive power is U class 2-6-0 No. A611.

inaugurated in July 1932 and was instantly successful. By 1932, the SR was able to point to a more reliable fleet of locomotives – monthly failures were down from 167 in 1923 to 46 – while more than three times as many gangwayed coaches were now in service.

The electrification to Brighton and Worthing was inaugurated on New Year's Day 1933, one basic feature being a train from Victoria to Brighton every hour from 9am to midnight every day of the week, on the hour and in an hour (some running times were 55min). Immediately prior to electrification there had been just seven down 60min trains, by then worked by 'King Arthur' 4-6-0s and the ex-LBSC Baltic tanks. The former departed to the Eastern

Section to replace 4-4-0s from some of the main line duties, and the latter were transferred to Eastbourne where they took command of express services. Baltic No. 333 *Remembrance* had worked the final steam working at 12.5am from Victoria to Brighton on New Year's Day itself. Displaced Atlantics were drafted to Bognor for the principal London services over the Mid-Sussex line. At the London end, the Brighton electrification brought the closure of Battersea shed, and transfer of its engines to the nearby Stewarts Lane.

Also ushered in by the New Year's Day 1933 timetables was the fastest time on record between Victoria and Eastbourne, 80min each way by the 10.45am 'Eastbourne Sunday Pullman' and its return working, and an equally good 82min by the 5.6pm from London Bridge to Eastbourne, including a stop at Lewes. Also new was a fastest ever scheduled run from Waterloo to Salisbury, in 87min non-stop by the 3pm from Waterloo; the insertion of a stop at Templecombe had spurred the timetable planners to shave time from the first stage of the journey.

In the July 1934 timetable, the Bournemouth line expresses were accelerated by 15min or so throughout to Weymouth, most of the time having been saved west of Bournemouth, or from the Bournemouth stop. The 'Bournemouth Limited' was accelerated to a 3hr timing each way between Waterloo and Weymouth. The next summer, the 'Bournemouth Limited' was accelerated to a 118min timing between Waterloo and Bournemouth Central each way, at an average speed of nearly 55mph, and the timing to Weymouth was similarly cut by 2min. October 1934 had seen the restaurant cars on the 'Limited' altered to run to/from Bournemouth West instead of Weymouth. In the Summer 1936 timetable, the process continued: a 116min booking for the down 'Bournemouth Limited', and to Weymouth in 174min, while the up 'Bournemouth Belle' was put on a 2hr timing, Southampton stop included. There were accelerations to the schedules of the semi-fast Bournemouth trains, and the

introduction of more or less regular 20min past departures of fast trains from Southampton to Waterloo.

With electrification of the Waterloo–Portsmouth services, the displaced 'Schools' migrated to Bournemouth in 1937 where they replaced 4-6-0s, and soon proved a great success on the 4.30pm down and 8.40am up 'Bournemouth Limiteds' which they worked to/from Weymouth. For this working and the 12.30pm from Waterloo and 5.37pm from Weymouth, refurbished Maunsell gangwayed stock was put into service from 1938, repainted, like the engines, in malachite green.

During 1934, six new 'Schools' had been allocated to Fratton shed to work between Waterloo and Portsmouth, and shortly afterwards were joined by another four. The result was to see the acceleration of the Portsmouth service from the Summer 1935 timetable when one down (11.50am) and two up trains (9.57am and noon) were put on 90min timings between Portsmouth & Southsea and Waterloo and the other best timings, with one or more stops, came down to 94-103min, some 6-12min faster than before.

At the same time, the down 'ACE' was put on an 87min timing to Salisbury, in common with the 3pm down, and now reached Exeter in 3hr 12min; the up train was 2min faster. The fastest time to Exeter (and

Residential trains between Thanet and London were running in late SE&CR days, let alone the Southern years. This is the 6.16pm Cannon St.–Ramsgate of 17 August 1931, with D1 class 4-4-0 No. A545 making smoky progress near Grove Park. Its train comprises the Thanet stock built by the SR soon after Grouping.

to Plymouth) was made by the 1.30am down newspaper train, in 3hr 9min; until the summer of 1939, this service was not publicly advertised east of Salisbury. More time-cutting followed in Summer 1936: an 86min schedule to Salisbury for the 10.35am North Devon section of the 'ACE' which now reached Exeter in the unprecedented time of 3hr 7min, and a fast overall timing to Ilfracombe of 4hr 57min. By late 1930s' summer Saturdays the down 'ACE' might run as nine separate trains departing Waterloo between 10.24am and 12.9pm. In the summer 1936 timetable the 7.20am from Exeter was now due in Waterloo at 10.59 instead of 11.10am, and the 10.28am reached Waterloo at 2.1pm, 8min earlier. Improvement came to the Plymouth–Brighton train in 1939 when it was retimed to leave 1hr later and to stop at Templecombe to connect to Bournemouth.

The main feature of the July 1935 timetable had been the start of electrified services between London and Eastbourne and, again, there were hourly departures for most of the day; with portions of the trains going forward to Hastings and Ore. With the introduction of the electric services came the decision, strongly criticised at the time, to curtail the through trains between the Brighton line, Ashford and the Kent Coast.

By the late 1930s, the Kent Coast services had undergone fewer changes than elsewhere on the SR. The fastest train between Victoria and Ramsgate in each direction took 110min with Margate and Dumpton Park as the only intermediate stops, but most trains also called at Bromley, Chatham and Faversham. The Sunday 'Thanet Pullman Limited' had been withdrawn with the Summer 1931 timetable. The expresses from Charing Cross to Folkestone and Dover continued round the coast to Thanet, with a best time of 150min. In summer, both Tonbridge and Chatham main lines were considerably busier, with the operation of a myriad of extra and excursion trains: in 1938, there were 29 down and 21 up extra trains in the Saturday timetable for the Tonbridge line. Among the through trains from outside the Eastern Section was a summer Sunday Kingston-upon-Thames–Ramsgate train which ran from 1930 to 1937.

By the mid-1930s the Continental traffic through Dover and Folkestone had picked up again. New business was encouraged by the introduction of the train ferry service between Dover and Dunkerque, the planning for which had started in 1932 although operations did not commence until 1936. Included was the 'Night Ferry' through sleeping car express

from Victoria to Paris Gare du Nord, featuring British loading gauge cars which were provided by Wagons-Lits. This service began on 14 October 1936 with the 10pm Victoria departure, and the next day with the 21.50 from Gare du Nord. Arrival in Paris was 8.55, and in Victoria, 8.30am.

The 'Night Ferry' soon loaded heavily. On Maundy Thursday, 1937, for instance, it was run in two portions – the first with the sleeping cars, the second with ordinary passengers. Closely following these were five portions of the 11pm Ostend boat train from Victoria, and a chartered special from Cannon St., all feeding into two sailings from Dover, one being the train ferry. Two other specials ran from Cannon St. to Folkestone Harbour for another sailing to Ostend. The weight of some of the boat trains caused problems, the 'Night Ferry' usually being double-headed with a pair of 4-4-0s. In 1938, Bulleid received Board sanction to build ten new express engines. In the same year, renovated standard stock went into use on the 'Golden Arrow'. Another VIP service started in 1937 when the Southampton Docks ocean liner expresses began to include Pullman cars for the passengers of flying boats using the base at Hythe, and from 1939 independent lightweight Pullman specials ran from/to Victoria.

Electrification schemes transformed the services between London and Portsmouth. The first, the Portsmouth No. 1 scheme, took in the former LSWR Portsmouth Direct line via Woking and Haslemere, and regular services between Waterloo and Portsmouth Harbour began on 4 July 1937. No. 2 scheme electrified the Mid-Sussex line from Dorking to Bognor, Littlehampton and Portsmouth, and the new timetable came in on 3 July 1938. One consequence of the increased service on the Portsmouth Direct line was that the through Bournemouth–Guildford trains were diverted to run via Winchester and Alton instead of via Fareham, Cosham and Havant.

A financial case could not be made for one major electrification scheme as in March 1938 the SR announced that the scheme for the Tonbridge–Hastings line would not proceed. Late 1938 saw the SR predicting electrification of the Oxted line to East Grinstead and Horsted Keynes. By this time the Brighton Atlantics were in use on Oxted line services including the 7am Brighton–Lewes–London Bridge, and the 3.55pm Victoria–Brighton/Eastbourne which ran non-stop to Oxted.

Until 11 September 1939, the SR continued to work normal summer services, but thereafter services were curtailed and decelerated, only to be

The last of the truly 'main line' electrifications carried out before 1939 by the Southern was the Mid-Sussex line. This typical down express over that route is leaving Sutton in the mid-1930s, headed by ex-LSWR L12 class 4-4-0 No. 430 with two Maunsell gangwayed sets in tow.

partially relaxed the following week and cut back again the following month. During this period, and for some time after, the SR was operating some of the fastest trains in Great Britain, having retained some schedules requiring 50mph average speeds; generally, the Railway had slowed its services less than the other Big Four. From late 1939, midday services on the Dover, West of England and Bournemouth lines were absent so as to allow troop and freight services to run. Loads on the Bournemouth line, for instance, increased to 16/17 coaches. During 1941, to provide more paths for military specials, some of the West of England services were combined, and then loaded to as many as 20 coaches on which Bulleid's new 'Merchant Navies' proved their mettle. All Western Section expresses now stopped at Woking in each direction, but even in these dark days there were accelerations, such as by a new 12.15pm Exeter–Waterloo introduced in the summer of 1941 which reached Waterloo 58min ahead of its previous schedule. Some intermediate timings of the West of England trains were particularly demanding given the heavy loadings involved.

With peacetime, the SR was quick off the mark in reintroducing prestige trains, if less so in restoring prewar schedules. From 15 April 1946, the 'Golden Arrow' began running again, complete with the new *Trianon Bar* car, but now taking 100min to Dover Marine. The first Paris–Victoria run of the 'Night Ferry' took place on 14/15 December 1947. Now made up to ten Pullman cars, the 'Bournemouth Belle' recommenced on 7 October 1946, at first to a 125min timing to Bournemouth Central and 120min in the up direction, but there were new trains as well. The most remarkable was the 'Devon Belle' which made its first run on 20 June 1947, FSSuMO initially, at noon from Waterloo and running to Wilton South where the Nine Elms and Exmouth Junction 'Merchant Navies' were changed over. Stopping only at Sidmouth Junction, on reaching Exeter Central the train divided into Plymouth and Ilfracombe sections, the latter including one of the unique Pullman observation cars. Both sections were taken on by 'West Country' Pacifics. The timings were 5hr 32min to Ilfracombe, and 5hr 36min to Plymouth Friary.

A fourth all-Pullman train was added on 31 May 1948 in the shape of the 'Thanet Belle'. That summer

The transfer of the 'Schools' to the Bournemouth line in the late 1930s resulted in some very lively running. No. 930 *Radley* approaches Byfleet in 1939 with a Waterloo–Bournemouth West express.

the train set out daily from Victoria for Ramsgate at 11.30am, but not Saturdays when it was retimed to 3.5pm. The down timing was 124min. The return journey started at 5.5pm, except Saturdays and Sundays when it was 6.15pm.

The Southern's postwar image was noticeably stronger than the other Big Four, not only on account of shrewd publicity and its fleet of Pullman workings, but bolstered by the eye-catching Bulleid Pacifics, and that designer's handsome gangwayed coaches with their attractive body profile, large windows and comfortable, well-planned interiors.

CHAPTER ELEVEN

THE LONDON MIDLAND & SCOTTISH RAILWAY

The first LMS timetable issue in April 1923 featured worthwhile accelerations of some of the principal services. A 3hr 30min timing was brought in for the 9.45am Manchester London Road and 6.5pm return from Euston, a 3hr 40min schedule for the 5.55pm Euston–Liverpool, and 4hr 5min for the 8.55am Birkenhead–Euston. In the 1923 summer timetable, the 5.20pm from Liverpool was accelerated to reach Euston at 9.5pm. That same timetable ushered in faster Anglo-Scottish services, the 10am down now arriving at Glasgow, Edinburgh and Aberdeen 15min earlier, the 1.30pm down into Glasgow and Edinburgh 10min earlier, and the 7.30pm and 11pm down sleeping car trains no less than 65min faster to Inverness, with similar improvements on the up trains. A connection off the 10am down and 2pm up Glasgow Anglo-Scottish trains was provided via Carlisle for the day sailings to Larne for Belfast. The Midland line Scottish trains were also accelerated.

In the Summer 1923 timetable, the Euston–Birmingham–Wolverhampton service gained an 8.30am down to Birmingham stopping at Coventry and taking 140min to Birmingham, and another 2hr train, up at 8.20pm from Birmingham. By late 1923, a Midland Compound was being tried out on the 2hr trains, and by the next year several of the class were at work between Euston and Wolverhampton, to be pitted against 'George Vs' and superheated 'Precursors'. These LNWR engines probably did better on the 270-ton loads of the hardest turns such as the 9.10am from Euston and 4.50pm from New St., with their 109min timings between Willesden Junction and New St.

During 1924, LMS-built Compounds began working on Euston–Manchester expresses via Stoke and via Crewe but the ex-LNWR 4-6-0 classes prevailed until 'Royal Scots' and 'Patriots' arrived in the early 1930s. Of the expresses, the up 'Mancunian' departed London Road at 9.45am behind a Fowler 2-6-4T, the train taking the Styal loop. On arrival at Wilmslow, a 'Royal Scot' would be waiting to work forward to Euston with the East Lancs and Halifax coaches which it had brought from Stockport. The 'Mancunian' was joined in January 1928 by another named train, the 'Lancastrian', which left Euston at 6.5pm and ran to Wilmslow where the East Lancs coaches for Colne and Halifax via Manchester Victoria were detached, together with one for Rochdale via Stockport, Ashton Oldham Road and Oldham Mumps. A return working left Rochdale at 8.45am for Stockport and was attached at Wilmslow to the up 'Mancunian'. The through coach from Euston to Northwich, Altrincham and Manchester London Road, which had been detached at Crewe from the 2.30pm down Liverpool, seemed to have ceased in 1927.

When the down 'Lancastrian' was accelerated to a 3¼hr schedule in September 1932, it lost the Rochdale and East Lancs coaches which were then worked north on the 6.10pm Preston train, detached at Crewe and taken forward separately to Stockport. The up 'Lancastrian' was the 12.5pm Manchester London Road–Euston via Stoke, this routing ensuring that a 'Claughton', and later a 'Patriot' or a 'Jubilee', was used as these were the heaviest classes permitted on the Potteries main line. An East Lancs portion was added to this train at Stockport.

The 4pm 'Mancunian' from Euston makes a fine sight on Camden bank as it begins its journey to Manchester London Road with 'Claughton' 4-6-0 No. 5913 *Colonel Lockwood* in command.

The 12.5pm Manchester London Road–Euston ran via Stoke-on-Trent and so was worked by a rebuilt 'Claughton' – as here – and later a 'Baby Scot' or 'Jubilee'. The express is seen near Wembley on 30 June 1934 behind No. 5993. Three of the new steel-panelled LMS corridor coaches are in the train.

The named Manchester expresses were joined in 1932 by the 'Comet', a name applied to the 11.50am from Euston. This train called at Crewe where a Liverpool portion was detached, then Stockport, and was due in London Road at 3.20pm. The up 'Comet' was the 5.40pm from London Road, routed via Styal, calling only at Stafford, and reaching Euston at 9pm. By the mid-1930s, the down 'Lancastrian' often loaded to 16 coaches on Fridays and Saturdays, and was then too long for London Road platforms so that the rear six coaches were detached at Wilmslow, to be worked forward by a tank engine. Another heavy train was the 10.30am Euston–Manchester/Liverpool which in the late 1920s often loaded to 15/16 coaches and was worked by a 'Royal Scot'.

A revision of the Euston–Liverpool service took place during the summer of 1929. The Liverpool portion of the 10.30am to Manchester/Liverpool was retimed to leave at 10.40am, had all its stops excised except Stafford, and was accelerated by 15min to a 3hr 35min schedule, the first to this timing since the World War I decelerations had affected the 5.55pm down. The running of a separate train seems to have been confined to summer only. The 8am from Liverpool lost all its stops except Mossley Hill – the Liverpool suburban calling-point – and Crewe and was now 20min faster to Euston while the 9.45am 'Merseyside Express' started 15min later and ran non-stop from Mossley Hill to Euston, but maintained its former arrival time. All told, the average time of the six expresses each way was improved by 6-10min to 3hr 53min. In 1932, the down 'Merseyside Express' and down 'Lancastrian' swapped departure times from Euston, so the former now left at 6.5pm and was booked to Mossley Hill in 3hr 20min, then called at Edge Hill to detach the through coaches for Southport.

Despite a reduction of traffic to/from Ireland during the Troubles, the LMS improved facilities at Holyhead station from 1925, but traffic levels were severely reduced and the 1.20pm and 10.15pm boat trains from Euston were never to be reinstated. From the autumn of 1927, through engine workings were instituted between Euston and Holyhead, using unrebuilt 'Claughtons'.

On the Midland Division improved connections were offered to Bradford in the Summer 1923 timetable, and restaurant cars were included in the 11.45am St Pancras–Harrogate and the 12.3pm up. From March 1925, the LMS introduced the 'Yorkshireman', the 9.10am Bradford Exchange–St Pancras and 4.55pm return, these expresses being routed via Low Moor, Heckmondwike Central and the Thornhill Junction–Royston Junction line to Sheffield, with an overall timing of 4¼hr. For the new working, a set of open vehicles was introduced, with an at-seat service of meals from a kitchen car. All were newly built vehicles, apart from the ex-MR clerestory brake opens at each end of the train.

Having acquired the London, Tilbury & Southend to gain access to Tilbury Docks, the Midland Railway left it to the LMS to try to develop rail/steamer services. Using secondhand LMS steamers from the Irish Sea services, a shipping company associated with the LMS launched a Dunkerque–Tilbury steamer service in May 1927. The LMS then advertised a St Pancras–Paris service, with connecting trains (initially provided with restaurant cars) to/from Tilbury via Barking and the Tottenham & Hampstead line, with a departure at 10.30pm from St Pancras. Travellers left Gare du Nord, Paris at 8pm. A through coach was provided c1927/28 between Tilbury and Glasgow St Enoch, conveyed on the 9.50am from St Pancras which at that stage was referred to by the LMS as the Continental Boat Express. From 1932, the Southern Railway bought out the LMS's share in the shipping line working to/from Dunkerque, and transferred the service to Folkestone. Thereafter, the only boat trains between St Pancras and Tilbury Docks were for cruises and ocean services, a traffic that increased markedly in the early 1930s.

Workings through Manchester Victoria changed very little from those of 1922 during the first years of Grouping, the longer distance express services being dominated by the Hughes 4-6-0s and L&YR's 2-4-2Ts working the shorter distance trains. The Club train to Blackpool remained, by 1930 made up of the low-waisted LMS coaches, open stock and two L&YR club saloons. A new Club saloon was built by the LMS in 1935. There was also a club train to Windermere from Victoria, and a Llandudno train from Exchange, both these Manchester stations now coming under the same station master.

With the enthusiasm shown by all Big Four companies at the time, the LMS named a number of its expresses during the summer and autumn of 1927:

the 'Royal Scot, 10am Euston–Glasgow Central/ Edinburgh and 10am return;
the 'Mid-Day Scot', the 1.30pm Euston–Glasgow Central/Edinburgh and 1.30pm return;
the 'Night Scot', the 11.45pm Euston–Glasgow Central sleeping car express and 10.30pm return;
the 'Royal Highlander', at 7.30pm from Euston–Inverness – the title was not carried in the up

The East Lancs side of Preston station with ex-L&YR 4-4-0 No. 10129 waiting to depart with the Liverpool Exchange portion of the 10.20am ex-Glasgow Central on 14 September 1930.

direction but the corresponding up train was the 4.15pm ex-Inverness;

the 'Thames–Clyde Express', 11.45am St Pancras–Glasgow St Enoch and 9.20am return;

the 'Thames–Forth Express' 9am St Pancras–Edinburgh Waverley and 10.5am return; the 'Irish Mail', applied to the 8.30am and 8.45pm Euston–Holyhead and to the 12.13am and 12.18pm return;

the 'Ulster Express', the 6.10pm SX, 6.40pm SO Euston–Heysham and 5.48am return;

the 'Yorkshireman' retained its title;

the 'Mancunian', the 9.45am Manchester London Road–Euston and 4pm return;

the 'London–Merseyside Express' (from 1928 the 'Merseyside Express'), at 10am from Liverpool Lime St–Euston and 5.55pm return;

the 'Lancastrian', at 12.5pm Manchester London Road–Euston via Stoke and the 6.5pm return;

the 'Sunny South Express', 'Pines Express' and 'Devonian' – see **Cross-Country services**.

Seasonal trains receiving names were the 'Welshman', the 11.10am Euston–North Wales, and the 'Lakes Express', the 11.35am Euston–Windermere/Keswick.

The train naming inspired a designation for the new LMS 4-6-0s introduced in 1927 to work the heaviest West Coast expresses which were beyond the

capability of the Midland-design Compounds in anything but favourable conditions. By late 1927, the 'Royal Scots' were at work on their namesake, and heading the 'Mid-Day Scot' and Liverpool expresses. The 'Royal Scot' itself was still under the influence of the 8¼hr schedule laid down in 1900. In the October 1923 timetable the Glasgow and Edinburgh portions of the train ran separately north of Crewe but, other than the introduction of LMS standard coaches the train had remained unchanged until March 1925, from when it ran in two portions throughout, at 10am from Euston for Glasgow only, and 10.8am for Edinburgh, Aberdeen and Dundee.

With the naming of the service from 11 July 1927 new stock was introduced, the train once more combining the Glasgow and Edinburgh portions, running non-stop to Carnforth for an engine change, and then on to Symington where the 'Royal Scot' divided. Similar arrangements applied for the up run. Once the 'Royal Scot' class was diagrammed to work the train, the first stop to change engines became Carlisle Citadel, and the inaugural working took place on 26 September 1927 using No. 6100 *Royal Scot.*

The LNER had announced its intention to run non-stop from King's Cross to Edinburgh from May 1928, and on the Friday before this was to take place – 27 April – the LMS divided the 'Royal Scot' with each portion, to Glasgow and Edinburgh, running non-stop, an audacious spoiling effort directed at the LNER. With the Summer 1928 timetable, the Carlisle stop was moved to Kingmoor on the down 'Royal Scot' and No. 12 signal box on the up, and the LMS's new low-waisted stock was introduced to the train, including some luxurious if unpopular lounge brakes.

The long non-stop runs ceased for the Winter 1928/9 timetable, the train then calling at Rugby, Crewe, Carlisle and Symington, with Aberdeen and Dundee (and, except for October–May, one for Stranraer) coaches detached/attached at Crewe. There were restaurant cars in each of the Glasgow and Edinburgh sections. The overall time was 7hr 55min. The pattern was now set for the winter and summer working: non-stop to Carlisle in summer, but otherwise four intermediate calls were made.

From May 1932, the 'Royal Scot' was accelerated to 7hr 40min to Glasgow, and that winter the time was 7hr 55min. From 1934, the train ran in two portions throughout on Saturdays, and Fridays, too, from 1935. By 1937, division of the up train had become a regular feature throughout the week in summer. Timings had been reduced to 7hr 25min for the up train, but the down train needed 20min longer to Glasgow and 25min more to Edinburgh. The formation was cut back from the Winter 1938/9 timetable so that north of Crewe the train loaded to nine coaches only.

The 2pm 'Corridor' remained largely unchanged from pre-Grouping days until 1927 when standard LMS coaches displaced the 1908 stock in the Edinburgh and Aberdeen portions, and then also in the Glasgow section. This change coincided with the naming of the train as the 'Mid-Day Scot' in September 1927, but the old stock was soon reinstated, to remain until 1930. Until Summer 1928, the train conveyed the well-established through coach for Whitehaven as far as Crewe where this and the Aberdeen portion were detached, to form a separate train northwards, and a through GWR coach from Plymouth to Glasgow was added in their place. At Carstairs the 'Mid-Day Scot' split into Glasgow and Edinburgh sections. In the up direction, leaving both cities at 1.30pm, the sections were combined at Symington, the train running non-stop in 176min to Crewe, and then on to Euston which was reached at 9.50pm.

From Grouping, the motive power for the 'Mid-Day Scot' included Hughes 4-6-0s, LMS Compounds, 'Royal Scots', and Pacifics from 1935 when through working between Euston and Glasgow was instituted.

With the ending of the 8¼hr timing in May 1932, the 'Mid-Day Scot' was accelerated by 25min throughout northbound, and 20min southbound. The down train now took 8hr 5min, the up train, 8hr, this timing being cut by 5min in September 1932. Major changes came in May 1936 when the down train became the fastest Euston–Glasgow day service,

The Edinburgh portion of the up 'Royal Scot' was usually run separately on Fridays and Saturdays in the summer of 1935, with a kitchen car serving to adjacent open coaches. 'Royal Scot' No. 6130 *The West Yorkshire Regiment* carries the '96' code of this train.

regaining once more its former 2pm departure and the Aberdeen coaches. It ran to Crewe in 163min. The next stop was Lancaster, then Penrith, with a taxing 59min schedule for the 51 miles between these stops. The train divided at Carlisle, the first section taking 116min to Glasgow Central (arr 9.35pm), and the remaining coaches going forward to Lockerbie where the Aberdeen and Edinburgh coaches separated, the latter reaching their destination in 7hr 55min from Euston. Strangely, the up train was not treated to such a dramatic acceleration.

Minor alterations followed until the decision in May 1937 to divide the train north of Crewe but, with the introduction two months later of the 'Coronation Scot', the 'Mid-Day Scot' no longer provided an *advertised* service between Euston and Glasgow. Through coaches were however provided, being accompanied from Crewe northwards by the GWR Plymouth–Glasgow coach. The train's role altered north of Wigan where through coaches from Manchester Exchange (dep 4.45pm) were added, and at Lancaster they were joined by those from Liverpool (dep 5pm). The train divided at Carlisle, and was non-stop to Glasgow, and to Edinburgh. Coming south, the 'Mid-Day Scot' retained through coaches from Aberdeen (dep 10.5am), Glasgow and Edinburgh, the first two sections combining at Law Junction, and the last at Symington. Arrival at Euston was 9.30pm, the service providing much quicker journeys than before to London from stations north of Perth.

The principal overnight train was the 'Night Scot', the 11.45pm Euston–Glasgow, diverted soon after Grouping to run from Carlisle over the former Glasgow & South Western line to Glasgow St Enoch, and worked by an ex-Caledonian engine. It reverted to the Beattock route in the summer of 1925, but a portion for Glasgow St Enoch was dropped off at Carlisle, and taking its place was one of the Pullman cars ready to provide a breakfast service, one of these cars being used on this working until 1936. By the winter of 1928, the 'Night Scot' was running non-stop from Glasgow to Crewe, and the formation included four first-class and one third-class sleepers. In 1934, the St Enoch portion had developed into a separate train, and in Winter 1935/36 the 'Scot' was retimed to leave 15min later in the up direction, and 10min later northbound, but retained its former arrival times.

The 'Royal Highlander', the 7.30pm Euston–Inverness, ran in three parts at the height of the summer, the first portion for Aviemore and Inverness, the second for Inverness by the Carr Bridge and Forres routes, and the third for Oban, and Highland line and Aberdeen line intermediate stations.

The LMS introduced third-class sleeping cars in 1928, as did the LNER and GWR, and here it might be interesting to comment on some less well-known sleeping car services. During 1928, a Holyhead–Liverpool car was run in connection with a sailing from Dun Laoghaire but was soon withdrawn. From July 1936, a Birmingham–Glasgow service was available using composite sleeping cars, out from Birmingham on the 10.50pm train, and returning on the 9.30pm from Glasgow. From at least 1929-39, through sleeping cars were worked in summer between Euston and Turnberry via Dumfries, Stranraer and Girvan, on the 8pm down sleeping car service.

A 1.50pm Glasgow Central–Liverpool/Manchester, with through coaches from Edinburgh attached at Strawfrank Junction (Carstairs) was introduced in September 1927, but otherwise the service between Manchester/Liverpool and Edinburgh/Glasgow was not really taken in hand until July 1937. Then new through portions were provided from Manchester Exchange and Liverpool Exchange, attached to the 'Mid-Day Scot', and between Liverpool and Edinburgh, giving a fastest-ever timing of 4hr 40min.

In 1926, the LMS decided to transfer to Heysham the steamer service between Fleetwood and Belfast. By now named, the expresses from Euston were simply transferred to run to/from Heysham, the down train leaving at 6.10pm, but from May 1936 the up train, formerly wending its way out of the port at 5.48am, was retimed to 7am and arrived in Euston no more 35min later than previously, at 11.35am. During the late 1920s, the 5pm St Pancras–Bradford conveyed a through portion for Heysham, attached at Leeds to the 9.30pm to Heysham. Meanwhile, improvements to the 'Ulster Express' continued. From July 1937, the down train was retimed to leave at 7pm, and ran the 234 miles non-stop to Morecambe in 4hr 12min, then to Heysham for an 11.30pm arrival. The docking time of the steamer at Belfast was unchanged. This summer arrangement continued in 1938/39.

The boat trains between Euston and Holyhead continued with scant change during most of the LMS period although some phenomenal loads were often noted, such as an August 1938 sighting of a 'Royal Scot' heading an 18-coach train up day 'Irish Mail'. The 'Irish Mail' restaurant cars were famed for their catering. In the Winter 1936 timetable, changes to the up 'Royal Scot' reacted on the up day 'Irish Mail'

Some of the up 'Irish Mail' formations of the late 1930s were enormous, and what at first sight seemed like undemanding schedules called for hard work by the engines. No. 6168 *The Girl Guide* is leading a 16-vehicle formation past Colwyn Bay in this scene from 1938/9.

which now left Holyhead 25min later, at 12.40pm. The running time was unaltered, but the train ran to Chester in 94min for the 85 miles, and had a concluding burst in 84min up from Rugby to arrive in Euston at 5.50pm. The down day 'Irish Mail' took 10min longer overall to Holyhead, but this, too, had some demanding timings, such as 68min from Watford Junction to Rugby.

The LMS put much effort into boosting travel to the Lakes and to North Wales. In the 1923 summer timetable there had been an 11.35am Euston–Blackpool/Windermere/Keswick, a weekdays seasonal working which persisted in one form or another throughout LMS prewar days. The year-round daily services were the 10.40am from Euston with through coaches to Windermere, and by connection to Keswick from Penrith, and by connections off the down 'Mid-Day Scot'. The principal service was the 'Lakes Express' which by 1934 ran FSO from May onwards at noon from Euston to Windermere, the portion for Keswick and Workington going forward from Oxenholme. On midsummer Saturdays, there were additional expresses from Euston such as the 9.30am from Euston via Northampton and Birmingham with through coaches for Windermere and Barrow while the 'Lakes Express' itself was divided, with the Barrow/Maryport portion running in advance of the Windermere/Keswick main section. The up SX train had the main section with restaurant car leaving

Windermere at 11.15am, to which at Oxenholme the Workington/Keswick portion was attached, but the journey to Euston was stately with the arrival not until 4.47pm.

The additional Euston–North Wales summer services of pre-Grouping days were maintained, the 1923 summer timetable having featured the 10.40am Euston–Pwllheli, the principal train which later became the 'Welshman'; by Summer 1938 it was leaving Euston on weekdays at 11.15am, booked non-stop to Rhyl where it divided into portions for Llandudno (with restaurant car) and Bangor/Portmadoc, the latter dropping off at Llandudno Junction a coach for all-stations to Bangor. The up 'Welshman' was the 9am from Portmadoc and 10.55am from Llandudno.

On Saturdays, the North Wales Coast services were sufficiently changed to warrant separate 'Saturdays only' pages in the timetable, and included numerous through trains from/to the North West and Midlands. The Summer 1923 timetable had included an 11.15am Manchester Exchange/12.10pm Liverpool–Portmadoc, the Manchester section reappearing at least as late as the 1938 summer timetable. To boost summer rail travel in the area, holiday contract tickets were available in North Wales for 10/- a week and there were locally promoted holiday excursion trains such as the 'Snowdonian', on Wednesdays from Chester to Llanberis, and the three journeys a day SX service between Llandudno and Rhyl known as the 'Golden Sands Express'.

In slow decline were the services to Central Wales from Euston and the North West, now without the accompanying through coaches to/from the Cambrian Coast. In the Summer 1923 timetable there had been two services from Euston, at 10.40am and 1.15pm Euston, departing so the publicity said, to the 'Spas of Central Wales'. Motive power for the Shrewsbury–Swansea services usually comprised LMS 2-6-4Ts, but from 1938, Class 5 4-6-0s took over. During the summer of that year, through coaches ran in Central Wales line trains to Euston (arr 3.5pm) on the 7.45am from Swansea Victoria, and from Euston at 10.40am, travelling through Wales on the 2.40pm from Shrewsbury; at 10.25am to Liverpool, and noon back from there, these services being provided with ex-LNWR tea car to/from Craven Arms; at 12.50pm to Manchester (and noon return from there). There was also the 6.45pm Swansea–York Mail, whose return working left Shrewsbury for Swansea at 3.30am. Other half-forgotten trains from the Welsh Borders include the fast Hereford–Merthyr train (dep 3.35pm in 1938) worked by a 'Prince of Wales' – and latterly an LMS '5' – to Abergavenny Brecon Road, and a Coal Tank thereafter. In 1938, the return working was at 6.47pm from Merthyr to Hereford. One wonders what use was made of it.

Blackpool was a major crowd-puller for the LMS and, during the summer of 1927, for instance, the resort attracted 3 million rail travellers, no less than 700,000 during that autumn's illuminations fortnight. Despite the growth of road traffic, rail carryings increased such that by 1935 some 6 million passengers were received at all the stations on the lines west of Preston into Blackpool and Fleetwood, and traffic increased throughout the late 1930s.

The through service between Blackpool and Euston was not remarkable, and in winter was restricted to coaches leaving at breakfast-time and attached at Crewe to a Liverpool–Euston train, and returning on the 5.20pm Fleetwood/Birkenhead express. In due course, the Fleetwood coaches were supplanted by the 'Ulster Express', but the Blackpool coaches remained. In July 1935 the 5.20pm was divided, the first section with restaurant car leaving 10min earlier and now bearing the name 'Fylde Coast Express'. It also conveyed the East Lancs coaches formerly passing on the 6.10pm Euston–Manchester. The new train was 33min quicker to Blackpool Central. The up 'Fylde Coast Express' was the 8.25am from Blackpool Central, into Euston at 12.50pm.

Meanwhile, the 5.20pm down retained its through coaches and restaurant car to Birkenhead and Holyhead, as well as to New Brighton, the last-named detached at Hooton and worked via West Kirby Joint station and Bidston. The return working was at 9.58am from New Brighton, both services providing a prestige job for a 3F 0-6-0T otherwise used on shunting duties.

Much of the LMS policy on passenger train services in the mid/late 1930s was derived from an exhaustive study carried out during the summer of 1934 of train working and punctuality on the Western, Central and Midland Divisions, under the direction of C. R. Byrom, the Chief General Superintendent. No thorough analysis of train working had been undertaken since Grouping, noted the authors, and travel conditions had altered greatly. On those parts of the Railway surveyed, the average lateness on Mondays–Fridays was 5min per train, but deteriorated on Saturdays to an average lateness of over 20min. The major causes of delay were signal checks, station overtime, engineering slacks and waiting connections.

The report recommended that special attention should be paid to improving signalling at Preston and through to Blackpool; to train working and the station layout at Carnforth; that greater use should be made of the Manchester–Hellifield–Settle & Carlisle route for through expresses between Manchester and Scotland, and that engine changing at Crewe station should be minimised. Before long, nearly all these recommendations had been implemented: Preston was resignalled, from the summer of 1935 Manchester–Scotland expresses were diverted over the S&C on Saturdays, and Carnforth's Furness platforms and layout were improved during 1937-9.

The LMS also instituted its 'On Time' campaign to improve train timekeeping, publishing praiseworthy efforts at time recovery in its *On Time* newspaper. In one four-weekly period in 1936 the LMS boasted that 93% of express passenger trains arrived right-time – 5min late – not up to 10min late, as today.

From the mid-1930s, the LMS embarked on a steady programme to accelerate services and improve its operations. The Euston–Birmingham 2hr expresses, usually continuing to Wolverhampton, featured prominently in the Winter 1935/36 speed-up when they were generally accelerated by 5min, and now boasted a number of mile-a-minute schedules, notably a 65mph run from Rugby to Watford Junction by the 6.20pm ex-New St. An additional 8.10am Euston–Wolverhampton came in July 1938, in 120min to Birmingham including Watford

Junction and Coventry stops. As yet, 'Patriot' 4-6-0s were more popular with the crews on these trains than the 'Jubilees' which only became dominant early in 1939.

The Liverpool and Manchester expresses shared in the accelerations of the 1930s. In the May 1935 timetable, the 8.30am from Manchester and the up 'Mancunian' were both promoted to 60mph schedules, the former running from Blisworth to Euston (62.8 miles) in 61min, the latter the 177 miles from Wilmslow to Euston in 172min. In September 1935, the East Lancs coaches of the down 'Lancastrian' were switched to the down 'Fylde Coast Express' and detached at Wigan, to be worked forward via Chorley, and arrived at Colne 30min earlier. In May 1936, the up 'Merseyside Express' was altered to start 10min later but still reached Euston at 1.30pm after a 3hr 9min non-stop run from Mossley Hill. At the same time, the 10.30am Euston–Manchester gained 5min overall.

From May 1937, the 4.10pm departures from Liverpool/Manchester to Euston, previously combining at Crewe, now ran independently, the first calling only at Nuneaton and reaching Euston in 3hr 30min from Liverpool, the second, taking 3hr 37min from Manchester; from September 1938 the Liverpool train was speeded-up by another 5min. In May 1938, the 2.20pm Liverpool–Euston lost its Manchester portion, and was booked non-stop over the 158 miles from Crewe in 152min, to arrive 30min earlier. The Manchester section ran as the 2.20pm via Stoke-on-Trent instead of Crewe, and arrived in Euston at 6pm. The 5.25pm Liverpool–Euston no longer stopped at Willesden Junction, and sped from Crewe in 148min, at an average speed of 64mph. Strangely, the journeys of the four fastest up Liverpool–Euston trains averaged some 15min faster than the down Liverpool expresses. From the summer of 1938, Pacifics were allowed to work into Manchester London Road, usually with the 10.30am from Euston and the up 'Comet', and indeed during 1939 two 'Princess Royals' were allocated to Longsight shed, a 70ft turntable having been recently installed there.

The most spectacular of the West Coast expresses was probably the 'Coronation Scot' introduced on 5 July 1937 and hauled by a streamlined Pacific. To work the service, the LMS built three nine-coach train sets (one was spare), all liveried in Coronation blue with horizontal silver bands. There were two kitchen cars in each set so that there could be an at-seat service of meals, and the coaches were pressure-ventilated. Leaving Euston and Glasgow Central at 1.30pm except Saturdays, the down and up trains made their journeys in 6hr 30min, with 4hr 43min timings between Euston and Carlisle, and booked in

A powerful image is evoked by this photograph of the down 'Coronation Scot' at Winwick Quay, north of Warrington in 1938 or 1939. The engine is 'Princess Coronation' Pacific No. 6223 *Princess Alice*.

The morning Glasgow Central–Birmingham New St. express descends Shap at speed behind 'Royal Scot' No. 6105 *Cameron Highlander* on 27 August 1937. The second vehicle behind the engine is a GWR Toplight composite bound for Paignton, and will be detached at Crewe.

105min between Carlisle and Glasgow. Soon the LMS was contemplating a design for a 4-6-4 to work trains of up to 500 tons on 'Coronation Scot' timings – or even as little as 6hr – between Euston and Glasgow. All the day Anglo-Scottish expresses would have been greatly accelerated but the project died with the outbreak of war.

On the Midland Division, the pattern of services after Grouping at first altered little and fell some way short of what had been done in 1914. Trains were worked by Midland and LMS-built Compounds (and Class 2 4-4-0s), but from the late 1920s 'Claughton' 4-6-0s were sent to work the Anglo-Scottish expresses between St Pancras and Carlisle, in turn giving way to 'Patriots' from the early 1930s. Through coaches were provided between St Pancras and Liverpool Central, and for Manchester Victoria, these being detached at either Cheadle Heath or Chinley from Manchester Central trains; by the late 1930s, other through Liverpool workings were via Manchester Central.

The St Pancras–Harrogate service was withdrawn during 1929, by which time the best St Pancras–Leicester time was 107min, to Nottingham, 135min and to Sheffield 3hr 7min. In contrast to MR days, the longest non-stop run was between Chesterfield and St Pancras, by the 2.10pm up which was booked in 163min. One curiosity of the early 1930s and until 1936 was the 2pm from St Pancras which divided at Nottingham, the first section running non-stop to Sheffield, then proceeding to Rotherham Masborough. By that time, the second portion which had taken the 'Old Road' from Tapton Junction had got ahead. The 'via Sheffield section' then made its way over the Royston Junction–Thornhill Junction line to Bradford Exchange while the other section went to Leeds and on to Bradford Market St.

From October 1932, there were at last some changes to the Midland route's Anglo-Scottish expresses, the 'Thames–Forth' having already been speeded-up in May, but now the 'Thames–Clyde' was accelerated to a 9hr journey to Glasgow St Enoch – 20min faster – the 11.45am Glasgow was retimed to noon, and also took 9hr to Glasgow/Edinburgh, being 25min faster overall; all but 10min of this gain was lost by deceleration in May 1935. The up expresses were also expedited in 1932, but less markedly.

Using Stanier's Class 5 and 'Jubilee' 4-6-0s, trial runs were conducted during April 1937 over the Midland Division to greatly accelerated 'test' timings. The outcome was a major revision of the main line timetables from October 1937, with a ruling principle of non-stop, mile-a-minute timings between St Pancras and Kettering, Leicester or Nottingham; even with two intermediate stops the St Pancras–Nottingham time was 132min.

A general smartening-up of the St Pancras–Manchester service aimed at relieving the Western Division service to Manchester, the best time being made by the 10.30am from St Pancras, in 3hr 35min and stopping only at Leicester and Derby. From early 1938, this train and the 4.25pm from Manchester became the 'Peak Express', while the 10am from Manchester and 4.30pm from St Pancras took the title of the 'Palatine'. Until July 1938, 'Jubilees' were not passed to work from Derby to Manchester because of weight restrictions and so Class 5s and Compounds were used. Cut-backs to this improved service came in the Summer 1939 timetables when the 6.20pm Manchester–St Pancras was withdrawn, its replacement gaining extra stops and being made generally slower, as was the down 'Peak Express' which gained five extra intermediate calls and a 21min longer run to Manchester.

Sheffield, the cause of such competitive striving before 1914, had been somewhat neglected by the LMS and LNER until the 1937 timetable when the former brought in 172min non-stop timings by the 5.10pm down 'Yorkshireman' and the 9.50am Leeds–St Pancras. The 19 trains in the St Pancras–Sheffield service now averaged 3hr 6min in journey time, but the improvements were not restricted to principal cities, intermediate journeys and connections generally also being made quicker. The non-stop runs between St Pancras and Sheffield lasted only until October 1938 when additional stops were inserted in the schedules of the two trains and services were trimmed somewhat.

By late 1937, out of a total of 51 'Jubilees' at Midland sheds some of the later, and better, examples were to hand, supported by almost as many '5s' and the engines had little difficulty in improving on schedules. Nonetheless there were some complaints arising from the loss of old services for although there was a 1pm St Pancras–Halifax restaurant car express its overall time was slower than by the former through coaches, and Luton seemed to have lost out.

Trials carried out during October 1937 between Bristol, Leeds and Glasgow with 'Jubilee' No. 5660 *Rooke* were the prelude to more accelerations of Midland route expresses. The up 'Thames-Clyde' was marginally accelerated but the down 'Thames-Forth', usually a light train of six or seven coaches north of Leeds, now had a fastest-ever timing of 123min from there to Carlisle, including a Skipton stop, but the time saved by so doing was frittered away on the Waverley route. Also bucked-up were the Sunday services, including the re-introduction of a Glasgow–St Pancras daytime express. Further

accelerations of all northbound daytime expresses on the Settle & Carlisle followed in October 1938 when through timings to Glasgow were 10min quicker, while the 5.30pm Glasgow St Enoch–Leeds was made non-stop Carlisle–Skipton and took 5hr 18min overall. The former MR West of England route services had been accelerated in 1933, and further limited accelerations took place in October 1937 and in the next winter timetable.

The Central Division benefited after the mid-1930s from the introduction of Class 5 4-6-0s and the capable taper-boilered Class 4 2-6-4Ts, the latter having water-scoops to replenish their side-tanks when working some of the shorter distance fast trains. The pattern of services did not greatly alter until May 1938 when the restaurant car set that had so long worked the Heysham–Leeds diagram – see **Lancashire & Yorkshire Railway** – was withdrawn and not replaced, the trains themselves remaining.

The Tilbury section was left to its own devices until May 1935, by which time the Stanier 2-6-4Ts were in use, additional slow lines had been provided between Barking and Upminster, and the LNER had remodelled and resignalled Fenchurch St station. From 1925, there had been through trains between Broad St. and Southend via Bromley but these were now withdrawn, and instead the basic Fenchurch St.–Southend service was redrafted and expanded, with trains at rush hours working to a skip-stop pattern to divide up the traffic. There were some accelerations, with a best time to Southend of 55min.

As yet, the LMS was very largely steam-worked, and the impressive recasting of main line services had been made possible as a consequence of the large-scale building programme of the Stanier standard classes. A 1936 plan considered dc electrification between Euston and Rugby. As another pointer to the future, in September 1938 a three-car articulated diesel unit was put into service between Oxford and Cambridge. It provided additional workings that were only advertised locally, including a fastest-ever timing of 105min for the 77¼ miles from Cambridge to Oxford, this on a route never noted for speed and over which the best existing timing was 148min. When the diesel unit failed, a 2-6-4T with two coaches substituted but was pushed to keep time. From March 1939, the set began working between St Pancras, Bedford and Nottingham covering 350 miles daily.

But war cast its pall over any forward planning. Although a peacetime Winter 1939/40 LMS timetable progressed to proof stage, normal summer services continued to the second week of September

A wartime view of a begrimed 'Princess Coronation' Pacific, No. 6235 *City of Birmingham*.

1939, apart from the 'Coronation Scot' which was withdrawn at the outbreak of war. Like the GWR and LNER, the war emergency timetables applying from late September brought services that were slower and less frequent, particularly so on the Midland Division where the average time booked time from St Pancras to Manchester was 6hr. Through Euston–East Lancs coaches were restored from June 1940, when the Euston–Manchester sleeper was making the longest non-stop journey on the LMS, of 183 miles to Stockport. The day 'Irish Mails' reappeared in September 1940. There had been a praiseworthy attempt that summer to provide a programme of holiday trains to resorts.

From February 1941 long-distance up evening 'expresses' made stops in the outer London area to try to reduce the number of passengers coming into central London. More normal working came in May 1941 when the number of main line trains actually increased and when, for instance, all six down expresses from Euston between 10.0 and 10.40 had restaurant cars. The same spring saw the first use of

'Royal Scots' over the Settle & Carlisle line, and from 1943 rebuilt 'Jubilees' and 'Scots' were put to work on this route. Despite restrictions on recreational travel, people were not dissuaded and in 1942 summer long-distance traffic on the LMS was some 74% above that for 1938.

Trains such as the wartime equivalent of the 'Royal Scot' had their restaurant cars restored in October 1945, but the train's honoured name was not reinstated until February 1948. October 1945 had also seen some massive accelerations of services, a few such as the 'Royal Highlander' actually becoming faster than in 1939. The Midland Division services were completely recast in October 1946 when a number of West Coast expresses were also speeded-up such as the 'Ulster Express'. But timekeeping was often abysmal, particularly after the severe winter of 1947. That summer some express running recovered almost to wartime standards but was soon inhibited by deteriorating track conditions which saw main line trains decelerated in the last months of the LMS.

CHAPTER TWELVE

THE LONDON &
NORTH EASTERN RAILWAY

While the other Big Four companies strove to integrate their constituent companies, the LNER chose to allow its components some independence. Even as late as 1939, the various sections of the LNER corresponding to the pre-Grouping companies pursued their own policies for the operation of passenger stock and for on-train catering, and the various LNER sectional working timetables retained their pre-1923 styles. Above all,

the LNER was dominated by the requirements of the East Coast services, the *crème de la crème* when it came to engines and stock, and for which policy was largely influenced by managers with a background of management in the Great Northern and North Eastern railways.

At Grouping, the Great Northern section was the operator of the twelve original Gresley A1 class Pacifics, the last of which entered service in

The Great Northern scene did not change much for most of the life of the LNER and was not finally expunged until the 1970s. Here is Peterborough North station in June 1925 with, what is believed to be the 9.50am Pullman service from Manchester London Road passing behind ex-GNR C1 class Atlantic No. 4459. Note the gas tank wagon to the left of the picture for servicing coaches and restaurant cars.

September 1923, and mostly based at Doncaster though this shed had just two daily diagrams to London. So the Ivatt Atlantics remained the predominant power for expresses on the GN main line although an attempt was made to find work for the impressive-looking ex-Great Central 4-6-0s which failed however to come up to scratch. One unusual regular working from the summer of 1923 brought an ex-North Eastern Z class Atlantic (and a Gateshead crew) to Grantham on the 8am Newcastle–King's Cross. The Z returned north with the fast 5.30pm King's Cross–Newcastle – see **East Coast Main Line services** – which ran non-stop between Grantham and Darlington. In due course, other ex-NER engines worked to London with special trains.

The general manager of the Great Eastern Railway, Sir Henry Thornton, had signed a 20-year agreement with the Pullman Car Co. in December 1919 for the operation of Pullman cars on GE express trains. The supplementary fare services proved unpopular with East Anglians and, having inherited an agreement with 17 years to run, the LNER needed to find more profitable employment for the cars.

At first, and apparently at the initiative of Harrogate Corporation, came the all-Pullman car 'Harrogate Pullman' between King's Cross (dep 11.15am) and Newcastle (arr 5pm) via Leeds Central, Harrogate and Darlington. This started running from 9 July 1923, made up to six cars and an

LNER bogie brake. Next, from 2 June 1924, there was introduced the 'Sheffield Pullman', at 11.5am from King's Cross via Nottingham Victoria to Sheffield Victoria (arr 2.20pm), returning at 4.45pm, to arrive in King's Cross at 8pm. Public response was so poor that its times were altered after just six weeks, and from July 1924 the train started from Sheffield at 10.30am, calling at Nottingham Victoria and arriving in King's Cross at 1.45pm; the return was at 6.5pm, and the Pullman got to Sheffield for 9.20pm. This arrangement lasted only until April 1925 when the train was altered to start from and terminate at Manchester London Road (out at 9.50am, arriving King's Cross at 2pm), and re-routed via Retford to Sheffield, rather than Nottingham. Down at 6.5pm, the train ran non-stop to Sheffield Victoria in 177min and got to Manchester London Road in 4hr 7min. So dismal was the public reception that on some runs the number of passengers was exceeded by Pullman stewards. This and the 'Harrogate Pullman' provided a chance to make better use of the ex-GCR 4-6-0s but they steamed fitfully, and from 1927 were replaced by GNR Atlantics and ex-GCR 'Director' 4-4-0s. By then, the 'Manchester Pullman' was no more: it last ran in September 1925.

The replacement for this ill-fated venture was a West Riding Pullman, at first untitled but later the 'West Riding'. This started in September 1925, initially leaving King's Cross at 11.10 (the 'Harrogate Pullman' was now away at 11.20), and

The 11.15am 'Harrogate Pullman' passes through Hadley Woods behind ex-Great Central 4-6-0 No. 6166 *Earl Haig*.

non-stop to Leeds Central (arr 2.35pm) from where a portion was worked to Bradford Exchange. For the southbound train, the cars were worked to Harrogate. Leaving there at 11.15am, the Bradford cars were picked up at Leeds, and the train was similarly timed to King's Cross as the down Pullman, in 3hr 25min. Next year, a stop was made each way at Wakefield where cars for Halifax Old station via Bradford were detached or attached, being worked via Batley.

In May 1928, the 'West Riding' was completely retimed to provide morning departures from the provincial cities and a late afternoon return from King's Cross, and could now be worked by a single set of Pullman cars. It now started from Newcastle at 9.10am, ran via Harrogate to Leeds, dep 11.27, collecting the Halifax cars at Wakefield and arriving in King's Cross at 3pm. Away from there at 4.45pm, the train reached Leeds at 8.15pm and Newcastle at 10.27pm.

Meanwhile, from July 1925 the 'Harrogate Pullman' had been extended beyond Newcastle to Edinburgh, reached at 7.50pm. Southbound, the train left there at 8.30am, to arrive at King's Cross for 5.5pm. But now there were two morning Pullmans to Leeds which was clearly a nonsense so, from September 1925, in each direction the 'Edinburgh Pullman' (but not officially so-named) was altered to run non-stop in 3hr 43min over the 199 miles between King's Cross and Harrogate via Shaftholme Junction, Church Fenton and Tadcaster. Edinburgh was now reached at 7.35pm and the southbound train arrived in King's Cross at 4.45pm.

The name 'Queen of Scots' was chosen in 1927, and the train began running to/from Glasgow Queen St. from May 1928. Then the two trains used for the 'Queen of Scots' were each made up of a set of new all-steel Pullman cars. Because of changes to the West Riding Pullman, the 'Queen of Scots' reverted to running via Leeds, non-stop at 11.15am from King's Cross, with a 3hr 25min booking, and reaching Glasgow at 8.45pm. The southbound run became later, with departures from Glasgow at 10.5am, and at 4.15pm from Leeds, to arrive at King's Cross for 7.35pm.

Despite of, or perhaps in view of all these changes, having once found a successful formula for the Pullmans the LNER left their operation well alone until the mid/late 1930s. There was a third train, the 'Harrogate Sunday Pullman' which commenced running in July 1927, at first with a 10.30am departure, but then made 30min earlier. Cars ran to Harrogate and Bradford. With a speedy turn-round, Harrogate was left at 3.15pm. From July 1938 the up

train was accelerated to a 4hr journey, to arrive in King's Cross at 7pm.

The Pullman cars featured then and during later LNER days on special trains from King's Cross, in connection with Nottingham races, and to Newmarket. The latter were a consequence of Grouping and ran non-stop via Hitchin and Cambridge, previously the specials having operated from St Pancras. Now they were worked by ex-GNR Atlantics and comprised spare Pullmans which were based on Southern Railway territory. Pacifics appeared on these trains from 1930. From 1927, they were also used throughout on Grand National day for the annual King's Cross–Aintree Pullman special, at first with the 'spare' Pullmans, but later those from the LNER-based fleet. Among the regular specials over the GN main line were the chartered Eason's Specials from Grimsby (later Cleethorpes) to King's Cross and worked by ex-GCR 4-6-0s.

The LNER participated in the naming of its express trains during 1927, having agreed that the names should appear in the timetable, and on engine headboards and coach roof-boards. The names agreed the previous October were the 'Flying Scotsman', the 'Scarborough Flyer' (11.50am from King's Cross and return working), the 'Aberdonian' (7.30pm sleeping car express), the 'Highlandman' (7.25pm seasonal sleeping car express) and the 'Night Scotsman' (10.25pm sleeping car express). The LNER seemed in doubt whether 'Flyer' or 'Flier' was correct, posters showing the former and train boards the latter!

The Great Eastern section of the LNER's Southern Area went much its own way through the mid-1920s, efforts being concentrated on improving the suburban rolling stock. New coaches had been built for the 'Hook Continental' in 1925, but the ordinary expresses were largely formed of ex-GER stock. Traffic was growing and, with no new engines built since 1923, the GE was in need of more powerful engines, but hampered by the section's limits on locomotive axle-loads and overall lengths. The short-term palliative was to build more GER-design 4-6-0s, then from late 1928 came the new B17 4-6-0s.

The top LNER management was concerned at the state of the GE section's rolling stock, and particularly at the competition offered by road coaches, such that investment was approved ahead of the normal building programme for 30 new coaches for use on the Liverpool St.–Cromer service, including restaurant cars with electric cooking equipment which had been standardised by the

The LNER inherited a contract drawn up with the Pullman Car Co. by the Great Eastern Railway. The only Pullman workings that prevailed on the GE section were the buffet cars in the Continental boat trains and the Sunday 'Clacton Pullman', seen here on 15 June 1924 forging through the suburbs behind ex-GER D15 class 4-4-0 No 8828.

Railway. The two sets of coaches went into service from July 1929.

As the source of the LNER's agreement with the Pullman Car Co., vestiges of Pullman operation remained on the GE lines, not only as buffet cars on the Continental boat trains, but in the shape of the Sunday 'Clacton Pullman' which operated to a 90min timing between Liverpool St. and Clacton. In 1929, the train was renamed the 'Eastern Belle', and on summer weekdays it now ran in turn to different East Anglian resorts and usually to fast timings, such as 2hr 53min to Cromer. From March 1929, new passenger and mail trains with TPO vans were introduced between Liverpool St. and Peterborough East via Ipswich, and Norwich–Liverpool St. At 8.30pm from Liverpool St., and back in early morning, the 'Hook Continental' was a weighty train of 400 tons tare, and its 82min timing to Harwich Parkeston Quay was the most testing working on the GE for a passenger locomotive.

The GC express services of the 1920s included a Mansfield–Marylebone train which had developed from being little more than a semi-fast to a full restaurant car train, and by the summer of 1925 left Mansfield at 8am, to arrive at Marylebone in mid-morning. The return working was at 4.50pm, and south of Nottingham the train called only at Aylesbury, Leicester and Loughborough; there was a 60mph booking from Aylesbury to Leicester. An Atlantic or 'Director' worked the trains between Mansfield and Leicester. In July 1929, the service was diverted to/from Sheffield, leaving 5min later in the down direction and, in 1930, extended to Manchester.

A Neasden 'Director' worked through to Manchester Central (arr 7.45pm) with the 3.20pm from Marylebone. At 212 miles, this was one of the longer through workings by engine and men in the late 1920s and, though not as speedy as in GCR days, was booked to Leicester in 109min start to stop, on to Nottingham in 25min and arrived in Sheffield Victoria at 6.26pm. The 3.20pm comprised five or six ex-GCR gangwayed coaches, including restaurant car, and an LMS through coach for Halifax which was detached at Sheffield. That coach came up on the 8.20am Manchester–Marylebone. Through coaches from/to Barnsley continued on the 2.20pm ex-Manchester and 6.20pm down Bradford.

From the late 1920s, new Gresley gangwayed stock began to supplant the stately GCR-design vehicles. Into the early 1930s the 'Director' 4-4-0s were well-represented on the London expresses, the big GC 4-6-0s being usually seen on less important workings. These included such trains as the midday Cleethorpes–Leicester working with its three coaches, and fish vans from Grimsby. Interlopers had also appeared on the GC scene in the shape of GN large Atlantics which had been allocated to Neepsend shed, Sheffield. From 1929, these engines worked westwards to Manchester and Liverpool on passenger trains such as those forming the Hull–Liverpool service, and on cross-country trains routed south over the GC main line.

The North Eastern Area received the first new D49 class 4-4-0s in 1927, and put them to work to and from Newcastle on one of its principal trains, the 8.55am Leeds–Glasgow and 4pm return. The D49s were also to be found on the Liverpool–Newcastle trains. From February 1931, the Leeds–Glasgow service received a new set of coaches which included very adequate dining accommodation, the same crew serving breakfast, lunch, tea and dinner during their long day on the move. Despite the attention paid to this service, it usually loaded lightly north of Newcastle. The 4pm from Glasgow became one of the faster LNER expresses when, in 1932, it gained one of a pair of mile-a-minute timings between Darlington and York.

New Gresley gangwayed stock was built from the early 1930s to replace non-gangwayed vehicles still in use on some of the York–Newcastle and Newcastle–Edinburgh fast trains. New stock was built for one of the NEA's principal through coach workings, between York and Perth, out at 10.5am, back at 8.30am.

The original Gresley Pacifics were still somewhat unsatisfactory, particularly in terms of their consumption of coal. This and other deficiencies were underlined during the locomotive exchange of April 1925 when the Great Western Railway's *Pendennis Castle* was pitted against LNER Pacifics Nos 4474 and 2545, the second of these A1s remaining on its home ground, and the former being used between Paddington and Plymouth. Long-lap valve motion and higher pressure boilers transformed the Pacifics from the late 1920s. When the LMS began non-stop working with the 'Royal Scot' between Euston and Carnforth in 1927, the LNER decided to react. The plan involved the summertime three-days-a-week 9.50am relief which preceded the 'Flying Scotsman' and it was made

non-stop between King's Cross and Newcastle – 268¼ miles. Engines and men worked throughout and the working began on 11 July 1927.

The LMS then retaliated by running non-stop to Carlisle – see **London Midland & Scottish Railway** – to which the LNER's riposte was to move to non-stop working between King's Cross and Edinburgh. This was made possible by pairing the A1 Pacifics with corridor tenders, the King's Cross and Haymarket (Edinburgh) crews changing over en route. The first day of the world's record non-stop run of 392¾ miles began on 1 May 1928, the 'Flying Scotsman' departing at 10am behind No. 4472 *Flying Scotsman*. New triplet articulated restaurant car sets with an extravagant interior in the first-class saloon to Louis XVI style was one innovation, another being a coach with its interior converted to provide a hairdressing salon, and a retiring-room for ladies.

The non-stop working lasted until the end of the summer only, but had proved a success operationally, helped by the undemanding 8¼hr schedule. In Summer 1930, for example, there were no engine failures on any of the 132 runs made. From 1928, the summer relief down 'Scotsman' was altered to follow rather than precede the 'Flying Scotsman', leaving at 10.5am and making the usual intermediate stops of its parent, and carrying the King's Cross–Newcastle passengers.

The higher standard of fittings on the 'Flying Scotsman' train sets encouraged the introduction of new gangwayed stock with entry by end vestibules only, and from 1930 these appeared in the 'Flying Scotsman' and afternoon Scotsmen train sets. Before long, pressure-ventilated first-class coaches were being built for the premier sets, and the end door stock for general use on East Coast day trains. In 1932, two of the hairdressing saloon/ladies retiring room coaches in the 'Flying Scotsman' sets were further modified by the addition of a cocktail bar.

From 1930 the LNER had experimented with radio reception on trains, and the two sets of coaches used for the afternoon 'Scotsmen', as well as the GNR-built quintuplet set used on the 10.10am King's Cross–Leeds and 5.30pm return, were fitted up with a receiving office for radio reception and a record-player, the other coaches being wired up with leads to headphones at seats throughout the train. The service was never very popular and ceased in 1935. The radio service, cocktail bars and the like did not pay for themselves, but the LNER justified their provision in terms of valuable public relations.

Another East Coast innovation was the 'Northern Belle' cruising train, first run in the summer of 1932.

The southbound summer 'Flying Scotsman' in the course of its non-stop run from Edinburgh Waverley makes its stately way into York station behind A1 class Pacific No. 2744 *Grand Parade* with some of the then new end-door coaches in the train.

This took the well-heeled tourist for a week's tour through the Lake District and Highlands of Scotland by rail (and coach). A staff of 27 ministered to 60 passengers who enjoyed on-train facilities including restaurant cars, a lounge, the hairdressing saloon car from the 'Flying Scotsman', and first-class sleeping accommodation. The 'Northern Belle' concentrated on cruising through the Highlands after 1936, and last ran in 1939.

More money was probably made from the passengers using the first-class Anglo-Scottish sleeping cars than on any other LNER service. Soon after Grouping, the LNER introduced a summer-only working between King's Cross and Lossiemouth, out on the 7.40pm 'Aberdonian' from King's Cross, at 608½ miles one of the longest-ever through sleeping car workings in Britain. Lossiemouth was reached at 10.20am in the late 1920s, the up working starting with the 4.5pm from Lossiemouth, with arrival at King's Cross at 7.30am the next morning. From 1930, first-class sleeping cars to a much higher specification began to enter traffic, all with pressure ventilation and some featuring a shower bath.

Third-class sleeping cars were introduced in September 1928 on trains already having first-class cars: on the 7.30pm down – one car for Aberdeen, one for Inverness; one car on each of the 10.25pm to Glasgow and 9.45pm return; and on the 10.45pm to

Newcastle and return. More cars were built for the Summer 1929 service to cope with the demand for third-class sleeping berths.

Since 1923, and with the exception of the Pullman trains, there had been little change to the GN main line train services. During late 1931, there were test runs to see whether accelerated schedules were feasible, and these duly materialised as from 2 May 1932, when the restrictive 8¼hr schedule for Anglo-Scottish day trains was dead and buried. At the top of the list were the 'Flying Scotsman', now 25min faster and taking 7hr 50min to and from Edinburgh. When the non-stop started running in July, its overall time was 7½hr, 45min quicker than before. The next winter, the 'Flying Scotsman' had another 5min pared from its timing.

The 1.15pm afternoon 'Scotsman' now left 5min later and reached Edinburgh at 9.15pm, instead of 9.35pm. Its counterpart departed Edinburgh at 2.5pm, 15min later, and arrived at King's Cross at 10, not 10.5pm. The non-stop runs by the 'Queen of Scots' between King's Cross and Leeds were reduced to 3hr 10min up, 1min faster down, and the trains' King's Cross–Edinburgh journey now took 8hr. But the speediest train was the famed but unofficially termed 'Breakfast Flyer', the long-established weekdays 7.50am Leeds–King's Cross express which was accelerated 15min, and allowed 160min

None-too clean Ivatt C1 class Atlantic No. 4404 smokes its way out of Scarborough with the up 'Scarborough Flier' in the 1930s.

up from Doncaster, including calls at Retford and Grantham. From the latter there was a 100min run to the capital which, at an average speed of 63mph, was currently the fastest non-stop run in Europe over 100 miles. In the Winter 1932/3 timetable, it was the turn of the principal King's Cross–Newcastle expresses, the 8am up being retimed to leave 15min later but to be 6min earlier into London, while the 5.30pm down was 13min faster overall.

The May 1932 timetable featured additional expresses between King's Cross and Cambridge. The LNER management was concerned at increased coach competition along the Great North Road, and a fall in revenue on the Cambridge route, and first considered a new service using Sentinel steam railcars. Chief General Manager Sir Ralph Wedgwood was more realistic and instead recommended 'lightweight' conventional trains made up of three coaches, one including a buffet counter, and all with armrests in the third-class, a feature then lacking in LNER main line stock. Five trains each way operated between King's Cross and Cambridge, advertised as 'Garden Cities and Cambridge Buffet Express' but soon familiarly known as the 'Beer Trains'. At first, stops were made only at Welwyn Garden City, Hitchin and Letchworth and the standard times were 82min down, and 77min up, times cut by 7 and 5min

respectively in 1933, by which time the LNER reckoned that at their stopping stations the buffet trains had helped to recover revenue earlier lost to road. Before long, the trains were increased to at least six coaches, and some fine performances were made by ex-GNR Atlantics and other classes, Pacifics often appearing on fill-in turns.

Some recovery from the depths of the Depression was clearly discernible and, when chairing a special meeting of LNER officials in February 1934, Sir Ralph Wedgwood set out his objectives of 'securing continuous economy . . . and continuous improvement in service to the public'. 'Each year', he said, 'should show some improvement in the matter of passenger train facilities.' The ideal was that every train running more than 50 miles non-stop should be booked at a 60mph average. But, he pointed out, the limit had been reached with present loads and punctuality had suffered since accelerated services had been introduced. Trains were 'too long and too heavy' and he urged that certain main line trains should be split. Coaches must be renovated, armrests fitted to main line third-class stock and cross-country services must be reviewed for acceleration. Certainly, some of the expresses were both heavy and complex. Typically, the 4pm from King's Cross loaded to 455 tons, had through portions for six destinations, and no less than seven brake coaches.

The upshot was the first in a series of test runs, conducted from November 1934, in which the opportunities for accelerating main line expresses were explored. That of 30 November 1934 took *Flying Scotsman* on four coaches to Leeds in a fraction under 152min, and back in 157¼min. Coming south, the engine was timed at 100mph. A more ambitious trial was staged in March 1935 in preparation for the introduction of a high-speed service between King's Cross and Newcastle. This time Pacific *Papyrus* attained 108mph down Stoke bank.

First came accelerations to the existing trains, particularly the 'Scarborough Flyer' which started its summer run on Saturdays only, then became daily in July. Leaving at 11.10am instead of the long-familiar 11.50am, it was booked to York in 190min, 5min faster than in 1934, and 20min quicker than in 1933; the same timing was made by the return train. Some of the other Saturday trains were speeded-up in the Summer 1935 timetable, as were the traditionally lethargic long-distance Sunday workings which were also bucked up.

The new high-speed express was the 'Silver Jubilee', at 10am Mondays–Fridays from Newcastle–King's Cross and 5.30pm return, and taking 4hr each way. From the Darlington stop, the 232¼ miles to King's Cross were scheduled to be run in 3hr 18min at an average speed of 70.4mph, bringing the train into King's Cross at 2pm. The schedule demanded speeds of 90mph over much of the route. A special set of seven articulated, pressure-ventilated coaches was built, with adequate catering facilities and, like the A4 Pacific at their head, liveried in distinctive silver-grey paintwork. A supplement was charged in first and third-class and, as on the crack East Coast Scottish expresses, a train attendant looked after seat reservations, tickets and passengers' welfare. The train went into service on 30 September 1935 and only one shed – King's Cross – was responsible for providing the crew and A4 motive power. Having established an enviable record for reliability, the 'Silver Jubilee' made its last runs on 31 August 1939.

Wedgwood made it clear that the 'Silver Jubilee' was to be regarded as an experiment, to be reviewed once it had been running for a while. After its first year of operation, he reported that the 'Silver Jubilee' had acted as a stimulus to a 12% rise in Newcastle–London passenger carrying and recommended to the Board two other high-speed trains, to Leeds/Bradford, and to Edinburgh. In 1938, when an extra coach was built to increase the capacity of the 'Silver Jubilee', the train was making a profit of 13/- each loaded train-mile run.

Wedgwood was careful not to refer to some of the operating consequences of the 'Silver Jubilee' whose introduction had spawned a number of other changes in the Winter 1935/6 timetable, some no doubt for the better. The existing 'West Riding Pullman' was withdrawn north of Harrogate, and to compensate a portion was run to/from Hull, and the train retitled the 'Yorkshire Pullman'. A new connecting service into the 'Jubilee' was provided between Middlesbrough and Darlington. The existing 5.30pm King's Cross–Newcastle and the 5.39pm King's Cross–Hull were combined as far as Doncaster, and retimed to 5.45pm. The 8.15am from Newcastle also attached a Hull portion at Doncaster. The existing 5.45pm departure for Leeds/Bradford was delayed 5min. Railways were reluctant to sanction any increase in train mileage, and the net increase arising from the introduction of the 'Jubilee' was just 237 miles per week. This represented some clever planning, but the timings of some 40 passenger and freight trains had been altered by the new service's introduction, and the list of alterations took up 12 pages of typescript.

Other consequences of the 'Jubilee' included the withdrawal of the through coaches between King's Cross and Saltburn, formerly conveyed on the 5.30pm down, and the replacement of the Atlantic on the 'Yorkshire Pullman' by an A1, so that the train could be accelerated to give a 3½hr timing between King's Cross and Hull. By now serving the East Riding, the 'West Riding Pullman' could legitimately change its title. The train now left at 4.45pm, ran to Doncaster in 156min, a time equalled by the up run. Experience soon showed that the new 5.45pm down to Newcastle/Hull was overloaded, and a bad timekeeper. From 1 January 1936, the Hull portion ran as a separate train and was timed to leave King's Cross at 7.15pm for Doncaster (10.3pm) and Hull (11pm), and included a portion for Leeds (arr 10.54pm). The new service met recent requests to the LNER from businessmen for a later evening train between the Capital and Yorkshire towns. Later stops were added at Peterborough and Retford.

The LNER's penchant for on-board 'novelties' spread beyond East Coast expresses. In May 1935, the first cinema car service began on the 10.10am King's Cross–Leeds and 5.30pm return, using a bogie brake van converted with projection equipment, screen, and 44 tip-up seats. From March 1936, a second car was put into service on the 9am Leeds–Glasgow and 4pm return, south of Edinburgh only. This car proved less successful, and in May 1937 was transferred to work between Doncaster and

UP MAIN LINE—WEEKDAYS—continued.   53

	524	530	532	536a	537	538	539		547	548	
	Mnl.	Exp. Pass.	Etles.	Etles.	Exp. Pass.	Exp. Pass.	Exp. Pass.		Mnl.	Exp. Pass.	
Class	B			O	A					B		
	MOQ	SX		Q		SX		SX	SO	MOQ		
	a.m.	a.m		p.m.	p.m.	p.m.	p.m.	a.m.	p.m.	a.m.	p.m.	a.m
YORK (Dringhouses) dep.		p11 19								11 30		11 45
Naburn "											.0	H.C.
Escrick "		H0										
Riccall "										pass		pass
ESLBY arr.	10.30 a.m. from Gascoigne Wood.	11 33		12 15						12 3		12 1
dep.												
Temple Hirst "										A arr. 12.46pm via Thorne Jct.		
Hock "												
Balne "												
Moss "	11 28	11 45	12 45							12 36		12 15
Shaftholme Junction pass	11 A49									1A10		
Arksey dep.												
DONCAS- Central arr.	pass 11 59	pass 11 49			pass 12 6		11 56 12 4	12 6 12 10		pass 12 39	12 15	12 21
dep.	A Arr. 11.37										e 12 25	
TER Bridge Jcn. dep.							12 8					
Mineral arr.		10.0 a.m. from Newcastle.										
dep.										1 50		
Decoy arr.	12 10											
dep.												
Rossington dep.	Does not run when 547 runs.		Worked by M.R. Area, Bentley Colliery arr. 12.80 p.m.				12 23	12 22		Manthorpe Jct. dep. 1.26 p.m.		
Bawtry "												
Scrooby "												
Ranskill "												
Barnby Moor and Sutton "			12.30 p.m. from Colwick, train 176, page 86, Nottingham Book.									
RETFORD arr.		pass 12 4			pass 12 21		12 35 12 47	12 34 12 47			pass 12 44	
dep.												
Gamston "												
East Markham "												
Tuxford North "												
Dukeries Junction "												
Crow Park "												
Carlton-on-Trent "												
NEWARK arr.		pass 12 20			pass 12 36		1 10 1 12	1 10 1 12			pass 1 1¼	
dep.												
Claypole dep.												
Hougham "						12 44½		1 25	1 20			1 11
Barkston South Junction pass		12 28½										
Barkston arr.		pass 12 32		1 55	pass 12 48		1 31 1 35	1 31 1 35			pass 1 16	
GRANTHAM dep.				2 20								
Great Ponton "		Does not run December 23rd to 27th and April 6th to 10th, inclusive.		2 48								
Highdyke "							2 5	2 5				
Corby "			SUSPENDED			Does not run December 23rd to 27th and April 6th to 10th inclusive.						
Little Bytham "												
Essendine arr.												
dep.												
Tallington "												
Werrington Junction "												
New England arr.												
dep.												
PETERBORO' Spital dep.							2 25 2 30	2 25 2 30	SUSPENDED		pass 1 44	
NORTH Station arr.		pass 12 55½			pass 1 11½							
Fletton dep.												
Yaxley and Farcet "												
Holme arr.												
dep.					2.4 p.m. from Cambridge.							
Abbots Ripton "												
Leys "												
HUNTINGDON NORTH arr.		pass 1 11½			pass 1 26½		2 52 2 54	2 52 2 54			pass 2 2	
dep.												
Offord and Buckden arr.												
dep.							3 5	3 5				
St. Neots "												
Tempsford "												
SANDY arr.							J Not advertised	J Not advertised	Pullman Cars.			
dep.												
Biggleswade arr.												
dep.												
Langford "												
Arlesey and Henlow "												
Three Counties "												
HITCHIN arr.		pass 1 32½			pass 1 47½		2 46 2 42	3 29 3 31	3 29 3 31		pass 2 26	
dep.												
Stevenage "												
Langley "								3J57	3J57			
Knebworth "												
Woolmer Green "												
Welwyn North "					2 58							
Welwyn Garden City "												
HATFIELD arr.		pass 1 44			pass 1 58½		3 3 3 4	4 7	4 7		pass 2 40	
dep.												
Brookman's Park "												
Potters Bar "							Will run Goods line Hitchin South to Stevenage South		Will run Goods line Hitchin South to Stevenage South			
Hadley Wood arr.												
dep.												
New Barnet "												
Oakleigh Park "												
New Southgate "												
Wood Green (Alex.Park) dep.												
Hornsey Sidings arr.												
dep.												
Hornsey "												
FERME PARK arr.												
dep.												
Harringay dep.							3 21 3 33	4 25 4C28	4025 4 28			
FINSBURY PARK arr.												
dep.												
EAST GOODS YARD arr.												
dep.												
Holloway arr.												
dep.												
KING'S CROSS (Goods) arr.					2 15		3C29	4 34	4 34		30 9	
" (Passenger) arr.		2 0										

Extract from the working timetable of the Great Northern main line, showing the timings for the up 'Yorkshire Pullman', 'Silver Jubilee' and 'West Riding Limited'.

King's Cross, returning in the newly introduced 7.15pm from King's Cross. The novelty soon palled, and the cinema cars gave their last showings in September 1938.

Passenger traffic on the East Coast services grew rapidly in the mid/late 1930s, to offset a decline in receipts elsewhere on the LNER. Several summer Saturday King's Cross–Edinburgh/Glasgow services, and Scarborough/Whitby workings were now a regular feature of the timetables but to cover these workings stock often had to be borrowed from other Areas. In 1937, approval was given for the building of six sets of coaches for the additional East Coast workings and two trains for the Scarborough expresses.

Early in 1935 the LNER passenger managers agreed that a better deal should be given to travellers between King's Cross and Newcastle Tyne Commission Quay, travelling to/from Norway. Up-to-date stock would be provided, the coaches being labelled as the 'Norseman' and worked down on the noon or 1.20pm trains from King's Cross (which sometimes loaded to 17 coaches) and usually running as a separate train in the up direction, depending on the docking time of the steamer.

The May 1936 timetable brought one major innovation and a number of service accelerations. The Railway at last attempted to cater for the growth in business travel from London by making it possible to travel to Teesside and Tyneside and back in the day. The York portion of the 7.25am from King's Cross was extended to run to Edinburgh, but it was 12.56pm before the day-tripping businessman got to Middlesbrough, and Newcastle was reached only at 1.10pm. The new timetable saw the 'Queen of Scots' speeded-up to a 7¾hr journey between King's Cross and Edinburgh.

That was nothing as compared to the July changes that year which reduced the schedule of the non-stop 'Flying Scotsman' to 7¼hr each way. A new connecting express from Edinburgh made a through journey to Aberdeen possible in 10hr 28min from King's Cross. With the LMS's striking acceleration of the 'Mid-Day Scot' in its May 1936 timetable, for its July timetable the LNER took a knife to the schedule of the 1.20pm King's Cross. It now ran non-stop north of Newcastle, to reach Edinburgh in 7hr 25min, 10min faster than the West Coast train. The up afternoon 'Scotsman' lost its Doncaster and Peterborough stops, and had a 7½hr journey. Another improvement was a fast 7.15am Grimsby–Peterborough, connecting into an up express to reach King's Cross at 10.28am, a 20min faster journey than previously.

Having demonstrably proved the case for high-speed trains, in October 1936 Wedgwood put forward two further proposals for high-speed expresses. Subject to Board approval, one would start in the summer of 1937, to be called the 'Coronation Train' and timed to Edinburgh in 6hr; and the other, scheduled to start in the autumn, would take 2¾hr to Leeds. In fact, planning for the Edinburgh train had started in May 1936 and at first it was envisaged as a seven-coach train, running to Aberdeen in 9hr. Proposed departure times were 12.15pm from King's Cross, and 9.15am from Aberdeen. For various reasons this was impractical, and the train was rethought as a London–Edinburgh service.

The 'Coronation' began running on 5 July 1937, and comprised a nine-coach train of special pressure-ventilated stock, of open layout throughout, and concluding with a beaver-tail ended observation car. To Norman Newsome of the LNER who was closely involved with the design of the stock, "The 'Coronation' was designed with a specific purpose in mind – feed the passengers at their seats and give them a comfortable ride". Supplementary fares were charged and all seats, except those in the observation car, were reservable, the LNER's publicity warning that the 'number of passengers is limited to the seating capacity of the train'. All aspects of its design were carefully worked out and with the matching liveried A4 Pacific at its head, the train represented a quantum leap forward in high-speed operation on British railways.

Leaving King's Cross and Edinburgh at 4pm and 4.30pm respectively, Mondays–Fridays only, at first the 'Coronation' called only at York in the down direction, and at Newcastle southbound; a Newcastle stop was added to the down train from March 1938 and in winter the observation cars were withdrawn. The Summer 1937 timetable saw another 15min cut from the non-stop 'Scotsman' which now took exactly 7hr on its journey, and the relief – 'Junior Scotsman' – was now accelerated to 7hr 20min, despite the up train having no less than five stops.

Very similar stock to that designed for the 'Coronation' was provided for the 'West Riding Limited' which started operation on 27 September 1937. Departing Bradford at 11.10am behind a pair of tank engines, the train left Leeds at 11.31am behind an A4, and arrived at King's Cross at 2.15pm, in the wake of the 'Silver Jubilee'. The down working took its cue from the 7.15pm introduced the previous year and left 5min earlier than that train, with arrivals at Leeds for 9.53pm, and Bradford,

The inaugural up 'West Riding Limited' of 27 September 1937 enters Peterborough North behind A4 Pacific No. 4492 *Dominion of New Zealand*. The Gresley articulated set built for this train was very similar to the sets provided for the 'Coronation'.

10.15pm. Introduction of the new train enforced a change to the routing of the up 'Yorkshire Pullman' which, from Harrogate (11.15am), now ran via York (dep 11.45am), and as before reached King's Cross at 3pm. The cars which went down to Halifax returned empty to Wakefield, then were worked on a King's Cross semi-fast to Doncaster, and attached there to the up 'Pullman'.

The East Coast services may have been transformed but the routine of GC main line expresses continued almost undisturbed. Their haulage remained in the hands of pre-Grouping 'Directors' and Atlantics, but from early 1936 these began to be replaced by a new series of B17 4-6-0s. All were named after Football Association clubs, and by the summer of 1937 had taken over the Manchester–Marylebone expresses, and most fast workings south of Leicester. In place of the light loads that had characterised GC main line services since their inception, the up morning workings to Marylebone such as the 7.30am Sheffield, 8.20am Manchester and 10am Bradford were regularly made up to 10 coaches. Such loadings were probably beyond the capability of the B17s north of Nottingham.

With the installation of 70ft turntables at Marylebone and Leicester it was possible to draft Pacifics to the GC main line, and in late September 1938 the first A1 started working regularly between Manchester and Marylebone, soon to be joined by a V2 2-6-2. It was not until the spring of the next year that enough of the large engines were available to cover the principal workings.

Symptomatic of the changing GC scene was the withdrawal of the last slip coach workings, those at Finmere and Woodford Halse (for Stratford-upon-Avon) off the 6.20pm Marylebone–Bradford. In December 1935, the Woodford slip had been involved in an accident when a fault in the slipping procedure led to a collision between the slip coach and the rear of the 6.20pm as it was braking to a stop at Woodford. The resulting inquiry seems to have brought the withdrawal of both slips from February 1936, and also the end of the Marylebone–Stratford through service.

Apart from the trains patronised by businessmen, by the late 1930s the other GC main line expresses were more in the nature of high-quality semi-fasts, noted for their smart running and excellent restaurant cars, and made up with the latest Gresley stock. The value of the route was enhanced by its use for cross-country expresses and special workings such as the

Marylebone–Immingham Docks specials connecting with Orient Line cruise sailings and, from May 1937, the cheap fare FSO 10.45pm Marylebone–Newcastle and 11pm return excursions. These were routed via the S&K Joint line to York, and via West Hartlepool and Sunderland.

Other than the introduction of the B17s, the rebuilding of the former Great Eastern B12 4-6-0s and introduction of Gresley rolling stock, into the early 1930s the GE main line services similarly kept out of the limelight. The Southend line services were improved during 1933 when some down trains were divided at Shenfield, and the fast portions were briskly timed on to Prittlewell. By Summer 1938, the best trains were doing the Liverpool St.–Southend run in just under the hour with a couple of stops.

The summer expresses to the East Anglian resorts, so much a feature of GER days, had continued, and the best was the 12.25pm SO Liverpool St.–Cromer which ran non-stop in 170min, faster than the pre-1914 'Norfolk Coast Express'. The 'Eastern Belle' made ten or so runs to Cromer during the summer, and was usually booked to run non-stop to Wroxham in 144min, called at North Walsham and reached Cromer in 179min, as did the up working which stopped at Ilford to 'put down' passengers. From

1936, five-day season tickets were available for the 'Eastern Belle' which during the week offered the purchaser daily departures from Liverpool St. at 11am to resorts such as Aldeburgh, Hunstanton, Cromer – and Skegness.

From July 1935, the first morning Cromer–Liverpool St. restaurant car express left from Beach station and travelled via Mundesley to North Walsham, there to combine with a portion from Sheringham. Alterations in the July 1936 timetable included a summer Saturday 10am Liverpool St.–Hunstanton in 155min, with stops at King's Lynn and Heacham only. The daily 11.50am from Liverpool St. and 5.28pm return were speeded-up by 30min or so and now took 3hr to/from Hunstanton. That same timetable also brought the fast 11.52pm SO train from Liverpool St. which with three stops was booked to Norwich in 141min – the fastest time to date. But still the GE section clung to the last slip workings outside the Great Western, at Waltham Cross from the 6pm from Liverpool St., and at Marks Tey (for Bury St Edmunds) off the 4.57pm Liverpool St.–Clacton. The first of these ceased in the spring of 1937, but the Marks Tey slip was made until July 1939.

Early in 1937, it was agreed to run a fast train between Liverpool St. and Norwich which would be

The Gresley big engines only came to the GC main line on the eve of war. This is the 8.20am Manchester London Road–Marylebone on 17 June 1939 with V2 class 2-6-2 No. 4828, seen just south of Wilford Bridge, Nottingham. Behind the engine is the through LMS coach from Halifax–Marylebone.

To overcome a shortage of powerful engines the LNER ordered a batch of GER-design B12 class 4-6-0s in 1928, and here is one of them, No. 8579, passing Chadwell Heath in July 1931 with an up Colchester line express, formed of ex-GER corridor stock.

similar in specification, but not speed, to the East Coast high-speed trains. No supplementary fares were to be charged as the overall journey time would only be 9min faster than the current best. A test train hauled by a rebuilt B12 had been run in July 1936, and in each direction its running times were 120min. With open layout coaches internally somewhat in the style of the 'Coronation', the new train was titled the 'East Anglian', and began running in September 1937. The times were 11.55am from Norwich, calling only at Ipswich, and taking 135min overall while the down working was at 6.40pm. From January 1938, 5min was chipped from the schedules and the up train retimed to leave at midday. The engines used were specially streamlined B17 4-6-0s. Even finer rolling stock was built to re-equip the 'Hook Continental' train as from October 1938, with at-seat service from two kitchen cars and two Pullman cars attached in addition.

The September 1937 timetable brought a more enterprising service to the Cambridge line with non-stop Liverpool St.–Cambridge trains made up of five coaches including buffet car. There were three workings each way in 65min, at 11.10am, 1.40, and 4.12pm down, and 11.50am, 2.20 and 8.30pm up. The 1.40pm down and 2.20 and 8.30pm up lasted only until the end of the Summer 1938 timetable. There was part-compensation in the Winter 1938/9

timetable with a new train at 7.25am from Ipswich to Bury St Edmunds, Cambridge and Liverpool St., its return run taking over the previous 4.12pm departure and that train's 65min booking to Cambridge.

Other lightweight trains with buffet cars were introduced, this time in the North Eastern Area. First came the use of such cars from the Winter 1937/8 timetable formed in new gangwayed sets which took over the hourly Newcastle–Stockton–Middlesbrough service, and on Leeds, York and Scarborough workings. Then buffet cars appeared on the Newcastle–Carlisle service which, from July 1938, was totally revised to feature an unprecedented time of 77min by the westbound noon train over the 60½ miles of this slack-infested and heavily graded route. Two other trains took 80min for the journey.

New rolling stock was entering service at a remarkable rate and, during the summer of 1938, it was the turn of the 'Flying Scotsman' which was re-equipped with pressure-ventilated stock, if still of the traditional Gresley teak-bodied construction. The sets included restaurant cars and a buffet lounge vehicle which took the place of the previous hairdressing salon/ladies retiring-room car. The non-stop run to/from Edinburgh now came down to 7hr for the 392¾ miles, and was made also on Sundays.

The July 1938 timetable also brought the daily division of the 1.20pm from King's Cross, the Tyne

Critics carped about the unadventurous running times given to the 'East Anglian' but the coal consumption of the streamlined B17s which hauled it suggested that they had to be worked hard to keep time. The LNER reckoned that the train had helped to fight off coach competition. No. 2859 *East Anglian* brings the up train through Goodmayes on 28 September 1937, the second day of its operation.

Buffet car expresses were introduced between Newcastle and Carlisle, and this is the 2.27pm from Newcastle west of Haltwhistle during the winter of 1937 behind ex-North Eastern C9 Atlantic No. 2171.

Crossing Croxdale Viaduct to the south of Durham on 16 February 1939, the up 'Flying Scotsman' epitomises the last days of the prewar LNER East Coast expresses. The coaches may still be teak-panelled, but are pressure ventilated, and the buffet lounge car features a number of clever innovations. The engine is – again – A4 No. 4492 *Dominion of New Zealand*.

Commission Quay portion leaving 10min earlier. The 4pm down Yorkshire express was also divided and a separate buffet car train now left for Cleethorpes at 4.5pm, and at the weekend included though coaches for Horncastle and Skegness. On the East Coast express workings there was now a tendency for engines to be diagrammed to make longer through workings, such as Grantham–Edinburgh. Early in 1939 one A4 was recorded as running 661 miles in just 12hr.

The first wartime timetables came into force in October 1939 when the East Coast Scottish day trains were reduced to just one each way, and the GC main line services were drastically cut back, to just two day and one night train each way, all four Marylebone–Bradford expresses being withdrawn. Cambridge and Hull lost most of their through trains to/from London. Before long, the East Coast services were supplemented by virtually regular relief trains while principal services were loading to 20 coaches. In January 1940, a separate 5.30pm King's Cross–Newcastle and 8am up reappeared and was booked to take just under 6hr each way. Yet, in May 1940, the scheduled main line service out of King's Cross was half that of prewar days. At first on-train catering had been suspended but it was soon restored, and the LNER in particular placed great reliance on buffet cars so that some 90 trains featured them in 1941.

The advertised wartime service was no clue to the number of trains actually run. One Friday night in September 1942, of seven expresses arriving at

King's Cross within 30min three were the main trains, the others their duplicates and in all they comprised 132 coaches. From March 1943, much longer non-stop runs were being made by East Coast expresses. The 9.50am King's Cross–Edinburgh, for instance, called only at Grantham, Darlington and Newcastle.

Not all the principal trains had been withdrawn on the outbreak of war and the 'Aberdonian' and 'Night Scotsman', for example, turned out to be two of the only four trains which retained their titles throughout hostilities. The latter ran between King's Cross and Edinburgh only but took no more than 37min longer than it had prewar.

The 'Flying Scotsman' was speeded-up from October 1945 when it was accelerated by 50min to an 8hr 5min schedule, the up train being 5min faster. Reinstatement of the 'Yorkshire Pullman' came from November 1946, but because of the coal crisis it was suspended between March and October 1947. The 'East Anglian' had recommenced running in October 1946, the only one of the prewar prestige trains to reappear, while the other GE line stalwart, the 'Hook Continental', was reinstated as early as November 1945, at first three times weekly but daily operation was resumed the following year. The LNER's top management was keen to see the high-speed expresses return to the East Coast main line but, with the heavy loadings of the early postwar years had to accept realities and leave the handsome rolling stock to gather dust in storage.

CHAPTER THIRTEEN

THE SCOTTISH RAILWAYS FROM GROUPING

The first proposals drafted for railway Grouping by the Ministry of Transport included a Scottish group, formed of the five railways, but opposition from interests in Scotland resulted in the five railways being joined as appropriate to the east and west coast English groups – LNER and LMS – with the promise of some element of cross-subsidisation. In looking at the Scottish main line services after 1923 it seems sensible to keep them together rather than 'losing' them among the wider interests of the Big Four.

Possibly a Scottish group might have tackled the rationalisation of duplicate services and facilities more quickly than occurred under the LMS and LNER. In the event, it was left until 1933 and 'pooling' of competitive traffic before much happened and, for instance, the LMS withdrew through coaches between Edinburgh Princes St. and Dundee West in favour of the LNER service. The jointly owned stations remained, at Aberdeen and Perth, the latter Scotland's major interchange point between railways. Comparing winter and summer there was a great disparity in traffic, and in the sort of services and through coach workings operated.

Despite the number of Caledonian 4-6-0s, 4-4-0s of pre-Grouping and LMS Compound design dominated the passenger workings on the LMS's Glasgow–Aberdeen main line into the early 1930s. Speeds were not particularly high on this route, even on falling gradients, and enginemen expended their efforts on maintaining satisfactory speeds uphill. The contract with the Pullman Car Co. inherited by the LMS from the Caledonian expired in December 1933, and the 22 cars built 1914-27 were purchased by the Railway to be used as restaurant cars on scheduled services and for excursions, some into England.

By late 1928, the 'Royal Scots' were working Anglo–Scottish expresses to Glasgow Central, but it was not until 1934 or so that those working to Perth from the South were purloined to work to Dundee and Aberdeen. For instance, a 'Scot' working into Perth on the down 'Royal Highlander' took an express to Aberdeen, returning with a fish train to Perth, and then returning south with the 10.5pm sleeper. From the Winter 1934/35 timetable, LMS Class 5s were being used on Glasgow–Aberdeen expresses, and in the July 1935 timetable there was a new pair of expresses: the 9.15am Aberdeen–Glasgow and 7.15pm return, the first taking 3hr 30min, the other, 6min more.

The LNER introduced new motive power to internal Scottish services, such as the D11/2 and D49 4-4-0s, into traffic from 1924 and 1928 respectively, but the services were not greatly altered. One innovation was the use of Pullman cars on former North British lines, displaced from the 'Queen of Scots' by the new all-steel stock. From the July 1929 timetable, and in subsequent seasons, a Pullman restaurant car – on which a supplementary fare was not charged – was introduced between Glasgow and North Berwick on the summer-only 'Lothian Coast Express'. It did not reappear for the 1932 summer service. In winter this car and another were at work on Glasgow–Edinburgh expresses.

More Pullman cars were added, between

Shandon, on the West Highland line, in 1936 with a Fort William–Glasgow Queen St. train headed by K2 class 2-6-0 No. 4684. There are three fairly recent LNER corridor coaches, and a tail of several fish vans!

Edinburgh and Perth (1932) and, by the summer of 1934, between Edinburgh and Carlisle, and between Glasgow and Dundee. By the winter of 1937, there were two journeys worked between Edinburgh and Glasgow, one between Edinburgh and Carlisle and two between Edinburgh and Perth. All were withdrawn on the outbreak of World War II. The 'Lothian Coast Express' had also ceased running after the summer of 1933. Other summer residential fast trains ran between Glasgow and Edinburgh and the Fife Coast, such as the 6.50am St Andrews–Queen St and 4.10pm return.

From the late 1920s, standard LNER gangwayed stock was put into service on Edinburgh–Glasgow and Aberdeen expresses. North of Edinburgh, an attempt had been made during the summer of 1928 to use the triplet restaurant cars from the 'Flying Scotsman' to work to/from Aberdeen but they had proved unsuitable and were diverted instead to/from Glasgow. For the Summer 1929 service, the LNER transferred ex-Great Northern restaurant cars to inaugurate on-train catering on the West Highland line. During the winter, when there were no more than two down and three up expresses, a car continued on the 5.5am Glasgow–Fort William and 4.5pm return, joined from September 1933 by restaurant service on the 3.43pm Glasgow–Fort William and the breakfast-time departure from there.

From October 1929, sleeping cars commenced running daily between King's Cross and Fort William. There was no Sunday train service on the West Highland line during the winter but, from the 1934 season, there were regular half-day excursions on Sundays from Bridgeton Cross via Glasgow Queen St., and from Edinburgh and some other stations, to Fort William and back. The bucket-seated LNER Tourist stock was used from the summer of 1935. Withdrawn in September 1939, these West Highland excursion trains returned in 1949.

Until bridge strengthening had been carried out by the LMS north of Kinnaber Junction in 1930, and so permitted the use of A1 Class Pacifics between Edinburgh and Aberdeen, the North British Atlantics were the largest engines that could be used. After the deceleration of the short-lived 3hr service between Edinburgh and Aberdeen introduced in 1906, nothing to comparable schedules had appeared until January 1935 when the LNER introduced a new 8.55am Aberdeen–Edinburgh express timed in 3hr 9min, and the extension of the 7.25pm Edinburgh–Dundee to run to Aberdeen (arr 10.43pm). This train provided a connection out of the down 'Queen of Scots', but the 8.55am up missed the up Pullman by no more than 45min. The through daytime coaches between St Pancras and Aberdeen had been withdrawn in May 1932.

Compounds were allocated to Kingmoor for express workings over the Glasgow & South Western main line from 1925, and others arrived in 1927. In June 1923, Pullman services had been extended to the Glasgow & South Western section, and new cars were built in that year, and in 1927. The LMS restored the daytime sailings between Stranraer and Larne, and from 1925 LMS restaurant cars – rather than Pullmans – came to the connecting 12.25pm Stranraer–Glasgow and 4.10pm return. The Pullmans were working to Stranraer by 1930, on the 5.10pm SX, 12.30pm SO from Glasgow–Girvan, and the 7.22am return. The following year, there was another change to the service, with an 8pm Glasgow–Stranraer boat train, and a 7.20pm Stranraer–Glasgow while the 5.10pm Ayr train was extended to Stranraer in place of the 4.10pm.

From Summer 1935, LMS 5P4F 2-6-0s began to work regularly on Carlisle–Stranraer and Stranraer–Glasgow expresses, all other Glasgow–Stranraer trains by then being worked by Compounds. Another innovation in the Summer 1935 timetable had been a first-ever, but short-lived acceleration of the 5.10pm from St Enoch to take 48min to Ayr. Later, 45min was the timing for the 8.27am ex-Ayr and 5.10pm from St Enoch, and by then 'Jubilee' 4-6-0s were used. It was the summer of 1938 before there were other accelerations, including 50min trains between

Glasgow and Ayr, including a Paisley stop. Summer 1937 had seen the morning and evening residential trains between St Enoch and Largs accelerated to 55min for the 42¾ miles. From spring 1939 Class 5s were being used between Glasgow and Stranraer, soon to be joined by 'Jubilees'.

There were two Carlisle–Stranraer Harbour trains, the first with through London coaches including the Turnberry sleeping car. The other had the TPO van for Stranraer off the West Coast postal, and the through coach from Newcastle-upon-Tyne, and as far as Dumfries included a TPO van for Ayr. With Compound haulage, the timings of the St Pancras–Glasgow trains had been smartened up in 1928, with no more than 56min allowed to the down 'Thames–Clyde Express' for the 48¾ miles from Dumfries to passing Mauchline. Further accelerations followed in the Winter 1932/3 timetable with two 145min, one 146min and two 150min timings for the St Pancras/Leeds–Glasgow expresses.

Services on the Great North of Scotland generally retained the pattern of 1922, but in summer the 7.45am Aberdeen–Inverness, with restaurant car, included the through sleeping car and coach from King's Cross to Lossiemouth. These worked south on the 4.30pm from Elgin via Craigellachie. The 2.20pm from Aberdeen carried the through Edinburgh–Lossiemouth coach while through

Out from Dumfries comes a down express of the mid-1920s hauled by an ex-Glasgow & South Western 4-4-0, No. 14206. These engines disappeared quickly in the next few years, supplanted by standard LMS designs.

During 1936, an Aberdeen–Inverness through train enters Elgin behind ex-Highland 'Castle' 4-6-0 No. 14692 *Darnaway Castle*, its train no more than three LNER gangwayed coaches and a bogie brake.

coaches from Inverness to Aberdeen were worked in summer on the 7.35pm from Elgin. By the late 1920s, the 7.45am from Aberdeen was a summer-only train, and the Inverness coaches normally passed on the 8.5am departure from there. There was a second Aberdeen–Inverness restaurant car working at 2.20pm. The restaurant cars on this route were jointly provided by the LMS and LNER. Up through coach workings from Inverness were on the 9.35am from Elgin, 1.3pm from Keith, and 4.30 and 7.35pm from Elgin.

The fast Speyside line excursions were running WSO at 1pm from Aberdeen (sometimes with a relief 5min later) and 8pm from Boat of Garten (the relief from Grantown on Spey). The down train ran non-stop to Dufftown in 84min for 64 miles. The GNoS 4-4-0s were not challenged on passenger work until the arrival of ex-NBR D31 4-4-0s from 1925 and, from 1931, ex-Great Eastern B12 4-6-0s, by which time standard Gresley gangwayed stock was in use.

In 1927/8, almost all of the Perth–Inverness principal services were worked by Highland 'Clan' or 'Castle' 4-6-0s, assisted by 'Loch' and 'Ben' 4-4-0s. One major change was the provision on nearly all principal trains of LMS restaurant cars or Pullman cars whose use had involved the transfer of

gangwayed stock to the Highland section from other parts of the LMS.

The Highland main line services included the 1.30am from Perth which took the through sleeper composite from Glasgow Buchanan St., and in summer through coaches for Wick and Thurso. From Inverness there was a connecting 6am Far North train for Wick and Thurso, with restaurant car as far as The Mound. The through sleeping cars from King's Cross and Euston were worked from Perth on the 6.25am down (with Pullman restaurant car) in winter, this train being preceded in summer by two workings with the through sleeping cars, respectively via Carr Bridge and Forres, the latter with restaurant car.

The 6.25am was also a complex train, splitting into three sections at Aviemore, fast and stopping to Inverness direct, and via Forres. It also connected at Inverness into the 10.10am Far North train, with restaurant car to Helmsdale, and the 10.20am to Kyle. The principal Scottish service was on the noon train from Perth, via Carr Bridge and via Forres, and with through coaches from Glasgow Buchanan St. and Edinburgh Waverley, and a Pullman car running from Buchanan St. to Aviemore. The last through day train from Perth was the 3.40pm down, with restaurant car and Glasgow (LMS) and Edinburgh (LNER) through coaches.

The principal up expresses from Inverness were the 8.30am without restaurant car; the 10am via Forres and 11am via Carr Bridge, combining at Aviemore and with TC to Glasgow and Edinburgh and restaurant cars; the 3.45pm with Pullman from Aviemore and through coaches for Edinburgh, Glasgow and, in summer from Wick; the 4.15pm with sleeping car to Euston, and restaurant car; the 4.35pm, the second sleeping car express, with through cars for Euston and King's Cross, and lastly the 11.20pm sleeping car train to Glasgow Buchanan St. The 11.20am Aviemore–Perth completed the service, with return Pullman car to Perth. On Sundays, no regular passenger trains operated over the line until the summer of 1929, although during the mid/late 1920s some half-day excursions were run from Glasgow to Inverness.

From the summer of 1928 the six 'River' 4-6-0s ordered by the Highland Railway, but sold to the Caledonian, began to work regularly between Perth and Inverness and, soon after, ten 5P4F 2-6-0s were also allocated to the Highland although the indigenous 'Clans' and 'Castles' retained some duties.

The Kyle line had been worked by 'Skye' bogie 4-4-0s until the mid-1920s but, in due course, the ex-HR Cumming Goods 4-6-0s took over. The service comprised three up and two down trains, one each way through from Inverness, and of which two up and one down were mixed trains. On the Far North line, a faster summer train between Aviemore and Wick had run in prewar days and was repeated for the 1923 season and, from the 1924 season onwards, it left from Inverness at 4.30pm; it was withdrawn in 1926 because of the General Strike. In 1927, it was running with restaurant car at 4.10pm FSO and with eight stops only took 5hr 25min to Wick, the complementary 9.25am SO up having seven stops and taking 15min longer. The down train connected out of the noon service from Perth, the up train into the afternoon sleeping car trains. Otherwise, the principal trains were the 10.20am Inverness–Wick, and 8.25am and 3.20pm from Wick, the 8.25 with through coaches in summer to Glasgow, and both with restaurant cars, the former from The Mound, the latter from Helmsdale.

In the summer of 1933, the additional summer trains on the Far North line had been named the 'John o'Groat' and ran three days a week. Naming also spread to other workings, and in 1936 the name 'Orcadian' was applied to the 6.45am from Inverness and the 3.30pm return train which connected with the

NIGHT TRAINS TO SCOTLAND FOR THE TWELFTH

The finest fleet of trains in the world steams North to Scotland every day and is specially augmented for the 12th. Day and night they leave Euston, King's Cross and St. Pancras with their restaurants and sleeping-cars (first and third class) and their excellent staffs of servants. Below is a full list of night trains. Times of day trains will be supplied on request at any L M S or L·N·E·R station or office.

FROM EUSTON (LMS)
WEEKDAYS

P.M.		A.M.	
7.20 AB	"The Royal Highlander"—Perth, Boat of Garten, Inverness, Aberdeen.	12.30 DE	Dumfries, Kilmarnock, Glasgow.
7.30 AB	Oban.	**P.M.**	**SUNDAYS**
7.40 AB	Stirling, Gleneagles, Dundee.	7.20 B	"The Royal Highlander"—Perth, Boat of Garten, Inverness.
8.0 A	Dumfries, Stranraer Harbour, Turnberry.	7.30 B	Stirling, Oban, Gleneagles, Perth, Dundee, Aberdeen.
9.25	Glasgow (On Saturdays, Third Class Sleeping Accommodation only).	8.30	Dumfries, Stranraer, Turnberry.
		9.30	Glasgow (Cent.).
10.50	Edinburgh, Stirling, Gleneagles, Perth, Dundee, Aberdeen, Inverness.	10.50	Edinburgh, Stirling, Gleneagles, Perth, Dundee, Aberdeen, Oban.
11.45	"Night Scot"—Glasgow	11.45	"Night Scot"—Glasgow.

NOTES: **A** Saturdays excepted. **B** Dining Car Euston to Crewe. **D** Saturday nights and Sunday mornings excepted. **E** Sleeping Cars to Kilmarnock.

FROM KING'S CROSS (L·N·E·R)
WEEKDAYS AND SUNDAYS

P.M.		P.M.	
*7.25 R	"The Highlandman"—Edinburgh, Fort William (Breakfast car attached en route), Perth, Inverness.	†10.35	Edinburgh, Glasgow. (North Berwick. First class only and on Friday nights only.)
*7.40 R	"The Aberdonian"—Edinburgh, Dundee, Aberdeen, Elgin, Lossiemouth.	A.M.	
†10.25	"The Night Scotsman" — Glasgow, Dundee, Aberdeen, Perth.	§1.5	After-Theatre Sleeping and Breakfast Car Train. Edinburgh, Glasgow, Dundee, Aberdeen, Perth, Inverness.

*Nightly (except Saturdays). †Nightly. §Daily (except Sunday mornings). **R** Restaurant Car King's Cross to York.

FROM ST. PANCRAS (LMS)

P.M.	WEEKDAYS	P.M.	SUNDAYS
9.15	Edinburgh, Perth, Aberdeen, Inverness.	9.15	Edinburgh, Perth, Aberdeen, Inverness.
9.30	Dumfries, Kilmarnock and Glasgow (St. Enoch).	9.30	Dumfries, Kilmarnock and Glasgow (St. Enoch).

With a return ticket to Scotland, you now have the choice of travelling back by the East Coast, West Coast, or Midland routes, with break of journey at any station.
PENNY A MILE SUMMER TICKETS are issued every day (first class only two thirds higher) for return any time within one month—break your journey at any station. Ask at any L·N·E·R or L M S Station or Office for Pocket Timetables and Programme of Circular Tours.
MOTOR CARS accompanied by one first-class or two third-class adult passengers are conveyed to include outward and homeward journeys at the reduced rate of 4½d. a mile charged on the single journey mileage for distances not less than 50 miles. Single journey charges at 3d. a mile.

IT'S QUICKER BY RAIL
LONDON MIDLAND & SCOTTISH RLY. ● LONDON & NORTH EASTERN RLY.

sailing to/from the Orkneys. In August 1939, the 'John o'Groat', at 10.10am from Wick, was taking 5hr 10min to Inverness, and the return 4.10pm, 4hr 49min to Wick.

A restaurant car was worked on the Skye line in 1928 on the 10.30am from Inverness as far as Achnasheen, to return on the mid-morning train from Kyle of Lochalsh. From 1933, the trains running on the Kyle line in connection with the MacBrayne's sailings to/from Stornoway were named the 'Hebridean' and 'Lewisman': the 7.25am from Inverness (TC from Glasgow) and 10.45am return, and the 5.5am from Kyle and the 10.15am to Kyle respectively: the second pair featured a through

Ready to do battle with the snow fiend, ex-Highland 0-6-0 No. 138, with sturdy plough, is leading Highland 4-4-0 No. 74 *Durn* at Wick on the 2.30pm departure for Inverness on 1 March 1924.

The LMS drafted the Hughes Moguls to the Highland lines, and a pair of them – Nos 13103 and 13101 – are seen in the early 1930s near Hermitage Tunnel, north of Dunkeld with the 3.40pm Inverness–Glasgow Buchanan St.

Displaced from their native lines by an influx of Stanier Class 5 4-6-0s, the Highland 'Clan' 4-6-0s were transferred to work the Oban line. Not long before they were ousted from there, too, No. 14764 *Clan Munro* pauses at Stirling on 14 July 1938 with a Glasgow–Oban train which includes several modern LMS coaches.

coach from/to Glasgow Buchanan St. In winter, the 7.25am ex-Inverness and 5.5am ex-Kyle were withdrawn.

The major change to the Highland lines was one of motive power, the all-conquering Stanier Class 5 4-6-0s having taken over many workings north of Perth from late 1934, and by 1936 even in summer dominating the passenger services, but with no change to schedules. The arrival of these engines displaced the 'Clans' to the Callander & Oban line which they were working in 1937 in league with 'Castles'; '5s' took over here, too, during 1939. Still in its original Pullman colours, the *Maid of Morven* observation car remained at work, a special fare of 20s 3d including all meals being charged from Glasgow to Oban and back. By late 1938, the Class 5s were at work through to Wick but the class was not passed to work to Kyle until 1948.

Behind the scenes, and despite continuing economies in operation, the LMS twice contemplated – in 1930 and again in 1936 – closure of the whole system north of Perth, or at least the lines beyond Inverness. The conclusion was that loss of revenue would narrowly outweigh any savings in costs.

From the Summer 1936 timetable, the LMS began speeding-up the Glasgow–Aberdeen service, with the down 'Granite City' and 1.40pm from Buchanan St. having most of their existing stops cut out north of Perth, the former now taking 3hr 12min, the fastest-yet regularly scheduled, and the latter, 6min more. Another couple of trains took 3hr 23min, the 7.15pm from Glasgow being a new service. A new 4.30pm Buchanan St.–Inverness was introduced at the same time and, by use of the 7.25am King's Cross–Edinburgh, this enabled the London–Inverness journey to be made in daytime.

The Summer 1937 timetable brought 180min timings for the Glasgow–Aberdeen expresses, by the 10.5am and 1.30pm down, and the 9.35am and 3.20pm from Aberdeen. Stops were made at Perth and Stonehaven only, but the 9.35am called at Forfar instead. These fast workings disappeared with the Winter 1937/8 timetable although their replacements were faster than before, in 3hr 30-50min with up to eight stops, and the 3.30pm from Aberdeen included the TPO vans for Euston, detached at Perth. Two 3hr trains each way – the 'Saint Mungo' – 9.35am ex-Aberdeen and 1.30pm return – and 'Bon Accord' – 10.5am ex-Glasgow and 3.20pm return – were reintroduced for the 1938 and 1939 summer

The massive Gresley P2 class 2-8-2s were a grand choice for the sleeping car trains which loaded to 550tons but often outgunned the other Edinburgh–Aberdeen workings. No 2001 *Cock o' the North* sounds its whistle as it passes Inverkeithing.

timetables. Their motive power was generally 'Jubilee' 4-6-0s on eight-coach trains.

Between Edinburgh and Aberdeen there was a 3hr express in the Summer 1936 timetable, at 5.15pm from Waverley and conveying the through coaches off the 'Flying Scotsman' while the 9am from Aberdeen was now booked in 3hr 4min only with four intermediate stops. By late 1936, the Gresley P2 class 2-8-2s were at work on the route, their loads varying from the 215 ton load sometimes found on the 9am ex-Aberdeen to the 500 ton-plus sleeping car trains. With the May 1938 timetable, the 6.40am Aberdeen–Edinburgh was accelerated to take no more than 3hr 9min with eight intermediate stops, and the 9am became a 3hr train. Another specialised Gresley design was produced for the West Highland line, in the shape of the K4 2-6-0s of which six were at work by early 1939. Although

timings were not reduced, their K4's value lay in the elimination of piloting on trains loaded up to nine coaches.

Much of Scotland was regarded as of strategic importance during World War II, and lines such as the Mallaig Extension were designated Prohibited Zones. Although train services were reduced, passenger train timings suffered less than in the rest of Britain. Indeed, those between Glasgow and Aberdeen were some of the fastest, and one at least of these trains was worked by a Crewe Pacific off a sleeping car train. Between Perth and Inverness, the 'Royal Highlander's' timing of 3hr 12min was the fastest ever northbound working. On the Highland section generally, although wartime ordinary passenger traffic was greatly reduced, the number of special trains run for service personnel redressed the balance.

CHAPTER FOURTEEN

CROSS-COUNTRY INTER-RAILWAY SERVICES 1923-47

Aberdeen-Penzance – East and West Coast

The East Coast's Aberdeen–Penzance service seems to have proved a disappointment in that, although it continued running until 1939, the through facilities were never developed. The new first-class sleeping cars supplied by the LNER for the working were withdrawn in May 1924, and that Company's NBR-built through coaches were criticised for being elderly during the early 1930s, and accordingly received a modest facelift. In place of the GWR restaurant car previously provided, from 1926 the catering facilities between York and Swindon comprised no more than a small buffet in one of the ex-GNR articulated twin brake composites, and it was not until 1939 that purpose-built restaurant-buffet cars were introduced by the LNER.

The Aberdeen–Penzance was one of the first duties on the GC main line for V2 2-6-2s which worked the train between Sheffield and Banbury and return. The Aberdeen/Glasgow–Penzance through coaches were withdrawn in September 1939 and not reinstated.

The competitive service from Penzance to Aberdeen via the West Coast route was withdrawn during the late 1920s.

North West to South West/South Wales
North and West via the Severn Tunnel
During the early 1930s, the two principal through expresses over the North & West route to/from the West Country were the 2.35am from Shrewsbury and 10.32am from Crewe, both to Plymouth, while the 1.10pm Crewe–Taunton and 4.7pm Crewe–Bristol conveyed through coaches from Birkenhead to Penzance, Liverpool–Penzance/Plymouth and Manchester–Paignton. Those on the 4.7pm were attached at Bristol to the 6.30pm Paddington–Plymouth, and comprised coaches from Liverpool, Birkenhead and Glasgow Central.

There were five northbound workings from the West of England, at 8.45am from Plymouth (TCs to Glasgow, Liverpool, Birkenhead and Manchester), and 7.45, 10.15am, 12.30 and 5.5pm from Penzance, variously with through coaches for Liverpool or Manchester or both, and to Glasgow – on the 12.30pm. The service was greatly expanded on summer Saturdays in the 1930s, as compared with the early days of Grouping. The overall times of these cross-country services remained slow, the overall time in 1938 from Liverpool to Bristol being 3hr 30min, or an average speed of no more than 36mph.

Until 1935, the through coaches between South Wales and the North West had mostly travelled on North & West expresses from/to the West of England, with the result that these were often heavily laden and slow. In July 1935, the GWR and LMS introduced a 'businessmen's' service, all trains with restaurant cars, at 7.45am and 5.5pm from Swansea to Manchester (arr 1.20pm and 10.30pm), and 8.20am and 6.17pm return in similar timings, all some 30-45min faster than before. Retained for the Winter 1935/6 timetable, this enterprising attempt at improving cross-country services did not last, one pair of trains being withdrawn after Summer 1937, and the 7.45am ex-Swansea and 6.15pm from Manchester were deleted as from the Winter 1938/9 service.

The GWR service between Birmingham and

With the arrival of the Stanier 4-6-0s the LMS West of England line trains were further accelerated, though time had been cut from the schedules in 1933 when Compounds were in charge. This Bristol–Sheffield express is seen climbing the Lickey Incline during 1938 with ex-MR 4-4-0 No. 508 piloting Stanier Class 5 4-6-0 No. 5285. Just one 3F 0-6-0 tank is banking.

South Wales via Worcester, Hereford and Pontypool Road which had been introduced in 1922 continued to 1939, with three trains each way. Their times of 3-3½hr between Birmingham and Cardiff compared with the fastest schedules of 140-145min made by the diesel railcar service between both cities which was routed via Honeybourne.

Nearly all the North & West route passenger trains were worked by GWR engines in the mid-1920s but one turn with the 1pm from Shrewsbury to Hereford and back with the 7.55pm mail train was worked alternately by a GWR 'County' 4-4-0 and an ex-LNWR 'Prince of Wales'. Later 'Saints', 'Castles' and 'Halls' were staple power.

Most other cross-country express services were either cut back or withdrawn entirely during World War II, but the North & West expresses remained almost unaltered, except that the Birkenhead and Glasgow through portions were withdrawn; indeed some trains were duplicated as from October 1941. The Birkenhead through coaches were not restored after 1945.

Sheffield–Bristol/Weston-super-Mare
The summer Sheffield–Weston-super-Mare and return restaurant car train had disappeared by the late 1930s, but there was a 'dated' Saturday 1.25pm Paignton–Sheffield (arr 9.24pm) routed via Bristol, Swindon, Oxford and Banbury.

South Coast to South Wales
Portsmouth–Cardiff/Plymouth/Reading
The restaurant car of the Cardiff–Brighton was withdrawn c1927 but the train continued to run through to/from Brighton. The complexities of the train were reduced by the early 1930s when the Plymouth coaches became a separate working, as did the Bournemouth service which, by Summer 1938, was running at 9.42am from Brighton, and 1.48pm return.

From 1927, the Brighton–Plymouth service, with restaurant car, was worked west of Salisbury on the 12.40pm from Waterloo–West of England, but ran separately at summer weekends. There was also a morning through coach working from Portsmouth to Plymouth, worked west of Salisbury on a London express.

In 1937, the Brighton–Plymouth ceased running into/out of Portsmouth & Southsea, and instead a through Portsmouth portion was joined to or removed from the main train at Fareham. The times were now noon from Brighton and 12.55pm from Portsmouth & Southsea, arriving Plymouth at 6.27pm, with the return at 11.10am and a Brighton arrival at 5.26pm.

By the mid-1930s, SR engines, usually 2-6-0s but later 4-6-0s, were working to/from Bristol, particularly on the 4.18pm from Salisbury and 8.45pm from Bristol. Times changed little on the Portsmouth–Cardiff trains from their introduction in 1896 into the late 1930s.

From 1920, there were through trains from Portsmouth Town via Basingstoke and Reading, at 8.22am to Birkenhead, and at 2.30pm/3pm to Birmingham, neither with a return working. In 1930, the earlier of these trains which had become the 8.45am from Portsmouth Harbour was curtailed north of Reading. In 1932, it began to convey a through coach to Manchester, attached at Eastleigh to the

A Cardiff–Brighton train near Dean on 26 September 1935, hauled by K10 class 4-4-0 No. 389. GWR and SR sets of coaches were used on these meandering cross-country workings.

Bournemouth–Birkenhead train – qv, and later developed as part of that train. By 1938, the Reading–Portsmouth through workings were very limited.

North East to South West/Wales
Newcastle/West Riding–Bristol/Torbay
The Bristol–Newcastle mails continued to run during World War II, but from late 1942 were diverted south of York to run via Selby to Milford Junction, and worked by LNER engines to/from Sheffield Midland.

Although some accelerated timings had been introduced on the West of England main line during 1933, and despite its naming as the 'Devonian' in 1927, the Bradford–Paignton express was not greatly changed until 1937 when the southbound train left Bradford at 10.25am and, after reversal at Leeds, called only at Sheffield before Derby. There it detached a through coach from Bradford to Bournemouth, and acquired one from Newcastle to Bristol in its place. There were smart timings on to Bristol Temple Meads, reached at 3.32pm. The Paignton coaches were then attached to a GWR express to Paignton, reached at 6.51pm after a journey of 8hr 26min.

Northbound, the GWR service to Bristol was not particularly fast, but matters changed once the 'Devonian' was on LMS metals, and there were tight timings to Gloucester, and from Cheltenham to Bromsgrove where the train stopped for a banker up the Lickey Incline; this second leg was a mile-a-minute booking. Eventually, Bradford was reached in 8hr 39min. On summer Saturdays the 'Devonian' was normally duplicated by the mid-1930s, the first part non-stop from Sheffield to Gloucester in 162min, and worked from Gloucester by a GWR engine, by-passing Bristol Temple Meads.

Withdrawn in 1939, the train was reinstated in October 1946, at first taking 8¾-9hr each way but decelerated during 1947 by a hour or so.

Newcastle–Barry
New stock was built for the service by the LNER in 1925. In due course, through coaches from/to Hull were reintroduced. With the introduction of the 'Silver Jubilee' in 1935, the Newcastle–Swansea was at first retimed to leave 15min earlier, at 9.20am, and to run slow line from Northallerton to Thirsk, in order to maintain the handover time to the GWR at Banbury. In due course, the train took up a 9.30am departure time from Newcastle.

The GWR Mogul, used for so long west of Banbury, was replaced from February 1938 by one of the new 'Manor' class 4-6-0s. Withdrawn in September 1939, the 'Ports-to-Ports' reappeared in October 1946, but now started and terminated at York and was rerouted each way via Oxford, Swindon and Severn Tunnel Junction. The times were 12.20pm from York, arriving in Swansea at 9.8pm; northbound at 8.15am, with a York arrival at 5.12pm.

The York–Bristol and 9.5pm Swindon–York were being worked from Sheffield to Swindon and back by an ex-GNR C1 Atlantic in 1925, this being a lodging turn for Sheffield Neepsend shed. From 1937, B17s were in charge, and these engines were timed up to 88mph or so between Swindon and Didcot. There were also Sunday Sheffield–Swansea trains, chiefly noted for their use by theatrical parties, with the scenery and props carried in vans.

During the 1930s, GWR express engines up to and including 'Castle' 4-6-0s worked to Nottingham from Oxford on SR excursions from the South Coast.

An example of the motive power combinations that came to the Midland Division with the transfer of the 'Claughtons'. Leading is ex-MR 2P 4-4-0 No. 385 but the 'Claughton' is unidentified although fitted with a ROD-type tender. The train is the down 'Devonian', at speed near Duffield.

The Newcastle–Swansea train waits at Sheffield Victoria on 29 August 1936, formed of GWR stock and headed by B17 class 4-6-0 No. 2848 *Arsenal*.

The Birkenhead–Deal through train descends Hatton bank in the late 1920s behind 'Saint' 4-6-0 No. 2904 *Lady Godiva*.

North West and West Midlands to Channel Ports
Birkenhead–Dover
Its reintroduction in Summer 1922 was regarded as a success by the GWR, and during 1923 through coaches between Birkenhead and Hastings were added, these being routed via Redhill, Brighton and Eastbourne. After 1923, the Birkenhead–Dover was often worked east of Reading by one of the SE&CR J class 0-6-4Ts, but later the SR 'River' 2-6-4Ts were used, in turn replaced by 4-4-0s and 2-6-0s.

The 1925 summer timetable featured a new through train, in the 9.45am Wolverhampton Low Level–Brighton–Eastbourne–Hastings (arr 3.37pm), and 12.20pm return from Hastings. Connections were provided from/to Birkenhead. The GWR passenger train services committee commented in its inimitable style: 'It has been the desire to inaugurate such a service for some time past . . . anticipated it will prove remunerative'.

With the opening in 1926 of the revised lines in the Ramsgate/Dover area, the Birkenhead–Dover was extended to run via Deal and Minster to Margate and back. Later a separate Margate portion was included, detached/attached at Ashford.

By the summer of 1937, there were three trains on Saturdays: the Margate–Wolverhampton (as introduced in 1925), the Deal–Birkenhead main train, and the Hastings coaches normally conveyed on that service forming a separate train to/from Birmingham.

On peak Fridays in summer there was also an overnight Wolverhampton–Eastbourne/Deal train.

The Birkenhead–Margate was an expensive train to work, requiring eight separate engine duties en route: changing engines at Chester (reversal), Wolverhampton, Reading, Redhill (reversal), Brighton (reversal), Eastbourne (reversal) and Ashford (division into two parts). The train was withdrawn in September 1939 and reappeared in September 1948 as a Birkenhead–Margate service, the Deal coaches detached at Ashford now being regarded as of lesser importance.

Late in 1940, a forces' leave train was introduced from Ashford (Kent) to Newcastle, routed via Reading, Banbury and the GC main line, and later being made available for civilians. This train was provided with a buffet car and often loaded heavily. Leaving Ashford at 8.45am, it took exactly 12hr to Newcastle; the return times were Newcastle 8.10am and Ashford, 8.32pm. For some of the war it was worked by a Southern engine through to/from Banbury. The train was withdrawn in May 1944.

Cross-country to East Anglia/Lincolnshire
Harwich–York/Liverpool
Major changes in operation came in May 1927, when an ex-GER B12 4-6-0 took up through working between Ipswich and Manchester and return while the eastbound working was retimed to leave Liverpool

25min earlier at 2.5pm, and the through coaches to/from York (and one to Glasgow) were detached at Lincoln to travel via Doncaster, rather than working via Sheffield. The coaches to/from Birmingham New St. continued to be detached/attached at March. In due course, standard LNER gangwayed stock was introduced, and the motive power changed to B17 4-6-0s. After arrival in Liverpool, the set of coaches worked to Hull, and back the next morning, in time to take up the eastbound working of the Harwich train. From 1935/36, the northbound York portion ran via Shaftholme Junction to Knottingley, returning as before via Selby. The service ceased on the outbreak of World War II, but was revived afterwards, although without either the York portion or the through Glasgow coach.

Colchester–Newcastle/Glasgow

To improve through journeys for service personnel, two trains were put on during 1940 between Colchester and Leeds, and Colchester and Edinburgh, both routed via March and Peterborough and the East Coast Main Line, rather than the GN/GE Joint line through to Doncaster.

By early 1941, there was a third service, this time a buffet car train between Colchester and York, and routed over the Joint line which since the start of the wartime timetables had been reduced to a stopping train service only. The northbound train left Colchester at 7.20am, running via Ipswich, and reached York at 1.30pm, in time to connect with the northbound 'Flying Scotsman'. The southbound train left York at 3.15pm, and arrived in Colchester at 10.10pm.

Manchester/Liverpool and York–Lowestoft GC/GE

The York–Lowestoft train was running in Summer 1938 with a 10.25am departure from York, and with a buffet car and with through coaches for Ipswich. The Lowestoft arrival was 4.34pm. The northbound train with buffet car departed Lowestoft at 10.3am. At March it attached a through coach for York which had arrived on the 10.8am from Harwich Town.

The morning Liverpool–Yarmouth/Lowestoft remained a fixture in the summer timetables of the 1930s, and included through coaches from Sheffield to Felixstowe which ran as a separate train on FSO.

Liverpool/Manchester–Yarmouth/Lowestoft via M&GN

Although the operation of services such as this is covered in **Midland & Great Northern Joint Railway until 1936**, this Saturdays-only train, which was introduced in the summer of 1923, was so complex in its running off M&GN territory that it merits separate coverage.

As at Summer 1930, a Liverpool Lime St. portion with restaurant car travelled to Crewe and used the former North Stafford main line via Stoke-on-Trent to Uttoxeter. There it combined with a Manchester portion which had travelled via Macclesfield, Leek and the Churnet Valley line. From Uttoxeter, and with a Longsight ex-LNWR engine in charge, the combined train ran non-stop to Nottingham via Willington Junction, Stenson Junction, Castle Donington and Trent. The same route was followed by the northbound train. The train ceased in 1939 and was not reinstated.

Birmingham/Nottingham–Skegness

LNER trains operated on summer Saturdays from Derby and Nottingham–Skegness, some of those from Derby taking the route via Daybrook and Gedling to avoid Nottingham Victoria. There was also an LMS Birmingham New St.–Skegness train routed that way having travelled via Burton-on-Trent and Derby Friargate. This train was reinstated in postwar years, but ran from/to Kings Norton.

North West to South Coast

The 'Sunny South Special'

Having established a pattern of working for the Liverpool/Manchester and Birmingham sections, the usefulness of the train was further extended not long after Grouping.

The Midland Railway had been keen to arrange a through working from East Midlands cities into the 'Sunny South' and, as Charlewood records, the first proposal was that these should be exchanged at Rugby where the track layout was ill-suited to through workings. As a result, the transfer was altered to the Market Harborough–Northampton line, with the coaches attached and detached at Northampton Castle station. The working started in Summer 1925, with through coaches from Bradford to Eastbourne and Nottingham–Ramsgate, working respectively on a St Pancras express and the Lincoln–Bournemouth train (qv) as far as Leicester, and then combined as a separate train to Northampton.

This development resulted in the splitting of the main train south of Northampton into Eastbourne and Ramsgate/Margate sections, and similarly for the northbound working. At Northampton the two northbound trains became three: for Liverpool/Manchester; for Birmingham, and for Leicester. The Midland line coaches remained a summer-only feature, and in July 1927 the Nottingham–Ramsgate coaches started back at Mansfield.

From November 1927, the 'Sunny South' became

a weekends only train, out on Saturdays, back on Mondays. Later, only the Eastbourne section ran throughout the year, the Kent Coast and East Midlands workings running only from Whitsun until October. In July 1929, the Eastbourne section was extended to run to/from Hastings.

By the late 1930s, the 'Sunny South Express' had become a major operation before and after August Bank Holiday when sometimes four trains were run to/from the South Coast. This contrasted with the winter when the Margate portion was no more than a couple of coaches worked to/from Willesden, and the Hastings portion ran once a week, twice-weekly from Whitsun to early July.

The 'Sunny South Express', so named in 1927, was withdrawn in September 1939, never to be reinstated in its old form.

North East to South Coast
Newcastle–Bournemouth
The train ran independently only on MFO in the summer of 1932, at 8am from Newcastle and at 11.15am from Bournemouth West. On TWThO, the coaches – including a restaurant car to/from York – only ran separately north of Basingstoke, working to/from that point on Bournemouth–Waterloo expresses.

For a time in the 1930s, the main train left Newcastle at 7.30am but a through brake composite for Bournemouth was also conveyed on the 8.15am Newcastle–King's Cross, and detached at York. A similarly 'detached' service ran northwards, with a 'fast-track' Newcastle coach detached at York from the main train, to be worked north on the 4pm from King's Cross.

The Newcastle–Bournemouth conveyed a through portion from/to Leeds Central which was introduced in 1927. Leaving Leeds at 10am, it was routed via Doncaster, Dukeries Junction, the former Lancashire Derbyshire & East Coast line to Clipstone East Junction, then via Mansfield, reaching Nottingham Victoria at 12.16pm where it joined the main train. A similar route was followed by the northbound working, leaving Nottingham at 5pm. The through coaches ceased in the early 1930s.

The Newcastle–Bournemouth train was withdrawn in September 1939, and revived in 1946, complete with restaurant car.

York–Southampton
The train continued unaltered until September 1939, with through coaches from Southampton Docks to Glasgow Queen St., but southbound between Glasgow and Basingstoke only, and on Saturdays from/to Scarborough. A restaurant car was provided between Newcastle and Oxford. When the sailing to Le Havre was operating, the Glasgow coach

The Eastbourne portion of the northbound 'Sunny South Express' is seen near Merstham in May 1925, worked by ex-LSWR L12 class 4-4-0 No. 421.

The northbound 'Pines Express' approaches Masbury summit on 17 March 1936, worked by LMS 2P 4-4-0 No. 630, and with a smart set of LMS coaches.

continued with the boat train from Waterloo to Southampton Docks. One change in the early 1930s was that the southbound train now ran non-stop between Basingstoke and Southampton Docks, to arrive at 10.49pm.

North West to Bournemouth
Manchester and Yorkshire–Bath–Bournemouth
Apart from the more customary workings featured in **Somerset & Dorset Joint Railway**, there was also a Nottingham to Sidmouth, Budleigh Salterton and Exmouth train introduced in 1929, routed via Templecombe and the SR main line westwards. It was shown as running in the Summer 1938/9 timetables as a 10.24 SO Derby–Sidmouth/Exmouth, and 9am Exmouth/9.20am Sidmouth return. A 10.40am Lincoln–Nottingham–Leicester–Birmingham–Bath was introduced in the summer of 1923, returning at 9.50am. The through coach working remained in the 1938 summer timetable as a facility on MTFO, and on Saturdays as a northbound through train.

The 'Pines Express', so named in 1927, ran via Birmingham New St. in winter, but at summer weekends, was diverted via Bushbury Junction to Walsall, then by the ex-MR line through Sutton Park to Saltley, there to join the ex-MR West of England route.

In 1939, the 'Pines' left Manchester London Road at 10.10am, and at Crewe gained a through section from Liverpool to Birmingham, and through coaches for Bournemouth and Southampton. At Birmingham

New St., the train was reformed, and had attached a through coach from Bradford that had come part of the way on the southbound 'Devonian'. At Cheltenham the Southampton coach was detached, and the 'Pines' next stopped at Gloucester before the run to Bath after which the train passed on to the S&D line.

Northbound, the procedure was the same, but in reverse, and the 'Pines' featured a 60mph timing between Cheltenham and Bromsgrove. After changing engines at Birmingham New St., but without reversal of the train, the 'Pines' departed via Aston and Bescot, thereby avoiding Wolverhampton, for a non-stop run to Crewe where it separated into Liverpool and Manchester portions. The summer weekend running via Sutton Park was continued.

Through trains over the S&D ceased from September 1939 only to be restored during 1940 in the shape of a 9.45am Bournemouth West–Bath semi-fast and an afternoon return train, both conveying through coaches to/from Derby and Bradford. The service ran for the rest of the war. By October 1946, the Manchester–Bournemouth was restored but the name 'Pines Express' was not officially used until 1949.

Manchester–Southampton
See **Midland & South Western Junction Railway**.

Birkenhead–Oxford–Bournemouth
By the summer of 1938, the train was running at

A Newcastle–Manchester express comes up to Croft Spa station behind C7 class Atlantic No. 737.

9.43am from Birkenhead and 10.10am from Manchester London Road, with a restaurant car in the first section. The train arrived in Bournemouth West at 5.31pm. Calls were now made at Basingstoke and Winchester, and at Eastleigh where the Manchester–Portsmouth Harbour section was detached/attached. The train was duplicated on FSO by a restaurant car train from Birmingham Snow Hill.

Northbound the departure from Bournemouth West was at 9.30am and Portsmouth, 10.4am, with arrivals at Birkenhead at 5.29pm, and Manchester London Rd, at 4.51pm. For both Manchester and Birkenhead sections, Southern Railway coaches alternated with those provided by the GWR. Usually a 'King Arthur' 4-6-0 worked the train between Bournemouth and Oxford.

North East to North West
Newcastle–Leeds–Liverpool, Liverpool–Hull
In May 1935, belated improvements came to the Newcastle–Liverpool service. There was a new 8.55am restaurant car express from Liverpool, routed via Darlington and York, and rising to a 43min schedule between these stations. Taking over the times of an existing train west of Leeds, the 8.55am reached Liverpool at 1.9pm, the 4hr 14min journey from Newcastle being some 15min better than the fastest time of 1914. The stock returned on the 5pm from Lime St. which previously ran to Leeds but was

now extended via Harrogate to Newcastle (arr 9.30pm). The set covering these workings was provided by the LNER, an LMS set working the 9am Liverpool–Newcastle and 4.17pm return.

There was considerable competition between the LMS and LNER for the Hull–Liverpool traffic, both railways introducing tea cars for a while in the mid-1920s. New stock was put into service in the early 1930s on the principal LNER trains, the 8.30am and 1.18pm from Liverpool, and 2.50 and 6.30pm return. The LNER route via Doncaster and Sheffield was the longer, at 141 miles, as compared with the 126 miles of the LMS route. The best timings in 1935 were by the LMS's 4pm from Hull in 3hr 10min, and the 2pm ex-Liverpool Lime St. in 3hr 15min. That year the LNER contemplated but did not proceed with an accelerated service, with a proposed running time of 2¾hr.

Newcastle–Wakefield–Liverpool
With the Summer 1938 timetable, the withdrawal of the former L&Y Fleetwood boat train set, and of buffet cars running between Manchester and York, left the Calder Valley main line with just the 10.45am Liverpool Exchange–Newcastle (arr 3.16pm), and 5pm return (arr Liverpool Exchange, 10.21pm) featuring on-train catering. The 10.45am retained a non-stop run between Manchester and Wakefield, but the 5pm made several intermediate stops.

CHAPTER FIFTEEN

WESTERN REGION

The West of England expresses featured in a notable speed-up introduced with the Winter 1948/9 timetable. The 3.30 and 5.30pm from Paddington to Penzance and Plymouth, respectively, were accelerated to a 148min timing between Paddington and Taunton for the 142¾ miles and this approached some of the prewar times. The 3.30pm now slipped a Weymouth coach at Heywood Road Junction, before taking the Westbury cut-off. The start to pass time from Paddington to Exeter of the down 'Cornish Riviera' was 184min for the 173½ miles, in the course of its 4hr 30min non-stop run to Plymouth North Road, as compared with the 189min including the Taunton stop of the two accelerated expresses. The 5.30pm was an innovation because in the 1939 timetable the last down daytime West of England train via the Berks & Hants line had been the 3.30pm ex-Paddington. In the up direction, the 1948/49 schedules were something like 2¾-3hr for the Taunton–Paddington run.

Holiday traffic to the South West grew markedly in the early postwar years. At the height of the Saturday peak in the early 1950s, expresses to/from the West were passing Whiteball summit, west of Taunton, at 8min intervals in each direction. The standard of punctuality was often dire. Some 25,000 passengers were crossing the Royal Albert Bridge in trains on the busiest peak Saturday, holiday-bound or travelling home. Not all the traffic to/from the West was connected with summer holidays. The boat train specials from Plymouth Millbay–Paddington possibly reached their apogee during this period. In October 1954, 'Castle' No. 5069 *Isambard Kingdom*

Brunel brought a five-coach train to a stand at Paddington in a record 3hr 37min for the 226 miles. This traffic was soon to decline and in April 1962 it was decided to abandon the Plymouth boat trains.

Business traffic, particularly from London, was developing fast as Britain recovered from the effects of war. In the Winter 1949 timetable, the first down trains from Paddington to Bristol were at 7.30am – arriving 10.21 – and 9.5am which with a Reading stop (and Bath slip working) did somewhat better in 138min. To Birmingham, the first presentable train was a 9am SX down to Wolverhampton, introduced to relieve the long-established 9.10am Birkenhead train. Picking up passengers at High Wycombe, the 9am was into Snow Hill at 11.15am. Its return working was the 4.20pm from Wolverhampton, taking 165min to Paddington. In October 1950, this service became the 'Inter-City', a name then derided as bereft of inspiration but destined to become a household word.

The 9.10am made all the principal intermediate stops on its way north, and also included a portion to Stratford-upon-Avon, no doubt intended to lure American tourists, but not getting them to Stratford until 12.7pm. For the 1951 summer season, and coinciding with the Festival of Britain, these through coaches switched to the 10.10am Paddington–Wolverhampton and 7.23pm return, both these trains being named the 'William Shakespeare'. The Stratford portion and the main train were made up of BR Standard stock. Despite an apparent potential, the through service did not flourish, and was not repeated.

Mention should be made of the seven so-called 'Festival of Britain' train sets which made their appearance in May 1951, and were composed of the brand-new BR Standard all-steel vestibuled coaches, 525 of which entered service during the year. The introduction of these coaches contributed significantly to improved safety standards. In addition to the 'William Shakespeare', the 'FoB' sets were employed on a clutch of other newly named services on four BR Regions. The Western Region boasted another 'FoB' working in the 'Merchant Venturer', a name applied to the 11.15am Paddington–Bristol and 5.25pm return. The other Regions' trains were the 'Red Rose', the 12.5pm Euston–Liverpool and 5.25pm return; the 'Heart of Midlothian', the 2pm Kings Cross–Edinburgh, and 2pm return; and the 'Royal Wessex' whose experience with the 'FoB' stock is related in the **Southern Region** section. Sets of BR Standard coaches also entered service on existing named trains in 1951/2, notably the 'Norfolkman' between Liverpool St. and Cromer and return, and also the 'Royal Scot'.

The September 1953 timetable returned 120min Paddington–Birmingham timings to the former GWR main line, the down 'Inter-City' being one of a pair of chosen services, the other being the 9am from Birmingham. The up 'Inter-City' missed being a 2hr train, and took 125min including Leamington and High Wycombe stops. At this same timetable revision, 5-12min was pared from other Paddington–Wolverhampton/Birkenhead trains. Meanwhile, the summer through train from Paddington–Aberystwyth/Pwllheli progressed from being a Saturdays only train to the named 'Cambrian Coast Express' of Summer 1951, to materialise in the 1954 timetable as a daily working with a 120min timing between Paddington and Birmingham in both directions. With the Winter 1955/56 timetable, extra time was allowed to most Birmingham line expresses, and the 2hr schedules disappeared, not to return until the winter of 1957/58.

Some progress had been made in returning other Western Region expresses at least to 1939 schedules. In the Summer 1952 timetable the 'Cornish Riviera' was put on a 4¼hr timing in both directions between Paddington and Plymouth. Compared with prewar days though the loads were reduced and, in winter, the down train was rostered for ten coaches only to/from Plymouth, Weymouth slip included on the down train. On the Bristol line, the 11.45am from Bristol via Badminton at last regained a 120min timing in the Winter 1953/4 timetable while the 1.15pm down was given a mile-a-minute timing to

Bath, in 106min, and took 127min to Bristol. The most favoured train at this stage was the 11.15am from Paddington to Weston-super-Mare which had been named the 'Merchant Venturer' in 1951, and also ran to Bath in 106min.

The WR was on the way to becoming the BR Region most enamoured of naming trains, sometimes with unfortunate results when decelerations took the shine off the service. From the Summer 1952 timetable, the Wolverhampton–Penzance express had become the 'Cornishman', a venerated GWR title, and in each direction its usefulness was increased by diversion at Gloucester to the former Midland line for a call at Eastgate station; previously, Honeybourne route expresses such as this had by-passed the city. The train had also been also accelerated, leaving Wolverhampton Low Level at 9.15am, and Birmingham 35min later, to reach Bristol at 12.28pm, and now entering the city by means of the former Midland route from Yate. Taunton was served by slip coach and the 'Cornishman' ran forward to Plymouth, and to Penzance where it arrived after an 8hr 40min journey from Wolverhampton. Northbound, the train left Penzance at 10.30am, and pulled into Wolverhampton at 7.28pm. In each direction, there were through coaches to/from Kingswear.

Behind the scenes, the Western Region's management was well-aware of the limitations of its train services, with a punctuality record at the bottom of the Regional league table. Although on selected routes locomotive performance was sometimes beyond reproach, in reviewing their express services' poor timekeeping the managers blamed the locomotives and bad coal.

In October 1953, the WR's mechanical and electrical engineer, R. A. Smeddle informed the operators that certain 'Kings' and 'Castles' had been 'modified to give improved performance . . . (there is) a possibility of accelerating trains on main routes. The loads being stipulated represent the maximum – there is no margin for additional coaches.'

Early in 1954, the accelerated timings were finalised, for introduction from the summer service. Such speeded-up trains depended on the availability of specially selected 'Castles' and 'Kings'. The first trains selected for special timings were the 10.55am Paddington–Pembroke Dock and 1.10pm return, the former non-stop to Newport in 141min for 133 miles, and the 8.55am Worcester–Paddington, to be booked in 65min from Oxford to Paddington. In addition, the 7.45am Pembroke Dock–Paddington, 8.20am ex-Neyland, 9.45am Paddington–Hereford and 11am return were accelerated but retained standard point-

The postwar image of the GWR – 'King' No. 6019 *King Henry V* makes good progress with the 'Cornish Riviera' near Kintbury in very early BR days. Most of the coaches are the new, slab-sided Hawksworth stock.

to-point timings. A penalty was paid as the accelerated 'Special Load' timings limited a 'Castle' to a maximum of 315 tons although the 'Pembroke Coast Express' (a new service, introduced along with its title in 1953) usually loaded to eight coaches.

Such retimings in the Summer 1954 timetable were to be overshadowed by the restoration of the 'Bristolian' to its prewar 105min timing to and from Bristol, making this Britain's fastest train. As before, the outward run was via Bath, the return over the Badminton route. Departure from Paddington was now at 8.45am, but the return journey started, as in 1935-39, at 4.30pm. More was offered on the Bristol service: a fast time of 99min to Bath, and 120min to Bristol by the 1.15pm from Paddington while 60mph timings start to stop, Saturdays excepted, were introduced between Chippenham and Paddington for the 1.50pm from Bristol and 4.35pm Weston-super-Mare, the up 'Merchant Venturer'. The latter was accelerated by no less than 29min from Bristol to Paddington, but slunk back to its old timings in the Winter 1954/5 timetable.

The changes made to the 'Cambrian Coast Express' in the Summer 1954 timetable have been mentioned already, but the 11.10am down also joined the ranks of Birmingham 2hr expresses. On the West of England main line, the noon 'Torbay Express' was speeded-up appreciably, and now took 174min down, and 1min longer eastbound, between Paddington and Exeter, but just failing to achieve a mile-a-minute booking. With the exception of the up 'Venturer', these improvements were sustained in the

Winter 1954/5 timetable which saw the 7.45am from Bristol timed to run from Chippenham in 92min, and retention of the previously summer-only 9.30am Paddington–Plymouth which was promoted to a 105min timing between Reading and Taunton which was reached in 148min from Paddington. Improvements also came to the up South Wales and Worcester line services with 'on the hour' departures from Cardiff and from Worcester respectively.

With the Summer 1955 timetable, the down 'Cornish Riviera Express' at last regained its prewar timing to Plymouth of 4hr. The 9.30am down was speeded-up, too, and reached Plymouth in 4hr 30min. Also, the down 'Pembroke Coast Express' was promoted to a better than mile-a-minute run from Paddington to Newport, in 128min, faster by 9min than any previous timing. Overall, the train took 25min less to reach Pembroke Dock.

The Summer 1955 timetable also promised the introduction of the 'South Wales Pullman', down at 9.55 am from Paddington, and back at 4.35pm from Swansea. But the inaugural run was delayed by the footplatemen's strike and only took place on 27 June. Although limited to eight Pullman cars, equal to 320 tons, the new service did not share, let alone surpass, the fast timings of the 'PCE'. The more familiar 8.50am departure of the down Pullman dated from 1957. On the Bristol line, the 4.15pm and 6.30pm down were made 14/10min faster respectively in the Summer 1955 timetable which brought a thorough revision to the Worcester line service where several trains were accelerated, the 4pm Worcester–Oxford train being extended to Paddington with a 60min timing, the first since 1939.

A modified scheme of the GWR's familiar two-tone coaching stock livery was applied to the Region's named trains from the Summer 1956 timetable, and initially confined to the 'Cornish Riviera', 'Bristolian' and 'Torbay Express'. The traditional livery was only approved by higher authority for application to named trains, and so the WR set about adding titles to trains. The 1.30pm Paddington–Penzance and 11am return became the 'Royal Duchy' from January 1957; the 8.30am Plymouth–Paddington and 5.30pm Paddington–Plymouth, the 'Mayflower' from June 1957; the 7.45am Hereford–Paddington and 4.45pm return, the 'Cathedrals Express' from September 1957. Earlier train namings had included the 'Red Dragon',

Carmarthen–Paddington and return – 1950; the 'Capitals United Express', Fishguard Harbour–Paddington and return – 1956, and the 'Cheltenham Spa Express', Cheltenham Spa St James–Paddington and return. These and the newcomers were decked out with brown and cream painted coaches, and looked superb – when clean.

The old Great Western fondness for slip coach workings had scarcely diminished, and nine remained in the Winter 1955/6 timetable, including three at Reading from up expresses, and for Weymouth at Heywood Road Junction, outside Westbury from a couple of down West of England expresses. Costly to provide and something of an anachronism, from the winter of 1958 the number of slip workings had declined to three and, in June 1960, to one only, the Bicester slip off the 5.10pm

A real attempt was made to improve the image of the WR by invoking the spirit of the GWR with the reintroduction of chocolate and cream livery, and painting as many engine types as possible in GWR-style green livery, typified by 'Manor' 4-6-0 No. 7802 *Bradley Manor* reposing on Aberystwyth shed on 16 May 1959. In the background is the stock of the 'Cambrian Coast Express' mostly in the traditional livery, and with a restaurant car.

A full set of chocolate and cream liveried coaches, and with one of the decorative headboards used for the WR named expresses, displayed on 'Castle' No. 5043 *Earl of Mount Edgcumbe* as it works the down 'Bristolian' near Bath.

Paddington–Wolverhampton. When this ran for the last time on 9 September that year, slip coach working had come to an end on the world's railways.

By cutting the odd minute or two from some previously accelerated schedules, the WR could boast of 17 weekday runs at 60mph or over in the Summer 1956 timetable, but the pace of change was slowing down. Those innovations that involved

steam services in the next few years were few: from June 1958 there were summer Saturday through trains from Abertillery and from Ebbw Vale to Paddington, but without return workings; a sleeping car service between Paddington and Milford Haven was introduced from December 1958; a 7.50am Birkenhead–Cardiff and 4.15pm return were proudly launched in April 1957, but never prospered and

Towards the end of their lives the 'Kings' were not at their best and neither was the Paddington–Wolverhampton service. Normally the 'Kings' worked only as far north as Wolverhampton, but they were used on the down 'Cambrian Coast Express' to Shrewsbury where No. 6015 *King Richard III* is being detached, so that the train can continue to the Welsh coast behind a 'Manor'.

were axed from 30 June 1958. They featured in a drive by the British Transport Commission to eliminate loss-making trains and the WR lost a number of secondary passenger services.

When the London Midland Region withdrew most of its Euston–Birmingham–Wolverhampton expresses in November 1959 in preparation for forthcoming electrification work, the WR augmented its own service by five/six trains each way giving a total of 14, and with slightly better than hourly frequency between 8am and 6pm. The loads of most expresses were increased but an apparent absence of confidence in the abilities of the 'Kings' meant that the timings of the Birmingham line expresses were distinctly lack-lustre. No more than one down, and two up trains featured 120min schedules between Paddington and Birmingham. The same November 1959 timetable increased the Paddington–Worcester–Hereford workings by one train each way, with trains at better-spaced intervals. Yet few timings were faster, and the overall result was unenterprising.

Meanwhile, dieselisation schemes proceeded apace, usually with more and faster trains than in the displaced steam service: Birmingham–South Wales, operated by diesel multiple-units from Summer 1957;

main line diesel locomotives introduced on Paddington–West of England services from the autumn of 1958, and on an accelerated 'Bristolian' from June 1959; the Paddington–Bristol and Paddington–Birmingham diesel Pullmans made their debut from September 1960; all Bristol expresses were dieselised from September 1961, and those on the Paddington–South Wales and Birmingham/Birkenhead services from September 1962. The last steam-worked express service was that between Paddington and Worcester/Hereford which (officially) went over to diesel haulage from September 1963.

The ending of once-familiar services included the withdrawal of independent Paddington–Weymouth trains as from September 1960. A strictly even interval service was brought in with the Winter 1961/12 timetable, by which time steam haulage was restricted to the Paddington–South Wales, Birmingham/Wolverhampton, Worcester/Hereford and Cheltenham/Gloucester services. None of these featured any accelerated trains in the new timetable, as extra stops were inserted and schedules were generally slower. There was just one Birmingham–Paddington 120min timing, and that by a Friday-only relief working.

1859–1959
Centenary
ROYAL ALBERT BRIDGE
SALTASH

PRICE ONE SHILLING & SIXPENCE

CHAPTER SIXTEEN

SOUTHERN REGION

If it had been left to the Southern Railway, all its lines east of Poole and Salisbury would have been either electrified or dieselised by the mid-1950s, but paradoxically this was to be the second to last Region to operate steam traction, and ran some of the fastest steam workings of the postwar years. For most of the period that it was operating steam, the SR restricted its timetable changes to a minimum, and train working settled down to predictable patterns.

On the Eastern Division, the Kent Coast services via Chatham and via Tonbridge hardly changed from the pattern of prewar years until the onset of the Hastings line dieselisation from June 1957, and electrification of the Chatham lines under the Kent Coast Phase 1 scheme of June 1959. One development had been the growth in commuter traffic. The once extensive holiday traffic to the Thanet Coast had declined steadily after the mid-1950s and the prestige workings disappeared with electrification.

In 1951, the summer 'Thanet Belle' had conveyed a portion for Canterbury East and accordingly the train was renamed the 'Kentish Belle' but the innovation was not repeated the next year, and the 'Belle' itself did not reappear after the summer of 1958. On winter weekdays, Pullman cars to Thanet were restricted to a couple of vehicles in the 11.35am Victoria–Ramsgate and 5.2pm return. In the last year of operation, to June 1959, the first of these took an interminable 159min for the 79¾ miles to Ramsgate, but the evening train was more fleet of foot and arrived at Victoria at 7.9pm.

The special workings so long associated with Kent, such as for hop-pickers, and their friends, died

with steam. On the former South Eastern main line, the Folkestone/Dover expresses might have been expected to have been speeded-up, but the main development was the naming as the 'Man of Kent', from late 1955, of the 1.15 and 4.15pm from Charing Cross, and the 9.40am and 12.40pm from Margate. From June 1956, the 1.15pm was promoted to a 66min timing between Waterloo Eastern and Ashford, the fastest on record for steam. An 80min timing between Charing Cross and Folkestone Central was restored to the 4.10pm down and up morning train in June 1959. Steam was replaced by electric working from June 1961 on Charing Cross–Folkestone–Margate expresses and boat trains alike, but to steam timings which were retained until a revised timetable came into force the next year.

The 'Golden Arrow' remained steam worked until June 1961. The train's traditional 11am departure had changed to 1pm (2pm in summer) with the Winter 1952/3 timetable, when it was diverted to Folkestone Harbour, there to connect with the afternoon sailing to Calais. The London–Paris time was lengthened by 45min to 7½hr, and patronage suffered by the changes, introduced to suit SNCF. To Folkestone Junction sidings, the time was 86min, with 92min allowed from Dover Marine to Victoria, the up 'Arrow' continuing to run from Dover. From Summer 1960, the 'Arrow' reverted to a its 11am departure from Victoria, and to a Dover routing both ways.

The 'Night Ferry' maintained its departure times from Victoria at 10pm and from Dover Ferry Berth at 7.20am, and worked via Tonbridge, but on weekdays from Winter 1954/55 the up train was diverted to run

Flags flying and arrows in place, the down 'Golden Arrow' is waiting at Victoria behind 'West Country' Pacific No. 34039 *Boscastle* on 1 August 1948.

In the days when it was routed via Tonbridge, the up 'Night Ferry' approaches Dunton Green on 25 July 1953, headed by 'Merchant Navy' Pacific No. 35030 *Elder-Dempster Lines*.

The down 'Devon Belle' passes Winchfield on 2 September 1949 behind 'Merchant Navy' Pacific No. 35013 *Blue Funnel* which is displaying the special nameboards that were affixed to the engine's smoke-deflectors.

via Faversham and Chatham. From June 1957, a sleeping car to/from Brussels joined the cars running to/from Paris. Electric locomotives took over haulage of the 'Night Ferry' from June 1959, displacing Bulleid 'Merchant Navies' or Light Pacifics.

On the Central Division, there were few scheduled fast steam workings once the regular Newhaven boat trains went to electric haulage from 1949. The main workings were on the Oxted line where an hourly service between Victoria and Tunbridge Wells West was introduced from June 1955, a regular interval timetable being applied to the Uckfield and Heathfield lines from June 1956. Three down and five up of the weekdays Oxted line trains were semi-fast north of Eridge, and ran from Victoria to Brighton/Eastbourne and return. The peak-hour trains had not been much affected by the changes, and included the heavy 6.10pm Victoria–Uckfield/ Brighton which was worked by a Bulleid Light Pacific. By 1960, diesel multiple-units were on order and steam was generally supplanted during 1962/23.

The main steam operations in postwar years were on the Western Division. Despite early promise the 'Devon Belle' proved a disappointment. In the Summer 1949 timetable, it ran from Waterloo on Thursdays and back from Devon on Tuesdays, as well as both ways Fridays-Mondays inclusive. The Plymouth section was withdrawn in 1950, and complete withdrawal seemed likely, but the down workings now became FSSuO, the up trains, SSuMO. From the Summer 1954 timetable, the 'Devon Belle' started from Waterloo on Fridays only at 4.40pm, and called at Salisbury in 85min, and also at Axminster, and was 19min faster to Exeter in 3hr 16min, to reach Ilfracombe at 9.48pm. On other days the 'Belle' continued to change engines at Wilton South, as a relic of the days until 1950 when the engines of all West of England expresses were changed at Salisbury. To little surprise, the 'Devon Belle' was withdrawn at the end of the Winter 1954/55 timetable.

The Southampton Docks boat train workings increased steadily through the 1950s, whether for scheduled ocean liner sailings, cruises or immigration traffic; some trains were named, and others included Pullman cars. During one July in the 1950s, 132 trains were operated, and a fine Ocean Terminal was opened at the Docks in 1953. There were also scheduled boat trains from Waterloo at 6.35pm in summer for the St Malo sailing, and one for Le Havre, and at 9pm for the Channel Islands. All Channel Islands boat services were concentrated on the SR from November 1959, with boat trains linking Waterloo and Southampton Docks or Weymouth Quay, and the boat trains to/from Paddington were withdrawn. All BR's Channel Islands sailings were moved to Weymouth from Summer 1961.

The Bournemouth line express service was largely

absent from the service alterations of the early 1950s. One major exception was the introduction of one of the 'Festival of Britain' train sets – see **Western Region** – coincident with the introduction in May 1951 of the 'Royal Wessex' named express. The trains involved were the 7.38am Weymouth–Waterloo, and 4.35pm return, both conveying through coaches between Swanage and Waterloo. As on other Regions, the new BR Standard stock used on the 'Royal Wessex' proved problematic. The three-car restaurant car set, and the luggage space provided in the new stock were in excess of the requirements of the 'Wessex', but the Southern Region persevered with its 'FoB' train set until the early 1960s.

In terms of significant changes to the timetable, the Bournemouth line had to wait until June 1954 when the 7.30pm Waterloo–Bournemouth West was accelerated by 11min. New trains brought in with the Summer 1956 timetable comprised a 9.30pm Waterloo–Bournemouth West (arr 12.5am) restaurant car train, and a 7.7am return, the latter calling at Bournemouth Central, Brockenhurst, Southampton and Winchester only, and arriving at Waterloo for 9.33am.

By now the SR was engaged in rebuilding the Bulleid 'Merchant Navy' Pacifics and, from the Summer 1957 timetable, seemed at last confident of reintroducing 120min schedules between Waterloo and Bournemouth Central including a stop at Southampton Central, with trains at 8.20, 10.30am and 6.30pm down, and up departures at 12.40, 2.40, 6.40 and 7.40pm, the last of these a summer-only train. The 10.30am down ran to Weymouth in 3hr. Neither the 'Royal Wessex', the 7.38am express from Weymouth with a through portion from Swanage and returning at 4.35pm, nor the 'Bournemouth Belle' was accelerated.

The 6.30pm down gained a Winchester stop in June 1959 and was slowed by 7min, while the 8.20am's departure was made 10min later in summer 1961. From the Summer 1963 timetable, in each direction the 'Bournemouth Belle' was put on a 120min schedule between Waterloo and Bournemouth Central, now 10min faster southbound and 6min faster to London.

The electrification of the Bournemouth main line beyond Sturt Lane Junction, Brookwood, and south of Basingstoke was authorised in September 1964. With the June 1965 timetable, all Waterloo–Bournemouth trains were decelerated to allow electrification and track relaying to proceed and were some 15min slower to Bournemouth, the fastest time being 135min. Most up expresses were altered to start earlier and to arrive in Waterloo 12min later than before. Britain's last steam-hauled express

'Merchant Navy' No. 35017 *Belgian Marine* nears Bournemouth West with the down 'Bournemouth Belle' on 11 April 1955.

On 23 September 1959, the up 'Atlantic Coast Express' passes through Seaton Junction station on one of the through lines, hauled by rebuilt 'Merchant Navy' Pacific No. 35003 *Royal Mail*.

passenger service lasted until 9 July 1967, although some weekday workings, notably the 'Bournemouth Belle', had been diagrammed for diesel traction from October 1966, and limited electric working began on other trains in April 1967.

Only in the summer timetable of 1952 was the 'Atlantic Coast Express' accelerated to better than prewar timings, and in so doing provided the Southern Region with its sole point to point run averaging 60mph or more – the down train's booking of 83min for the 83¾ miles from Waterloo to Salisbury. The rest of the 'ACE's' timings were also speeded-up, with the result that to most destinations, other than Plymouth, overall journey times were 10min or so shorter than prewar. For the next decade the timings were largely unchanged.

On the West of England route, most of the point to point bookings in the basic two-hourly service of five/six express trains each way were reasonably generous. In the summer Saturday timetable of the 1950s/early 1960s there was an extensive programme of extra trains with no less than 14 departures from Waterloo, at an average of 20min intervals, all for Sidmouth Junction and beyond.

Neither locomotive nor coaching stock utilisation was intensive.

The 'ACE' was in a class apart when it came to through portions and coaches. As late as the Winter 1959/60 timetable its booked formation was: second corridor and composite brake for Ilfracombe; composite brakes for Torrington, Padstow and Bude; second brake and composite brake for Plymouth; restaurant car pair detached at Exeter Central; composite brakes for Exmouth and Sidmouth detached at Sidmouth Junction and finally, a composite brake for all stations west of Salisbury (advertised to Honiton, but running to Exeter) which was detached from the 'ACE' during the Salisbury stop.

The Summer 1957 timetable brought an isolated acceleration of the 4.30pm from Exeter Central, with a cut in its journey time of 19min and excision of its Woking stop. More significant was the introduction of a pair of new trains in the 1957/58 winter timetable. Departing 1hr earlier than the first previous up express, the 6.30am from Exeter Central called at Axminster, Yeovil Junction, Sherborne, Gillingham, Salisbury and Basingstoke, to arrive in the Capital at 10.8am. The balancing working was the 7pm from

Waterloo, non-stop to Salisbury in 85min, then calling at Yeovil Junction and Axminster to reach Exeter Central at 10.18pm. A section of the 7pm continued to Plymouth, in place of that on the 6pm from Waterloo which was now curtailed at Exeter.

Next change came in 1959 with public advertisement for the first time of the second summer portion of the 'ACE'. That summer, this 'dated' train ran on Mondays to Fridays from 21 July to 3 September and included, as it had previously done if not publicly advertised, the Padstow, Bude and Plymouth portions. It called also at Axminster. The balancing working was the 10.15am from Exeter Central. The other innovation during this period was the summer Surbiton–Okehampton car carrier train which made its appearance as from 18 June 1960, and lasted for five seasons.

The Summer 1961 timetable featured acceleration of the up 'ACE' by 2min to a 83min booking from Salisbury to Waterloo, to give another mile-a-minute run to the SR's tally. Then, with the coincident introduction by the Western Region in the 1961/62 winter timetable of a strictly even-interval service for its main routes, the SR cut the timings of the 'ACE' in each direction between Waterloo and Exeter. Overall, the journey time was 178min in the down direction, and 1min slower coming up. To achieve these times, there were 80min bookings both ways between Waterloo and Salisbury and, over the next section to Sidmouth Junction, 75min down and 74min up. At the time, the late C. J. Allen adjudged the new 'ACE' timings as 'the hardest schedules in Great Britain today which are regularly operated by steam power'.

Yet signs of retrenchment came in the new timetable. In future, the 9am down would convey through coaches for Plymouth and Barnstaple Junction only, instead of for Ilfracombe and Torrington. The process of cutting back on through coaches continued in the Winter 1962/63 timetable, with the withdrawal of all through coaches from Waterloo to East Devon resorts, Padstow and Torrington, except for those conveyed on the 'ACE'; the through weekday Lyme Regis coach conveyed on the up 'ACE' and 1pm down had been axed in 1960. The premier train lost only the coach for all stations to Honiton, detached at Salisbury. As from September 1962, the 4.30pm from Exeter regained its Woking stop, but at the cost of 8min added to its overall time. With the Summer 1963 timetable, the down and up summer weekday relief 'ACE's' were the subjects of modest acceleration in timings, resulting in 60mph average bookings – 82min Salisbury–Waterloo and 61min Salisbury–Axminster.

As from 1 January 1963, all SR lines west of Wilton South were ceded to the Western Region, quickly followed by a debate regarding the future of the Reading–Westbury–Taunton and Salisbury–Exeter routes. For the moment, the Waterloo–West of England service was the last in Britain to be completely steam-worked but it represented no more than a stay of execution while strategies were finalised.

The Winter 1963/64 timetable saw a further reduction in the through portions carried by the 'ACE', now restricted to those for Ilfracombe, Padstow and Exeter only, the through coaches for Sidmouth and Exmouth being cut out; those for Bude and Torrington had been axed at the start of the Summer 1963 timetable. The Ilfracombe portions of the 1pm from Waterloo, and 2.30 and 4.30pm from Exeter were replaced by dmu connecting services as from the Winter 1963/4 timetable.

In the Summer 1964 timetable, the last to be worked by steam, the 6.30am from Exeter was retimed to leave 5min earlier and to make additional stops, but with an unchanged arrival time at Waterloo. Its companion working, the 7pm from Waterloo, was altered as a result of the decision to terminate the 6pm down at Yeovil Junction, and for that train to run all stations from Salisbury. Additional stops were added to the schedule of the 7pm down and the train now terminated at Exeter St Davids.

Western Region diesel locomotives started work on the West of England expresses during August 1964, and a revised, diesel-operated Waterloo–Exeter service was introduced the next month. Some Saturday holiday trains between Waterloo and Exmouth/Sidmouth were partially steam worked in the Summer 1965 timetable.

The cross-country trains running within the Region comprised those between Brighton and Bournemouth and Brighton and Plymouth. The former never loaded well, and left Brighton at 9.40am, running non-stop between Chichester and Southampton. In 1961, its return from Bournemouth West was altered from 1.50 to 6.35pm, and later it changed to diesel haulage, but only to be withdrawn at the end of the 1962 summer season. The 'Plymouth' departed from Brighton at 11.30am, complete with restaurant buffet car, a portion from Portsmouth & Southsea being added at Fareham. Diesel traction replaced steam from 1964, and for a time the train was diverted to Fratton where one of the former Southern electric locomotives gave way to steam. Early in 1966, Bulleid Pacifics took over again between Brighton and Salisbury and back, and lasted until that April.

CHAPTER SEVENTEEN

LONDON MIDLAND REGION

The first main line timetables to be issued by British Railways began on 31 May 1948, and the LMR's most notable contribution was resumption of a daytime service between Euston and Ireland, via Holyhead, but now to be in summer only. The 'Irish Mail' was, after all, probably the World's oldest named train and had just achieved its centenary.

In the Winter 1949/50 timetable, the evening expresses from Euston to Manchester and Liverpool exchanged departure times, the former now 5.55pm, the latter 6.5pm, and also acquired their former names of 'Mancunian' and 'Merseyside Express', but overall times at 3hr 55min and 4hr 5min were well below prewar best. Other names restored from the same timetable were the 'Mid-Day Scot', 'Ulster Express', 'Thames–Clyde Express' and 'Comet'. The 12.5pm Euston–Liverpool and 5.25pm return became the 'Red Rose' from the summer of 1951 and were worked by one of the 'Festival of Britain' train sets – see **Western Region**.

Having regained its title in February 1948, the 'Royal Scot' soon reverted to the pattern in summer of a publicly advertised non-stop run between Euston and Glasgow. For the summer of 1949 the train had an easy timing of 8hr 25min between Euston and Glasgow, with one 5min stop only to change engine crews, at Kingmoor, Carlisle. That pause had a significance on 1 June 1949 when the 'Royal Scot' was worked to Glasgow without a stop by the LMS/English Electric main line diesel locomotives Nos 10000 and 10001. In the Winter 1950/1 timetable, the down 'Royal Scot' with just three stops, at Rugby. Crewe and Carlisle, needed 8hr 35min to Glasgow, and the up train, 8¼hr to Euston.

At this stage, some of the timings of West Coast expresses were a curious mixture, fairly demanding over one stretch, but slow elsewhere, and not helped by the imposition of speed restrictions over sections affected by mining subsidence, such as Warrington–Preston. North of the Border, the timings of the Anglo-Scottish trains were more adventurous. From New Year 1951, the up 'Mid-Day Scot' was retimed to leave Glasgow Central 15min later, at 1.30pm, but to retain its 10.9pm arrival at Euston. The journey was no less then 54min slower than in 1939. Matters hardly improved in the next couple of years. For the winter of 1953/4, although the down 'Royal Scot' returned to an 8hr 10min schedule, with the same stops the up train had retained its 7½hr summer schedule.

The 5.20pm Euston–Holyhead was speeded-up in the Winter 1950/51 timetable by 17min overall, to a 5hr 33min timing, and regained its through coaches for Birkenhead Woodside, as did the corresponding up train. Through coaches to/from Southport Chapel St. and Euston had also been restored to the Liverpool expresses. One feature of this period was the operation of very heavy trains on the Western Division, of 15, 16 or 17 coaches, not infrequently hauled by rebuilt 'Royal Scot' 4-6-0s.

Pressure from Midlands' civic bodies and businessmen for an improved service between London and Birmingham drew a guarded promise from the Railway Executive that a target of 130min with one stop was in prospect. With the Winter 1950/1 timetable, the 8.5am SX Euston–

The 10am Glasgow Central–Euston 'Royal Scot' of 2 June 1949 passes Wembley behind the LMS/English Electric diesel locomotives Nos 10001 and 10000 working in multiple, the train painted in the then new BR carmine and cream livery.

Wolverhampton and 10.55am return were new services, trains at these times not having featured in the prewar timetables. The new 10.55am up and the existing 5.45pm down were distinguished by the name 'Midlander'. 'Royal Scots' were drafted to Bushbury in place of 'Jubilees', but improvements were short-lived as the shortage of coal led to the suspension of a number of Euston–Wolverhampton and other Western Division trains during early 1951.

The Summer 1951 timetable brought the promised acceleration of the Euston–Wolverhampton service with 130min timings between Euston and Birmingham including a stop at Coventry for the 12.40, 2.15, 5.45 and 6.55 pm down, and 7.50, 9.55, 10.55 and 11.55am and 3.55pm up from Wolverhampton. Overall journey times were upwards from a minimum of 160 min. The speeding-up coincided with the transfer away of the 'Scots', in exchange for 'Jubilees'!

In the Summer 1953 service came a new 8.50am SX Euston–Wolverhampton, with a non-stop run from Watford Junction to Birmingham New Street, at an average speed of 60.8mph. Except on Saturdays, there were better than even-time average speeds – 94 miles in 93min – for the Euston–Coventry (and vice versa) runs of the 12.50, 2.20, 5.50 'Midlander' and 6.50pm down. Just under the 60 mph average were

the Coventry–Euston bookings, again Saturdays excepted, of the 8.30, 11.30am and 12.30, 2.30 and 4.30pm ex-New Street.

Birmingham having regained the 2hr schedules of prewar days to/from Euston, the Railway Executive congratulated itself that 'a prewar service at comparable speed had been restored for the first time since the War'. One other development was the alteration of departure times to provide 'clockface' times of 30min past up from Birmingham and 50min down from Euston. In the Winter 1954/55 timetable, the 1.55pm from Wolverhampton was accelerated to run from Rugby–Euston in 79min for the 82½ miles, at an average speed of 62.7mph, at the time, the fastest start-to-stop booking of any train on the LMR. The Winter 1958/9 timetable featured expanded schedules and the demise of the 2hr trains, with 7–8min added to the Euston–Wolverhampton timings and no less than 16-20min southbound.

Nine years after the end of the war, the June 1954 timetable had at last offered some worthwhile improvements in services to the North West. The 7.55 (former 8am) Euston–Liverpool and Manchester ran the 140½ miles from Watford Junction to Crewe in 136min, at 62.5mph. The 4.30pm Euston–Liverpool was altered to start 25min later, and to run non-stop in 3hr 27min, the fastest

There are 14 coaches behind 'Royal Scot' No. 46124 *London Scottish* which, on 26 May 1955, is passing alongside the GPO's Hillmorton radio station, south of Rugby with the up 'Manxman'. This was a summer-only working between Euston and Liverpool and, as the name suggests, was run in connection with the Isle of Man sailings.

down journey ever tabled, It was named the 'Shamrock' as this and the 8.10am return from Liverpool connected with the Belfast and Dublin steamship services. The 8.10am formerly included a Manchester portion which was made a separate train, non-stop from Crewe and into Euston for 11.45am. The previous 4.30pm departure from Euston was now used for a Manchester express.

Other bright timings were by the 9.45am down 'Comet', accelerated by 10min to become a 3½hr train to Manchester and the retimed 6.30pm to Preston and Colne, non-stop to Stafford in 140min for the 133 miles. The 'Ulster Express' was altered to leave at 6.20pm, its previous timing was cut by 35min, and the arrival time of the steamer in Belfast was advanced by 85min; the up train was spruced up in the Summer 1955 timetable, to leave at 7am and arrive in Euston at 11.35am.

From the Winter 1954/55 timetable, the up 'Red Rose' had 10min cut out of its timing and with its 3hr 25min schedule became the fastest train on the Liverpool service, and one renowned for fast running with Stanier Pacifics. Trimming of the up 'Comet's' schedule by 5min to become a 3½hr service at first sight seemed unexceptional, but the train now made an additional stop at Watford Junction and was booked to run from Crewe to there in 137min. Another naming from the same timetable revision

was that of the 5.35pm down 'Emerald Isle Express', principally an evening Euston–North Wales Coast express but also allowing travellers to join the Dun Laoghaire steamer at Holyhead at a civilised hour rather than detraining at 2.30am from the 'Irish Mail'. The up 'Emerald Isle' was the 7.30am Holyhead–Euston.

The 'Royal Scot's' summer schedule for 1954 was 7¼hr each way with the usual engine changing stop outside Carlisle. One of the problems of this and other Anglo-Scottish expresses derived from combining portions for Glasgow and Perth. But with the Winter 1954/55 service, there was a marked improvement from other winter seasons, the 'Royal Scot' now taking 7hr 40min, with a tight 80min timing between Euston and Rugby, then leaving its Perth portion at Crewe, and keeping ahead of the Birmingham–Glasgow train to which the 'Scot's' Perth section had been transferred. The up 'Royal Scot' retained its summer 7¼hr timing with Carlisle stop only. In the Winter 1954/5 timetable, the down 'Mid-Day Scot' was accelerated by the similar expedient of transferring its Perth section to the 1.35pm from Euston, previously for Blackpool only, then detaching it at Crewe to run forward separately. The same was done south of Carstairs with the up 'Mid-Day Scot', the Perth section previously added there now continuing as an independent train. The down 'Mid-Day Scot' had its overall time cut by 20min, the up train by 45min.

One of the poorer relations among the LMR's express services was that between Birmingham and Liverpool/Manchester. It was made halfway presentable in the Summer 1955 timetable, by provision of additional trains and some accelerations, including a best time of 107min over the 82 miles between the cities by the new 3.45pm Birmingham–Manchester. Four years later the equivalent train took 135min!

From 1955/56, the pace of improvements began to slacken on the Western Division. Far from returning to its pre-1939 time of 3¼hr each way Euston–Manchester, in the summer of 1956 the 'Mancunian' was decelerated by 5min each way from previous schedules of 3hr 25min by the up non-stop train, and 3hr 35min of the down service with one stop at Wilmslow. One reason for the addition of time to schedules of Manchester via Crewe services from 1956 was the start of electrification work. Somewhat belatedly, the craze for train naming took in the 7.55am Euston–Manchester and 4pm back which revived the prewar name of 'Lancastrian' from the Winter 1957/58 timetable.

Late in 1955, there were reports that a fast Euston–Glasgow service was on the cards, to be timed in 6¼hr, and comprising a 300 ton train worked by a 'Duchess'. The familiar pleading of 'operating difficulties', but usually taken to mean inter-Regional disagreements, meant that the train did not materialise until the summer of 1957. Named the 'Caledonian', its timing was in fact 6hr 40min each way, and the load was restricted to eight coaches, not nine. Leaving Glasgow at 8.30am, and Euston at 4.15pm, the only intermediate stop was Carlisle. To make way for the flyer, in a way that was typical of the 'operating-led' management of the time, the 3.45pm down Manchester was hustled to Nuneaton, to arrive there 7min earlier and where its passengers contemplated the station for 17min to let the down 'Caledonian' pass! Another consequence was that the up 'Mid-Day Scot' was retimed to leave Glasgow at 3pm and, by giving up its Crewe stop, now ran non-stop between Carlisle and Euston.

A second pair of 'Caledonians' was added from the summer of 1958, timed in 6¾hr: at 7.45am down, calling at Crewe and Carlisle, and at 4pm up with Carlisle and Stafford stops. Its pathing had the effect of enforcing some improvement to the timings of the morning Manchester and Liverpool–Edinburgh/Glasgow expresses, but a fair description of their journey times of 5hr or so for a 225-mile run was lethargic, despite which their timekeeping was poor. In any event, the down morning and up afternoon

One reason for the slow timings of the Manchester/Liverpool–Glasgow expresses was that they were limited to Class '6' motive power, at least into the late 1950s, and the engines were hard put to keep time on the normally heavy loads. 'Jubilee' No. 45712 *Victory* leaves Preston in July 1953 with the afternoon service for Glasgow and Edinburgh.

A classic study of the down 'Caledonian' in 1958 with 'Duchess' Pacific No. 46257 *City of Salford* seemingly taking the climb to Shap in its stride.

'Caledonians' were dropped with the Winter 1958/59 timetable.

Enterprise was soon stamped out by a major programme revealed in the Winter 1958/59 timetable of padding-out the schedules of nearly all Western Division expresses with recovery times, and back-timing departures of expresses, to suit the demands of the engineers for electrification works. Effectively, this spelt the end of the steam age express service on the West Coast Main Line, as morale suffered and, by the time the reconstruction of the main line had been completed, steam was on the way out. Some semblance of former timings returned during the summer of 1959, but by then the damage had been done. Worse, the public timetables took to showing arrivals considerably later than the working times. The dieselisation of the principal Euston–Liverpool and Manchester expresses followed close behind.

One strategy adopted to offset adding time to schedules was to limit train loads strictly, and from the winter of 1959/60 the 'Royal Scot', 'Mid-Day Scot' and 'Caledonian' were all formed of eight coaches only, all being seats reservable. With departures at 9.5am, 1.5 and 3.45pm down, and 10am, 1.15pm and 8.30am up, all three trains ran to the same timings of 7¼hr between Euston and Glasgow, and were non-stop

to/from Carlisle. Free from the electrification work now in progress south of Weaver Junction, the through trains between Lancashire and Scotland were accelerated from the winter of 1959/60, yet the best time, by the 4.30pm from Glasgow and Edinburgh was still a shade over 5hr.

Also in the timetable of 2 November 1959, its introduction delayed by a printing strike, the majority of Euston–Birmingham–Wolverhampton expresses were withdrawn and the Western Region service augmented in their place. The effect was to reduce the remaining Euston–Birmingham–Wolverhampton trains to four each way, most routed via Northampton.

In the early postwar days, express trains on the Midland Division generally made long and weary journeys, and their timekeeping was often very poor. One adverse influence from the Winter 1950/51 timetable was the addition of 35-40min or so to the schedules of expresses between Nottingham or Trent and Leeds alone, now that speed restrictions had been imposed on sections suffering from coal-mining subsidence. The restoration of through coaches to/from Buxton and St Pancras and a 37min acceleration of the up Edinburgh and St Pancras express from November 1952 were about the only positive developments.

No doubt emitting that characteristic hollow, even bark, 'Duchess' No. 46256 *Sir William A. Stanier, F.R.S.* climbs Beattock bank on a summer morning heading a Euston–Glasgow Central sleeping car express, with a banking engine providing assistance.

Late 1950s' Midland Division express power – 1: with the 1957 accelerated timings, a driver was entitled to ask for an assisting engine if his train loaded outside the limit. That meant having a stock of supposedly suitable engines, and various ex-Midland and LMS 2P 4-4-0s were brought out of idleness to work at speeds up to 80mph. The 2.15pm St Pancras–Bradford Forster Square is hammering up to Sharnbrook summit on 3 May 1958 with Midland 2P No. 40420 and 'Jubilee' No. 45619 *Nigeria*.

Late 1950s' Midland Division express power – 2: one of the last steam-worked expresses to be named was the morning service from Nottingham Midland–St Pancras and afternoon return, and this became the 'Robin Hood'. The train is seen near Manton Tunnel on the Kettering–Nottingham line, worked by 'Royal Scot' No. 46157 *The Royal Artilleryman*, these engines having been replaced by diesels on the Western Division.

In the Summer 1954 improvements to LMR services, the only significant Midland Division change was the retiming of the 7.10pm St Pancras–Sheffield to 6.33pm, its diversion to run via Leicester and a non-stop booking to Derby in 140min. Sheffield was reached in 3hr 22min from London. Even in late 1954 there were just two expresses on the Midland Division with mile-a-minute timings. In the winter of 1955/6 Sheffield at last regained a 3¼hr service with the noon departure from St Pancras via Leicester and Trent.

Somnolent for so long, the Midland Division came to life from the winter of 1956/7, with the restoration of a 99min timing between Leicester and St Pancras, a new 1.55pm from Derby, non-stop runs between St Pancras and Nottingham in 127/128min, and a 3hr 10min timing to Sheffield by the 2.10pm St Pancras–Bradford which was now 15min faster overall.

All this was a prelude to the rewriting of the Midland timetable in June 1957 which reflected what had been done 20 years earlier. Clockface departures from St Pancras were broadly on the basis of 15min past for Leicester, Nottingham and Sheffield, and

25min past for Derby and Manchester. The fastest St Pancras–Manchester time was slashed to 3hr 44min, by the 2.25pm down which was inexplicably denied catering facilities. Average cuts to schedules – not just by specified trains – ranged for 35min between Manchester and St Pancras to 15min between Sheffield, Nottingham and Leicester, and St Pancras. Five trains down and two up ran non-stop between St Pancras and Nottingham with the fastest at 123min. Now named the 'Waverley', the morning St Pancras–Edinburgh train via Leeds and the Settle & Carlisle was accelerated by 40min going north, and 26min coming south. The cross-country trains over the West of England main line were taken in hand, too, from the Summer 1957 timetable – see **Cross-Country services**.

From 1957/58, the 7.55am St Pancras–Manchester and 2.25pm return became the 'Palatine', and early in 1959 the 8.15am Nottingham–St Pancras and 4.45pm return were titled the 'Robin Hood', the second-rate afternoon train taking 2¾hr overall on its journey. One curiosity arising from electrification work on the Western Division was the diversion from the winter of 1959/60 of a quartet of Manchester trains to/from St Pancras, the day trains at noon from Manchester London Road, and 1.55pm from St Pancras running non-stop from/to Stoke, and routed via Stenson Junction and Castle Donington.

The withdrawal of the Great Central route's Marylebone–Sheffield, Manchester and Bradford expresses from January 1960, and their replacement by just three semi-fast trains each way between Marylebone and Nottingham only, had repercussions for the Midland route. Through coaches were put on from/to Halifax and St Pancras in part-compensation, returning on the 5.5pm from London. One return to past glories for the GC route came in the Winter 1962/63 timetable when the sleeping car service between London and Manchester was diverted via Sheffield, worked by steam south of Nottingham for a couple of years.

With the general introduction of 2,500hp diesel locomotives on the Midland lines from early 1961, it was only a matter of time before a revised timetable was introduced, and that occurred in November 1962. As a footnote to previous services, the daytime through trains between St Pancras and Edinburgh were withdrawn in winter as from the 1964/65 timetable, to be replaced by through coaches conveyed south of Carlisle on the 'Thames–Clyde Express'.

Conspicuous by its absence in any postwar service accelerations was the Central Division. Most of the features of its prewar services remained, despite fast-changing circumstances. Four Blackpool–Manchester 'residential' services operated each way, also running on Saturdays when they returned from Manchester at midday, and two were non-stop between Lytham or Layton and Salford. Another flow of residential trains linked the Fylde Coast and the East Lancashire towns, some with through coaches to/from Liverpool. The Calder Valley service retained its LBL – Liverpool–Bradford–Leeds – trains but the best times between Manchester and Liverpool were now 48/49min. The Liverpool Exchange–Newcastle restaurant car express remained in the timetables, leaving at 10.30am, but now made half-a-dozen calls before Wakefield was reached and, having run via Stockton and West Hartlepool, was scheduled in 5hr 48min overall; the 5.10pm return was at least 25min faster.

From March 1962, the previous long-standing

Just three weeks before the date of this photograph – 25 February 1958 – control of the former Great Central main line to London passed to the London Midland Region. This is the up 'Master Cutler' pausing at Nottingham Victoria behind V2 class 2-6-2 No. 60911. In September 1958 the train's title was transferred to a new Pullman service between King's Cross and Sheffield.

An example of the Central Division's residential trains is provided by this afternoon Rochdale–Blackpool Central Class '1' arriving at Preston in July 1957 behind LMS Compound 4-4-0 No. 41193.

pattern of Central Division services over the Calder Valley main line passed into history when diesel multiple-units were introduced. Among the greatly reduced number of steam workings east of Manchester Exchange/Victoria there remained two or so trains each way conveying through coaches from/to Colne and Euston, via Burnley and Blackburn. This link between East Lancs and the Capital was lost in September 1962.

On 1950s and 1960s' summer weekends, the volume of extra trains along the North Wales Coast from Chester and from Preston to/from the Fylde Coast resorts was truly amazing. It was not unusual for 40 holiday trains to pass through Preston in an hour. Along the North Wales Coast the railway retained a commanding presence in the tourist industry, with LMR staff literally touting for traffic from holidaymakers promenading at Rhyl. There were special workings in the summer season, some dating from prewar inspirations, such as the 'Snowdonian' to and from Llanberis, two land cruise trains, and the 'Welsh Dragon' shuttle service between Rhyl and Llandudno.

Footnotes in the demise of steam included the drastic reduction in workings between Manchester/ Colne–Blackpool in August 1964 which saw the end of the steam-worked Blackpool Club trains; the

diversion of the 'Northern Irishman' Euston–Stranraer boat train via Mauchline, Ayr and Girvan from June 1965 following closure to traffic of the Dumfries–Stranraer line, and with steam haulage north of Carlisle; the introduction of the electrified services between Euston and the North West in April 1966 which brought an end to many traditional workings such as the Windermere–Manchester Club train; and continuance of the 'Cambrian Coast Express' as a steam working west of Shrewsbury until March 1967. After that, steam remained at work on some scheduled West Coast Main Line trains north of Crewe for a few more years.

In relating the story of main line services in the steam age, there is a special place for the 'Belfast Boat Express'. This was the unofficial title for the 6.15am Heysham–Manchester Victoria and 8.55pm return, both trains stopping at Bolton, Preston, Lancaster and making a reversal at Morecambe. By New Year 1968, this was the last daily steam-hauled Class '1' train on British Rail, and Stanier 'Black Fives' were kept at work on this train up to and including 5 May that year. The very last steam-worked Class '1' workings on BR were through portions between Preston and Blackpool/Liverpool of West Coast expresses and they made their last runs on 3 August 1968.

CHAPTER EIGHTEEN

EASTERN AND NORTH EASTERN REGIONS

The last day of May 1948 saw the restoration of the 'Flying Scotsman's' non-stop running between King's Cross and Edinburgh, for which the timing was 7hr 50min. Two new sets of coaches had been built for the service, all with pressure ventilation, and including a special restaurant buffet car. In August that year, the worst floods for many years in the Borders washed away bridges and embankments on the East Coast Main Line between Reston and Grantshouse, such that through trains were diverted via the Newcastle–Carlisle and Waverley Route line, or in the case of the 'Flying Scotsman', from Leeds via the Settle & Carlisle line. After a fortnight, the route from Tweedmouth, Kelso and St Boswells to Edinburgh was used and this was adopted by the 'Flying Scotsman' which, on eight occasions, set up a record non-stop run of 408½ miles between King's Cross and Edinburgh.

For the following year, the non-stop was renamed the 'Capitals Limited', and was taking 8hr overall. During the 1952 season, only one engine failure occurred during the eleven weeks that the train ran. In honour of the Queen, the train was retitled the 'Elizabethan' as from the 1953 season when the schedule each way came down to 6hr 45min, and for 1954 to 6hr 30min. The train was worked by A4 Pacifics from King's Cross and Haymarket sheds.

September 1948 saw the first new winter BR timetables and with them came the introduction of the 'Tees–Tyne Pullman' from King's Cross to Newcastle, and the 'Norfolkman' between Liverpool St. and Norwich.

A second Pullman service was restored to the East Coast lines on 5 July 1948 when the 'Queen of Scots' pulled out from King's Cross at 11.30am. The 'Yorkshire Pullman' was running at 4.45pm from King's Cross, altered to 5.30pm a year later, and at first with portions for Harrogate, Leeds and Hull only; Bradford came later. Attempts to find suitable services on which to use the rakes of prewar high-speed coaches from the 'Silver Jubilee' and other trains came to nothing, and instead a new Pullman service was introduced in September 1948. This was the 'Tees–Tyne Pullman', at 9am from Newcastle, with a 5hr 16min timing to King's Cross, and 4min longer northbound. It left King's Cross at the 'Jubilee's' former time of 5.30pm, but later swapped with the 'Yorkshire Pullman' for a 4.45pm departure. Overall timings came down to 4hr 54min. The special prewar stock never again operated as complete trains although freshly repainted in BR carmine and cream livery some vehicles were used on the the newly titled 'West Riding' which began running in 1949 with the 3.45pm down, running non-stop to Wakefield.

With the Winter 1949/50 timetable, the southbound 'Tees–Tyne Pullman' came down to a 4hr 7min run between Darlington and King's Cross, the northbound train being 4min slower. The other Pullmans were also given faster point-to-point times so that the 'Queen of Scots' made its King's Cross–Leeds journeys in 3hr 42min (down) and 3min more up, and the 'Yorkshire Pullman', 172min to Doncaster and 178min up. The three Pullman expresses were generally unchanged until new stock was put into service from 1960 and they began to be worked by 'Deltic' locomotives from 1962. One

A gleaming turn-out for the up 'Tees-Tyne Pullman' which has slowed down to 20mph for the passage of Peterborough North station on 25 April 1949, with A3 No. 60073 *St Gatien* leading the set of Pullman cars.

By the time that A4 No. 60017 *Silver Fox* was photographed passing Doncaster, the 'Tees-Tyne Pullman' was one of the more exacting duties on the East Coast Main Line. The date is 15 June 1958 and No. 60017 is working through from Newcastle to King's Cross.

Watchful eyes follow A4 No 60034 *Lord Faringdon* as it threads York station at slow speed with the down non-stop 'Flying Scotsman' in the summer of 1948.

notable exception was acceleration of the 'Tees–Tyne Pullman' to a 3hr 49min timing southbound, 3min more northbound as from the Summer 1953 timetable; a York stop was added to the northbound run in October 1953.

The Winter 1951/52 timetable introduced clockface departures from King's Cross, on the hour for Newcastle and Scottish expresses, and at 18min past for Leeds/West Riding trains. However, the new, fast King's Cross morning express to Leeds/Bradford which was put on from the Winter 1952/53 timetable left at 8am, calling only at Hitchin and Doncaster, and reaching Leeds at 11.31, and Bradford at 11.55am. From Summer 1953, the departure time was made 7.50am, and that October a Newcastle portion was added, worked forward separately as a lightweight express from Doncaster. Its return working was as the 5.3pm from Newcastle, joining up at Doncaster with the Bradford section.

As on the West Coast Main Line, the recovery from wartime schedules only made real progress after 1953. Typical was the acceleration of what was to become a principal businessmen's train in the timetables, the breakfast-time departure from Newcastle. From October 1953 this was altered to leave at 7.45am, and arrive at King's Cross for 12.46pm, 32min quicker than in the summer timetable, and calling at Durham, Darlington and Peterborough.

The schedules of the 'Flying Scotsman' hardly altered until Summer 1955 when the down train was changed to run non-stop to Newcastle in 4hr 40min, and the up train in 4hr 36min. North to Edinburgh, the best times were made not by the 'Flying Scotsman' but the 'Queen of Scots' and 'Heart of Midlothian', both these expresses being booked in 127min from Newcastle. But the speeded-up 'Scotsman' lasted no more than three months and in the Winter 1955/6 timetable no less than 30/35min were added to the overall timings with just one additional stop, at Grantham. Highlighting the trend towards increasingly busy weekend operations, on summer Saturdays in 1956 the Eastern and North Eastern Regions combined to offer an hourly service between King's Cross and Newcastle from 8.40am to 3.40pm, and at a two-hourly frequency to Edinburgh between 9am and 2pm. This meant 55 long-distance departures from the terminus in 10hr – one every 11min.

It took until September 1956 for a high-speed train to return to the East Coast, and it was named the 'Talisman', a 6hr 40min train in each direction between King's Cross and Edinburgh. It left either terminal at 4pm, and called only at Newcastle, non-stop northbound in 4hr 28min, southbound in 3min less. Restricted to eight coaches only, including a twin open first formerly used on the 'Coronation', the new service was worked by A4 Pacifics. Insertion of a fast train such as this into an existing timetable was bound to cause changes, as indeed had happened in 1935 with the 'Silver Jubilee'. So it was with the 'Talisman' and, to keep out of its way, the 3.45pm 'West Riding' now left 5min earlier, while the 3.52pm to Leeds was diverted to run slow line from Potters Bar to Welwyn Garden City. The 'Queen of Scots' also took up a noon departure (11.50am from Winter 1957/58). These altered times were largely to remain into the early 1960s.

As on the West Coast, the late 1950s saw an apparent reversal of the drive towards faster trains. Electrification work was not to blame on the East Coast though, rather it was the operators' keenness to impose recovery time on schedules, ostensibly to improve timekeeping but often serving to depress it, particularly as an unaffected, fast point-to-point timing might be followed by one padded out with recovery time. The process meant that all but two East Coast expresses in the Summer 1957 timetable lost their mile-a-minute timings.

New from 17 June was a 'Morning Talisman' service, at 7.45am from King's Cross, and 7.30am from Edinburgh. One advantage was that only two sets of coaches were needed: the down morning train to Edinburgh formed the afternoon up service, and vice versa. Also, the up 'Night Scotsman' was advertised as running non-stop Edinburgh–King's Cross and accelerated to an 8hr schedule.

The down 'Morning Talisman' did not load well and, from September 1957, an attempt was made to capture new traffic by extending the train to run to and from Perth via the Forth Bridge. Why this should have helped is unclear, and it meant that rolling stock utilisation worsened. Departure from King's Cross was made 7.50am, and the train displaced the Newcastle portion of the former Bradford/Newcastle train. Into Perth at 4.18pm, the return working of what was now called the 'Fair Maid' left at 6.40am, was 60min later than the up 'Morning Talisman' from Edinburgh, and arrived in King's Cross at

3.20pm. That was not all. The down 'Heart of Midlothian', retimed to 1pm, was also run onwards to Perth (arr 10.24pm), this time via Falkirk Grahamston and Stirling. Its return was at 11.25am, and away from Edinburgh at 2pm it reached King's Cross at 9.52pm. From the Winter 1958/9 timetable, the 'Fair Maid' workings were cut back to Edinburgh, and the trains retitled 'Talisman'. Similarly, the 'Heart of Midlothian' no longer ran to Perth.

The other changes to Anglo-Scottish trains in the September 1957 timetable were equally radical. The 'Flying Scotsman' was changed to run non-stop to Newcastle in winter, as had been tried before, in a time of 4hr 44min. The Aberdeen coaches went forward from Edinburgh in a new 5.10pm express, their return next morning on the similarly new 7.5am from Aberdeen meant that the arrival at Edinburgh was too late for them to travel on the 'Flying Scotsman' and instead were transferred to the 9.30am Glasgow Queen St.–King's Cross.

There were now three trains with sleeping accommodation from King's Cross to Aberdeen: at 7.45pm, with through coaches for Elgin; at 10.15pm, sleeping cars only, taking the 'Aberdonian' name from the earlier train, and at 10.30pm. Southbound, the King's Cross sleeping car trains left Aberdeen at 7.5, and 8.35pm. The 'Night Scotsman' to/from Edinburgh comprised first-class sleeping cars only, down at 11.35pm and up at 10.50pm, and both journeys being accelerated to 8hr only.

Other changes in Winter 1957/58 included cutting out some of the intermediate stops made by the King's Cross–West Riding trains, the speeding-up of the 7.30am from Leeds by 33min, to arrive at 11.7am, and running the former early evening train from Newcastle to King's Cross at 5.5pm. It now had a 40min timing between Darlington and York, and retained its Retford–Hitchin run with a mile-a-minute average speed. Also, new tightly-timed trains, termed semi-fast by the Region, were brought into the timetable, with the object of serving Hull. The northbound departures were 8.20am, 2.10pm (also for York) and 6.35pm down. Southbound there were a 7.43am from York, and trains at 1.33 and 6.30pm from Doncaster (both with TC from Hull).

All told, these changes generated a pretty formidable increase in train mileage, but also provided the basis of the East Coast/West Riding services that lasted into the 'Deltic' era. From Summer 1958, the 10.10am King's Cross–Glasgow became the 11am down, the 6.20pm down Leeds was altered to a 6.12 departure, and the 6.35pm left 9min earlier. Main line services benefited greatly by the May 1959 completion of the Greenwood–Potters Bar four-tracking which removed a troublesome bottleneck.

The diesel era on the GN main line began in September 1958 with the introduction of the 'Master Cutler' Pullman between Sheffield Victoria and King's Cross, featuring fast up morning and a down evening workings in 165min, and in addition a slower off-peak return trip to Sheffield.

One latter-day addition to the steam worked services was the 'Tees–Thames', a through train to King's Cross from Saltburn at 7.5am via Middlesbrough, the same set of coaches returning at 2pm to Saltburn. Introduced in September 1959, the service lasted only until the Winter 1961/62 timetable, and the start of regular operations with the 'Deltics'. By the following summer, the East Coast operators were once more offering 6hr timings between King's Cross and Edinburgh, for the first time since 1939.

A new service dating from the early postwar days comprised the up morning and down evening Cleethorpes–King's Cross trains, worked throughout by B1 4-6-0s from March 1950, and unusual power for main line services otherwise dominated by Pacifics of prewar and postwar classes. Two more through trains were added in June 1954, at 6.55am from Grimsby Town and 6.18pm return. From 1961, 'Britannia' Pacifics replaced the B1s, and all four trains were accelerated by up to 26min, the down trains becoming the 4.12 and 6.50pm, the up ones leaving Grimsby at 6.54 and 8.43am.

From December 1948, a revived service of four 'Cambridge Buffet Expresses' each way had begun, taking 82min at best and calling at Welwyn Garden City, Hitchin and Letchworth; some trains stopped also at Baldock or Royston. Much the same pattern remained until 1959 and the onset of dieselisation which ironically coincided with the inclusion of extra stops and slower timings.

During the 1950s, the Eastern Region made use of normally freight-only lines for regular holiday trains and excursions, notably summer Saturday Cleethorpes–Leicester and Scarborough or Mablethorpe–Basford North trains routed over the former Lancashire, Derbyshire & East Coast line which had lost its daily services in 1955. Two summer Saturday trains each way between Leicester Belgrave Road and Skegness, and Mablethorpe which traversed the Great Northern & London and North Western Joint line which had closed to regular public services in 1953.

With the announcement that the new British Railways Standard steam classes would include a Pacific design, first reports were that 15 of these would be allocated to the former Great Eastern lines of the Eastern Region. The GE eventually ran 23 'Britannias', having received later deliveries during 1952/53.

As the Railway Executive's report for 1951 put it:
New standard locomotives of the 'Britannia' class were introduced on the Liverpool Street–Ipswich–Norwich services which were completely reorganised to give standard departure times and

The 'Cambridge Buffet Expresses' were restored at the end of 1948, and regained something of their prewar reputation. On 14 June 1954, a down working comes past Belle Isle, and the entry to King's Cross Goods and engine shed, with B17 class 4-6-0 No. 61640 *Somerleyton Hall* at the front end.

Bank Holiday and summer only trains ran over some otherwise freight-only lines in the Eastern Region. This is a Leicester Belgrave Road-bound service returning from Skegness, and passing Scalford on 10 July 1954, worked by J39 class 0-6-0 No. 64798.

considerably quicker journeys and adjustments of branch line connections enabled the accelerated services to be enjoyed by many outlying places in East Anglia.

The new timetable between Liverpool St. and Norwich began on 2 July 1951 and provided for hourly departures from Liverpool St. between 8.30am and 7.30pm; however, the 2.30pm ran to Ipswich only. Up from Norwich there were hourly trains from 7.45am until 6.45pm, with the exception of the 10.45am. In each direction some trains made several stops, but there were fast workings which called only at Ipswich, down at 9.30am – the 'Norfolkman'; 12.30; 3.30 – the 'Broadsman'; 5.30; and the 6.30pm – 'East Anglian'. The up fasts were the 7.45 – 'Broadsman', the 11.45am – 'East Anglian', the 2.45, 5.45pm – 'Norfolkman', and 6.45pm, all booked to take no more than 130min for the 115 miles. The 5.30 pm down called also at Chelmsford. For the fast trains the 'Britannias' were limited to 9 coaches, or 300 tons. BR promised that 2hr schedules between Liverpool St. and Norwich would be introduced once the backlog of track renewals had diminished.

The average acceleration of trains as compared with the previous timetable was 22min, but individual accelerations were often dramatic. The 5.30pm Liverpool St.–Cromer was now 63min faster to its destination and the 5.45pm from this Norfolk coast resort was 45min quicker to London. One of the 'Britannias' covered the up and down 'Hook

Continental' from/to Harwich Parkeston Quay, and the engine regularly provided was *Britannia* herself, the intention being that Continental visitors would not fail to miss a patriotically named engine at the head of this prestige train.

The 'Norfolkman' was one of the 'Festival of Britain' trains (see **Western Region**) and made its first run with the new BR Standard corridor stock on 7 May 1951 in advance of the summer timetable and the accelerated Liverpool St.–Norwich services.

The Great Eastern had to wait until the Summer 1953 timetable before a similar reorganisation could be applied to its Cambridge line express service. Once again, radical reshaping of the timetable brought appreciable savings in resources, and also benefited the Colchester line as a result of the interworking of locomotives and stock. No less than 10 engines, 14 train-crews and 36 coaches were saved, as compared to the previous timetable.

The new Cambridge line timetable comprised a variety of trains including Liverpool St.–Ely– Norwich expresses which were now handled by Pacifics on timings allowing for 400-ton loads. Regular interval departures applied from London and Cambridge in the up direction. The Pacifics were diagrammed to cover the 8.24am, 12.24, 2.24, 5.54 and 7.14pm from the capital, and the 10.4am, 12.15, 3.45, 4.45 and 7.15pm departures from Cambridge.

Schedules were less dramatically improved than had been the case with the Colchester main line, a

The 'Easterling' was a summer holiday train, and was worked by B1 and B17 class 4-6-0s until 'Britannias' were available in the late 1950s. B1 No. 61234 departs from Liverpool St. with the down train in 1951.

combination of a maximum line speed of 70mph, and compounded by curvature south of Cambridge as well as difficulties in pathing fast trains over a route dominated by an intensive flow of goods trains between Whitemoor and Temple Mills.

In December 1957, with an imminent prospect of the delivery of Type 4 diesels, the ER announced that the 'Britannias' displaced from the Norwich expresses would be employed in speeding up the Liverpool St.–Clacton service. By Spring 1958, the diesels were at work on the Norwich trains and 'Britannias' were beginning to appear between Liverpool St. and Clacton. Until the civil engineering restrictions were lifted, the Pacifics were restricted to 40mph between Colchester and Clacton.

With the Summer 1958 timetable, the diesels were handling all the Norwich trains except for the 11.30am, 4.30, 5.30 and 7.30pm down, and a similar number of up trains. 'Britannias' from Stratford depot had several diagrams based on Clacton. Four evening Clacton residential trains from London were

now worked by 'Britannias', and star of the service was the down 'Essex Coast Express', a newly named train. This stopped only at Colchester and Thorpe-le-Soken in its 70-mile journey, to reach Clacton in an unprecedented time of 86min. 'Britannias' were also available for some of the East Suffolk line expresses, too, including the summer 'Easterling', at 11.3am from Liverpool St. to Yarmouth South Town and 7.17pm back.

More changes came in the Winter 1958/59 timetable, and Norwich now had three 2hr trains each way. The Liverpool St.–Cambridge–Norwich day trains were withdrawn and the Cambridge line fast trains comprised a recast and largely diesel-worked Liverpool St.–Ely–King's Lynn service.

Yet more rethinking came in January 1959 with dieselisation of most GE line branch passenger services, and the replacement by dmu connections of the through coaches formerly provided to most coastal resorts. Only the 'Broadsman' now worked beyond Norwich, to Sheringham and back.

Economies were made in rolling stock utilisation, four sets of coaches being able to make two return London–Norwich trips daily. For the first time, there were hourly trains through the day on this route, 2hr trains every three hours, and the acceleration of the semi-fast trains to a general time of 150min down and 155min up. Three East Suffolk line trains each way were in the hands of 'Britannias', the class also heading the three off-peak Liverpool St.–Clacton expresses in each direction. Three of the 2hr Norwich trains remained steam hauled.

During the summer of 1961, the first batch of English Electric Type 3 locomotives was being delivered. These locomotives took over the haulage of the 'Hook Continental' and the Harwich–Liverpool boat train, and then displaced the 'Britannias' from their remaining turns with the Norwich expresses.

Having had the former London, Tilbury and Southend section transferred to its control in 1949, the Eastern Region soon reintroduced 50min timings between Fenchurch St. and Southend. On the former GE Southend line, the fastest timings in postwar years were 68min and the supper cars of 1914 were long-forgotten. Electrification at 1,500V dc was extended from Shenfield to Southend Victoria, and the last steam workings ran on 30 December 1956.

In May 1958 the Eastern Area Board decided that in view of the losses being made it would proceed with the closure of the major part of the Midland & Great Northern lines. Closure was implemented as from 29 February 1959, the last services running the previous day, including the 9am Yarmouth Beach/Cromer Beach–Leicester and 3.15pm return through trains, with their through coaches to/from Birmingham New St.

In the autumn of 1947, the 7.40am Sheffield–Marylebone and the 6.25pm return were named the 'Master Cutler'. With the Summer 1948 timetable, the Great Central section regained one through train each way between Bradford, Huddersfield and Marylebone, at 10am from Bradford and 4.50pm from Marylebone, and these became the 'South Yorkshireman'. The GC main line sheds had received brand-new B1 4-6-0s but, as business traffic recovered, so the loads of the expresses into/out of Marylebone increased, and the crews working the B1s were hard pressed to maintain schedules.

In February 1949, Pacifics returned to the GC section and, despite the prevailing difficulties, also imparted prestige to the main line's expresses. The 'Master Cutler' featured a distinctive headboard and this train, and the 'South Yorkshireman', were allocated some of the best rolling stock available on the Eastern Region.

The timetable current at November 1949 comprised down expresses from Marylebone to Manchester at 10am, 12.15pm, 3.20pm and the 10pm Mail, the last having through coaches and vans to Liverpool Central which were detached at Godley Junction. The other expresses were the 4.50pm 'South Yorkshireman' to Sheffield and Bradford Exchange, and the 6.15pm 'Master Cutler' to Sheffield Victoria. Up trains to Marylebone comprised 'The Mail' at 10.25pm from Manchester London Road (and including through coaches at 9.30pm from Liverpool Central); the 7.40am from Sheffield Victoria, the 'Master Cutler' ; the 10am 'South Yorkshireman' from Bradford Exchange, and the 8.25am 11.30am and 3.46pm from Manchester London Road. Some trains ran via Aylesbury, others via High Wycombe.

The timings of the GC trains to and from Leicester and Nottingham compared favourably with the Midland main line expresses, but only the 'Master Cutler' was really competitive for journeys to Sheffield and the North. The punishing climb over Woodhead to Manchester contributed to the lengthy journey times of 5-6hr for the 206 miles to/from Manchester.

From September 1954, the Manchester–Sheffield line was electrified but few changes were made to the timings of the Marylebone expresses. The 11.30am Manchester–Marylebone was later replaced by the 2.10pm. In Summer 1955, there was a belated acceleration of the 'Master Cutler' in each direction, 13min by the down train which now left at 6.18pm and arrived in Sheffield at 9.55pm, and 10min by the up train which started at 7.50am but retained its 11.25am arrival at Marylebone.

With the introduction of the diesel-worked Pullman service between Sheffield and King's Cross in September 1958, the title of 'Master Cutler' was stripped from the GC route trains which at first were slated for withdrawal. By now, control had passed to the London Midland Region for much of the GC main line's length, and the end of the Marylebone–Sheffield/Manchester expresses was widely expected. This was confirmed in May 1959 with publication of the Region's Passenger Plan. One last change in September 1959 saw the 6.18pm down retimed to start at 7.15pm, routed instead via Aylesbury and not reaching Sheffield until 11.13pm.

On 4 January 1960, all through expresses between Marylebone and Sheffield, Manchester and Bradford were withdrawn, to be replaced by semi-fast service as far as Nottingham only. The night trains – and cross-country expresses – survived for longer, but the

The 'South Yorkshireman' was one of the earliest new postwar named trains introduced by the Eastern Region. Eight coaches, but two LMS Class 5s on this occasion in the 1950s when the train was photographed at Heaton Lodge Junction behind Nos 45210 and 44982.

through coaches to/from Liverpool Central by the mail trains were withdrawn from March 1962.

Marylebone was also the London terminus for the cheap fare, guaranteed-seat 'Starlight Specials' which operated on Fridays between 1953 and 1962 to/from Edinburgh and Glasgow St Enoch. These made use of the so-called cafeteria cars, introduced by BR from 1952. Converted from a variety of vehicle types, the cars were originally intended for excursion trains, and were arranged for self-service.

Although the North Eastern Region's main passenger services ran over the East Coast Main Line and were jointly operated with the Eastern, and/or the Scottish Regions, its main contribution was in making best use of the splendidly graded main line between York and Darlington. By October 1953 there were two runs in 42min and 13 slower ones, only by up to 3min. The process of accelerating the line's services continued so that by 1957 there were 24 runs between Darlington and York at 44min or better, the blue riband held by the 5.5pm Newcastle–King's Cross of Summer 1958 with its 39min sprint.

The Region's crack train was the 'North Briton'.

This held the distinction of being the first BR service of postwar days with a 60mph timing which was introduced between Darlington and York in winter 1949. By November 1949, the train was running at 8.48am from Leeds City and, after calls at York, Darlington, Newcastle and Edinburgh, arrived at Glasgow Queen St. for 3.8pm. Away again at its old time of 4pm, the train called additionally at Dunbar and Berwick, and by 10.28pm was back in Leeds City. By 1952/3, the 'North Briton's' timings had been improved almost to 1939 standards with the overall journey times both ways down to 6hr or so.

One former route used by express services declined rapidly in the 1960s. This was the Leeds Northern line north of Harrogate to Northallerton which lost nearly all the Liverpool–Newcastle trains by 1964, the 'Queen of Scots' being withdrawn in the same year.

Elsewhere the NER set out to replace steam by diesel units on semi-fast and stopping services. That between Newcastle and Middlesbrough went over to diesel in Summer 1956, and between Newcastle and Carlisle in 1959.

CHAPTER NINETEEN

SCOTTISH REGION AND CROSS-COUNTRY EXPRESSES

One attempt to demonstrate the advantages of a unified network came in 1949 with a summer-only Glasgow Queen St.–Oban and return service routed via the West Highland line and the spur linking with the Callander & Oban at Crianlarich. It did not last long. Some years were to pass before the duplication of facilities was rooted out and a more effective train service was introduced throughout Scotland.

Immediately after nationalisation the Region was in the news on account of its relatively fast schedules. Between Forfar and Perth, a 34min timing southbound, and 35min northbound were introduced with the Winter 1949/50 timetable, the latter as part of a 104min run – including two stops – between Perth and Aberdeen by the down Postal which included through coaches from Glasgow Central which had left at 4.5am. The usual allowance for Glasgow–Aberdeen trains north of Perth was 125-138min with five or so stops.

The up Postal, at 3.30pm from Aberdeen, and with limited passenger accommodation, at one time in 1948/9 featured a 106min booking from Aberdeen to Perth including the Forfar stop. At the same time, the 50min St Enoch–Ayr timing was reintroduced on the time-honoured 5.10pm down. Throughout the Region there was a line speed limit of 75mph or lower, and in the 1950s the fastest scheduled runs were between Carlisle and Glasgow.

Passenger traffic had declined noticeably on former Great North of Scotland Railway territory in the 1950s, some trains having been suspended during the fuel crisis of 1951 and not restored. Services were also thinned out in 1954, such as on the Buchan line to Fraserburgh. Overdue accelerations were applied in the Summer 1954 timetable and bucked up the timings of through Aberdeen–Inverness workings, never known for their speed. The 8.8am Aberdeen–Inverness was retimed to 7.50am, with a new section for Inverness routed from Keith via the former Highland line to Elgin, as well as one via Buckie, and now reached Inverness 29min earlier, at 11.6am. The 7.40am and 4pm from Inverness also took the same route and their through journeys to Aberdeen became over 1hr quicker, in 3½hr or so. The usual power for these trains were B1 4-6-0s working to Inverness.

In 1956, the ScR gave a clue to the future of main line services on BR when it rationalised workings on the former Caledonian Railway main line between Glasgow Buchanan St. and Aberdeen, and to Dundee West. From 11 June, no less than 26 intermediate stations were closed, and all stopping trains withdrawn. In their place came an accelerated service – give the odd gap or two – from Buchanan St. at 15min past the hour, hourly to Perth, and alternately bound for Aberdeen or Dundee, with corresponding return trains at clockface intervals. The average time between Glasgow, Aberdeen and Dundee was cut by nearly 30min. North of Perth, the trains from/to Glasgow called at all six remaining stations.

The star turn of the weekday trains was the 12.15pm 'Bon Accord' with a best time of 3hr 15min to Aberdeen – a 3hr schedule had applied in the summers of 1937-9 – and two trains ran non-stop Glasgow–Perth. A few more minutes were chipped

The attractive coaches from the prewar 'Silver Jubilee' found limited employment on the summer only 'Fife Coast Express' between Glasgow and St Andrews in the late 1940s/early 1950s. D11/2 class 4-4-0 No. 62684 *Wizard of the Moor* is seen near Dysart with the 4.7pm from Glasgow Queen St. in 1954.

from the timings from down expresses – but not up ones! – in the winter of 1956/57, so that there were three Glasgow expresses to Aberdeen in 3½hr, or slightly less. As part of a system-wide cost-cutting drive, from July 1958 the fast 12.15pm from Buchanan St. and 11.30am from Aberdeen were withdrawn, except on Saturdays.

The through daytime service between Glasgow and Inverness comprised just a couple of trains in the mid-1950s, morning and afternoon, and leaving Inverness in mid-afternoon and early evening. In addition, there were morning trains between Perth and Inverness and return, the night-time Glasgow–Inverness and return sleeping car trains, and the 'Royal Highlander' from/to Euston. A through Edinburgh–Inverness and return sleeping car was introduced in June 1959. Another innovation for the Perth–Inverness line was the introduction early in 1961 of a griddle car on the 8.30am Inverness–Edinburgh and 4.3pm return. Vehicles of this type saw limited service on other Regions, too, the intention being to serve grilled dishes, snacks and drinks rather than the full meals for which the demand was decreasing.

The Edinburgh–Glasgow via Falkirk High service went over to operation by diesel multiple-unit from January 1957, and the completion of engineering

works on this route permitted the reintroduction of 55-60min timings for the through steam express workings.

On the West Highland and Oban lines, an attempt was made to encourage tourist traffic by employing the pair of observation cars built by the LNER for the prewar 'Coronation' service, and on which a supplementary fare was payable. First used from July 1956 between Fort William and Mallaig, by Summer 1957 another car was at work between Stirling and Oban. Then the Pullman observation cars from the 'Devon Belle' came to Scotland and a third observation car service was brought in, between Glasgow and Fort William. Another service, between Inverness and Kyle of Lochalsh, began in the summer of 1961.

On the former Glasgow & South Western lines, the principal services remained the through trains to/from St Pancras and the Glasgow–Leeds and return workings, and the 5.30pm St Enoch–Plymouth. On the Ayr line, there were the through 'Irishman' trains to/from Stranraer Harbour, at 9pm from St Enoch and 9.15pm back. These were worked by 'Jubilee' 4-6-0s and had overall journey times of around 2½hr. Still retaining some of their erstwhile status were the 5.10pm from St Enoch non-stop to Ayr and the morning return train. Diesel multiple-

Double heading in the Highlands: a Fort William–Mallaig train heads away from Mallaig Junction on 17 September 1956 behind a pair of LNER design Moguls – K1 No. 62034 and the rebuilt K1/1 No. 61997 *MacCailin Mór*. At the rear of the train is one of the former 'Coronation' observation cars then making their debut on the line.

The A4 Pacifics enjoyed an Indian summer in Scotland. No. 60007 *Sir Nigel Gresley* was photographed near Bridge of Allan on 10 August 1964 with an Aberdeen–Glasgow express.

units replaced steam on most Glasgow–Ayr–Stranraer workings from late August 1959.

Also from the end of August 1959, diesel locomotives took up duties on Edinburgh–Aberdeen expresses, as a prelude to the introduction from April 1960 of two 3hr timings each way, and the general acceleration of other expresses on the route from that summer. The same timetable also saw the closure of 24 intermediate stations north of Inverness on the Far North line, and accelerated timings for Inverness–Wick trains, steam having been almost eliminated in the area with the first stages of dieselising the Highland lines. An experimental service of diesel units introduced 2½hr schedules to the Inverness–Aberdeen service from July 1960, and was made permanent early in 1961. Dieselisation of the Glasgow–Fort William–Mallaig, and Perth–Inverness services allowed greatly accelerated services to be introduced in June 1962.

But all was not lost for steam north of the Border. When announcing details of the summer services at a press conference just before Easter 1962, no less than the Scottish Area Board's Chairman confirmed that the four new 3hr trains between Glasgow and Aberdeen would indeed be steam worked. This was to be the only example of an accelerated express passenger service introduced during the later Modernisation Plan years with steam traction.

Compared with the 3hr summer-only expresses run from 1937 to 1939 by the LMS, the 1962 trains operated on weekdays throughout the year and made four stops in each direction: Stirling, Perth, Forfar and Stonehaven. Formed of seven-coach sets, and running on weekdays from September 1962, the new trains were the 8.25am Glasgow–Aberdeen – the 'Grampian'; the 5.30pm Glasgow–Aberdeen – the 'Saint Mungo'; the 7.10am Aberdeen–Glasgow – the 'Bon Accord' and the 5.15pm Aberdeen–Glasgow – the 'Granite City'.

These were existing trains accelerated and retimed, and the reductions in journey time were impressive. The 'Bon Accord' left 50min later than before but was accelerated by 60min overall while other trains had running times reduced by 25-34min. The new workings required some tightly timed intermediate bookings, notably 31min for the 32½ miles between Perth and Forfar. Some recovery time was built into the schedules, but the limiting factor on time recovery was the 75 mph speed restriction in force throughout the ScR.

One of the most unsuccessful diesel designs was the North British Locomotive Co.'s Type 2 diesel-electric. By April 1961, they were being deployed in

pairs to work Glasgow–Aberdeen expresses but their appearances during the rest of that year were problematic. So much so that instead of completing their introduction the ScR decided to stick with steam traction – ex-LNER Pacifics – for the 3hr trains and other Glasgow–Aberdeen workings.

From April 1964, the 8.25am Glasgow–Aberdeen and 5.15pm return went over to diesel traction, but in due course Aberdeen's Ferryhill shed boasted an allocation of 11 A4 Pacifics to cover the 7.10am Aberdeen–Glasgow and 5.30pm return, as well as other trains on the route such as the 1.30pm Aberdeen–Glasgow and 11pm return, and the West Coast Postal between Aberdeen, Perth and Carstairs and return. The Glasgow-based turn reverted to steam power during the summer of 1965, and A4s and other types continued to appear on all four trains until September 1966.

The pattern of services changed with the closure of Glasgow Buchanan Street station in November 1966, and transfer of the Glasgow–Aberdeen and Dundee trains to Queen St. In September 1967, the line from Stanley Junction to Forfar and Kinnaber Junction was closed to passenger traffic and the Glasgow–Aberdeen service re-routed via Dundee and Montrose.

Cross-Country Inter-Regional Services 1948-67

Glasgow–Plymouth/Penzance

Although the Aberdeen–Penzance was never reinstated, nor the through coaches between these points via the Severn Tunnel, a new service began running in the late 1940s – though unadvertised until Summer 1954 – between Glasgow St Enoch (dep 5.30pm, except Sundays) and Penzance (arr 1.40pm) via Dumfries, Carlisle, Crewe and the North & West route. The through coaches ran as far as Plymouth only on Saturday night/Sunday morning, but otherwise formed a separate train as far as Carlisle where they were attached to the 5.40pm Glasgow Central–Crewe, and from there added to a North & West route train. The return working comprised a through Glasgow section on the noon train from Penzance to Bristol and beyond.

With the Winter 1958/9 timetable, the former 5.40pm Glasgow–Euston was retimed to 6.50pm, accelerated throughout, and thereafter took over from the 5.30pm ex-St Enoch the through coaches to Penzance and Plymouth. From then onwards the 5.30pm ran as far as Carlisle only, although still known to railwaymen as the 'Plymouth'.

A through coach continued to be provided at 10.15am from Glasgow Central–Plymouth, and 8am return, in both cases routed via the Severn Tunnel and North & West route.

North West to South West/South Wales
North and West via the Severn Tunnel
Much of what was a prewar pattern of working, modified somewhat during wartime, continued until the winter of 1953/54 when the morning Plymouth–Liverpool was appreciably accelerated. The train now left at 8am instead of 8.45am, and reached both Liverpool and Manchester over 70min earlier than before, and at Crewe the connection into the down 'Mid-Day Scot' was restored.

By the mid-1950s, there was a daily through service each way between Swansea and Manchester, but from Cardiff there were five services, the 1.13 and 7.20pm being worked through to Shrewsbury by Cardiff engines.

From Summer 1962, and the start of dieselisation, the North & West services were reorganised and accelerated. To avoid time wasted in remarshalling the principal midday trains from Liverpool/Manchester and Plymouth/Torquay, these were rearranged to carry either Liverpool portions or Manchester portions only, eg the new 9.5am Liverpool Lime St.–Kingswear and 12.5pm Manchester–Plymouth, and the 8am from Plymouth now to Liverpool only, and the 10am to Manchester only.

South Coast to South Wales/South West
Portsmouth–Cardiff/Plymouth/Reading
The 11am Brighton–Cardiff picked up a Portsmouth & Southsea portion at Fareham. On alternate days, the set working from/to Brighton was provided by the Southern and Western Regions. The return working was at 1pm from Cardiff. A Southern engine worked as far as Salisbury, usually changing there to a Western Region 'Hall'. The train ceased running with the end of the Summer 1962 timetable.

From January 1958, an economy drive cut short three Bristol–Portsmouth trains each way at Salisbury, but most were restored for the summer. From early 1959, there remained the 10.30am and 4.25pm Cardiff–Portsmouth, and 9.33am and 5.45pm return; like the Brighton train these were worked by WR engines as far as Salisbury. There were a number of extra summer Saturday trains between Cardiff (or Swansea), and Bournemouth and Portsmouth.

North East to South-West/Wales
Newcastle–Bristol and South West
After 1948, the former Midland West of England

main line unquestionably became the principal artery for cross-country trains between the North East, Yorkshire and the Midlands, and Bristol and the South West. The evening Newcastle–Bristol and return mail trains still ran, but were now joined by other through expresses from Bristol to Leeds, York and Newcastle.

The northbound 'Devonian' of 1956 was routed into/out of Bristol by the former GWR route via Filton Junction, and was over 30min slower between Bristol and Birmingham than the prewar train. Among the few notable accelerations of the period was the 7.32am Bradford–Bristol whose Birmingham–Bristol schedule was cut by 16min in the winter of 1956/57, to arrive 16min earlier.

An 8.5am Birmingham New St.–Newcastle train began running during the 1950s, its return working being retimed from the winter of 1957 to leave Newcastle at 3.34pm, accelerated throughout and with a New St. arrival at 8.11pm.

Major changes were made to the service in the summer of 1958, by which the southbound 'Devonian' changed to a 10.15am departure from Bradford, 25min later than before, but was only 3min later into Bristol. Northbound, the service was accelerated 17min to Bradford from Bristol. The 8.35am from Bristol was retimed 10min later, and extended from Sheffield to York (arr 1.59pm). The 10.20am Bristol–Newcastle now left 10min later, and was 28min faster to York. The 4.45pm Bristol was altered to a 5pm start but had recovered its old timings by Birmingham. In the reverse direction, the 7.32am from Bradford was retimed 8min later, but was now 10min earlier into Bristol, and the midday service from York picked up 16min on its previous schedule.

York–Swindon–Swansea
The night-time York–Swindon trains via Leicester and Oxford were continued through the 1950s until September 1966. In addition, there were the Sundays York–Swindon and 9.20am Sheffield–Swindon–Swansea workings, these however ceasing in March 1963. By the late 1950s, the times of the weekday trains were: from York at 6.40pm (from Scarborough in midsummer) and 10.22pm, and from Swindon at 7.30pm to Sheffield only, and 9.40pm to York. A fair description of them at the time was glorified parcels trains.

Newcastle–Swansea
The Newcastle–Swansea train via Banbury and Cheltenham was rerouted as a result of the closure of

Cross-country trains were expensive to work, particularly in this case when the Birkenhead–South Coast train has detached no more than a couple of Ramsgate via Dover coaches, seen here getting away from Ashford on 17 September 1958 behind 'Schools' 4-4-0 No. 30916 *Whitgift*.

the Banbury–Cheltenham line for through traffic. As from 30 June 1952 there was a Cardiff–Gloucester–Birmingham New St.–Derby–York–Newcastle and return express. Except on Saturdays, through coaches were provided at 8.45am from Bristol Temple Meads, and back in the evening. The Cardiff service used Gloucester Central, so that the Bristol portion was worked over the GW lines between Engine Shed Junction, Gloucester and Standish Junction.

A Swansea–Oxford–Sheffield–York train was introduced in the late 1940s, restricted to Mondays, Fridays and Saturdays only after 1951, and then to summer operation only. By Summer 1958, it was running FSO, at 8.10am from Swansea, with buffet car, to York on Saturdays, and on Fridays to Newcastle (arr 7.44pm). The return workings were at 12.26pm FO from York, and 10.8am from Newcastle.

North West and West Midlands to Channel Ports
Birkenhead–Margate/Deal
From the winter of 1951/52 the train ran on Fridays and Saturdays only, and a daily working was not reinstated until September 1956. It was withdrawn again after 31 October 1959 and suspended until May 1960, thereafter running south of Wolverhampton only.

From the spring of 1962, the South Coast section

was cut back to run to/from Eastbourne only instead of to and from Hastings. Diesel traction was used from September 1962 on a curtailed service between Wolverhampton and Margate only which ran throughout the year until September 1963, thereafter being suspended. The train reappeared for the summer Saturdays of 1964, but it was withdrawn for good on 5 September that year.

Cross-country to East Anglia/Lincolnshire
Harwich–Liverpool
With the Winter 1957 timetable, there was a short-lived attempt to speed-up the train which, now leaving Harwich Parkeston Quay at 8am, lost its calls at Bury St Edmunds, Ely and Spalding, so resulting in a non-stop run between Ipswich and March. The missing calls were soon reinstated but the faster timings were retained. Southbound, the Liverpool start had been made 25min later, at 1.15pm. The restaurant car now ran between Harwich and Sheffield only, out and back in the same day and, like the engine, covering the Harwich–Sheffield return working in a day.

Colchester–Newcastle/Glasgow
By the late 1950s, the services were at 7.20am Colchester–Newcastle and 12.5pm return, both

running via the GN/NE Joint line from March to Doncaster, routed northbound via Darlington and southbound via the Coast line, and the 5.15pm Colchester–Glasgow and 10pm return. This latter pair of trains ran via Peterborough and the East Coast Main Line. The 12.5pm Newcastle–Colchester was accelerated in Winter 1957/8 to connect at March into the Liverpool–Harwich, accordingly restoring a through service from York and the North which had been lost in 1939 when the York portion of the Liverpool–Harwich train was withdrawn.

Manchester/Birmingham–Clacton-on-Sea

On summer Saturdays in the 1930s there had been 9.33am Manchester Central–Clacton and 10.45am return through trains which ran via Sheffield Victoria, Lincoln, Ely and Ipswich.

From the mid-1950s, a new summer Saturdays service to Clacton was started, from Birmingham and Leicester to Clacton via Kettering, the former Midland line to Cambridge, Long Melford and Colchester. In due course, this working became two trains, the Summer 1958 times for which were 8.14am from Leicester Midland and 10.50am from Clacton, these sticking to the former route, and an 8.5am Birmingham New St. and 11.10am return which were routed via Rugby Midland, Peterborough East, Ely and Ipswich.

By Summer 1958, the workings had changed, with an additional 7.10am Clacton–Manchester Central and 1.43pm return workings following the line via Marks Tey to Long Melford, and then to Bury St Edmunds and Ely. However, this arrangement lasted only for one season, after which it was replaced by a 12.10pm Clacton–Sheffield train. With the closure of the Kettering–St Ives line, the Leicester train was diverted via Peterborough, Ely, Bury and Marks Tey.

York–Lowestoft GC/GE

The normal pattern of working involved buffet car trains at 10.15am from York, and 10.10am from Lowestoft, worked by no less than four different engines each way: from York to Lincoln and back,

A Saturday Yarmouth Beach–Nottingham train that has travelled over the M&GN line now rattles along between Stanton Tunnel and Plumtree behind LMS 4F 0-6-0 No. 4412 on 24 July 1948.

Lincoln–March and back, March and Norwich, and Norwich and Lowestoft. In summer, there were through coaches from/to Newcastle, and duplicate trains ran on Saturdays from Doncaster, Leeds and Sunderland.

Liverpool/Manchester–Yarmouth/Lowestoft via M&GN

Apart from the Birmingham/Leicester–Yarmouth/ Cromer weekdays year-round train, there were numerous summer-only workings in the 1950s, including an 11.55pm FO Mansfield–Yarmouth Beach, and some ten other Saturdays only through trains each way from Birmingham, Chesterfield, Leicester and Derby, the majority serving both Yarmouth Beach and Cromer Beach, and principally catering for the holiday camps and camp-sites north of Yarmouth.

With the closure of the M&GN in February 1959, the summer trains were rerouted via Peterborough, Ely and Norwich, nine replacement trains being run each way.

Birmingham/Nottingham–Skegness/Cleethorpes

The summer Saturday Birmingham–Skegness via Burton-on-Trent train of 1939 was restored early in postwar years, and in 1959 was running as an 8.50am Kings Norton–Skegness and 2.20pm return. The ex-GNR Nottingham–Derby route also featured a Leicester Central–Nottingham Victoria–Derby Friargate–Llandudno and return service.

From late 1948/9, an Immingham-based B1 4-6-0 began working to Nottingham and Leicester with a through train from Cleethorpes via Lincoln St Marks. This later developed into the 6.52am Cleethorpes–Birmingham New St. semi-fast and 4.50pm return which ran until the early 1960s.

North West/Midlands to South Coast

Although the 'Sunny South Special' did not reappear after 1945, a number of summer Saturday trains between the South Coast and Midlands routed via Kensington Olympia and Willesden Junction were soon established, notably from 1949 an SO Birmingham–Brighton and Hastings and return train which ran until 1963. There was also a Leicester via Northampton to Brighton and Hastings and return train, and a Friday night train from Manchester via Stoke to Eastbourne, later switched to run via Sheffield, Leicester, Banbury, Bicester and Old Oak Common.

After 1948, the GC main line became the principal route for summer Friday night/Saturday expresses between the Midlands and the South Coast. These included an 11.35pm FO Derby Friargate–Ramsgate and 12.10pm SO return; 11.44pm FO and 7.35am SO Sheffield Victoria–Hastings and 10.14am SO return; 10.15am SO Bradford–Poole and 10.25am SO return, and 10pm FO Sheffield–Portsmouth Harbour and 4.57pm SO return. All tended to be duplicated at peak summer weekends.

North East to South Coast
Newcastle–Bournemouth

Reintroduced in 1946, this train ran in Winter 1949/50 as a Bournemouth–York service, and in 1951 was restricted to Saturdays and Sundays only. From Summer 1958, a Western Region engine, usually a 'Hall', worked the southbound service throughout from Banbury to Bournemouth, and northbound a WR engine worked Oxford–Leicester Central.

From October 1959, the York–Bournemouth was withdrawn south of Banbury, and replaced between York and Banbury and return by a North Eastern Region based diesel multiple-unit which worked out and back in the day. A loco-hauled train reappeared between Easter and September 1960 and from Summer 1961 the York–Bournemouth was reinstated as a year-round service. Diesel locomotives took over north of Banbury from the Winter 1962/63 timetable, but steam was used south of there until September 1966 when, with the closure of the GC main line, the service was initially rerouted from Oxford via Worcester and the Midland lines, then via Banbury and Birmingham New Street.

North West to Bournemouth
Manchester, Yorkshire and Midlands–Bath–Bournemouth

Restored as a through train in October 1946, and as a named train in 1949, the 'Pines Express' now carried a Sheffield portion which ran as a separate train at summer weekends. In the summer of 1948 there were seven other through trains each way over the S&D to/from Bournemouth and Bradford/Leeds, Sheffield, Nottingham and Lincoln.

Weekend holiday traffic over the S&D was busiest in the mid-1950s. During 1954 peak summer Saturdays, there were 15 southbound expresses – inclusive of four Friday night trains from the North – and 12 northbound trains. On certain Saturdays, such as before the August Bank Holiday, there might be six or seven additional relief trains. In fact, the S&D was the most important route in the late 1950s for inter-Regional through trains to the South Coast.

By the time a satisfactory type of engine was available to work the heavy cross-country expresses using the Somerset & Dorset line, the end was already in sight for these through workings. BR 9F 2-10-0 No. 92245 heads south near Bailey Gate with one of the holiday trains on 16 June 1962, not long before they were withdrawn from the S&D.

The Lincoln–Bournemouth train of late 1930s' summers had echoes in a 6.57am Cleethorpes–Derby–Bournemouth and 11.40am return, extensions of the daily Cleethorpes–Birmingham New St. train. The summer Saturdays through train from Sidmouth/Exmouth–Derby via the S&D was partially replaced by an Exmouth–Manchester service routed via the Severn Tunnel but, during 1960, the Cleethorpes train was diverted to run to Exmouth and Sidmouth.

By 1960, the number of through holiday trains over the S&D had declined and Saturday, 8 September 1962 saw the last scheduled through workings over the S&D, including the 'Pines Express' which was afterwards rerouted via Southampton, Oxford, Birmingham, Market Drayton and Crewe to Manchester/Liverpool. For a year or so, the train was steam worked throughout between Bournemouth and Wolverhampton, thereafter and until 1965 south of Oxford only.

Birkenhead–Oxford–Bournemouth
From November 1959, with the augmented Paddington–Birmingham–Birkenhead service, the

Bournemouth train was reduced to six coaches and, between Banbury and Wolverhampton, combined with coaches forming the 12.10pm from Paddington, and 12.20pm from Birmingham. From Winter 1960/61, the Birkenhead–Bournemouth was once again an independent train throughout, and the following winter it was retimed to leave Bournemouth West at 8.35am, instead of the well-established time of 9.30, to run to Wolverhampton. It left there at 11.5am, 75min earlier than before. The service was withdrawn in 1962 with the rerouting of the 'Pines Express'.

North East to North West
Newcastle–Leeds–Liverpool, Liverpool–Hull
Having changed hardly at all after 1948, the existing steam-worked service was swept away in January 1961 when greatly accelerated diesel-hauled Newcastle–Liverpool workings were introduced, supported by a Hull–Liverpool service of Trans-Pennine diesel multiple-units.

The Hull–Doncaster–Sheffield–Manchester–Liverpool trains were withdrawn east of Sheffield in September 1962.

The Bournemouth–Birkenhead service had an uneventful life, and here it is on the first stage of its journey on 3 September 1955, near Hinton Admiral, with a set of WR stock hauled by 'King Arthur' No. 30736 *Excalibur* which will work the train as far as Oxford.

Newcastle–Wakefield–Liverpool

The 10.30am Liverpool Exchange–Newcastle and 5.10pm return were withdrawn with the January 1961 introduction of the new diesel-worked Liverpool–Newcastle trains via the Diggle route.

North East–Blackpool/Keswick

From 1932 to 1939, through summer trains had operated between Newcastle and Blackpool/Southport via the Stainmore line, and on Sundays from Newcastle to Keswick and return via Carlisle.

These workings developed during the 1950s so that the Stainmore route saw a 7.32am South Shields/West Hartlepool–Blackpool train (introduced in 1949), an 11.20am Newcastle–Blackpool, transferred in 1953 from a via Carlisle and West Coast Main Line routing, and a Darlington–Blackpool train, and their return workings. These passed to/from the London Midland Region at Tebay, were limited to eight coaches and were double-headed over Stainmore. On Sundays, there was a regular Saltburn–Penrith excursion which connected with the Newcastle–Keswick train.

The Stainmore route trains made their last runs at the end of the 1961 summer season, after which the Newcastle train was rerouted via Carlisle and the West Coast Main Line, and the service from Darlington to Blackpool was worked via Harrogate and Skipton.

ACKNOWLEDGEMENTS

In preparing this book, reference was made as much as possible to original sources. The custodians of the major archives relating to train services are the Public Record Office, Kew, and the Scottish Record Office. The staff at both locations were always ready to provide the material requested and it was a pleasure to work there.

Chris Bishop has most kindly read the manuscript and made a number of helpful suggestions, as well as picking me up on 'literals'. I am most grateful to him.

I would like to include a special 'thank you' to Brian Stephenson for allowing me access to Rail Archive Stephenson, for his interest, and care in making available some excellent prints for reproduction in this book. I hope that this book might be of value in his endeavours. Similarly, Graham Stacey was tireless in leading me through the Ken Nunn Collection held by the Locomotive Club of Great Britain, and kindly made available some excellent prints, backed up with carefully prepared captions.

As usual, I would like to thank my family, Carol, Edmund and Georgia for their interest and patience, and for their many helpful suggestions and unstinting interest.

References
The principal sources of reference were those held at the PRO, in particular, the minutes of the traffic committees, train services committees, timetable meetings, and conferences of traffic officers of the various railways and, for example, the minutes of the meetings of the LNER Superintendents and Passenger Managers. More general material that was consulted included the deliberations of the Railway Clearing House meetings of superintendents.

Particularly valued as references were the volumes of E. L. Ahrons' *Locomotive and Train Working in the latter part of the Nineteenth Century* (Heffer, 1953), *Extracts from British Locomotive Practice and Performance from Railway Magazine articles 1902-8*, compiled and edited by Charles Fryer (PSL, 1990) and Professor Jack Simmons' *The Origins and Early Development of the Express Train* (Thomas & Lochar, 1994).

Finally, many useful references have come from study of the following journals: the *Bulletin of the International Railway Congress*, 1907; *The Railway Gazette*; *The Railway Magazine*; the golden jubilee issue of the *Railway News*, 1914; *Railway World* and *Trains Illustrated/Modern Railways*.

INDEX

* Denotes train service.

Aberdeen Joint station 99, 100, 163
*Aberdeen–Ballater 99, 100
*Aberdeen–Elgin 98, 99, 100
*Aberdeen–Inverness 99, 100, 101, 165, 166, 210
*Aberdeen/Glasgow–Penzance via East Coast 97, 98, 112-114, 115, 171, 213
*Aberdeen–Penzance via West Coast 114, 171
'Aberdonian', The 151, 154, 162, 204
Allhallows on Sea 130
Anglo–Scottish train services 31-34, 59-63, 76-79, 91, 94, 97-99, 100, 101, 103, 104, 105, 106, 112, 144, 145, 154, 160, 162, 213, 214
    Abolition of meal-stops 59
    Balfour agreement 31, 59
    World War 1 34, 62
*Ashford (Kent)–Newcastle 175
'Atlantic Coast Express', The 129, 132, 190, 196

'Ballater Express', The 100
*Barry–Llandrindod Wells 13
Barry Railway 12
'Belfast Boat Express', The (GWR) 120
'Belfast Boat Express', The (LMR) 200
*Birkenhead–Bournemouth 19, 110, 112, 118, 178, 218
*Birkenhead–Cardiff 184
*Birkenhead–Deal/Dover/Margate 29, 107, 109, 115, 175, 215
Birmingham Snow Hill station 11
*Birmingham–Bournemouth 18, 19, 80, 111
*Birmingham–Glasgow/Edinburgh 61, 141, 194
*Birmingham–Hereford–Brecon–Swansea 82
*Birmingham–Manchester–Liverpool 195
*Birmingham–Rugby–Peterborough 67
*Birmingham–South Wales (GWR) 8, 12, 114, 123, 124, 171, 184
*Birmingham/Leicester/Derby–Skegness 34, 176, 205, 217
*Blackpool–Colne 87
*Blackpool–Liverpool 87
'Bon Accord', The 170, 210, 213
'Bournemouth Limited', The 130, 132
'Bournemouth Belle', The 130, 132, 189, 190
*Bournemouth–Leeds via Birmingham 82, 111,173, 217
*Bournemouth–Manchester 19, 20, 82, 111, 112, 118, 178, 217
*Bradford–Glasgow/Edinburgh 78
*Bradford–Paignton 115, 173

Brecon & Merthyr Railway 13
*Brighton–Cardiff/Bournemouth/ Ilfracombe 18, 106, 115, 172, 214
*Bristol–Birmingham–Glasgow 76, 77
*Bristol–Birmingham–Sheffield–Leeds 80, 82, 84, 146, 214
*Bristol–Birmingham–York/Newcastle 80, 106, 115, 118, 173, 214, 215
*Bristol–Bournemouth 19, 20
*Bristol–Edinburgh via Midland Rly 98
'Bristolian', The 123, 182, 184
British Railways 180-219
    Cafeteria cars 209
    Griddle cars 211
    Standard coaching stock 180, 181, 189, 206
'Broadsman', The 206
*Broad St–Birmingham 66

Caledonian Railway 89-93
    Coaching stock 90
    Competition with G&SWR 90, 93
    Competition with NBR 90, 96, 97
    Forfar–Perth line 89
    Pullman cars, use of 90, 91, 92
    Slip coaches 90
'Caledonian', The 195, 196
Callander & Oban line 89, 92, 93, 94, 169
'Cambrian Coast Express', The 121, 181, 182, 200
Cambrian Railways 13, 70
    Coaching stock 71
'Capitals Limited' The 201
'Capitals United Express', The 183
*Cardiff–Manchester/Liverpool 13, 105, 114
*Cardiff–Yarmouth 10, 108
*Carlisle–Bullgill–Keswick 73
'Cathedrals Express', The 183
*Charing Cross/Cannon St–Hastings 27, 126, 130, 133, 186
*Charing Cross/Victoria–Dover boat trains 28, 29, 30, 126, 127, 130, 134
*Charing Cross/Victoria–Folkestone Harbour boat trains 27, 28, 107, 186
'Cheltenham Flyer', The 120, 121, 122
'Cheltenham Spa Express', The 183
Cheshire Lines Committee 57-58
*City/Baker St–Aylesbury/Verney Jct 52
*City-GWR stations 53
'City Limited', The 24, 25
'Clacton Pullman', The 152
*Cleethorpes/Derby–Exmouth 178, 218
*Cleethorpes–Leeds/Sheffield/Manchester 55

*Cleethorpes–Leicester 56, 153
*Cleethorpes–Nottingham–Birmingham 217, 218
Club Trains 64, 86, 138, 200
*Colchester–Newcastle/Glasgow 176, 215
'Comet', The 138, 144, 192, 194
'Cornishman', The 8, 123, 181
'Cornish Riviera Express' 9, 10, 11, 120, 123, 124, 180, 181
'Cornish Riviera Limited', The
'Coronation', The 157
'Coronation Scot', The 141, 14, 147
*Crewe–Derby 74
Cross-Country to East Anglia 108, 116, 175, 215

*Deal–King's Cross 29, 108
*Deal–Manchester/Bradford via Mid Rly 29
*Deal–Manchester via LNWR 109
*Derby/Lincoln–Bournemouth 19
*Derby–Llandudno 74, 75
'Devon Belle', The 134, 188
'Devonian', The 115, 173, 178, 214
'Dutchman', The 9

*Ealing Broadway–Southend 84
'East Anglian', The 43, 160, 162, 206
'Eastbourne Sunday Limited', The 25
'Eastbourne Sunday Pullman', The 131
East Coast Joint Stock 31, 33, 34
East Coast main line services 31-34, 60
'Easterling', The 207
'Eastern Belle', The 152, 159
Eastern & North Eastern Regions (BR) 201-209
    Introduction of 'Britannias' 205
    Train schedules 204, 209
East London Railway 25, 26
*Edinburgh Princes St–Glasgow Central 89, 91
*Edinburgh Waverley–Aberdeen 95, 96, 97, 98, 164, 170, 213
*Edinburgh Waverley–Elgin 98, 99, 100
*Edinburgh Waverley–Inverness 211
*Edinburgh Waverley–Perth 95, 96, 163
'Edinburgh Pullman' 151
'Elizabethan', The 201
'Emerald Isle Express', The 194
'Essex Coast Express', The 207
*Euston–Aberdeen 59, 60, 61, 63, 136, 141
*Euston–Altrincham 61, 67, 136
*Euston–Birkenhead/New Brighton 67, 136, 143, 192
*Euston–Birmingham–Wolverhampton 11, 64, 65, 66, 68, 69, 136, 143, 184, 192

*Euston–Blackpool 66, 69, 143
*Euston–Buckingham–Banbury 67
*Euston–Buxton 67, 74, 75
*Euston–Central Wales–Swansea 64, 66, 67, 69,
  143
*Euston–East Lancs towns 66, 67, 86, 136, 144,
  147, 200
*Euston–Edinburgh 59, 60, 61, 77, 136, 138,
  139, 141
*Euston–Fleetwood 63, 68
*Euston–Glasgow 59, 60, 61, 63, 136, 138, 139,
  141, 144, 192, 194, 195
*Euston–Gourock 61
*Euston–Halifax 88
*Euston–Heysham 139, 194
*Euston–Holyhead 63, 66, 68, 138, 141, 192,
  194
*Euston–Inverness 60, 62, 63, 101, 104, 138,
  141, 166
*Euston–Leamington/Warwick 66
*Euston–Liverpool Lime St 63, 64, 66, 67, 69,
  136, 138, 144, 181, 192, 193, 196
*Euston–Liverpool Riverside boat trains 63, 66
*Euston–Manchester via Crewe 64, 66, 67, 136,
  138, 144, 147, 192, 194, 195, 196
*Euston–Manchester via Stoke 64, 66, 74, 75,
  136, 138, 144
*Euston–Melton Mowbray 67
*Euston–North Wales resorts 63, 64, 68, 69,
  139, 142, 194
*Euston–Oban 60, 63, 141
*Euston–Perth 60, 61, 63, 194
*Euston–Southport 66, 138, 192
*Euston–Stranraer 60, 140, 200
*Euston–Stratford upon Avon/Towceter 69
*Euston–Thurso 103
*Euston–Turnberry 141, 165
*Euston–Welshpool/Cambrian Coast 66, 67, 69,
  70, 71
*Euston–Whitehaven 61, 64, 69, 71, 72, 140
*Euston–Windermere/Keswick 64, 66, 69, 136,
  139, 142

'Fair Maid', The 204
'Fastest Train in the British Empire', The 40, 41
*Fenchurch St–Southend 84, 146, 208
*Fleetwood/Heysham–Leeds 86, 146
'Flying Scotsman', The 31, 34, 151, 153, 154,
  157, 160, 162, 170, 201, 203, 204
  Non-stop summer running 153, 157, 160
Forth Bridge, opening of 94
Furness & Midland Joint line 71
Furness Railway 71-73
  Promotion of tourism 72
'Further North Express', The 102
'Fylde Coast Express', The 143

('Garden Cities &) Cambridge Buffet
  Expresses', The 155, 205
Glasgow & South Western Railway 93-94
*Glasgow–Aberfeldy 92
*Glasgow–Ayr 93, 94, 165, 210, 211
*Glasgow–Clyde Ports 90, 93, 94
*Glasgow–Crieff 92
*Glasgow–Dundee 89, 91, 210
*Glasgow–Fife Coast 164
*Glasgow–Fort William/Mallaig 95, 97, 164,
  213
*Glasgow–Gullane/Dunbar/North Berwick 96,
  97, 163
*Glasgow–Inverness 92, 101, 166, 211, 213
*Glasgow–Oban 89, 91, 169, 210
*Glasgow/Edinburgh–Perth–Aberdeen 89, 90,
  91, 163, 169, 170, 210, 213
*Glasgow–Plymouth 114, 140, 141, 171, 211,
  213
*Glasgow–Stranraer 93, 165, 211
*Gloucester–Lowestoft/Yarmouth (GWR/LNWR
  routing) 52
'Golden Arrow', The 130, 134, 186
'Grampian', The 213
'Grampian Corridor Express', The 90, 95
'Granite City', The 169, 213

*Grantham–Uttoxeter 36
'Granville Express', The 28, 30
Great Central Railway 54-57
  Cross-country services 54, 55, 56, 107, 110,
  112
  Dining cars 54, 55, 56
  Fay, Sam 54
  Newspaper trains 56
  Slip coaches 55, 56
  Water troughs 54
Great Eastern Railway 42-47
  Coaching stock 43, 44
  Dining cars 43, 44
  Off-peak traffic 45
  'Poppyland' 43, 47, 52
  Pullman cars, use of 46
  Radical Alterations timetable 1914 45, 46
  Slip coaches 44
  Thornton (Sir) Henry 45, 149
  Water troughs 43
Great Northern/North Eastern Joint services 33,
  35, 38
Great Northern Railway 34-37
  Atlantics 35, 36
  Coaching stock 34, 35
  Pacifics 37
  Rolling stock 36, 37
  St Leger traffic 37
  Working agreement with GCR 35
Great North of Scotland Railway 90, 98-100
  Coaching stock 100
  Connections with the South 99
  Slip coaches 100
  Speyside excursions 99, 166
Great Western & Great Central Joint line 56
Great Western Railway 7-12, 119-125
  Allen, T. I. 9
  City of Truro 9
  Competition with LSWR 9
  Dining cars 8, 12
  'Dreadnought' stock 10
  Locomotives working to Manchester 124
  Morris, Joseph 9
  New lines 7, 9, 10, 122
  Relations with Cambrian Railways 70, 71
  Relations with Midland Railway 10, 82
  Royal train 9
  Sleeping cars 8, 12, 121
  Slip coaches 8, 10, 11, 12, 27, 107, 113, 120
  Timetable reorganisation, 1924 119
  'Toplight' stock 10
  Train speeds 122
  Water troughs 9
Grouse-shooting season 31, 32
*Guildford/Deal–Bournemouth 18, 133

'Harrogate Pullman', The 149, 151
*Harwich Town/Parkeston
  Quay–Manchester/Liverpool/
  Birmingham/York/Glasgow 43, 55, 56, 58,
  67, 88, 108, 116, 175, 176, 208, 215
'Heart of Midlothian', The 181, 203, 204
'Hebridean', The 169
*Hereford–Merthyr 143
Highland Railway 100-104
  Difficulties in operation 100
  Dining car, use of 104
  Improvements to main line 100
  Sunday services 104, 167
  Through CR Pullman cars 104
Holiday camps, traffic to 52, 217
'Hook Continental', The 151, 152, 160, 162,
  206, 208
Hull & Barnsley Railway 41
*Hull–Sheffield 41

'Ilfracombe boat express', The 12
'Inter City', The 180, 181
*Inverness–Kyle of Lochalsh 102, 167, 169, 211
*Inverness–Strathpeffer 102
*Inverness–Wick/Thurso 102, 166, 167, 213
'Irish Mail', The 63, 66, 139, 141, 142, 147, 192
Isle of Wight railways 22, 126

'John o'Groat', The 167

'Kentish Belle, The 186
King's Cross station 35, 37
*King's Cross–Aberdeen 31, 32, 33, 97, 154,
  157, 170, 204
*King's Cross–Blackburn 34, 35, 37
*King's Cross–Bradford 34, 35, 37
*King's Cross–Cambridge 37, 155, 162, 205
*King's Cross–Cromer 34, 37, 47, 51, 52
*King's Cross–Edinburgh 31, 32, 33, 34, 139,
  153, 154, 156, 157, 160, 162, 181, 201, 204
*King's Cross–Fort William/Mallaig 95, 97
*King's Cross–Glasgow 32, 33, 151, 154, 157
*King's Cross–Grimsby/Cleethorpes 34, 36, 51,
  151, 162, 205
*King's Cross–Harrogate 35, 37, 39, 149, 151,
  156, 157
*King's Cross–Hull 34, 35, 3, 156, 162, 204
*King's Cross–Inverness 32, 33, 101, 166, 169
*King's Cross–Lossiemouth 154, 165
*King's Cross–Newcastle 31, 33, 34, 35, 38, 41,
  149, 154, 155, 156, 157, 162, 201, 203
*King's Cross–North Berwick 33
*King's Cross–Nottingham 33, 35
*King's Cross–Perth 32, 33, 204
*King's Cross–Saltburn 156, 205
*King's Cross–Scarborough/Whitby 33, 38, 151,
  156, 157
*King's Cross–Sheffield/Manchester 34, 35, 55,
  149, 205
*King's Cross–Skegness 34, 37
*King's Cross–Sunderland 41
*King's Cross–West Hartlepool 38
*King's Cross–West Riding 33, 34, 35, 36, 154,
  156, 157, 201, 203, 204
*King's Cross–York 33, 37
*kingston upon Thames–Ramsgate 133

'Lakes Express', The 139, 142
Lancashire & Yorkshire Railway 37, 85-88
Amalgamation with LNWR 88
  Coaching stock 86, 87, 88
  Slip coaches 87
  Through services and coaches 86
Lancashire Derbyshire & East Coast Railway 56
'Lancastrian', The 136, 138, 139, 144, 195
*Leamington–Nottingham 67
*Leeds–Bournemouth via GC main line 177
*Leeds–Carlisle–Edinburgh/Glasgow 77, 146,
  165, 211
*Leeds–Edinburgh/Glasgow
via East Coast 38, 40, 41, 153, 156, 209
*Leeds/Bradford–Morecambe/Carnforth 80, 84
*Leeds–Scarborough/Bridlington 39, 40
*Leicester/Sheffield–Llandudno/Blackpool 110
'Lewisman', The 169
*Liverpool Exchange–Manchester–
  Bradford/Leeds 86, 199
*Liverpool Exchange–Manchester Victoria 86,
  87
*Liverpool Exchange–Wakefield– Newcastle 88,
  112, 179, 199, 219
*Liverpool–Hull both routes 39, 56, 58, 88, 153,
  179, 218
*Liverpool/Leeds–Newcastle via Diggle 39, 64,
  88, 112, 118, 179, 209, 218
*Liverpool/Manchester–Blackburn–Glasgow 76,
  77, 79, 80
*Liverpool St/St Pancras–Cambridge 42, 44, 45,
  46, 160
*Liverpool St–Clacton 43, 44, 46, 159, 207, 209
*Liverpool St–Cromer 43, 44, 46, 47, 151, 152,
  159, 181, 206
*Liverpool St–Felixstowe 44
*Liverpool St/St Pancras–Hunstanton 45, 46,
  159
*Liverpool St–kings Lynn 42, 46, 207
*Liverpool St–Colchester–Norwich 42, 43, 45,
  46, 159, 201, 205, 206
*Liverpool St–Ely–Norwich 42, 206, 207
*Liverpool St–Parkeston Quay boat trains 27,
  43, 44, 46, 151, 152, 206

*Liverpool St–Peterborough East 152
*Liverpool St–Sheringham 51, 52, 159
*Liverpool St–Southend 43, 44, 45, 46, 159
*Liverpool St–March–York 43, 44, 46
*Liverpool St–Yarmouth/Lowestoft 43, 44, 46, 47, 208
London & North Eastern Railway 148-162
    Agreement with Pullman Car Co 149
    Boat trains from Marylebone 159
    Organisation 148, 151, 155
    Pullman cars used on race meeting specials 151
    Pullman excursions 46, 152, 159
    Rolling stock 151, 153, 155, 156, 157, 158, 160
    Sleeping car services 154
    Slip coaches 158, 159
    Traffic to Tyne CQ 157, 162
London & North Western Railway 63-69
    Competition with Midland Railway 60
    Dining/tea cars 69
    Liverpool Special stock 66
    London–Dublin/Belfast services 63
    New lines 68
    Relations with Cam Rlys 70
    Slip coaches 65, 67
    Train loadings 65, 68
London & South Western Railway 14-18
    Competition with GWR 9, 15, 16
    Competition with LBSCR 15, 22
    Dining cars 15, 16, 17, 18
    'Eagle' stock 16
    Fay, Sam 15
    'Ironclad' stock 18
    Military traffic 14
    New lines 15
    Salisbury accident, 1906 16
    Sleeping cars 16
    Water troughs, absence of 17
London Brighton & South Coast Railway 22-25
    Ashurst spur 25
    'Balloon' stock 24
    Electrification 23
    Finlay Scott, F. 24
    Proposed electric railway, effect of 23
    Pullman cars, use of 23, 24
    Quarry line 23
London Midland & Scottish Railway 136-147
    Diesel unit 146
    Expiry of agreement with Pullman Car Co 163
    Investigation into train working 143
    Midland Division accelerations, 1937 145, 146
    Possible closure of Highland lines 169
    Recovery from wartime 147
    Sleeping cars 141
    Traffic to Blackpool 143
    Use of Pullman cars 141, 165, 166, 169
London Midland Region (BR) 192-200
    Acceleration of Midland Division services from 1957 198
    Electrification works 196
    North Wales holiday traffic 200
London Passenger Transport Board 52
London Tilbury & Southend Railway 69, 84, 85, 138
    Coaching stock 84, 85
    Proposed electrification 85
    Train working 84, 85
'Lothian Coast Express', The 96, 97, 163, 164
*Lowestoft/Yarmouth–Birmingham 50, 51, 52, 208
*Lowestoft/Yarmouth–East Midlands 47, 50
*Lowestoft/Yarmouth–Manchester/ Liverpool 50, 176, 217
*Lowestoft/Yarmouth–West Riding 50, 51

*Manchester–Blackpool 86, 87, 138, 199
*Manchester–Deal via GCR 110
*Manchester Central–Chester Northgate 58
*Manchester Central–Liverpool Central 57, 81

*Manchester Central–Southport Lord St 58
*Manchester Exchange–Liverpool Lime St 64
*Manchester L Rd–Southampton 21, 112, 178
*Manchester/Liverpool–Brighton/ Eastbourne 109, 176
*Manchester/Liverpool–Cambrian Coast 70
*Manchester/Liverpool–Lowestoft 108, 116, 176, 216
*Manchester/Liverpool–North Wales/Holyhead 64, 141, 142
*Manchester/Liverpool–Plymouth 105, 106, 114, 171, 214
*Manchester/Liverpool–Preston–Scotland 60, 61, 62, 63, 141, 143, 195, 196
*Manchester/Birmingham–Clacton 216
*Manchester/Bradford–Bournemouth via GCR 110
*Manchester/Bradford–Deal/Portsmouth via Midland Rly 109
*Manchester/Halifax–Bristol/Ilfracombe 106
*Manchester/Salford–Colne 86, 88
*Manchester–Llandudno 64
*Manchester–Morecambe 64
*Manchester–Scarborough 87
*Manchester–Southport 86
*Manchester–Swansea 124, 171, 214
*Manchester–Windermere 64, 71, 138
*Manchester–York 86
'Manchester Pullman', (LNER) 149
Manchester Sheffield & Lincolnshire Railway 52, 54, 57, 69
'Mancunian', The 136, 139, 144, 192
'Man of Kent', The 186
'Manxman', The 194
*Margate–Brighton 126, 133
*Marylebone–Barnsley 57, 152
*Marylebone–Bradford 54, 55, 56, 88, 152, 158, 162, 199, 208
*Marylebone–Edinburgh/Glasgow 209
*Marylebone–Halifax 152
*Marylebone–Leeds 54, 55
*Marylebone–Liverpool Cen 58, 208, 209
*Marylebone–Manchester 54, 55, 56, 57, 152, 158, 199, 208
*Marylebone–Mansfield 57, 152
*Marylebone–Newcastle 159
*Marylebone–Scarborough 55
*Marylebone–Sheffield 54, 56, 57, 152, 158, 199, 208
*Marylebone–Stratford upon Avon 55, 56, 69, 158
Maryport & Carlisle Railway 73
'Master Cutler', The 205, 208
'Mayflower', The 183
'Merchant Venturer', The 181, 182
Mersey Railway 107
'Merseyside Express', The 138, 139, 144, 192
Metropolitan & Great Central Joint Committee 52, 56
Metropolitan Railway 52-53
    Pullman cars, use of 52
'Mid-Day Scot', The 138, 139, 140, 141, 192, 194, 196
Midland & Great Northern Joint Railway 47-52
    Closure of M&GN section 208
    Control passes to LNER 52
    Single-line working 47, 50
    Use of other railways' stock 51
Midland & South Western Junction Railway 20-22
    Emigration traffic 20
    Military traffic 20, 21
'Midlander', The 193
    Midland & Scottish Joint services 76, 79, 93, 94, 95
Midland Railway 76-79, 80-84
    Acquisition of LTSR 84
    Anglo-Scottish services 59, 76-79
    Coaching stock 84
    Competition with LNWR 60, 78, 81
    Competition with West Coast/ East Coast 77
    Dining cars 82

Hope Valley line 80
    Lake District expresses 79, 83, 84
    Lengthy non-stop runs 78, 83
    Pullman car services 76
    Sleeping car services 76
    Slip coaches 83
    Third-class Scotch expresses 77, 79
    Train working 82
    Water troughs 78, 82
    1908 timetable 83
Midlands to North West (trains) 110
*Moffat–Glasgow 91
'Morning Talisman', The 204

*Newcastle–Barrow 39, 72
*Newcastle–Carlisle 39, 41, 160, 209
*Newcastle–Middlesbrough 160, 209
*Newcastle–Sheffield 40
*Newcastle–Stranraer 39, 93, 165
*Newcastle–York 39, 153
*Newcastle/Hull–Barry/Swansea 12, 106, 108, 115, 173, 214
*Newcastle/North East–Blackpool/ Keswick 220
*Newcastle/York–Bournemouth 110, 112, 117, 177, 217
'Night Ferry', The 133, 186
'Night Scot', The 138, 141
'Night Scotsman', The 151, 162, 204
Norfolk & Suffolk Joint line 51
'Norfolk Coast Express', The 44, 46, 159
'Norfolkman', The 201, 206
*Northampton–Newark 67
*North & West route trains 8, 172
North & West via the Severn Tunnel (trains) 105, 114, 214
North British Railway 94-98
    Coaching stock 95, 96
    Delays in new Edinburgh–Aberdeen service 95
    Dispute with NER 95
'North Briton', The 209
North East to North West (trains) 112, 118, 179, 218
North East to South Coast (trains) 110, 117, 177, 217
North East to South West/Wales (trains) 106, 115, 171, 172, 173, 214
North Eastern Railway 37-41
    Coaching stock 40, 41
'Northern Belle', The 153
'North Express' (Cam Rlys) 70
North London Railway 69
'North/South Express' (MSWJR) 21
North Staffordshire Railway 74-75
    Coaching stock 75
North West & West Midlands to Channel Ports (trains) 107, 115, 175, 215, 217
North West to Bournemouth (trains) 111, 178, 217
North West to South Coast (trains) 109, 116, 176
North West to South West/South Wales (trains) 105, 114, 124

'Orcadian', The 168, 169
*Oxford–Cambridge 146
*Oxford–Leicester 8, 110

*Paddington–Aberystwyth/Cambrian Coast 70, 71, 121, 181
*Paddington–Birmingham–Birkenhead 8, 9, 10, 11, 12, 119, 120, 121, 123, 180, 181, 182, 184, 185, 218
*Paddington–Brighton 11, 23
*Paddington–Bristol/Weston super Mare 7, 9, 10, 12, 119, 124, 125, 180, 181, 182, 184, 185
*Paddington–Fishguard Harbour 10, 119, 120, 123
*Paddington–Gloucester–Cheltenham Spa 8, 119, 121, 123, 183, 185
*Paddington–Ilfracombe 11, 123
*Paddington–Penzance/Cornish resorts 7, 10, 11, 119, 121, 122, 180, 183, 184

*Paddington–Plymouth/Ocean Liner specials 9, 12, 120, 123, 124, 125, 153, 180, 183
*Paddington–Southampton 7
*Paddington–South Wales 9, 10, 119, 123, 124, 182, 185
*Paddington–Stratford upon Avon 10, 11, 121, 180
*Paddington–West Wales 8, 119, 121, 181, 183, 184
*Paddington–Weymouth 7, 9, 119, 181, 185
'Paddy'/'Paddies', The (boat trains to Stranraer) 93 211
'Palatine', The 146, 198
Passenger-rated traffic 52
'Peak Express', The 146
'Pembroke Coast Express', The 182
Perth station, train working at 89, 92, 163
'Pines Express', The 20, 178, 217, 218
Portpatrick & Wigtownshire Joint Railways 93
*Portsmouth/Brighton–Plymouth 17, 18, 133, 172, 191
*Portsmouth/Bristol/Cardiff 106, 115, 172, 214
*Portsmouth–Reading 172
'Ports to Ports Express', The 12, 106, 173
'Pullman', the 94

'Queen of Scots', The 151, 154, 157, 163, 164, 201, 203, 209

Races to the North 1888, 1895 31, 59, 98
*Reading–Margate 27
*Reading–Redhill/Charing Cross 29
Reading West station 110
'Red Dragon', The 183
'Red Rose', The 181, 192
Rhondda & Swansea Bay Railway 13
Rhymney Railway 13
*Richmond (Surrey)–Salisbury 16
'Robin Hood', The 198
'Royal Duchy', The 183
'Royal Highlander', The 138, 141, 147, 163, 170, 211
'Royal Scot', The 138, 139, 140, 147, 181, 192, 194, 196
'Royal Wessex', The 181, 189
Royston–Thornhill line 83, 84, 138, 145

*St Pancras–Aberdeen 79, 97, 98, 164
*St Pancras–Barrow/Windermere 71, 80
*St Pancras–Blackburn/Hellifield 80, 84
*St Pancras–Buxton 80, 196
*St Pancras–Edinburgh 59, 76, 98, 196, 198, 199
*St Pancras–Fort William 77
*St Pancras–Glasgow 76, 77, 145, 146, 165, 211
*St Pancras–Halifax 146, 199
*St Pancras–Harrogate 80, 138, 145
*St Pancras–Heysham boat trains 81, 141
*St Pancras–Leeds/Bradford 80, 83, 84, 138, 141, 145, 146, 198
*St Pancras–Liverpool 80, 81, 83, 84, 145

*St Pancras–Manchester 80, 81, 83, 145, 146, 147, 198
*St Pancras–Nottingham 82, 84, 145, 146, 198
*St Pancras–Perth/Inverness 77, 78, 79
*St Pancras–Sheffield 81, 82, 146, 198
*St Pancras–Southend 84
*St Pancras–Stranraer 77, 93
*St Pancras–Tilbury boat trains 84, 138
*St Pancras–Tilbury–Paris 138
'Scarborough Flyer', The 151, 156
*Sheffield–Bridlington 41
*Sheffield–Weston super Mare 114, 172
'Snowdonian', The 142
South Coast to South Wales (trains) 106, 115, 172, 214
*South Wales–Aberystwyth through trains 13, 70
'Sunny South Special/Express', The 109, 116, 176, 217
*Swansea–York 67, 143

Taff Vale Railway 13
'Talisman', The 204
'Tees–Thames', The 205
'Tees–Tyne Pullman', The 201
'Thames–Clyde Express', The 139, 145, 146, 165, 192
'Thames–Forth Express', The 139, 145, 146
'Thanet Belle', The 134, 186
'Thanet Pullman Limited', The 30, 133
*Tilbury–Glasgow 138
'Torbay Express', The 182
'Torbay Limited', The 121
'Torquay Limited', The 119, 121
'Torquay Pullman (Limited)', The 121, 122, 130
'Tourist', The 22

Uckfield line services 25, 133, 188
'Ulster Express', The 139, 143, 147, 192, 194

Victoria station (London) 25
*Victoria–Dover Marine/Folkestone Harbour boat trains 126, 127, 129, 133, 134
*Victoria–Newhaven Harbour boat trains 23, 25, 127, 188
*Victoria–Paris via Dover/Dunkerque ferry 133
*Victoria–Queenborough boat trains 27, 108
*Victoria/Holborn Viaduct–Dover 26, 27, 28, 30, 133
*Victoria/Holborn Viaduct/Cannon St–Margate/Ramsgate 26, 28, 29, 30, 126, 127, 133, 135, 186
*Victoria/London Bridge–Brighton 23, 25, 126, 127, 131
*Victoria/London Bridge–Eastbourne/Hastings 22, 25, 126, 127, 131, 135
*Victoria/London Bridge–Portsmouth 22, 24, 25, 126, 131, 133

*Waterloo–Bournemouth–Weymouth 15, 16, 17, 18, 130, 132, 134, 188, 189
*Waterloo–Guildford–Redhill 18
*Waterloo–Portsmouth 15, 17, 18, 126, 132, 133
*Waterloo–Southampton Docks boat trains 17, 18, 130, 133, 188
*Waterloo–Swanage 16
*Waterloo–West of England 15, 16, 17, 18, 126, 129, 132, 134, 188, 190, 191
*Waterloo–Weymouth Channel Islands boat trains 15, 188
Watkin, Edward 52
Waverley Route 95, 96, 164
'Waverley', The 198
'Welshman', The 139, 142
West Coast Joint Stock 59
    Dining cars 59, 62
    1900 stock 62
West Coast main line services 59-63, 89-93
    'Corridor', The 59, 62, 89, 109
    Sleeping car services 60, 63
    Up and Down Special Mails/West Coast Postal 63, 210, 213
West Highland Railway/line 94, 97, 164, 170, 210
    Mallaig Extension 95, 170
West Midlands to Channel Ports via Victoria (trains) 108
'West Riding', The 201, 204
'West Riding Limited', The 157
'West Riding Pullman', The 149, 151, 156
*Weymouth–King's Cross 17
Widened Lines, The 53, 110
'William Shakespeare', The 180, 181
World War 1 – train services during 12, 17, 19, 25, 29, 34, 37, 41, 46, 51, 56, 62, 69, 79, 83, 100, 103, 109, 110
World War 2 – train services during 124, 125, 133, 146, 162, 170, 178
Western Region (BR) 180-185
    Chocolate and cream liveried stock 183
    End of Plymouth boat specials 180
    Holiday traffic 180
    Slip coach workings 183, 184
    Train operating 181
*Wolverhampton–Hastings 175
*Wolverhampton–Penzance 10, 12, 122, 124, 125, 181
*Wolverhampton–Victoria 11, 108

*Yarmouth–Peterborough/York 43
York, traffic to 37
    *York–Lowestoft 108, 116, 176, 216
    *York–Perth 98, 151
*York–Swindon/Swansea 115, 173, 214
*York/Glasgow–Southampton 110, 118, 177
'Yorkshireman', The 138, 139, 146
'Yorkshire Pullman', The 156, 157, 162, 201

'Zulu', The 8